Fester

The publisher and the University of California Press Foundation gratefully acknowledge the generous support of the Peter Booth Wiley Endowment Fund in History.

Fester

CARCERAL PERMEABILITY AND CALIFORNIA'S
COVID-19 CORRECTIONAL DISASTER

Hadar Aviram and Chad Goerzen

UNIVERSITY OF CALIFORNIA PRESS

University of California Press
Oakland, California

Library of Congress Cataloging-in-Publication Data

Names: Aviram, Hadar, author. | Goerzen, Chad Lyman, 1979– author.
Title: Fester : carceral permeability and California's Covid-19 correctional
   disaster / Hadar Aviram and Chad Goerzen.
Description: Oakland : University of California Press, 2024. | Includes
   bibliographical references and index.
Identifiers: LCCN 2023031753 | ISBN 9780520386112 (hardback) |
   ISBN 9780520386129 (paperback) | ISBN 9780520386136 (ebook)
Subjects: LCSH: COVID-19 (Disease)—Law and legislation—California. |
   Prisoners—Legal status, laws, etc.—California. | COVID-19 (Disease)—
   Health aspects—California. | Prisoners—Health and hygiene—
   California.
Classification: LCC KFC613 .A99 2024 | DDC 365/.66709794—dc23/
   eng/20231002
LC record available at https://lccn.loc.gov/2023031753

33 32 31 30 29 28 27 26 25 24
10 9 8 7 6 5 4 3 2 1

In loving memory of Haim Aviram

נדר/אברהם שלונסקי

על דעת עיני שראו את השכול
ועמסו זעקות על ליבי השחוח
על דעת רחמי שהורוני למחול
עד באו ימים שאיימו מלסלוח
נדרתי הנדר: לזכור את הכל
לזכור—ודבר לא לשכוח.

דבר לא לשכוח—עד דור עשירי,
עד שוך עלבוני, עד כולם, עד כולם,
עדי יכלו כל שבטי מוסרי.
קונם אם לריק, יעבור ליל הזעם.
קונם אם לבוקר אחזור לסורי
ומאום לא אלמד גם הפעם.

By accord with my eyes, which witnessed bereavement,
Piling their cries on my burdened, bowed heart
By accord with my pity, which taught to forgive
Till days came that found my compassion unmet
I took on the vow: to remember it all
To remember—and naught to forget.

Not a thing to forget—till tenth generation,
Till insult assuages. Till all, until all,
Till all my morality whips are consumed.
Damned if in vain the rage night is unwound.
Damned if at sunrise my sins I resume
And learn naught, again, this time around.

AVRAHAM SHLONSKY, *"Vow"*

(translated from the Hebrew by Hadar Aviram)

CONTENTS

ILLUSTRATIONS

TABLES

PREFACE AND ACKNOWLEDGMENTS

The day after California's attorney general, Rob Bonta, appealed the Marin Superior Court decision *In re Hall*—which attributed the catastrophic COVID-19 outbreak in San Quentin to deliberate indifference on the part of California's prison authorities, but offered no relief to the prison population—Hadar gave a phone interview about the litigation. Halfway through, she began wheezing and feeling chest pains. Initially, she wondered if it was a heart attack; the appeal was incomprehensibly enraging, as there was nothing *to* appeal. It seemed like the culmination of the gratuitous cruelty that characterized the institutional approach to the COVID-19 correctional crisis. Then it occurred to Hadar that her symptoms probably had a more mundane explanation. Within minutes of arriving home, Hadar, Chad, and our son, Rio, tested positive for COVID-19.

Hadar's symptoms, while not grave, were discomfiting. She slept fitfully, haunted by feverish nightmares of ailing in a filthy prison cell, with no hygiene, household comforts, nutritious food and beverages, or helpful friends nearby. For two years, we—Hadar and Chad—had strongly felt that the COVID-19 prison catastrophe should have shaken the world into realizing the universality of human suffering and the interconnectedness of all living things. Our own COVID-19 bout made this sentiment visceral for us both.

Work on *Fester* began early in the pandemic, when Hadar and Chad were drawn into the #StopSanQuentinOutbreak coalition. Chad began to collect, map, and model the data for California prisons and the surrounding counties, in the little time he had off from his work as a senior research engineer at the Autonomous Rotor Project, first as a contractor for the San José State University Research Foundation and then as a civil servant with the US Army. Hadar turned to full-time COVID-19 activism while teaching a full

load at UC Hastings, writing op-eds and articles; organizing press conferences, panels, and events; and offering analysis and commentary in the
media. She was also honored to be counsel of *amici curiae* the ACLU of
Northern California, and 17 of her colleagues, in the San Quentin COVID-
19 litigation, and to be part of the legal team that achieved the short-lived
landmark victory *In re Von Staich* at the First District Court of Appeal.

Since the early 2000s, our multifaith household has celebrated Passover
with a large and gregarious group of Bay Area friends. In the last few years,
we celebrated via Zoom, using a PowerPoint Haggadah that we designed
ourselves. Engaging with the ancient texts from the book of Exodus and the
Talmudic interpretations provided historical depth to the story in *Fester*. The
story of Exodus features an otherized, feared, and despised community, perceived as a growing, multiplying threat, enslaved and saddled with hard labor,
and treated cruelly and heartlessly. It also features fearless leaders who face
the seat of power with a demand for freedom, as well as complicated ideas of
plague, sanitation, isolation, and protection. Even without our epigraphs, our
readers are sure to recognize the universal potential of fear and loathing to
dehumanize and debase, as well as the everlasting human spirit, yearning to
be free and to free others from bondage.

We extend our deepest gratitude to all the people who worked in the
trenches of the COVID-19 correctional crisis—first and foremost, residents
of prisons and jails who, against all odds, fought to protect themselves and
their friends from illness and death, educated themselves about the vaccine,
pulled off astonishing feats of *pro se* lawyering, and took serious personal
risks to communicate the situation they faced to us on the outside. For several months, we received numerous calls daily from behind bars, and we can
only imagine the sacrifice, stress, and upheaval that went into obtaining a
phone line or using a smuggled cell phone. We deeply apologize to anyone
who went to considerable lengths to contact us to no avail, and to anyone
whom we were unable to help.

We also heard a lot from recently incarcerated people who had many
friends to worry about still inside, and from worried and overwhelmed family members who spent an enormous amount of energy and resources to
advocate. Our paths crossed with several people and organizations that led
the advocacy on behalf of incarcerated people: UnCommon Law (particularly Keith Wattley and Susan Kim), the Ella Baker Center for Human
Rights (notably, Isabella Borgeson, Elliot Hosman, and James King),
Re:Store Justice (especially Adnan Khan), Root and Rebound, the Anti-

Recidivism Coalition (especially Sam Lewis, who did considerable heavy lifting on vaccine advocacy), infectious disease expert Dr. Peter Chin-Hong, and the courageous physician group AMEND (especially Drs. Brie Williams and Leah Rorvig). We also crossed paths with lawyers for the Prison Law Office and from the law firms Rosen, Bien, Galvan & Grunfeld, LLC (notably, Michael Bien), and Keker, Van Nest & Peters LLP (notably, Khari Tillery), as well as with Charles Carbone, the First District Appellate Project (notably, Richard Braucher and Brad O'Connell), Alex Post from the State Public Defender's Office, and Danica Rodarmel, Rebecca Rabkin, and Tom McMahon from the San Francisco and Marin Public Defender's Offices. Some people from within the institutional apparatus, such as Mary Izadi of the Orange County Jails, Michael Romano, chair of Governor Newsom's Penal Code Revision Commission, and others who spoke to us on condition of anonymity, had their hearts and minds in the right place and moved mountains to try to help. Justice Anthony Kline of the First District Court of Appeal also stands out as a heroic, outspoken decision-maker, whose example continued to light the litigation path even after petitioners' fortunes were reversed. Also in the struggle were first-rate journalists, who truly deserve a Pulitzer Prize for their reporting on this disaster: Jason Fagone, Megan Cassidy, Nora Mishanec, Bob Egelko, and John Diaz of the *San Francisco Chronicle*; Sam Levin of the *Guardian*; Wes Venteicher of the *Sacramento Bee*; Elena Goorey and Richard Winton of the *Los Angeles Times*; Brooks Jarosz of KTVU; Kathy Novak of KCBS; Mitch Jeserich of KPFA; Hana Baba of KALW; and many others.

We are also grateful to everyone who, in the absence of robust contact tracing and reliable official data collection, collected and analyzed information we relied on in this book: the UCLA Law COVID Behind Bars Data Project (spearheaded by Sharon Dolovich and Aaron Littman; we are also deeply grateful to Neal Marquez); the COVID-19 in Custody Data Project (spearheaded by Aparna Komarla, whose superb assortment of data we are honored to host at hadaraviram.com); the UCI Prison Pandemic Project and their thousands of collected testimonies (spearheaded by Keramet Reiter); the staff who authored the Office of the Inspector General reports on COVID-19 in California Department of Corrections and Rehabilitation facilities; and the mountains of inside information collected by Allison Villegas, Darby Aono (author of the Santa Rita Jail database), Olivia Campbell (who exposed an unflinching picture of the misery at the California Medical Facility at Vacaville), Tammy Ingram, and many others who shared their knowledge, backed up by screenshots and emails, on social media.

We are exceedingly grateful to everyone who saw, and commented on, early drafts and presentations of sections of this book: Ashley Rubin, Keramet Reiter, Emily Murphy, W. David Ball, Aaron Littman, Aparna Komarla, Binyamin Blum, Dorit Reiss, Nancy King, Margo Schlanger, Lee Kovarsky, Jonathan Abel, Katie Young, the participants of the Prison Law Roundtable, the participants of the UC Hastings Works-In-Progress colloquium, and the participants of the Virtual Workshop on Contemporary Parole. We received useful feedback on chapters presented at the American Society of Criminology, Law and Society Association, and Western Society of Criminology annual meetings. Excerpts from *Fester* were published by *Tropics of Meta*, *Boom: California*, the *Hastings Journal of Crime and Punishment*, and the *Case Western Reserve Law Review*, where we benefited from great editorial advice. Some of Hadar's op-eds throughout the crisis appeared in the *San Francisco Chronicle*, the *Los Angeles Times*, the *Daily Journal*, the *Recorder*, and the UC Press blog. We are, of course, grateful to everyone at UC Press, especially our editor Maura Roessner, for their unfailing excellence and professionalism. We are also grateful to our research assistant, Miriam Yarde, for her excellent work on our bibliography; to our reviewers, Terry Kupers and Jonathan Simon; to Erica Olsen for meticulous copyediting; and to Anneke Toomey for her comprehensive indexing.

In the last steps of this book's production, we experienced the tragic, unfathomable loss of Hadar's father, Haim Aviram, after a brutal battle with a rare lung disease. His sparkling intellect, rare and multidisciplinary talents, noble heart, and rolling laughter lit up even the most forlorn corners of the world; his wisdom and goodness live on in our memories and will illuminate our path forever as we try to do justice to his legacy of service and world-improving work.

Working on this book as our first joint professional venture deepened our two-decade-long journey of love, affection, and commitment, and expanded it to encompass mutual and profound professional respect. We are grateful to each other for the brainpower and heartfelt commitment each of us put into this project. We are also grateful to our wonderful son, Rio Aviram-Goerzen, for filling a stressful period for our family with joy, laughter, and hope, and to our cats, Gulu and Inti, for providing levity and cuddles. We are also deeply grateful to the Aviram and Goerzen families for their love and support; to the SOMA Childcare Center at Yerba Buena Gardens for being a beacon of normality and bravery (especially to teachers Saima, Winnie, Lady, and Jasmin); to our friend Raúl Zappella for keeping our home clean and tidy; to our friend Ruth Hernández for her loving and reliable babysitting; to our friend Brandon Tomlinson of Albert & Eve for providing us nourishing vegetables and fruit; to the Northern California Naginata Federation for supporting Chad's martial arts training and teaching; and to San Francisco Recreation and Parks, coach Celeste St. Pierre, the Mermaid Series Athlete Program, and everyone at Kaiser Permanente's Sports Medicine Clinic for supporting Hadar's multisport athletic endeavors.

In the book, we provide a theoretical framework for understanding how the catastrophe unfolded, synthesizing carceral geography and correctional epidemiology. But first and foremost, we want to bear witness to the immense, unnecessary, and preventable suffering unleashed on tens of thousands of our fellow human beings, and to warn everyone in California and beyond of the disastrous consequences of thinking and policymaking constrained by fear and indifference—pathologies that, unaddressed, will doom us to similar mistakes with the next pandemic.

Introduction

And you are to love those who are foreigners, for you yourselves
were foreigners in Egypt.

SMORGASBORD

Imagine yourself inside a cell.

*You don't know how you got there, or how long it's been. In fact, you have no
memories at all. But imagine yourself liking it inside the cell. It's a good kind of
cell for you.*

*Unbeknownst to you, you are very lucky indeed to be in that particular cell.
It's an epithelial cell inside a nose. This nose, part of a human being, is aboard a
bus going through a gate. You don't know what any of these things mean. You're
a virus, and like all viruses, you know just one thing: how to enter an epithelial
cell, hijack its internal machinery, make hundreds of copies of yourself, move on
to other cells, and repeat. And here you have hit the jackpot. This is a fantastic
opportunity for you, as you will soon find out.*

*It's getting cramped inside your cell; you've been multiplying like crazy in
here. Pop! You and your band of brothers burst the cell's outer membrane and
spread out. A timely sneeze sends you all flying out into the air like a multitude
of tiny parachutists. You don't have much time left to exist, as the droplet you are
in is rapidly evaporating.*

*Riding the air currents, you come across another human body. You brace
yourself. This part would be terrifying, if you were the sort that could be terri-
fied; here come the first defense lines—the skin, mucus, and stomach acid.
Mucus in the new nose might trap you and try to expel you; if you are in a*

mouth, swallowed, stomach acid may kill you. Even if you sail through, the host could send more troops after you: phagocytes wage war and release interferon to protect surrounding cells. If they cannot destroy you, they might raise the alarm and call the lymphocytes. These old-timers might remember your predecessors—anyone that was serious enough to bring them into the battle—intelligence that can help them fight an enemy they know. Many of your brothers will succumb. But your kind are not powerless: you can deceive and manipulate your way past the enemy's defenses.

The spoils of this combat are magnificent. You can't tell, but a human would know that you've passed through a wrought iron gate that reads "California State Prison, San Quentin—Ron Davis, Warden." Only they can tell whether the host whose nose you were in, whose cells you luxuriated in, was wearing a khaki uniform or prison blues. They are so close to each other—just a little leap, just a short conversation, or even a few hours on a tray slid into a prison cell. You don't care, do you, whether these cramped rooms bear memories of a petty offense or a serious one; whether this host might someday be injected with a lethal chemical, whether other humans will rejoice or tear up when they hear of his demise. What matters is this: you're staying, because the hosts aren't going anywhere, and you're in the vicinity of so much potential. Your odds of finding a new host are good: potential hosts are confined together in overcrowded buildings, always indoors where you will not be assaulted by the sun's rays. They are always close together, they sleep in the same rooms, they eat meals together in large halls. Here are showers, where you can brave the heat and stay on a surface for a while, just waiting for a touch. Here's an inadvertent hand on the back, or perhaps a fight just broke out, or the khaki uniforms are manhandling the prison blues. No gloves, no masks, no barriers; no big leaps to make. This world is your oyster.

Behold—more hosts! New ones, ones you haven't seen before. Such variety; a revolving door of faces, noses, mouths, lungs—some of them so worn from years behind bars that they are no match for your feats. You can already tell you're going to thrive here. You, or others, can stay here; you can head out in a host, stop while she gets takeout on the way home, sneak back in with someone else. The feet step in, the cars roll through the gates. Sometimes, the thermometer they use to detect your presence is broken, sometimes no questions are asked, sometimes cursory answers are offered. You can't read the penal code, you can't tell the good guys from the bad guys, you don't care about who's violent and who's nonviolent. There's so much to do here, so many places to be. It's a smorgasbord of opportunity.[1]

This is likely not, dear reader, how you would experience a trip into San Quentin, whether as a prisoner, a prison worker, or a visitor. You would likely not see it as a place of opportunity—except, perhaps, for its attractive location on San Francisco Bay and real estate potential. No, what you might notice first would be the visual markers of transition: the gate, the guards, the inspection at the entrance, the towers. As Erving Goffman explains in *Total Institutions*,[2] your mode of entering the prison and the rituals of your introduction would clearly communicate the rung you occupy in the prison hierarchy. Being "inside" would be markedly different from being "outside," and much would be made of terms such as "behind the prison gate" and "behind bars."

But the exercise is instructive. Its lesson is that the administrative, physical, and symbolic markers of the prisons might not bear the meaning or wield the power that our criminal justice and correctional systems have vested in these spaces, and that our understanding of prison spatiality is partial and flawed. This is the point of departure of *Fester*. We set out not only to bear witness to the most catastrophic medical scandal in US prison history but also to learn how viewing disease, risk, and pathology in a new way can upend the apparent firmness of the distinction between "inside" and "outside" and shed constructive light on correctional philosophies, designs, and practices. We by no means intend to trivialize the harsh realities of being in prison—quite the contrary. We argue that the COVID-19 prison disaster problematizes the assumption that outside communities are safer from the incarcerated "others" when they are behind bars than when they are in the community.

The virus, as many millions around the world learned to their detriment, is not a kind teacher. Like the Zen teachers of yore, who used to slap their disciples into enlightenment, it has wreaked death, illness, poverty, and hardship throughout the world. The gross mismanagement of the COVID-19 threat in the United States,[3] compounded by the excesses of petulant, selfish leadership[4] and deep pockets of noncompliance stemming from political polarization and disinformation campaigns,[5] generated, as of February 21, 2023, 103 million infections,[6] claimed 1.12 million lives,[7] led to an unemployment spike that eclipsed the one resulting from the Great Recession of 2008,[8] left countless people homeless, upended the education of millions of US children, and deepened gender, class, and race gaps by medically and economically worsening the situation of already vulnerable segments of the population.

Even against this sobering background, the horrific outbreak in San Quentin State Prison—2,239 cases and 28 deaths at a facility designed to hold 3,082 people—has stood out as the worst outbreak site in the nation.[9] The entire California prison system has been ravaged by COVID-19: as of February 21, 2023, it has seen 91,591 infections (some of which are reinfections) and 260 deaths. Thousands of additional infections and illnesses plagued California's county jail system. California was not unique in having a correctional COVID-19 disaster: nationwide, between the start of the pandemic and February 2023, prisons and ICE facilities reported 663,196 cases and 3,181 deaths.[10] Prisons surpassed the case rate in the US population on April 14, 2020. By June 2020 the COVID-19 case rate for prisoners was 5.5 times higher than the US population case rate of 587 per 100,000; even when adjusting for age (individuals aged 65 years or older, who accounted for most deaths in the overall US population, were underrepresented in the prison population), the difference was still stark: prison mortality rates were three times higher than in the US population.[11]

The staggering rate of infections and deaths in prisons generally, and in California prisons in particular, indicates that the designation of "inside" and "outside" spaces is far from meaningless. But the problem runs far deeper than mismanagement or even indifference. It stems from a basic misapprehension about the nature and function of prison boundaries, which we refer to here as the myth of prison impermeability.

THE MYTH OF PRISON IMPERMEABILITY

On May 30, 2020—three months after the global outbreak of the novel coronavirus—200 men were transferred from the California Institution for Men in Chino, which was experiencing a serious outbreak at the time, to San Quentin and Corcoran prisons. This fateful transfer would later be regarded as the cause of the horrific outbreak at San Quentin.[12] Two days later, Dr. Matthew Willis, the top health officer of Marin County (home to San Quentin) contacted the warden.[13] Dr. Willis expressed grave concerns about the implications of the transfer on the prison population and on the surrounding county and urged the warden to sequester the incoming population and administer COVID-19 tests. As Willis later explained in a letter to Judge Geoffrey Howard of the Marin Superior Court,[14] this conversation would be the first in a series of public health recommendations to be issued and summarily dismissed by prison officials. The California Department of Corrections and Rehabilitation (CDCR) didn't even directly address Willis's concerns; what they did was forward him a letter from their general counsel, which was addressed to county officials in Kings County. Apparently, health officials there had similar concerns about the earlier outbreak in Avenal State Prison, which, months before the San Quentin outbreak, had already infected more than 1,000 people and claimed 5 lives. This outcome was already known when CDCR officials repurposed the letter and forwarded it to Willis. The letter read in relevant part, "[t]he State is not an entity under local health officers' jurisdictions, and thus local health officer orders are not valid against the State."

This outrageous occurrence is emblematic of an extremely common perspective among politicians, policymakers, prison administrators, and the general public, who assume prisons are largely impermeable spaces. Theoretically, the notion of prison impermeability is a simplification of Erving Goffman's aforementioned characterization of prisons as "total institutions," finding the prison to be ". . . a place of residence and work where a large number of like-situated individuals, cut off from the wider society for an appreciable length of time, together lead an enclosed, formally administered round of life."[15] The classic studies of prison culture in the 1960s and 1970s looked at the prison as a closed unit of analysis, which required enculturation to its unique norms[16] and embeddedness in its endemic economy,[17] and which inflicted unique forms of suffering as a consequence of its closure.[18]

Under the logic of prison impermeability, the only important interfaces of prison with the outside occur at the entrance (incarceration) and at the exit (reentry). Both contact points raise serious problems, which the literature has discussed in detail: on the front end, criminalization, mass plea bargaining, the impact of pretrial detention and the cash bail system, and the racially discriminatory aspects of policing and courtroom dynamics; and on the back end, lengthy sentences, exacerbated recidivism through incarceration, the stigma of criminal records, and the lack of a rehabilitation-reentry continuum. But between entry and exit, confinement is perceived as impermeable. This idea underpins the philosophy of incapacitation, widely regarded since the 1980s as the most accessible goal of punishment: put people behind bars, and they will not endanger the community.[19] Thus, prisons are praised by some as spaces that incapacitate dangerous people by keeping them away from "the outside" and critiqued by others as spaces that remove people from participation in civil society (temporarily or permanently, with severe racial and class disenfranchisement implications).

While studying prison culture is a valuable endeavor, it is an oversight to do so at the exclusion of the continuities and connections between prison and the surrounding community. Practically speaking, prison impermeability is a myth; criticizing Goffman's framework, Keith Farrington found it to be "fairly inaccurate as a portrayal of the structure and functioning of the ... correctional institution," explaining that the prison "is not as completely or effectively 'cut off from wider society' as Goffman's description would lead us to believe."[20] Dominique Moran characterizes prisons as "having a relatively stable and on-going network of transactions, exchanges and relationships which connect and bind them to their immediate host communities and to society more generally."[21] Indeed, the membrane between prisons and their surrounding communities is quite thin: various people (correctional officers, prison workers, volunteers, visitors, tourists), things (money, goods, factory raw material), and intangibles (tax money, critique) pass through the membrane on a daily basis. Some of these exchanges are rooted in the basic functions of prison as an institution and an economic unit; others vary based on transparency.

This model of the prison is crucial to understanding the California COVID-19 prison crisis. For this purpose, our analysis utilizes the concept of *carceral permeability*—a perspective on carceral space that increases the salience of continuity and flow. We view the boundary between the carceral and the noncarceral as porous and fluid, both for the purpose of understanding viral contagion and for considering issues like overcrowding and release strategies. Replacing narrow political constructions of impermeability with this holistic understanding of spatial continuity allows us not only to comprehend how the COVID-19 catastrophe was allowed to occur, but also to critique it and to offer a way forward. The concept of carceral permeability lies at the intersection of theoretical perspectives on carceral spatiality and continuity: insights from carceral geography, situational crime prevention, and the social history of disease and contagion in prisons.

PRISON AND COMMUNITIES AS A GEOGRAPHICAL CONTINUUM

Carceral geography, a field examining the spatial dimension of incarceration and confinement, is deeply influenced by Michel Foucault's *Discipline and Punish*.[22] In his analysis of the shift from centralized, public displays of corporal punishment toward sites of supervision and a disciplining "gaze," Foucault coined the concept of "the carceral archipelago"—the notion that the distinction between the prison and the outside is not binary, and there are multiple settings of varying degrees of confinement and moral surveillance, designed to internalize notions of normality and deviance amid the surveilled population. Building on this notion of carceral gradation, Malcolm Feeley and Jonathan Simon identified the emergence of a "new penology,"[23] a sequel to Foucault's disciplinary carceral in that it incapacitates according to actuarial considerations but features the same array of gradual, continuous regimes of "selective incapacitation."[24] Other influences on carceral geography include Giorgio Agamben's work on "bare life" and spaces of exception[25] and the work of Loïc Wacquant on the continuum between the ghetto and the hypercarceral regime in the United States and Western Europe.[26]

The difficulty of using the term "carceral state," as Ashley Rubin and Michelle Phelps explain, lies not only in the term's multiple meanings but also in the simplistic suggestion that there is a single, unified, and actorless state responsible for punishment. This contradicts the thrust of recent punishment literature, which emphasizes fragmentation, variegation, and constant conflict across the actors and institutions that shape penal policy and practice.[27] The use of "the carceral" by geographers overcomes this challenge through its spatial focus.

Rather than characterizing a discrete, physical location, a "carceral space," according to geographer Dominique Moran, satisfies three necessary conditions. The first is "detriment"—a space must inflict suffering, harm, or punishment, experienced as such and regardless of intent. The second condition is that of an involuntary imposition of detriment via confinement (which would exclude, for example, choosing to confine oneself to a gated community "prison"). The third condition brings in the material, virtual, or imagined space or spaces to which these relate.[28] Moran identifies three themes within carceral geography: the nature of carceral spaces and experiences within them, the spatial geographies of carceral systems, and the relationship between the carceral and an increasingly punitive state.[29] All three themes problematize the idea of clear, impervious boundaries between the "carceral" and the "noncarceral," in ways that are essential to this project.

The first theme illuminates the ways in which prison structure and architecture, as well as mobility within prison or between prisons, deeply impact carceral experiences. Prison design researchers illuminate how historical and contemporary physical plants[30] reflect the institution's philosophy and the system's perception of its planned inhabitants.[31] Moran highlights this connection between function and design by examining the "Prison Design

Boycott" launched in 2005 by Architects/Designers/Planners for Social Responsibility against the planning and construction of death chamber and supermax prisons.[32] Prison ethnographies examine how incarcerated people emotionally and somatically experience carceral spaces, particularly the lack of privacy[33] and the stresses and conflicts stemming from prison overcrowding.[34] Special attention is paid to techniques of resistance, ranging from personalizing the space,[35] through inhabiting and maintaining one's own body,[36] to the "dirty protest."[37]

The second theme challenges the understanding of prisons as static and immobile. As prison geographers show, mobility is a constant feature of carcerality, be it between the prison and the outside, between prisons, or within prisons. The shape mobility takes is a key facet of what Moran describes as the "power geometry of everyday life" in carceral space:[38] the freedom to move[39]—and the amount of control individuals exert over the direction, medium, and conditions of their own mobility—varies greatly with the social role of the institutional inhabitant.[40]

The second theme highlights the oft-obscured connections between prisons and their surrounding communities.[41] Many studies examine the hesitation[42] of communities to reorient their economy around prisons, fearing rising crime rates,[43] undesired changes in local ambience[44] and infrastructure,[45] and declines in property value.[46] Other studies show community enthusiasm for prison siting, based on assumptions (warranted and unwarranted)[47] that the prison and related industries will produce economic growth.[48] Some of these important works feature Susanville, home to three California prisons and the recipient of the apt moniker "Prison Town, U.S.A."[49] Ruth Wilson Gilmore's pioneering work *Golden Gulag*[50] documents the process by which prison entrepreneurs presented prison siting within the town as an economic opportunity, and how local legislators were "sold" on the idea—even as the promise did not yield the promised local economic growth.[51] Becoming a prison town, however, changes the character and cultural norms in the community,[52] to the point that Karen Morin compares prison towns to cattle towns.[53]

The third theme offers an even broader interrogation of the "carceral space" concept. In *Prison Land*,[54] Brett Story illuminates the omnipresence of the carceral state far beyond prisons, into seemingly "outside" settings such as gentrifying downtown Detroit, neighborhood politics in Brooklyn, Appalachian mined mountaintops as potential correctional settings, statewide overnight buses, spatial restrictions on sex offenders and gang members, and electronically monitored homes. Story's sophisticated geo-economic analysis demonstrates the superficiality of postrecession reforms: an ostensibly benevolent push for urban renewal through a tech tycoon's purchase of downtown buildings also marginalizes and segregates poor people of color; an apparently well-meant effort at neighborhood justice as an alternative to incarceration serves more as a public relations stunt for law enforcement than as a true solution for the problems that produce crime; and efforts to create jobs in a vanishing world of coal mining hide an underbelly of prison capacity enhancement.

Story's book is especially valuable as a companion to her documentary *The Prison in Twelve Landscapes*,[55] which depicts the carceral state without showing a single prison: here, a master chess player who learned to play in prison teaches chess in Central Park; an Appalachian town's librarian discusses the impact of a prison escape on the town; California prisoners fight fires without any postrelease job prospects as firefighters; and warehouses in the Bronx are chock-full of goods for prisons. Story's depiction of the "prison in-between"—the overnight buses that take visitors to remote, rural prisons—drives home the physical discomfort, expense, and time of the travelers/visitors as sacrifices that extend the realm of the carceral to the bus visit and increase the visibility of the neoliberal hand of the market, through the companies that run the buses.

Alongside Jonathan Simon's *Governing through Crime*,[56] several important works examine how the carceral experience transcends obvious criminal justice institutions and permeates schools,[57] workplaces,[58] and families.[59] Wacquant's notion of the ghetto[60] and Davis's notion of the "carceral city"[61] are additional examples. These spaces are creatures not merely of the state but also of the private sector; several works examine the contribution of technological tools to the creation of invisible, but insidious and powerful, carceral spaces with racial underpinnings,[62] such as through software for predictive policing;[63] the racialization of surveillance in commerce;[64] limitations on financial mobility through credit monitoring;[65] and employing surveillance tactics, offered by loss-prevention corporations, on employees in the retail industry.[66] Some scholars draw important analogies between different kinds of carceral spaces: Karen Morin's provocative comparisons of prisons and factory farms shows how "[t]he process of 'animalization' in particular subjugates both certain humans and certain nonhumans into hierarchies of worthiness and value."[67] For some scholars, carcerality is a structural element of the neoliberal state, providing rationales and technologies to manage the underclass[68] or the locus for utilizing and investing surplus land, labor, and capital.[69]

These studies, which refute the myth of prison impermeability, are directly relevant to COVID-19 in prisons. They highlight the immense importance of prison architecture and design to the pandemic spread and prevention strategy behind bars, making the locus of any incarcerated person a defining characteristic of their pandemic experience. The particular case of forced, botched transfers is a case in point. Carceral geography also illuminates the folly of containment strategies that assume a separation between contagion behind bars and the surrounding counties. Finally, these studies highlight the continuum of carceral spaces between "the outside" and prison, in a pandemic scenario in which the public at large experiences considerable limitations on movement and quality of life, and interrogate the implications of these quasi-carceral experiences for humanizing incarcerated people and engendering empathy for their tragic plight.

CONTAGION, PLACE, AND OPPORTUNITY: INSIGHTS FROM SITUATIONAL CRIME PREVENTION

Another body of literature concerned with human experiences within spatial environments is situational crime prevention (SCP), a cluster of criminological theories that focus on how physical environments impact criminal behavior. The emergence of SCP, according to criminologist David Weisburd, was the consequence of despair of grand theories, which excavated personal histories and psychological makeups of people who committed crimes to understand (in vain) the causes of their behavior.[70] SCP is not agnostic, though, about human behavior: rather, it adopts a rational choice approach, whereby crime is not the manifestation of personal or social pathology but a rational response to one's environment. One of the unique aspects of rational choice theory is the duality that David Garland referred to as "criminologies of the self" and "criminologies of the other."[71] Even where people's situations are deeply constrained by their social and demographic circumstances, rational choice theorists are interested in the repertoire of choices they do have,[72] leading some to see rational choice theory as a general theory of crime.[73]

The intersection of human agency and its surrounding environs is evident in Marcus Felson and Lawrence Cohen's routine activities theory.[74] Felson and Cohen see crime as the product of three factors: an accessible target, the lack of a capable guardian, and a motivated offender. The accessibility of the target is a function of its value, inertia, visibility, and access (VIVA), as well as its characteristics: concealable, removable, available, valuable, enjoyable, disposable (CRAVED). The presence of a capable guardian might involve a human element (effective policing, private guards, a neighborhood watch) or surveillance technologies. Even the notion of "motivated offenders" does not involve delving into their psychological makeups but rather their assessment of the suitability of the target and the absence of a capable guardian.

SCP and its companion, crime prevention through environmental design (CPtED), have deeply transformed public and private spaces. Per SCP pioneer Ron Clarke,[75] carefully manipulating the physical environment can result in reduced criminal opportunities and rewards. The success of SCP is so ubiquitous that it is invisible: if you have ever seen a display wall at a sneaker store featuring a single shoe out of each pair,[76] experienced surveillance cameras or metal detectors, seen a park bench interspersed with armrests,[77] or noticed changes in street lighting, you have been subjected to SCP-informed architecture, engineering, or design. Civil engineers, urban planners, and retail designers put themselves in the shoes of potential burglars, vandals, or robbers and factor the possibility of criminal opportunities into their designs,[78] inviting SCP specialists to provide expertise. A wonderful example is Geoff Manaugh's masterful *A Burglar's Guide to the City*,[79] which examines the interface between urban planning and criminal opportunities, using examples of historical and current crimes ranging from the mundane to the outlandish.

SCP and carceral geography can be seen as two ideological sides of the same coin. While both perspectives focus on the interaction between humans and their spatial environment, they attach diametrically opposing values to spatial design: what SCP advocates see as successful crime prevention, carceral geographers see as the creation of carceral spaces or the transformation of urban environments to serve the neoliberal, hypercarceral state. The other commonality between the two theories is the element of choice and opportunism. As explained above, carceral geographers critiqued and developed Foucault's and Agamben's respective concepts of carcerality and exclusive spaces by paying attention to human adaptation to carceral spaces, particularly emotionally and somatically; some geographers see these adaptations as resistance.[80] Because of its rational choice roots, SCP is even more explicit about the available repertoire of choices even in circumstances rife with limitations and constraints, and consciously aims to shape space in a way that either curtails illegitimate opportunism or offers legitimate alternatives.

This matters greatly for our project. First, it is crucially important (and conceptually refreshing) to see prison as a site of coexisting and contradictory functions—a locus of human constraint and deprivation and, simultaneously, a rich opportunity for contagion to fester and thrive. Dialectically accepting closure and confinement, permeability and opportunity, is challenging: it brings to mind Rubin's famous optical illusion, in which one looks at a drawing and can discern either a face or a vase, but not both simultaneously. The policy problems of managing contagion and disease behind bars stem directly from this challenge: where politicians and prison officials are anxiously attached to a view of prison as confining, protecting the outside world from the enterprise and opportunism of incarcerated people, epidemiologists view the prison as an incubator of disease, a place where the viral equivalent of "rational choice" thrives and threatens.

Second, given the scale of the COVID-19 prison catastrophe, it is tempting (and, to a great degree, accurate) to think of people behind bars—incarcerated people, prison workers, and correctional officers—as the powerless recipients of contagion, neglect, and indifference. Suffering and lack of agency are important; Karen Morin's comparative analysis of carceral institutions and factory farms reminds us that "the process of animalization itself subjugates both certain human and certain nonhumans into hierarchies of worthiness and value."[81] This insight crystallizes the lower we descend in the Maslow hierarchy of needs, toward what Giorgio Agamben referred to as "bare life"[82] and Jonathan Simon criticized as "total incapacitation."[83] But the indignation at the prison authority's failed response to the pandemic must be supplemented by an examination of the variety of creative ways in which people behind bars have resisted, and adapted to, the calamity visited upon them. Somatically, these adaptations include health preservation strategies behind bars, such as social distancing, makeshift protective equipment, and negotiation of boundaries. They also include political organizing behind bars and on the outside and, of course, legal challenges to the state's iatrogenic shaping of the prison environment. And they include questions of compliance and buy-in that emerged as the prospect of a COVID-19 vaccine drew near. Imbuing the humans experiencing the COVID-19 tragedy with agency is not an ideological choice—it reflects how human ingenuity works with, around, and against spatial restrictions to improve its chances of survival.

This brings us to the third relevant body of literature: scholarship at the intersection of carcerality and disease. This category includes studies of miasma theory, which literally and metaphorically situate contagion within prisons, or even see carcerality itself as a contagion.

MIASMA, CONTAINMENT, AND SANITATION: INSIGHTS FROM SOCIOHISTORICAL STUDIES OF PRISON CONTAGION

In *American Contagions*,[84] John Witt draws a useful distinction between "quarantinist" and "sanitationist" state approaches toward contagion and disease. Authoritarian states, he explains, adopt a quarantinist approach: they "exercise forceful controls over the bodies and lives of their subjects, locking down communities, neighborhoods, and cities and imposing broad quarantine orders, often backed by the military." By contrast, "[a] sanitationist state employs liberal policies designed to eliminate environments that breed disease." Witt sees the United States as an amalgam of both approaches—"one approach for those with political clout, and another for everyone else":

> For middle-class white people and elites, public health policy typically reflected liberal sanitationist values. The law has protected property rights for the wealthy and attended to the civil liberties of the powerful. At the nation's borders, however, and for the disadvantaged and for most people of color, the United States has more often been authoritarian and quarantinist. American law has regularly displayed a combination of neglect and contempt toward the health of the powerless. But that is not all. Epidemics make visible the ways in which even the ostensibly neutral and libertarian rules of American social life contain the compounded form of discriminations and inequities, both old and new. The most basic rules of American law—from the law of private property to the law of health insurance to the law of employment— structure the social experience of disease and infection.[85]

The writings on the history of prisons and disease echo the tension between sanitationist and quarantinist approaches, linking social oppression and inequality in general and epidemic-combating strategies in particular. Perhaps the epitome of the enlightened, sanitationist approach can be found in the writings of 18th-century prison reformer John Howard—endowed not only with a considerable fortune but with an inquisitive eye and a compassionate heart—who toured more than 100 prisons in England and Wales. His resulting book, *The State of the Prisons*, opens as follows:

There are prisons, into which whoever looks will, at first sight of the people confined there, be convinced, that there is some great error in the management of them; the sallow meagre countenances declare, without words, that they are very miserable; many who went in healthy, are in a few months changed into emaciated dejected objects. Some are seen pining under diseases, "sick and in prison;" expiring on the floors, in loathsome cells, of pestilential fevers, and the confluent small-pox; victims, I must say not to the cruelty, but I will say to the inattention, of sheriffs, and gentlemen in the commission of the peace.... The cause of this distress is, that many prisons are scantily supplied, and some almost totally unprovided with the necessaries of life.[86]

Howard's concerns about the spread of disease in jails hearkened back to the Black Assize of 1577, in which prisoners awaiting trial were brought from jail to an Oxford courthouse. "Within forty hours," he wrote, more than 300 people who had been at court were dead from "gaol fever." Long before germ theory was fully understood, Howard expressed concerns about the risk of infected people carrying contagion back to their communities upon their release. His later adventures bolstered the connection between incarceration and disease: after a brief stint as prison reform administrator, he returned to his travels, experiencing people's fear of the plague and finding himself imprisoned at a Venetian lazaretto.

Howard's ideas and recommendations were popularized in the United States by Philadelphia reformer and physician Benjamin Rush.[87] As prison historian Ashley Rubin notes, a significant impetus for constructing the first prisons in the United States was the goal of preventing the spread of disease, which was common in the overcrowded and violent jails of the colonial era.[88] These facilities, whose physical structure and public/private ownership varied greatly, functioned not as a form of punishment but as a space to confine debtors, vagrants, or convicted people awaiting corporal punishment or transports, and were not designed for lengthy detentions. They did not conform to the now-conventional practice of segregating confined populations by age and gender,[89] which contributed to violence and exploitation.

Inspired by Howard's ideas about hygiene and segregation, Rush and his colleagues refashioned Philadelphia's Walnut Street Jail, which in 1794 became one of the nation's first state prisons. Michael Meranze's study of Walnut Street shows that the emphasis on clean clothing and bedding was as much a practical effort at preventing disease as it was a moral effort to curb vice.[90] Elsewhere in the late 18th century, Mississippi (like several other states) made special provisions for removing prisoners when disease erupted in jails.[91]

But these Enlightenment-era sanitationist notions were supplanted by quarantinist approaches in the period surrounding the Civil War, in both the North and the South. When smallpox broke out in Washington, DC, in 1862, the Medical Division of the Freedmen's Bureau blamed freedpeople. Healthy and infected freedpeople alike were forced into crowded, unsanitary prisons and tented communities, where disease raced through the population.[92] Witt places these approaches in the context of quarantinist strategies controlling poor people of color generally and shows their rise to prominence as prisons became loci of disproportionate containment of African Americans—as evidenced by the quarantinist approach during the parallel rise of the AIDS epidemic and mass incarceration.

The distinction between sanitationist and quarantinist approaches engages with the insights of carceral geography and SCP, because the two approaches differ in their perceptions of prison permeability. A sanitationist approach sees prisons and their surrounding communities as a continuum, both in recognizing the possibility of transmissivity and acknowledging that returning from prison is natural and normal. By contrast, a quarantinist approach upholds the myth of prison impermeability, providing the public health version of the incapacitative argument: the idea that "we" (the community outside) are safer from "them" (incarcerated people) when they are contained inside.

The tension between the two approaches is evident not only in the literal approaches toward disease but also in the use of contagion, disease, and miasma metaphors to describe criminality itself. As Rubin notes, even Howard himself found this idea captivating: in *The State of the Prisons*, he described how young "innocents"—the children of people jailed for debt or those awaiting trial for a petty offense—were "infected" by their proximity to career criminals and their enticing stories. Since then, referring to prisons as "criminogenic" has become so ubiquitous among prison scholars that many probably no longer notice the epidemiological metaphor underpinning it. Scores of experimental studies find correlations between incarceration and recidivism—be it incarceration itself,[93] its conditions,[94] or its effect on particular prison populations.[95] Not only is criminality infectious, but the stigma of criminality also follows the incarcerated person after release.

The disease metaphor is used in the service of critique even further with the popular references to mass incarceration itself as an epidemic. In *The Plague of Prisons*, public health scholar Ernest Drucker takes the analogy seriously and analyzes the proliferation of incarceration using basic public health concepts: "incidence and prevalence," "outbreaks," "contagion," "transmission," and "potential years of life lost." Drucker concludes that mass incarceration features the same contagious and self-perpetuating features of the plagues of previous centuries.[96]

CARCERAL PERMEABILITY AND THE CALIFORNIA COVID-19 PRISON CRISIS

What can this theoretical framework teach us about the COVID-19 prison catastrophe in California? In this book, we argue that the prison as a pandemic locus can only be fully comprehended spatially, as a site of opportunity and peril whose obviously porous nature is misperceived and misrepresented for political purposes. Our argument in the book is threefold.

First, we argue that *the myth of prison impermeability and the corresponding philosophies of warehousing and incapacitation are to blame for California's mismanagement of the prison outbreak.* These myths persist in California for political and geographic reasons. As Vanessa Barker explains in *The Politics of Imprisonment,*[97] California's unique mix of polarization and populism produces an appetite for punitive policies, which have resulted in exceedingly long sentences, which Hadar has elsewhere[98] referred to as "the trifecta of extreme punishment": a gargantuan death row under moratorium, thousands of people serving life without parole, and tens of thousands of lifers whose prospects of parole are dim because of political expediency and posturing. The idea that criminals are incapable of change can be exemplified by the cliché "lock them up and throw away the key." This mindset has produced the geographical spread of California's prison system, where most prisons are in remote, rural areas (San Quentin is a notable exception),[99] and many incarcerated people are serving lifelong or indeterminate terms. This out-of-sight, out-of-mind carceral scenery rendered invisible the abysmal population glut, to the tune of 200 percent of design capacity. The overcrowded conditions resulted in abysmal health conditions in California prisons, including (but not limited to) contagious diseases, and in aging and infirm people suffering and dying from preventable, often iatrogenic conditions.[100] After the Supreme Court's decision in *Brown v. Plata*[101] and the Public Safety Realignment of 2011,[102] the population glut shifted into county jails, which offered a different permeability problem: while these smaller institutions were located closer to urban communities, they were relatively independent and decentralized, which hampered visibility of the conditions within. Notably, this shift in carceral strategy reflected and reinforced the recession-era approach that Chris Seeds refers to as "bifurcation nation":[103] the idea that the only deserving recipients of compassion, release, or alternatives to incarceration are so-called "nonviolent inmates," whereas the so-called "violent ones"—many of whom are aging, infirm people who have spent decades behind bars for crimes committed during their adolescence and early adulthood—are irredeemable.

As we show in *Fester*, the obstinacy of state officials and prison management in the face of the COVID-19 threat represents an unrelenting fixation on the idea that any strategy that challenges the scale of statewide incarceration must be rejected, and that the only practical population changes should be cosmetic and target the so-called "nonviolent inmate" population. The scope and trajectory of the pandemic in prisons has repeatedly confronted CDCR and the Office of the Governor with the urgent need to prioritize aging, infirm people for release from a public health standpoint—and, time and time again, policy choices took the wrong turn. This attachment to the myth of prison impermeability has cost the lives of hundreds and the health of tens of thousands.

But the myth of prison impermeability affects Californians on the outside as well, which is the focus of our second claim. We argue that thinking of prisons as fixed, impermeable places perpetuates the myth that "we" (meaning the outside community) are safer when "they" (incarcerated people) are inside. The COVID-19 outbreak has been a powerful, albeit unkind, teacher in this respect. While it is impossible to provide a clean causal inference without contact tracing, *our spatial analysis suggests the opposite—that the quarantinist approach that emphasizes containment of the disease within prison walls actually increases the dangers to the surrounding community.* It reflects a contamination of what should have been a sound model of medical isolation with the punitive containment strategies that characterize California's incapacitative regime. Thinking of contagion through the tools of rational choice and opportunity theory sheds a completely different light on the meaning of the prison gate, and raises questions about prison workers, correctional officers, and the involvement of county public health authorities that the impermeability paradigm obfuscates.

Our third claim addresses the political appeal and persistence of the myth of impermeability, and the successes and limitations of different strategies— media outreach, political protest, and legal action—to expose its harms. Similarly to Garland's "criminologies of the self" and "criminologies of the other," we identify the hypocritical distinction between "pandemics of the self" and "pandemics of the other." In November 2020 the *San Francisco Chronicle* reported on two large private parties, held on two consecutive nights at the exclusive French Laundry restaurant; these parties were attended, respectively, by California governor Gavin Newsom and by San Francisco mayor London Breed and their entourages. The *Chronicle*'s food critic, Soleil Ho, encompassed the incongruence between those making the law and those subjected to it in this scathing paragraph:[104]

> You're getting ready for your big dinner party at one of the finest restaurants in the country, an occasion that you and your colleagues have planned for ages. So there's a pandemic—of course you're on top of that! You're a good, safe person who believes in science, you think as you check your makeup in the mirror. Not like those troglodyte COVID deniers storming retail outlets, demanding to be let in without masks on, banging on glass doors and insisting that they're important. These are the people the rules are for. You on the other hand know the rules so well—you are kind of in charge of explaining them, after all—that you know specifically, to the letter, why your situation is an exception to those rules.

We argue that *characterizing incarcerated people as "others" is an erroneous and unfair mindset that crystallizes the deep inequalities that have characterized the spatial distribution of both pandemic harms and supplemental harms due to pandemic prevention.* Our discussion of the state's litigation strategy shows that the misperception of carceral space is laced with deep-seated dehumanization, which has been the leitmotif of state strategy throughout the pandemic—from the careless preventive approach to the cruelty of the vaccine prioritization strategy.

Our goals, beyond bearing witness to the horrors of the COVID-19 prison disaster, are threefold. Theoretically, we set out to refute the idea that prisons should be lauded or critiqued as places of confinement, separate from their spatial context. We hope to create a conversation about prison permeability and the interfaces between the prison and the community, which will melt disciplinary silos and convene carceral geographers, prison epidemiologists, environmental criminologists, legal advocates, and sociolegal punishment scholars. We also hope to infuse this conversation with the important insights of community organizers, many of whom have acquired an understanding of prison permeability through personal or familial experience.

Policy-wise, we want aspiring correctional reformers to treat prisons as part of the physical communities where they reside. This has implications far beyond coordinated health-care strategies. Correctional culture and discipline, rehabilitative programming, staff training, and prison labor should be shaped to facilitate smooth, continuous transitions between prison and the outside. Weekend sentences and prison vacations, widely used in other countries and in low-level sentencing, should be incorporated into prison life to acknowledge permeability and rely on it as a positive rehabilitation motivator.

Litigation-wise, we offer thoughts about how a framework of permeability—particularly, treating prison as you would any congregated setting in the free world—can help us break through the stagnation, deference, and restraint that usually characterize prison litigation.[105]

BOOK PLAN, METHODOLOGY, AND SOURCES

Fester employs a multimethod, triangulated research design. Each chapter features different methods, sources, and approaches, to provide a fuller picture of the correctional COVID-19 experience.

Our first chapter, "Triggers and Vulnerabilities," sets the stage for one of the important missions of *Fester*: bearing witness to the unfolding of the COVID-19 tragedy. It starts with a framework borrowed from Ben Bernanke's "triggers and vulnerabilities" analysis of the 2008 financial crisis: mapping the chronic conditions that rendered prisons so vulnerable to the acute threat of the pandemic (this is why we are calling the book *Fester*, rather than *Outbreak*). We examine California's polarized and populistic political culture, the pre-*Plata* health-care crisis, and the decades-long correctional battle with the valley fever epidemic. We also examine the extent to which the myth of impermeability was entrenched and reinforced through the *Plata* and Realignment approaches to the overcrowding problem: the bifurcation between so-called "violent" and "nonviolent" inmates and the notion that decentralized county facilities are better than state facilities for controlling prison populations. We then show how ideas of prison insularity, irredeemability of people serving long sentences, and jurisdiction-over-geography blind spots led prison authorities to ignore warnings from medical and correctional experts about the outbreak potential in prisons. We show how jurisdictional grandstanding, which perceived prisons as their own institutional network, disconnected from the counties in which they reside and which they border, led politicians and prison officials to ignore opportunities for collaboration with neighboring communities and with the private tech and biomedical sector.

Chapter 2, "Petri Dish," turns to the pandemic tragedy itself. The theoretical framework for this chapter is Gresham Sykes's classic "The Pains of Imprisonment," which expanded the notion of carceral suffering beyond the legally prescribed deprivation of liberty. We show that this vast, diverse array of suffering is even truer in times of health crises. Through first-person accounts of the COVID-19 crisis by currently and formerly incarcerated people, their family and friends, prison activists and lawyers, and prison workers (particularly physicians), we construct a picture of COVID-19 correctional policies and strategies. We examine the practical impossibilities of social distancing and isolation, the resistance to sensible preventative measures, and the limitations of quantitative data collection due to erratic and primitive testing schedules and practices. We rely on inspector general reports, reports by the physician group AMEND, and professional grievance documentation to show ineffective gatekeeping, the powerlessness of prison worker unions, and the complete political capture of the correctional officers' union, which resulted in numerous hospitalizations and the death of one correctional officer.

Chapter 2 consists of content analysis, using modified grounded theory, of reports from the digital archive UCI Prison Pandemic, collected by faculty and graduate students in UC Irvine's Criminology, Law & Society Program. The archive includes thousands of firsthand reports from all of California's correctional facilities and is publicly accessible.[106] This chapter also uses journalistic accounts of the crisis, including op-eds by currently and formerly incarcerated authors, and the detailed reports compiled by the Office of the Inspector General. All these materials are in the public domain.

Chapter 3, "Bottleneck," turns to the equivalent experience in county jails. Our point of departure is Margo Schlanger's warning that the Realignment, designed to bring California prison populations into compliance with the *Plata* decision, would sprout a "hydra problem" of inadequate health care and contentious litigation against individual jails. In describing the inherent problems of decentralized jails, we argue, based on Robert Proctor's concept of "agnotology," that the paucity of information on COVID-19 policies and outcomes in jails is a social fact, rather than happenstance. Through a triangulation of data from the Board of State and Community Corrections (BSCC) database (which came into existence only in August, five months after the outbreak) and nongovernment efforts to collect data by the UCLA

Law COVID Behind Bars Data Project and by Darby Aono, currently a law student at UC Berkeley, we show how the decentralized framework and lax involvement of the BSCC led to disturbing outcomes in various jails, including Folsom, Riverside, and Santa Rita. We then show the tainted fruit of the "hydra problem" through the failed effort to litigate against the flawed precaution measures at the Orange County Jail in *Barnes v. Ahlman*.

Our analysis in chapter 3 relies on primary data collected by the Covid-in-Custody Project, which is freely available on Hadar's blog.[107] It also relies on data and information collected by Darby Aono, whose data is available as a Google document.[108] We also rely on secondary data compiled and analyzed by the Public Policy Institute of California and by the BSCC.

Chapter 4, "Elixir," hails the advent of vaccines and tells the story of vaccine acceptance and resistance in California's correctional facilities. This chapter depicts the uphill advocacy battle to designate prisons and jails as priority vaccination sites and the strategies employed by advocates and activists to encourage vaccine acceptance among the prison population. Despite initial fears that the complete collapse of trust in CDCR's administration would hinder vaccine acceptance, this chapter presents the prison population's vaccination as a success story mostly attributable to the incarcerated people themselves. By contrast, the prisons' and jails' custodial staff were stubbornly resistant to vaccination, and this chapter documents the complicity of the California Correctional Peace Officers Association, the prison guards' union, in this fiasco.

This chapter is a narrative/journalistic account based on news reports, as well as on participant observations at activist and advocate meetings in which Hadar participated and assisted as a public intellectual and blog owner. The videos recorded by formerly incarcerated advocates are hosted on Hadar's blog.

Having told the story of COVID-19 behind bars, in chapter 5, "Incubator," the book shifts gears to the surrounding and neighboring counties. After reviewing the scholarship documenting "zero-sum" thinking on prison conditions, we highlight the efforts of county officials to coordinate pandemic responses with prisons and jails within their territory and show how shortsightedness and grandstanding short-circuited cooperation precisely when it could have saved lives. To refute these impermeability assumptions, we use the Bradford Hill criteria, a widely accepted set of epidemiological principles for showing causality. Our model geographically superimposes prison data onto statewide data. By breaking continuous space into concentric rings, we can show temporal correlations between prison outbreaks and surrounding and neighboring counties. We also provide a counterfactual transmissivity model that, while falling short of telling an airtight causal story (nothing short of contact tracing can do so with sufficient confidence), confidently refutes the myth that Californians are safer when some of them are behind bars.

The CDCR data for our model were extracted from CDCR's own tracker.[109] Even though the data became publicly available only a few months into the pandemic, CDCR authorities updated it retroactively. Chad scraped this information daily from the CDCR website until January 2022, when the data ceased to be reliable due to CDCR's incomplete and vague reportage of reinfections. Our state data relies on the *Los Angeles Times* website.[110] As with the CDCR data, Chad coded this data daily.

Chapter 6 and chapter 7 turn, respectively, to the legal and the political efforts to obtain relief from the plague. Based on participant observations and court documentation in the federal case *Plata v. Newsom* and in two state litigation efforts (*In re Hall et al. before the Marin Superior Court* and *In re Von Staich before the California Court of Appeal*), chapter 6, "The House Always Wins," examines how the myth of prison impermeability (which is at the heart of legal barriers, such as the Prison Litigation Reform Act on the federal level) hindered judicial policymaking, despite the compassion and sympathy of some state and federal judges. We review the litigation in *Plata*, focusing on Judge Tigar's horror at the COVID-19 tragedy, amplified by the sense that his hands were tied. We also examine the two state cases, showing how CDCR adopted a divide-and-conquer strategy to postpone injunctive relief that could be of any utility to the incarcerated petitioners. This chapter refutes the idea that judicial helplessness is the product of statutory structure at the federal or the state level, ascribing it instead to the widespread antipathy and apathy toward incarcerated people.

Chapter 6 relies on participant observations of COVID-19 prison litigation in open court. Hadar participated in litigation of the San Quentin cases (*In re Von Staich*) at the California Court of Appeal as counsel for *amici curiae* the ACLU of Northern California and Criminal Justice Scholars, and attended the evidentiary hearing at the Marin Superior Court (*In re Hall et al.*) as a spectator. She also attended, as a spectator, the case management conferences (CMCs) held in *Plata v. Newsom* at the Federal District Court. Both cases were litigated via Zoom and open to the public through links on the respective courts' websites. This chapter also extensively cites court documents, also available on the courts' websites.

Chapter 7, "Fear and Loathing," focuses on the efforts, organization, and challenges of the #StopSanQuentinOutbreak coalition, which sought to persuade the governor's office to pursue emergency releases. Through participant observations and documentation, we explain the shortcomings of the statewide release strategy: assumptions based on the myth of prison impermeability generated a policy that was too modest, dated on the very day it was proposed, too individualized, and too restrictive. We particularly contrast the political construction of long-term aging prisoners as risky prospects for release (out of fear of political backlash), especially against the prospect of postpandemic rising crime rates, and the actual medical-to-recidivist risk equation, which, based on robust empirical evidence, strongly suggests that about a fourth of the California prison population presents less risk (for them and for the surrounding community) in the community than they do behind bars.

The demographic information in chapter 7 is publicly available through CDCR's Office of Research: CDCR's annual report and the weekly and monthly prison population counts. This chapter also relies on participant observations in publicly observable protests and actions by the #StopSanQuentin coalition. To preserve the trust and confidentiality of the coalition members, as well as that of our many interlocutors, we do not use any information obtained without proper notification and consent to use in the book. Our experiences working with the coalition, however, provided deep background that informed the categories for analysis in chapter 2.

Chapter 8, "The Next Plague," concludes with important implications for theorizing, policymaking, and litigating prison condition and health-care cases. Letting go of the myth of prison impermeability offers hope and opportunity for profound criminal justice reform. On the scholarship level, it opens up a range of possibilities for examining prison/community interface and creating theoretical connections between existing bodies of literature currently siloed into insular subfields of correctional research. It also offers essential and practical revisions to Goffman's seminal work on total institutions. On the policymaking level, it calls for a realistic, pragmatic culling of the prison population and for a prison-community continuum in programming, health-care, and family life. And on the litigation level, the permeability of prisons has much promise in shaking up the stagnant framework of deference and restraint that characterizes Eighth Amendment case law on prison conditions.

ONE

Triggers and Vulnerabilities

The children of Israel were fruitful, and increased abundantly,
and multiplied, and grew exceedingly mighty; and the land was
filled with them.

EXODUS 1:7

IN HIS EXPLANATION of the 2008 financial crisis, Ben Bernanke, director
of the Federal Reserve, offered a framework of triggers and vulnerabilities.[1]
The triggers were the particular, immediate causes that ushered in the market
crash, such as developments in the subprime mortgage market; the vulnerabilities, by contrast, were the structural, fundamental weaknesses in the
financial system and its federal regulation. "The distinction between triggers
and vulnerabilities," he said, "is helpful in that it allows us to better understand why the factors that are often cited as touching off the crisis seem disproportionate to the magnitude of the financial and economic reaction."

Triggers and vulnerabilities are an apt framework for understanding why
California correctional institutions were a fertile petri dish for the COVID-
19 crisis. In the introduction, we discussed the inherently disease-prone
nature of correctional facilities; the centuries since *The State of the Prisons*
have done little to change this scenario worldwide. As of 2021, United
Nations experts conservatively estimated that more than 527,000 prisoners
had contracted the virus in 122 countries, with more than 3,800 fatalities in
47 countries.[2] In Brazil prisoners have rioted and fled facilities, furious about
their exposure to COVID-19 risks.[3] As early as March 2020, Iran released
85,000 prisoners in preparation for outbreaks.[4] Chase Burton attributes this
affliction to the general conditions in prisons, as well as to the diminished
health of those entering correctional facilities and governmental unwillingness to provide for this population:

> [I]t is impossible to socially distance in prisons. Prisoners nearly everywhere
> share common facilities, spaces, and dining areas, and it is not unusual for
> prisoners to share sleeping areas or sanitary facilities as well. In addition,

prisoners often have high levels of comorbidities and underlying health conditions, such as substance abuse disorders and autoimmune diseases, which
weaken the immune system and make them a vulnerable population for
the spread of disease ... [A]lthough the health of people in prisons would
be more than enough reason to take action, we must also understand that
diseases which spread in prisons do not stay in prisons.[5]

If anything, California, a state with a culture of anticipating natural
calamities, should have been prepared for taking emergency measures in the
face of a looming pandemic. In 1968, against the backdrop of the upheaval
and turmoil of the Summer of Love, Joan Didion wrote: "All that is constant
about the California of my childhood is the rate at which it disappears ...
California is a place in which a boom mentality and a sense of Chekhovian
loss meet in uneasy suspension."[6] Didion wrote about the inevitability of fire
and drought in the lives of Californians, of the normality of seeing a hill
engulfed in flames during one's morning commute, of emergency evacuation
kits by the door. In an interview in 2000, Didion said, "I think people who
grew up in California have more tolerance for apocalyptic notions."[7]

Nevertheless, California's prison system careened into calamity utterly
unprepared because of its existing vulnerabilities. This emblematic inability
to provide minimal health care in prisons is inexorably tied to California's
political culture. In *The Politics of Imprisonment*, Vanessa Barker compares
the political cultures of three states: California, Washington, and New
York.[8] Barker attributes the different degrees of punitiveness in these three
states to their civic engagement styles. California's political culture, which
Barker terms "polarized populism," is characterized by right-left polarization
and by an emotion-driven referendum system, frequently used by well-funded
parties with private interests. In contrast to Washington's town hall–style
deliberative democracy, and to New York's elite-driven policymaking,
California's culture renders it vulnerable to arguments based on high emotional valence.[9] In this environment, "redball crimes"—violent, heinous
crimes, as rare as they are shocking—have a strong rhetorical pull, which is
effectively marshaled to introduce punitive voter initiatives,[10] particularly by
California's powerful prison guard union and its partners, victims' rights
organizations.[11] These characteristics prime our state conversations about
criminal justice to revolve around, on one hand, a laissez-faire attitude and,
on the other, a fear of crime (and so-called "criminals"), and particularly a
reluctance to seriously consider nonpunitive reforms to sentencing and incarceration, especially for violent crime.

These tendencies were exacerbated by California's pioneering transition to determinate sentencing in 1977, which curtailed judicial discretion in sentencing and greatly limited the authority of parole boards to set prisoner release dates. Before this reform, California's prisons, by contrast to Arizona's[12] and Texas's[13] "cheap justice" farm- and plantation-like institutions, were large bureaucratic creatures, driven by rehabilitative ideas fostered by therapeutic professionals who toiled in obscurity within the prison. The transition to determinate sentencing shifted the power from these professionals to elected officials: legislators, who responded to public emotions and demands by proposing punitive bills, and prosecutors, authorized to choose charging offenses. Gradually, felony sentencing in California increased in length, largely due to the creation of sentencing enhancements and aggravating conditions, resulting in the largest prison population in the United States and in grossly overcrowded institutions.

At the heart of this punitive approach, with its ramifications for health care, was a constant perception that prisons are a world apart, inhabited by people undeserving of even the basic provisions and kindnesses, and unaffecting the remainder of the state. This approach persisted even when financial and other ramifications made the connection between the inside and the outside salient. The myth of prison impermeability characterized not only the problem, which has persisted for almost two centuries, but also the dramatic solution fashioned for it by federal courts and affirmed in the Supreme Court's landmark decision *Brown v. Plata*. In the paragraphs that follow, we survey the health-care situation that was endemic to California prisons, as reflected in the *Plata* and *Coleman* litigation. We then analyze the outcome in *Plata* and its ramifications as an example of "homeopathic justice": a step forward that, while dramatic in scope and a deviation from the usual judicial deference to prison administrations, was a low-concentration form of the very problems it sought to resolve.

TRIGGERS AND VULNERABILITIES IN CALIFORNIA'S PRISONS: PRISON HEALTH CARE BEFORE *PLATA*

The California prison apparatus was vulnerable to outbreaks of disease from its inception. The horrifying ravages of the 1918 influenza pandemic, at the time known as "Spanish flu," strikingly foreshadowed the COVID-19 pandemic. L. L. Stanley, the prison physician, reported of "an epidemic of unusual severity, with 101 patients admitted to the hospital, of whom 7 developed broncho-pneumonia, and 3 died."[14] The precautionary steps taken by the prison reflect concerns about compliance, quarantinism, and prevention that would be relevant for many subsequent decades:

> Masks were not used in this last epidemic, since, from the previous experience of the October visitation it was believed they were of little value because the prisoners would not use them.
>
> It was considered better to warn the inmates against close contact and congregating in enclosed places. All assemblages were prohibited.
>
> As soon as an inmate reported ill he was immediately placed in the hospital and quarantined. Here he was held for at least 10 days after subsidence of symptoms. To provide against introduction of the influenza into the prison by possible carriers, it was arranged to place all new arrivals in isolation for at least four days before allowing them to be turned loose in the yard with the other men. It was also arranged that masks should be worn by all prisoners who had receptions with friends or relatives. At these receptions the visitor sits at a narrow table opposite the prisoner. It was believed that masks would prevent a possible carrier from infecting the prisoner.
>
> Probably as a result of these precautions there was no return of the epidemic, although surrounding cities had many cases after December.[15]

Stanley drew several conclusions from the epidemic waves at San Quentin:

1. Each epidemic was apparently introduced by a recently infected entrant.
2. Close contact in crowded, poorly ventilated show rooms probably spread the infection.
3. The incubation period is from 48 to 60 hours.
4. The second epidemic was less severe than the first, and the third less severe than the second, as shown by the number diseased, number of pneumonia cases, and number of deaths in each.
5. The infection spread in definite groups by close contact, as shown by its course in the rooms where night school was held.
6. The disease in the first and second epidemics attacked more prisoners between ages 20 to 25, but in the third, more between the ages 25 and 30 as well as 40 to 45 became ill.
7. The most effective means available for combating the spread of the disease in this prison were hospitalization, quarantine, isolation, and closure of congregating places.
8. From the first epidemic it is seen that 5 per cent developed tuberculosis.

9. It appears that those men who entered prison after the April epidemic were attacked in greater numbers than those who had come before, although there were more of the latter than the former.[16]

This 1919 account reads contemporary and fresh because, in the hundred years that followed, not much changed in California's correctional facilities to reduce contagion risks. Relenting on mask mandates within the facility but insisting on them for contact with the outside reflected a quarantinist notion that what really mattered was minimizing any interface with the outside. This notion would continue to inform California's approach to health care, as reflected in two landmark cases concerning the pathologies of prison health care services: *Plata v. Schwarzenegger*, over physical care, and its predecessor by a decade, *Coleman v. Wilson*, over mental health care.[17] These deficiencies were not a function of scant funding: as explained above, California differed from other sunbelt correctional systems in that its bloated correctional colossus ate up millions of dollars, with little to show for it. Nor was the health care price tag meager compared to other carceral expenditures: despite consuming more than a fourth of the California correctional budget, the healthcare system was a reign of chaos and neglect. During the litigation in *Plata v. Schwarzenegger*, the case that would later be hailed as a prison rights victory, experts appointed by the federal district court toured the prison and wrote a report, which judge Thelton Henderson described as "shocking":

> The experts reported that they observed widespread evidence of medical malpractice and neglect. When they attempted to review a backlog of 193 death records, the experts encountered prisons where records could not even be located. Among the records they were able to review, the experts found 34 of the deaths highly problematic, with multiple instances of incompetence, indifference, neglect, and even cruelty by medical staff.[18]

The report found that "[m]any of the [prison] physicians have prior criminal charges, have had privileges revoked from hospitals, or have mental health related problems,"[19] and "[e]xpert review of prisoner deaths in the CDCR shows repeated gross departures from even minimal standards of care."[20] Findings such as these continue in excruciating detail for nearly 50 pages.

In Aaron Rappaport's review of the *Plata* litigation,[21] he explains that, following this report, the court decided to visit one of the prisons to gain a firsthand view of the conditions. The court toured San Quentin on February 10, 2005, one year after the prison was supposed to have achieved compliance with the minimum standards of care.[22] The visitors were horrified:

[The Outpatient Housing Unit] was in deplorable condition. The cells were dirty, the nursing station is beyond sight or sound of the cells, and there is no examination room on the unit so that examinations are often performed on the cell floors or even through the food slots. The pharmacy was in almost complete disarray (with unlabeled cardboard boxes piled in no particular order, antiquated and dirty computers, wiring suspended like a drunken spider's web, and extremely frustrated nurses and technicians), and there was an obvious shortage of medical supervisory and line staff.

The physical conditions in many CDCR clinics are completely inadequate for the provision of medical care. Many clinics do not meet basic sanitation standards .... For example, the main medical examining room lacked any means of sanitation—there was no sink and no alcohol gel—where roughly one hundred men per day undergo medical screening, and the Court observed that the dentist neither washed his hands nor changed his gloves after treating patients into whose mouths he had placed his hands.[23]

Judge Henderson concluded: "[I]t is an uncontested fact that, on average, an inmate in one of California's prisons needlessly dies every six to seven days due to constitutional deficiencies in the CDCR's medical delivery system."[24]

Eventually, the federal three-judge panel summarized the situation in the following words:

"California's correctional system is in a tailspin," the state's independent oversight agency has reported. Tough-on-crime politics have increased the population of California's prisons dramatically while making necessary reforms impossible. As a result, the state's prisons have become places "of extreme peril to the safety of persons" they house, while contributing little to the safety of California's residents. California "spends more on corrections than most countries in the world," but the state "reaps fewer public safety benefits." Although California's existing prison system serves neither the public nor the inmates well, the state has for years been unable or unwilling to implement the reforms necessary to reverse its continuing deterioration.[25]

Indeed, as judges, lawyers, criminologists, public policy scholars, and correctional administrators would agree, the situation in California prisons had become unsustainable. As of 2005 and subsequent years, housing more than 170,000 people[26]—the largest state prison population in the country with the largest prison population[27]—California's prison system was operating at almost 200 percent of its design capacity.[28] In an effort to house even more people, prison officials resorted to makeshift solutions, converting gyms and hallways into gigantic dormitories containing double- and triple-bunked beds. Therapy sessions were conducted in bathrooms, medical beds were placed in hallways, and prisoners received medical treatment in cages.[29] Even as San Quentin's dilapidated death row was being refurbished, its residents were double-celled, despite the risks and security problems inherent in such an arrangement.[30]

Unsurprisingly, the overcrowded conditions directly contributed to health-care problems. Correctional medical personnel were difficult to hire and retain because of California's unattractive correctional geography: large institutions in remote, rural locations.[31] Providing for necessities such as housing, clothing, and feeding on such a scale required considerable compromises in quality, hindering preventative health measures.[32] This problem was compounded by California's increasingly lengthy sentences: the number of people serving life sentences, due to sentencing inflation and enhancements, ballooned to a fourth of the prison population, producing an aging population in poor health, requiring intensive, pricey health care.[33] Registration and pharmaceutical services were overburdened and disorganized. Even when people finally received medical appointments, they would be required to wait for long hours in tiny holding cages without access to bathrooms. Taking prisoners to medical appointments often required lockdowns, which in turn created more delays and administrative hassles. Medical complaints were regularly trivialized and disbelieved—not, usually, out of sadism but out of fatigue and indifference in the face of profound need. Every six days, a prisoner would die from a preventable condition.[34] The case's namesake was emblematic: Marciano Plata was injured in 1997 while working in the prison kitchen. Unable to get adequate medical attention because of insufficient medical staffing, Plata's condition worsened to the point that his knee required surgery, which took years to schedule.[35]

Alongside the physical health-care pathologies, the prison mental health-care system faltered. As Rappaport explains,[36] relying on the original *Coleman* transcripts and documents, the federal panel found that the state had no "systematic program for screening and evaluating inmates for mental illness," resulting in "thousands of inmates suffering from mental illness either undetected, untreated, or both."[37] The court found persistent and extensive "delays in access to necessary mental health care," which in some prisons reached a "crisis level."[38] This was partly due to chronic understaffing in CDCR's mental health-care roster.[39] Where services were offered, they were frequently substandard: medication was haphazardly distributed, and the court found serious problems in recordkeeping, "'including disorganized, untimely and incomplete filing of medical records, insufficient charting, and incomplete or nonexistent treatment plans at most prisons.'" Additionally, "inmates [were] typically transferred between prisons without even such medical records as might exist."[40] Moreover, the prison system had no means to identify or correct these defects because it had no "quality assurance" program to ensure the competence of their mental health-care staff and the adequacy of the services.[41] These kinds of findings led the *Coleman* court to conclude that California prisons lacked the "basic, essentially common sense, components of a minimally adequate prison mental health care delivery system," including "proper screening; timely access to appropriate levels of care; an adequate medical record system; proper administration of psychotropic medication; competent staff in sufficient numbers; and a basic suicide prevention program."[42]

THE *PLATA/COLEMAN* LITIGATION: A PATTERN OF STATE INTRANSIGENCE AND SABOTAGE

Litigation in the *Coleman* and *Plata* cases from 2000 to 2008 was characterized by intense resistance and a strong recalcitrance to make any changes to California's prison health-care administration, let alone consider population reduction. Correspondingly, federal courts, increasingly transcending their natural deference to prison administration,[43] tried to resolve the problem through a slew of remedial orders of increasing severity, to the point of taking many aspects of the health-care apparatus out of the state's hands.

In *Coleman*, Judge Karlton ultimately appointed special masters to supervise the mental health system and begin an arduous process of reform.[44] Publicly reminiscing about the lawsuit in 2009, he lamented that, nearly two decades into the suit, he was still forced to issue remedial orders to require the state to provide a sufficient number of beds to care for mental health patients.[45] Donald Specter, in his own presentation, noted the state's seemingly passive-aggressive efforts to forestall reform. After 2006 the state agreed it would be better to let the receiver handle the construction of the new bed plan, since the receiver could act more quickly and efficiently. However, as Specter noted, even before the receiver could act, the state "went to court to actually block the Receiver from constructing the very beds that they agreed were necessary." When Judge Karlton responded by asking the state for its plan to construct the beds, state attorneys asked for several weeks to devise a plan, and then asked for a further 90-day extension. Judge Karlton was furious, stating it was incomprehensible that after 14 years, the state still did not have a bed plan. According to Donald Specter, Judge Karlton declared that the state had demonstrated "an unacceptable lack of commitment to its constitutional duty much less towards this court."[46]

A similar scenario played out in *Plata*. The state agreed to a stipulated settlement that required it to adopt medical policies and procedures at all institutions,[47] which was to be implemented on a staggered basis: seven prisons would implement changes in 2003, with five additional prisons implementing changes each succeeding year until all 33 prisons were rehabilitated.[48] The state also "agreed to the appointment of medical and nursing experts" to advise the court on the progress of the reforms.[49] But when the court reviewed the state's progress in 2004, it found that not a single prison had successfully implemented the plan.[50] Worse, the court received a report from its appointed experts according to which there was an "emerging pattern of inadequate and seriously deficient physician quality in CDC facilities," such as a retired surgeon that continually made serious life-threatening mistakes, inadequate peer review, and insufficient physician supervision.[51] A 2005 report on conditions at San Quentin was equally damning. The report noted "multiple instances of incompetence, indifference, cruelty, and neglect"[52] rising to the level of preventable deaths. Eventually, on June 30, 2005, the *Plata* court ruled that it would appoint a federal receiver to oversee the California health-care system.

Accustomed to consent decrees and less drastic orders, the court itself perceived this step as "a drastic measure"[53] that rose to the level of "the largest federal takeover of a state prison medical care system in our country's history."[54] Rappaport explains that a receiver is "authorized by the court to make whatever changes he or she deems appropriate to bring the system into compliance with constitutional norms." Moreover,

> the Receiver need not ask the court for approval each time he or she acts. That means the Receiver can hire or fire staff, reorganize an agency, and even demand funds from the state treasury . . ., the Receiver's authority is derived from the federal courts and the U.S. Constitution, thereby giving it the power to ignore or suspend state law.[55]

The first appointee, Robert Sillen, proposed an ambitious and expensive plan for reforming the health-care system, including the construction of seven new health centers or hospitals and the upgrade of all prison facilities.[56] Fully implemented, the plan would generate 10,000 new hospital beds—5,000 earmarked for medical care and 5,000 for mental health care—and would cost $8 billion.[57] Sillen's aggressive stance and animosity toward the state prison bureaucracy went as far as threatening state officials with serious repercussions for noncompliance—including flouting state laws requiring minimum wage.[58] When the state refused to fund certain prison construction projects, Sillen declared that if the state did not act soon, he would drive a van to the state treasury and start loading money into the back.[59] After two years on the job, Sillen was fired by Judge Henderson;[60] it later turned out that Sillen and his employees were overpaid to the tune of hundreds of thousands of dollars.[61] Clark Kelso was appointed his successor on January 23, 2008, a move that did not alleviate the animosity between the custodial side of the prison apparatus, consisting of state officials, and the federal overseers of the medical side. When Kelso requested $200 million to begin implementing the turnaround plan,[62] the state refused to comply; Kelso then filed a motion in federal court to hold the governor and the state controller in contempt of court.[63] The state reciprocated by filing a motion to terminate the receivership. It argued, among other things, that the receivership was unlawful under the Prison Litigation Reform Act (PLRA).[64] The opening paragraph of the receiver's January 2009 report gave a hint of the nadir of state-receiver relationships: During the reporting period, the governor and the attorney general . . . executed a "flip-flop" and "bait and switch." The immediate victims of the state's turnabout, wrote Kelso, were four federal district courts and respect for the rule of law; "the ultimate victims are the tens of thousands of class members who are waiting for constitutionally required improvements in their medical care as well as the citizens of the State of California."[65] Meanwhile, state officials viciously attacked the receiver. The attorney general, for example, declared that the "Receivership has become a government unto itself, operating without accountability, without public scrutiny and without clear standards."[66]

A possible breakthrough seemed to occur in the spring of 2009, when Kelso agreed to scale back his $8 billion plan: rather than building 10,000 new beds, he unveiled a new plan to construct only two hospitals with a capacity of 3,400 beds. The cost under this revised plan would drop substantially, to $1.9 billion.[67] Kelso also agreed to retract his motion to hold Governor Schwarzenegger in contempt and, in return, demanded that the state provide the required funds and end efforts to terminate the receivership. But the thawing of the federal-state relationship ended up bringing the litigation to a breaking point. The negotiations between Kelso and CDCR secretary Matthew Cate led nowhere; eventually, Judge Karlton scolded the government's lawyers for their "intolerable" failure to approve the tentative agreement. Karlton also warned that if the state failed to sign the agreement or propose a reasonable, fully funded alternative, he would start "eating into their budget in a real dramatic way." The judge continued, "[t]hose are orders of the court that must be obeyed—not hoped for, not prayed for—obeyed. I'm not kidding."[68] The state lawyers repudiated the agreement, making a zero-sum argument emblematic of the myth of prison impermeability: they quoted Schwarzenegger, who said that he "[could not] agree to spend $2 billion on state-of-the-art medical facilities for prisoners while we are cutting billions of dollars from schools and health care programs for children and seniors." This position was typical of Schwarzenegger's zero-sum thinking, which frequently juxtaposed prison and education expenditures; at some point, he even proposed legislation according to which it would be impermissible to spend more on the former than on the latter, which the Legislative Analyst's Office severely criticized as reductive.[69]

The *Plata/Coleman* litigation exemplified some of the inherent problems of the myth of prison impermeability: judicial resistance to interference in prison management, accompanied by the sense that essential, last-resort interventions might be too sweeping and backfire; disconnect, and sometimes bitter animosity, between the custodial and the medical authorities of the correctional apparatus, as well as between state officials and federal overseers; and clunkiness, to the point of indifference, when rapid responses are needed to save lives.

An apt illustration of the chaos wrought by the struggle between the receiver and state authorities was the tragic mismanagement of a previous serious prison pandemic—valley fever. On February 1, 2022, Judge Tigar (who would also preside over the COVID-19 class action *Plata v. Newsom*) granted the current and former federal receivers of the prison health-care system, Clark Kelso and Robert Sillen, a motion to dismiss a class action involving the valley fever outbreak of 2005.[70] At the heart of the problem was the significant increase of valley fever cases in California facilities, particularly among Black and Filipino people. The receiver commissioned an investigation, which found that

Pleasant Valley State Prison had 166 Valley Fever infections in 2005, including 29 hospitalizations and four deaths. The infection rate inside the prison was 38 times higher than in the nearby town and 600 times higher than in the surrounding county. According to the report, "the risk for extrapulmonary complications [was] increased for persons of African or Filipino descent, but the risk [was] even higher for heavily immunosuppressed patients." The report then explained that physically removing heavily immunosuppressed patients from the affected area "would be the most effective method to decrease risk." The report also recommended ways to reduce the amount of dust at the prisons. After receiving the health department's recommendations, the Receiver convened its own committee. In June 2007, the Receiver's committee made recommendations that were similar to those from the health department.

In response, the receivership adopted a statewide exclusion policy that went into effect in November 2007, which identified six clinical criteria to identify those most at risk of death from valley fever, but race was not included—even after the policy was refined in 2010. Because race was, indeed, a risk factor for valley fever—which was known to the authorities given the 2005 report—the results were predictable:

> In April 2012, the prison system's own healthcare services released a report examining Valley Fever in prisons. The report concluded that despite the "education of staff and inmates" and the "exclusion of immunocompromised inmates," there had been "no decrease in cocci rates." The authors found that Pleasant Valley State Prison inmates were still much more likely to contract Valley Fever than citizens of the surrounding county. From 2006 to 2010, 7.01% of inmates at Pleasant Valley State Prison and 1.33% of inmates at Avenal State Prison were infected. By comparison, the highest countywide infection rate was 0.135%, and the statewide rate was just 0.007%. From 2006 to 2011, 36 inmates in the Central Valley prisons died from Valley Fever. Prison healthcare services also found that male African-American inmates were twice as likely to die as other inmates. Each year, about 29% of the male inmates in California are African-American, but 50% of the inmates who developed disseminated cocci between 2010 and 2012 were African-American, and 71% of the inmates who died from Valley Fever between 2006 and 2011 were African-American.[71]

Consequently, incarcerated people infected with valley fever attempted to sue CDCR officials for mismanaging the outbreak. The lawsuit failed due to qualified immunity: the officials prevailed because they followed the orders of the receiver. The valley fever victims pursued the receivership, also, for its neglectful preventative approach; the receivers countered that, as officers of the court, they had quasi-judicial immunity. The plaintiffs attempted a sophisticated attack on this argument, claiming that the receivers should not have directed CDCR's preventative policies, and that their mandate was limited to providing medical care. The argument failed: Judge Tigar found that "prevention of disease is, and always has been, within the Receivers' jurisdiction."

Ironically, it was precisely this wide mandate that aided the receivers' success in dismissing the case. Because they were acting within their authority, wrote Judge Tigar, and because said authority was quasi-judicial, they could enjoy immunity. Oddly, the decision mentions that "Plaintiffs do not argue that the other exception to judicial immunity—for actions 'not taken in the judge's judicial capacity'—applies here"—an odd omission, as Sillen and Kelso were acting as medical officials rather than judicial ones.

The valley fever epidemic, and the outcome in *Hines*, illustrate the Byzantine nature of California's correctional health-care system. Ironically, the effort to create patchwork remedies for the system's own ineptitude then stands in the way of recourse for this very ineptitude. A similar pattern would emerge, on a larger scale, in the *Plata* litigation.

THE ERA OF *PLATA*: RECESSION-ERA REFORMS AND THEIR LIMITATIONS

The years 2008–9 ushered in transformation not only in California but nationwide, due to a confluence of events. The 2008 financial crisis plunged state and local governments into a deep recession, which awakened interest in local budgets, of which correctional expenditures were a considerable share.[72] The realization that mass incarceration was financially unsustainable facilitated bipartisan coalitions at the state and federal levels,[73] dovetailing with the Obama administration's focus on criminal justice reform and racial justice.[74] Part and parcel of these coalition-building efforts was the politically expedient consensus to focus on low-hanging fruit, in the form of politically palatable populations, such as nonviolent drug offenders, which received the bulk of reformist attention on the right[75] as well as on the left.[76]

The *Plata* panel's population reduction order of 2009, while historically important, was in step with these new winds. Under the Prison Litigation Reform Act (PLRA), the panel ordered a reduction of California's prison population to 137.5 percent of system-wide design capacity—admittedly, a drastic population cut that the state would continue to fight tooth and nail all the way to the Supreme Court—but shied away from specifying how the population reduction was to be done. Theoretically, the state could have built more prisons to alleviate overcrowding, but recession-era cuts impeded this course of action.[77] Another possibility, relying on private contractors, was blocked by conflicting political interests.[78] In 2011, as *Plata* made its way to the Supreme Court, Governor Brown continued the path charted by his predecessor[79] and signed extensive legislation—the Criminal Justice Realignment.[80] Now, people convicted of "non-non-non" offenses—nonviolent, nonsexual, nonserious—would serve their sentences in county jails, rather than in state prisons, eliminating the "correctional free lunch" problem of sentencing at the county level and spending money on the state level.[81] Judges were given more sentencing discretion and, in most cases, parole supervision functions were transferred to community probation offices.

Brown's anticipation of the Supreme Court's affirmation of the *Plata* order proved prescient: the decision, which upheld the mandate to considerably reduce California's prison population, is widely regarded as a watershed moment in US prison litigation. The resulting jurisdictional shift was viewed as "the greatest experiment" in American correctional policy[82] and interpreted as "the second coming of dignity."[83] These optimistic perspectives were buoyed by the emotional, evocative tone of the decision: Justice Kennedy, by no means a bleeding-heart liberal, but a humane judge with a soft spot for correctional horrors,[84] wrote the majority opinion. It is, notably, the first Supreme Court opinion ever to include photographs; each depiction of the horrific overcrowding throughout the CDCR facilities is truly worth a thousand words (see figure 1).[85] The decision outright rejected the state's contention that the three-judge panel was convened incorrectly, stating that the time that had passed and the lack of relief necessitated this step. Documenting the standard of care, the abundant vacancies for medical and mental health staff, and the shortfall of resources, Justice Kennedy stated that the court had waited long enough before recurring to this admittedly drastic step. Justice Kennedy supported and affirmed the three-judge-panel conclusion that overcrowding was the dominant reason for the violations, as well as their conclusion, after considering many other options, that other remedial efforts had not borne fruit and therefore the only recourse would have to be reducing the population.

While the population reduction is of "unprecedented sweep and extent," wrote Justice Kennedy, "so too is the continuing injury and harm resulting from these serious constitutional violations." Justice Kennedy devoted a large portion of the opinion to a detailed description of the overcrowded

Appendix B to opinion of the Court

B

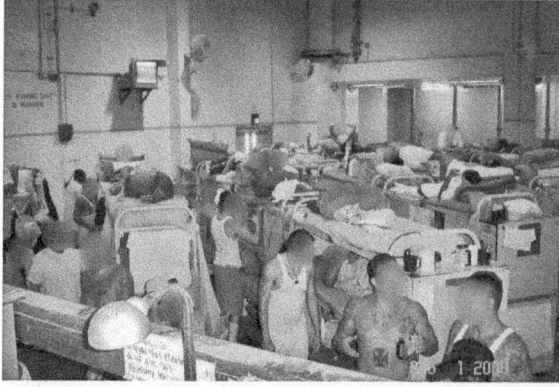

Mule Creek State Prison
Aug. 1, 2008

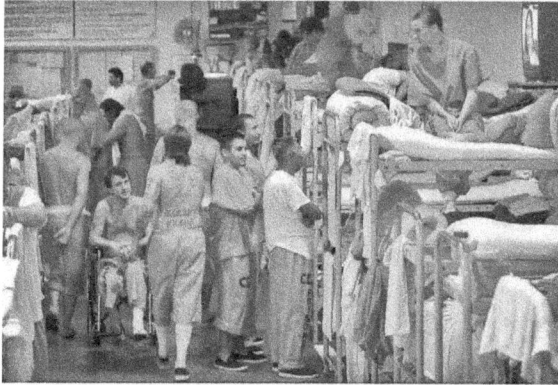

California Institution for Men
Aug. 7, 2006

FIGURE I. Images of overcrowding in California prisons before *Brown v. Plata* (*Brown v. Plata*).

conditions, mentioning the San Quentin converted gym and describing numerous incidents of appalling mental and physical care. He also provided details of the history of both cases, *Coleman* and *Plata*, and how the various measures to which the state resorted throughout the years failed to improve conditions. In this part, he relied extensively on data from the receiver and the special master, as well as the three-judge-panel decision. His description of how overcrowding was a direct and indirect cause of the abysmal health care closely followed the original panel order, citing, among other factors, the unsanitary conditions and the reliance on lockdowns, both discussed extensively in the original order.[86] This resulted in Eighth Amendment violations because "[a] prison that deprives prisoners of basic sustenance, including adequate medical care, is incompatible with the concept of human dignity and has no place in civilized society."

As far as its practical implications, the decision was a mixed blessing. Readers looking for an unequivocal statement on behalf of decarceration were disappointed. Justice Kennedy cautiously mentioned that "[t]he order leaves the choice of means to reduce overcrowding to the discretion of state officials. But absent compliance through new construction, out-of-state transfers, or other means—or modification of the order upon a further showing by the State—the State will be required to release some number of prisoners before their full sentences have been served." Through this framework, Justice Kennedy set the stage for the state to avoid early releases by recurring to damaging, malignant techniques, which proceeded to delay incarceration in the long run (and played out in a most unsavory way in the COVID-19 cases).

Other aspects of the decision seemed to bode well. Justice Kennedy was seemingly persuaded by the evidence presented to the original panel about the possibility of reducing population without causing an increase in crime and endangering public safety. He also affirmed the panel's estimate as to the extent of the reduction. His decision was a vote of confidence in the panel's work, comparing their projection that a 137.5 percent capacity would be reasonable under the circumstances to the situation in other states and in the federal prisons.

Justice Kennedy was careful to cut the state some slack in the timing of its plan. He encouraged the state to "move for modification of the ... order to extend the deadline for the required reduction to five years from the entry of the judgment of this court, the deadline proposed in the State's first population reduction plan ... [t]he three-judge court, in its discretion, may also consider whether it is appropriate to order the State to begin without delay to develop a system to identify prisoners who are unlikely to reoffend or who might otherwise be candidates for early release." For this purpose, an extension of time was encouraged, suggesting patience and the need to compromise.

If the majority opinion could be hailed as a victory for dignity, the dissent was the exact opposite. Justice Scalia bemoaned the fact that the court failed to "bend every effort to read the law in such a way as to avoid that outrageous result." His perspective was not wholly unpredictable: during the oral argument, when a horrified Justice Sotomayor made an impassioned comment about human beings lying in their own excrement, Justice Scalia told her off, saying, "don't be rhetorical." Echoing Justice Holmes's notorious eugenic, dehumanizing comment in *Buck v. Bell*, according to which "three generations of imbeciles is enough,"[87] Scalia mocked the complaints of prison residents subjected to medical neglect by observing that "[m]ost people to be released under the population reduction order will not be prisoners with medical conditions or severe mental illness; and many will undoubtedly be fine physical specimens who have developed intimidating muscles pumping iron in the prison gym"—commentary that evokes lurid literary and film exploitations of prison life.

If the *Plata* opinion fell short of being "the second coming of dignity," it did, at least, curb California's incarceration appetite, an improvement by all accounts. A closer look at the opinion, however, reveals numerous weaknesses, which share values and premises with the very situation that *Plata* sought to remedy: an atomistic, jurisdictional view of how incarcerated populations flow from place to place; a focus on the "low-hanging fruit" of nonserious, nonviolent offenders; and a focus on system-wide change without regard to the actual living conditions in each individual facility. We turn to these now.

FROM STATE TO COUNTIES: ORIGIN OF THE "HYDRA PROBLEM"

The implementation of Realignment meant that many thousands of people, formerly under the auspices (and financial responsibility) of the state, would now be housed, clothed, and fed at the county level. Many scholars and policymakers who welcomed this jurisdictional shift thought that counties would be better positioned to connect people with rehabilitation and reentry services because of their stronger ties to the home communities of incarcerated people, and that health care at the state level was so dire that the counties would surely do better.[88]

But the assumption that jails would be an improvement neglected to consider several factors. The first of these, which law professor Margo Schlanger referred to as the "hydra problem," was the concern that a decentralized health-care system would be difficult to monitor and improve: that is, rather than following the health-care instructions and practices in one jurisdiction (the state), prison rights advocates would now have to follow—and litigate—incarceration conditions and mismanagement in each county. Additionally, jails, originally built as short-term housing (pretrial or for less than a year), could not cater to a population in need of both acute and chronic health care. The extent to which counties rose to the occasion varied greatly: while some counties made efforts to reduce incarceration well ahead of *Plata*, others, in panic, started building jails[89] or changing revenue structures to roll expenses onto the inmates themselves. Such structures included "pay to stay" jails, in which people pay for their own incarceration (as if paying for a hotel stay) through liens on their postincarceration earnings, or more opaque practices: monetizing and charging for haircuts, food, and some health-care services.[90] The gaps in implementation were also reflected in divergent reliance on incarceration among judges in different counties.[91] These divergent patterns were unfortunately exacerbated by the formula for funding the newly burdened county systems, which was initially based on the counties' respective incarceration rates; this funding mechanism rewarded counties that relied more on incarceration and penalized those that avoided it, disincentivizing courts, sheriff's departments, and probation services from investing more in noncarceral options.[92]

BIFURCATION AND THE VIOLENT/NONVIOLENT DICHOTOMY

The Realignment's focus on rehousing the "non-non-nons," a more sympathetic population and therefore an easier "sell" from a political optics perspective, was emblematic of the bifurcation element of recession-era reforms: they applied to nonviolent offenders and retrenched negative public opinion about so-called violent offenders.

This distinction was based on several unfounded myths, the first of which was that mass incarceration resulted mostly from the needless incarceration of nonviolent offenders. In fact, drug offenders—the recipients of bipartisan sympathies, and justifiably so given racial disparities in drug enforcement—never exceeded a fourth of the state prison population nationwide, whereas people convicted of "violent" offenses constituted a majority of those in state prisons.[93] In California, especially after the legislative changes in 2011 and 2014, three-quarters of the prison population have been people convicted of "violent" crimes.[94] A related myth was the perception that violent offenders posed a greater risk to public safety—which proved to be untrue.[95] In California, specifically, the focus on the crime of conviction led the legal system to ignore a fourth of the prison population—the people serving the state's three most extreme sentences: incarceration on death row, life without parole, and life with parole. Because of the rarity of executions in California and the rarity of release on parole, these three punishments merged into an "extreme punishment trifecta,"[96] consisting of decades behind bars. Greatly overlapping with this category were prisoners aged 50 and above,[97] who, due to serving extremely lengthy sentences, had not only aged out of crime[98] but also incurred disabilities and chronic health conditions. Well-meaning reforms, therefore, calcified public opinion against the people who were wrongly perceived, because of their crime of commitment, to pose risks to public safety while, at the same time, facing increased risks to their own health because of their age and the prison conditions they have endured during their lengthy sentences. California's aforementioned political culture[99] is sensitive to emotional arguments building on heinous (albeit very rare) violent crimes, and public opinion has been remarkably resistant to the idea of distinguishing between, and extending compassion to, people convicted of violent crimes.

SYSTEM-WIDE POPULATION REDUCTION

Another well-meaning aspect of the *Plata* reforms was that the court order set a population reduction benchmark for the system as a whole, rather than for each individual institution. Part of the vagueness of the order was due to the already extreme measure of relying on the PLRA to require an enormous statewide effort. However, the choice of litigation strategy also mattered. By contrast to European and international standards, which measure humane incarceration standards based on a minimal square area per prisoner,[100] the order in California did not go so far as to ensure that each person would have adequate space—only that the average person in the entire system would. For years after the *Plata* decision, there was considerable variety in the occupation rates of state prisons, with some prisons still at pre-*Plata* capacity while others were at capacity or even slightly below. The decision, therefore, did not impact everyone equally.

The predictable challenge of protecting incarcerated people from contagion and illness should have, in itself, alerted state officials to the need to prioritize prevention, but there were also specific warnings regarding the threat of COVID-19, widely published months before the outbreak at San Quentin, in the early weeks of the pandemic. On March 23, 2020, the World Health Organization (WHO) published guidelines to protect prison populations worldwide from infection.[101] Declaring that health care for people in prisons was "a state responsibility," the WHO guidelines listed a few commonsense principles for prisons:

- People in prisons and other places of detention should enjoy the same standards of health care that are available in the outside community, without discrimination on the grounds of their legal status.

- Adequate measures should be in place to ensure a gender-responsive approach in addressing the COVID-19 emergency in prisons and other places of detention.

- Prisons and other detention authorities need to ensure that the human rights of those in their custody are respected, that people are not cut off from the outside world, and—most importantly—that they have access to information and adequate healthcare provision. Enhanced consideration should be given to resorting to non-custodial measures at all stages of the administration of criminal justice, including at the pre-trial, trial and sentencing as well as post-sentencing stages. Priority should be given to non-custodial measures for alleged offenders and prisoners with low-risk profiles and caring responsibilities, with preference given to pregnant women and women with dependent children.

- Similarly, refined allocation procedures should be considered that would allow prisoners at highest risk to be separated from others in the most effective and least disruptive manner possible and that would permit limited single accommodation to remain available to the most vulnerable.

- Upon admission to prisons and other places of detention, all individuals should be screened for fever and lower respiratory tract symptoms; particular attention should be paid to persons with contagious diseases. If they have symptoms compatible with COVID-19, or if they have a prior COVID-19 diagnosis and are still symptomatic, they should be put into medical isolation until there can be further medical evaluation and testing.[102]

Similarly, the Centers for Disease Control and Prevention (CDC) issued commonsense guidelines in early April, as a response to the first COVID-19 cases in Louisiana prisons. These were published and communicated on CDC outlets and included the following:

> 1) suspension of transfers of incarcerated and detained persons and visitation; 2) access to hand hygiene supplies, including running water, for both incarcerated or detained persons and staff members; 3) symptom screening and 14-day quarantine of incarcerated or detained persons upon intake to the facility before joining the general facility population; 4) symptom screening for staff members at the beginning of each shift; 5) dedication of space for medical isolation and quarantine; 6) symptom screening and coordination with local public health officials before release of incarcerated or detained persons; 7) personal protective equipment (PPE) use by staff members and incarcerated or detained persons who have duties that could involve exposure to an incarcerated or detained person with COVID-19; and 8) assignment of staff members to specific housing units.[103]

Popular outlets published warnings and guidelines from criminal justice and corrections experts. While these predictions were dismissed as alarmist at the time, they turned out to be accurate forecasts. On March 11, Premal Dharia of the International Legal Foundation wrote:

> Keeping people trapped inside facilities under heightened restrictions will do less, not more, to protect the greater community. Movement between people on the inside and on the outside is ceaseless. And because carceral facilities cannot operate without staff, who move in and out of these spaces every day, heightened restrictions are largely futile. The only meaningful way to keep the most people safe is to decrease the number of people incarcerated.[104]

On March 16, the *New York Times* published an opinion piece by Amanda Klonsky, with dire warnings about the contagion potential in prison. Klonsky advocated for a "one-time review of all elderly or infirm people in prisons, providing immediate medical furloughs or compassionate release to as many of them as possible."[105]

On March 23, putting North Carolina's correctional system on notice, criminal law scholar Brandon Garrett and social medicine expert Lauren Brinkley-Rubinstein warned about the risks to "people [who] have been jailed across the state for inability to pay cash bail, not because of pressing public safety concerns." These people, who are "presumed innocent . . . now find their health and lives imperiled through their involvement in the justice system." They also warned that "correctional facilities should consider releasing people who are infirm or elderly."[106]

On March 27, prison law scholars Margo Schlanger and Sonja Starr warned that "[w]e are on the verge of catastrophe—for incarcerated persons, staff, and their families, obviously, but also for the general public. Some officials have been sounding the alarm, and we're beginning to see some action—but not nearly enough, and not fast enough." Schlanger and Starr listed four commonsense strategies, one of which was to

> [c]ommute all sentences due to end within a year . . . Inevitably, hundreds of thousands of people will be released from prisons and jails during this emergency because they are due to be released. Keeping them behind bars until the crisis ends is not an option. Everyone will be safer if they are released *now* . . . The public safety risk would be minimal, and far outweighed by the benefits of reducing coronavirus spread. Many of those due for release within a year were convicted of misdemeanors or minor felonies and had short sentences to begin with. Others are people who have already served most of a longer sentence. Some have even already been granted parole but are awaiting various administrative steps for release. But all are due to be released soon anyway—the question is whether they bring the coronavirus with them.[107]

Schlanger and Starr also urged public officials to "release older and chronically ill individuals. Many older people behind bars are serving long sentences for long-ago violent crimes and are left out of steps targeting minor offenders. But even if past crimes were significant, nobody deserves the death sentence that COVID-19 could very likely become. Moreover, the vast majority pose no risk to the public now (except as virus vectors)."

In late March, Arizona State University's podcast *Legalese* published an episode on COVID-19 in the criminal justice system, including warnings anticipating pandemic spread in prisons. Law professor Valena Beety and guests discussed the urgency of releases and guaranteeing safety: "if safety means mass releases, then it's mass releases . . . we should release the people that we can. Certainly people incarcerated are at risk just as people outside are at risk, and we need to get at least the high risk people out of the jail . . . in order to protect them."[108] The podcast guests emphasized that "[i]f we're going to talk about flattening the curve, then prisons, jails, and detention centers have to be part of the conversation."

On April 20, Sharon Dolovich, the director of UCLA's Center on Prison Law and Policy (who would later lead UCLA's COVID Behind Bars Data Project), wrote:

> COVID-19 is already moving through prisons and jails across the country, and confirmed cases are growing exponentially ... In every facility, once the virus takes hold, it will spread quickly. Untold numbers of people will die, effectively sentencing them to the death penalty, whatever their crime. Every public official with the power to decarcerate should exercise that power now, to the fullest extent. If they do, they will save countless lives, including those of staff. And in the process, they may show us by example how to begin, finally, to dismantle mass incarceration for good.[109]

On April 23, the *New York Times* editorial board reminded the public that "[n]o one deserves to die of Covid-19 in prison or jail." They advised that "[i]nfection hot spots appearing in prisons is not a fait accompli. The spread of the virus can be curbed if prisons send home eligible inmates ... Releasing these prisoners during this crisis is not just an act of mercy to protect prisoners' health, and the health of the prison staff. Fewer sick inmates means less strain on the already burdened prison hospital system."[110]

On May 29, legal scholar Andrea Armstrong and colleagues at the Interdisciplinary Research Leaders Blog participated in a project providing guidance to correctional facilities on testing, contact with families of incarcerated people, decarceration efforts, and other important initiatives, commenting that "[m]ost of the work that we have done over the last few months to support the health of people incarcerated is applicable nationwide."[111]

These are just a few examples of the many editorials, pleas, and public commentaries widely available months before the San Quentin outbreak. In addition, other California prisons—some newer, less crowded, and better ventilated than San Quentin—had seen serious outbreaks, hundreds of cases, and several deaths months before the San Quentin outbreak. And so, in March 2020, unprepared prisons with indifferent administrators, overseen by political agents unmotivated to consider drastic measures, let alone population reduction, were sites of ticking bombs, waiting for the calamity to fully manifest.

TWO

Petri Dish

These are the Ten Plagues which the Holy One, blessed be His name, brought upon the Egyptians, namely as follows:

Blood.
Frogs.
Lice.
Wild Beasts.
Pestilence.
Boils.
Hail.
Locusts.
Darkness.
Slaying of the First-born.

THE PASSOVER HAGGADAH

ON JULY 11, as the pandemic tore through California's prisons, members of the #StopSanQuentinOutbreak coalition watched the rising numbers with concern. On the phone, loved ones told heartbreaking stories of illness, neglect, and callousness inside. Worried family members could hear coughing, screaming, and "Man down!" shouts in the background.

Two members of the coalition were all too familiar with this landscape. James King, the state campaigner for the Ella Baker Center for Human Rights, had been incarcerated himself; San Francisco public defender Danica Rodarmel, deeply involved in the struggle for better prison conditions, had an incarcerated loved one. They coauthored an op-ed pleading with Governor Newsom to release more people:

> We appreciate Gov. Newsom's statements that he is willing to visit San Quentin—a community he has lifted up and supported in the past—and hope he will do so in order to see the full extent of the human rights travesty that is occurring there. We trust that being faced with such devastating human suffering, the governor will be motivated to continue on the path to redemption and reduce the prison population to protect us all.[1]

What was the scope of this "human rights travesty," and in what ways did it exceed, or differ from, the worldwide suffering wrought by the virus? That a massive public health crisis produced many harms, particularly to already disadvantaged communities, is hardly news. But in the context of incarceration, paying attention to a diverse range of special harms matters for both legal and sociological reasons.

Legally speaking, mishandling of health care within prisons is regarded not as an inevitable aspect of the prison experience but as an additional infliction of harm that might constitute a constitutional violation. The Eighth Amendment, which prohibits cruel and unusual punishment,[2] has been extensively used in prison conditions litigation. In the context of health care, the legal test for "cruel and unusual," according to the US Supreme Court, is "deliberate indifference": the prison authorities' deliberate exposure of incarcerated people to "substantial risk."[3] In assessing the "substantial risk," courts have considered "(1) whether a reasonable doctor or patient would perceive the medical need in question as important and worthy of comment or treatment; (2) whether the medical condition significantly affects daily activities; and (3) the existence of chronic and substantial pain."[4] In addition, a condition evincing "serious medical need" is one that "has been diagnosed by a physician as mandating treatment or . . . is so obvious that even a lay person would easily recognize the necessity of a doctor's attention."[5]

The "deliberate indifference" standard evokes two philosophical perspectives. The first is the classic, welfarist duty of care that the state owes to its wards, people who involuntarily relinquish their autonomy over their own safety and well-being. The second is the formalist legal notion that our penal codes prescribe, as punishment, the deprivation of liberty and nothing more; therefore, to the extent possible, the incarceration experience must be stripped of any additional harms. Both perspectives are continuously eroded and attacked. As many commentators have observed, the capitalist engine of the prison system means that prisoners are increasingly seen less as wards and more as quasi-voluntary consumers of services, for which they are charged.[6] And many sectors of the public, particularly in populistic states, register vocal resistance to any effort to improve prison conditions, often through the rhetoric of imposing on people just deserts.[7] Nevertheless, the aspiration to separate the loss of liberty from its insalubrious corollaries permeates many aspects of Eighth Amendment litigation: for example, it is hard to attack the constitutionality of the death penalty, which was pronounced constitutionally compliant by the Supreme Court in 1976,[8] and therefore death penalty litigation focuses on the adjacent suffering, in an effort to divorce the death itself from its constitutionally questionable corollaries, such as pain or execution of members of special, vulnerable populations.[9]

Sociologists, on the other hand, have known for decades that severing the technical core of punishment from its penumbra was, practically, an impossible task. The notion that imprisonment encompasses a range of harms beyond mere deprivation of liberty was a big part of the prison ethnography boom of the 1960s. Inspired in part by Goffman's observation-based study of prisons and mental health hospitals,[10] and aided by lax regulation on human subjects research,[11] sociologists entered prisons and conducted observations. These studies characterized prisons, as we explained in the introduction, as self-contained institutions, governed by internal logics, rules, and adaptations. Goffman coined the term "total institution" to capture the absolute subjection of the person to the environment, beginning with the branding rituals that turned the person into an "inmate" and continuing with the clandestine economy, adaptation strategies, and staff-inmate relations. In 1965 the seminal prison scholarship anthology *The Sociology of Punishment and Corrections*[12] was published, with many of its chapters destined to be penology classics, such as Donald Clemmer's concept of "prisonization"— socialization to life inside.[13] Among these works was a short but fundamental text by criminologist Gresham Sykes titled "The Pains of Imprisonment." This was an excerpt from Sykes's book *The Society of Captives*,[14] based on his ethnography at a New Jersey prison.

As Victor Shammas explains in a retrospective,[15] Sykes was far from the first observer of the misery and suffering inflicted on residents of prisons and jails; author Charles Dickens and journalist Henry Mayhew extensively illuminated the anguish of incarceration in the 19th century. However, Sykes's contribution was its assertion that prisons went far beyond depriving people of their liberty, which was merely the first of five "pains of imprisonment."

Sykes's description of this first pain went beyond the obvious limitation to the confines of the prison (and control measures like cells, checkpoints, and passes). He included the dissolution of bonds with family and friends due to restrictions or difficulties associated with receiving visitors, sending and receiving mail, or placing telephone calls.

The second pain, deprivation of goods and services, consisted of a decline in the material standard of living compared to life on the outside: unpaid or very poorly compensated labor, few personal possessions, and a decline in the quality of shelter, clothing, diet, and health care.

Today, Sykes's third pain, the deprivation of heterosexual relationships, reads as somewhat antiquated; Sykes's understanding and framing of homosexual relationships and intimacy behind bars was fairly limited.[16] Nevertheless, his sensitivity to the notion that involuntary celibacy could create emotional, psychological, and physical problems in the inmate population was prescient. He believed an involuntary loss of sexual relations produced tension, anxiety, and a worsened self-image.

The fourth pain, the deprivation of autonomy, consisted of denying prisoners the ability to make even the most basic decisions about their daily life, such as when and what food to eat, when and how bodily functions should be taken care of, and when and how to move within the restricted confines of the prison. Sykes believed the loss of autonomy was harmful because it reduced inmates to a childlike state through a series of public humiliations and forced acts of deference.

Finally, the deprivation of security, according to Sykes, consisted of subjecting prisoners to a violent, unsafe environment, in which they were vulnerable to assaults, sexual victimization, substance abuse, and disease.

Sykes's typology of pains yielded an extensive body of literature. Later commentators added considerable nuance to his analysis and, in some cases, modified his findings. One example is Benjamin Fleury-Steiner and Jamie Longazel's *The Pains of Mass Imprisonment*, which offers a mass incarceration-era update rife with awareness of the increased salience of problems exacerbated by overcrowding and racial injustices. Much had changed, they argued, since Sykes conducted his ethnography in the mid-1950s, beginning with the scope of the system: At the time of Sykes's research, there were approximately 250,000 prisoners in the US (state and federal) prisons and jails. As of 2010, there were more than 2.2 million—that is, just about nine times as many prisoners.[17] This era, according to Fleury-Steiner and Longazel, ushered in an inventory of harms beyond Sykes's original formulation: the exacerbation of deprivation of liberty in the mass-containment era; the evolution of forced poverty into monstrous exploitation for financial profit "by, for example, making them engage in low-wage labor under often dangerous conditions"; the enhanced risk of sexual abuse of a rising population of women behind bars; an exaggerated form of loss of autonomy in the shape of "the isolation of exorbitant numbers of prisoners in the brutal conditions of solitary confinement, utterly stripping away the humanity of many prisoners"; and the ways in which vulnerability to fellow prisoners is exacerbated "as prisoners are subjected to numerous forms of prison guard brutality."[18]

Other commentators have expanded Sykes's framework to encompass the unique deprivations and indignities experienced by special populations, such as incarcerated immigrants,[19] trans prisoners, aging men[20] and women,[21] prisoners with HIV,[22] and fat prisoners.[23] As this chapter demonstrates, even these more extensive lists of harms for the mass incarceration age do not fully account for the panoply of unique and heightened suffering wrought not only by the COVID-19 pandemic but also by the measures taken and not taken to address it. Recall John Witt's sanitationist and quarantinist approaches to contagion.[24] Prisons are intrinsically quarantinist—their raison d'être in normal times[25]—which creates unique challenges and forms of human suffering that are not experienced, or experienced to a much lesser degree, in the free world even under pandemic conditions. We begin by broadly sketching the experience of COVID-19 in California's prisons. Then, we present a typology of the pains of COVID-19 imprisonment, with categories that broadly correspond to those created by Sykes and by Fleury-Steiner and Longazel. We detail and reveal these harms through the words of the people who suffered them firsthand: incarcerated people themselves.

Our primary source is the University of California, Irvine's repository UCI Prison Pandemic, a digital archive in the public domain collected and managed by faculty and graduate students at UC Irvine's Criminology, Law & Society Program.[26] The archive, containing thousands of stories, dates to 2020 and tracks stories submitted by incarcerated people, families, and prison workers:

> We collected stories in three ways. First, individuals called our hotline to tell their stories (staffed Monday through Friday from 5pm to 9pm PST). Second, individuals mailed letters, artwork, and other contributions to us ... Third, individuals submitted stories via the submission section of the PrisonPandemic homepage. As of March 2022, we stopped staffing the hotline. We still receive letters via our P.O. Box and website submission form.

The stories collected by UCI Prison Pandemic closely align with the many stories we heard, over the course of three years, from currently and formerly incarcerated people and their families. Because these people called Hadar during a time when she was a vocal advocate for COVID-19 relief as well as a litigant, and often asked for help with concrete problems wrought by the

COVID-19 crisis that she could address in her advocate capacity, we refrained, for ethical reasons, from using these direct conversations as cited sources in this book. Rather, we used the themes that emerged in these calls as deep background to develop the categories according to which we coded the stories in the digital archive. The coding was therefore a two-step process, or a version of "modified grounded theory": we formed a few initial codes using the information we were already familiar with through advocacy and proceeded to develop additional codes, subheadings, and connections from the materials in the archive.

We also relied on multiple secondary sources, including exemplary investigative journalism in California newspapers; in choosing these sources, we prioritized op-eds and exposés that featured firsthand accounts of COVID-19.

We considered several taxonomical approaches. A critical look at Steiner and Longazel's inventory of oppression and suffering reveals that the roots of this deprivation were already present in Sykes's time, and this was true for our source material as well. Reading reports, listening to recordings, and participating in phone calls with incarcerated people and their families throughout the COVID-19 pandemic—sometimes several a day—showed that COVID-19 merely exposed the already rampant neglect, abuse, fear, and deprivation and created new manifestations of old pains and difficulties. We considered the nomenclature of the categories secondary to telling the story of the COVID-19 disaster in as streamlined and comprehensive a fashion as we could, and so, rather than contorting the personal accounts to fit the categories, we chose to frame the categories along the narrative told by the tapestry of personal accounts.

The suffering that these stories reveal is vast and painful to read, and therefore likely to engender some resistance. At the end of the chapter, we address a few possible critiques of our "pains" inventory, which largely stem from the myth of prison impermeability: the idea that health-care problems are part and parcel of incarceration (which we accept as a descriptive premise, rather than a call for complacency); the notion that the pandemic hurt everyone and thus did not have special manifestations in prison (which we believe these first-person accounts refute); the notion that the behavior of prisoners contributed to their own suffering (also factually refutable); and, finally, the notion that we must accept heightened suffering in prison because relief from disease is a zero-sum game that must take into account moral deservedness (an idea we object to, both morally and practically).

As of February 21, 2023, most of California's prison population had been infected with COVID-19. There have been 91,591 cases—an unverifiable number of them reinfections—and 260 deaths of incarcerated people. Fifty staff members have died.[27] Ninety-four percent of the population at Avenal State Prison had tested positive for COVID-19;[28] more than 75 percent of the San Quentin population contracted COVID-19; and, in the winter of 2020–21, as the Delta variant began spreading, every single prison in the CDCR system had an active outbreak, more than half spanning hundreds of cases.

THE SPREAD OF COVID-19: CARELESS TRANSFERS, FLAWED GATEKEEPING

The virus spread through prisons in two main ways: through careless transfers and through staff. The most dramatic example of the former was the botched transfer from the California Institution for Men to San Quentin and Corcoran Prisons.

The Botched Transfer to San Quentin

San Quentin hearkens back to the gold rush era, when it began its history as San Francisco's city prison aboard "the stranded hulk of the brig *Euphemia*."[29] In 1851 former Mexican general Vallejo presented plans for a permanent prison to the California legislature. After some controversy, the hulk was dragged to Point Quentin, where the people incarcerated aboard the *Euphemia* built the prison on land. San Quentin's plant remains more or less the same as it was in the 1850s; consequently, the decrepit cellblocks do not have appropriate ventilation or solid doors as in more modern facilities.[30] But despite the dilapidated plant, San Quentin offers advantages: its proximity to the Bay Area's progressive, academic, and affluent enclave has yielded a wealth of volunteer activity and rehabilitative programming unavailable elsewhere in CDCR.[31] Indeed, long before the 2008 financial crisis, the gap between programmatic offerings in San Quentin and in other prisons was palpable to the point that people wanting to make parole—approximately a quarter of the entire California prison population—sought to be incarcerated at San Quentin despite the dire physical conditions.[32]

Another unique feature of San Quentin is the largest death row in the country, which, until recently,[33] housed more than 700 people.[34] Since the reestablishment of California's death penalty in 1978, and up to the eve of the pandemic, 13 people had been executed[35] while many dozens on death row died of natural causes.[36] The rarity of executions, alongside the size and dilapidated conditions of death row, has created a unique problem of elderly, infirm people who would be difficult to transfer, would be suboptimal candidates for rehabilitative programming and work, and require constitutionally mandated, costly legal representation.[37] In 2019 Governor Newsom declared a moratorium on the death penalty in California and ordered the death chamber dismantled, but litigation on behalf of those condemned to death continued.

San Quentin's COVID-19 outbreak during June 2020 was the consequence of a botched transfer, revealed in a journalistic exposé[38] and a subsequent investigation by the California Office of the Inspector General,[39] as well as through the evidentiary hearing in *In re Hall*.[40] San Quentin, already overcrowded to 113 percent of design capacity,[41] received an influx of 122 people transferred from the California Institution for Men (CIM) in Chino. The inspector general inquiry yielded damning details. Alarmed by the rapid infection rate at CIM, custodial and medical officials there sought to mitigate the spread by reducing prison population. The transferees—200 people intended for San Quentin and Corcoran Prisons—were not tested prior to their transfer. On the morning of the transfer, several transferees told nurses that they were experiencing COVID-19 symptoms (fever and coughing). Email correspondence between health officials shows that they were aware of this and nonetheless decided to pursue the transfer. No effort was made to facilitate social distancing within the buses; the transferees heard and felt their neighbors cough throughout the lengthy journey to the destination facilities.

The virus spread quickly throughout San Quentin, and by the end of June, more than three-quarters of the prison population had been infected and 29 had died—28 prisoners and 1 worker.[42]

As we explained in the introduction, the fast spread of COVID-19 at San Quentin alarmed Marin County's top public health official, Dr. Matthew Willis. Having worked with the prison during prior health crises, such as the Legionnaires' disease outbreak of 2015,[43] Willis contacted the warden, expressing concern that the contagion would spread into the surrounding county and imploring him to isolate and test the incoming transferees from

CIM. Willis's entreaties fell on deaf ears. After a few futile communications, prison officials did not even dignify him with a personalized response: they forwarded him the letter that Avenal State Prison had sent to the top health official in Kings County, which, as we described, tersely claimed that the state facility was not bound or beholden to a county official.

On June 4, 2020, a group of physicians belonging to the organization AMEND (UC Berkeley– and UC San Francisco–based physicians monitoring public health behind bars) visited San Quentin at the invitation of the federal receiver. They were horrified by the reach of the pandemic and by the custodial ineptitude they witnessed. Following their visit, the physicians issued a document titled "Urgent Memo,"[44] the most important recommendation of which was a 50 percent population reduction for the purpose of enabling social distancing:

> There are currently 3547 people in total incarcerated at San Quentin, approximately ~1400 of whom have at least one COVID-19 risk factor (as do many, unknown, staff members). This means these individuals are at heightened risk of requiring ICU treatment and/or mortality if infected ... We therefore recommend that the prison population at San Quentin be reduced to 50% of current capacity (even further reduction would be more beneficial) via decarceration.[45]

Among AMEND's other recommendations were the need to appoint a dedicated pandemic response team; dramatic expansion of testing practices; speeding up testing results (which were so slow at the time that they impeded contact tracing); and developing medically appropriate space for isolation and quarantine, because "quarantine strategies relying on the Adjustment Center or cells usually used for punishment may thwart efforts for outbreak containment as people may be reluctant to report their symptoms."[46]

The prison administration ignored AMEND's recommendations.

As we explain in chapter 6, by October, when the California Court of Appeal decided *In re Von Staich*, the first wave of the pandemic had already run its course through the facility, infecting the vast majority of its residents.

Other prisons, alarmed by the San Quentin fiasco, completely halted transfers from county jails, a move that made sense in the early days of the pandemic but caused a chain reaction of outbreaks and ineptitude in county jails (as we explain in detail in chapter 4). Epidemiologists have found a significant association between weekly transfers (which continued throughout the pandemic)[47] and positive COVID-19 cases, concluding that "[t]he number of COVID-19 cases was positively correlated with the number of transfers three to five weeks [prior to the transfer]."[48] Additionally, despite the inability to argue strong causality (due to the absence of contact tracing), epidemiologists have found that staff members' COVID-19 prevalence—and through them, that of the larger community—has had a direct relationship on the prevalence of COVID-19 among incarcerated individuals, lending strong support to the common-sense hypothesis that staff members are an important node of infection transmission in prisons.[49]

The legacy of the botched transfer was so tragic that people in other prisons, despite the suffering stemming from lockdowns, were grateful that this risk, at least, was minimized in their institution:

> After seeing the deaths have risen in the hundreds to thousands on the news in different states, wow. I'm just glad this prison did the best to the fastest way to get everyone vaccinated when they stopped the transfers to visits as I see it. Instead of expanding it, they accomplished it.[50]

Flawed Gatekeeping

Beyond the transfers, prisons contributed to the spread of the contagion in several tragic ways. In their first report,[51] California's Office of the Inspector General (OIG) uncovered lax and careless screening practices at the entrances to several prisons. Heeding warnings from the WHO and CDC, Governor Newsom instructed CDCR to take preventative measures to prevent the spread of COVID-19 in prisons. As early as March 11, CDCR suspended all visits to the prison but continued to allow some essential visitors, including contracted workers, attorneys, and OIG staff, to enter prisons, in addition to thousands of the department's staff who did so each day. On March 14, the suspension policy was supplemented by a directive to verbally screen all staff and visitors by querying them about signs and symptoms of COVID-19. Later in March, CDCR added required temperature checks to the verbal queries.

Admittedly, designing gatekeeping proceedings for prisons is complicated by their far-from-straightforward structure. As the report explained, most prisons have multiple gates and entrance points, varying in security level. Administrative offices, warehouses, industries, and other areas are often behind the main gate but outside of an internal, secured entrance point. Any aerial photograph of a prison will feature clearly visible structures that are not part of the inner perimeter of the prison, as well as multiple buildings within the complex that are accessible only through their own secured gates. Staff, essential visitors, and incarcerated people employed throughout the prison mill about through these multiple gates on a daily basis, coming in contact with each other, a situation that requires careful screening at the entrance to each correctional complex.

Unfortunately, CDCR institutions failed to conduct effective screening. The OIG report found "vague screening directives" that "resulted in inconsistent implementation among the prisons":

> Specifically, we found prisons took different approaches to implementing the same departmentwide directive. Some prisons funneled every car to a single screening location, where prison staff conducted verbal and temperature screenings of the cars' occupants. Other prisons screened staff at certain pedestrian entrances to the prisons. We found that this second approach increased the risk that staff or visitors may have walked into or through other workspaces without having been screened.

Visiting OIG staff experienced these inconsistencies firsthand, passing through prison gates with no delays or screenings—observations supported by the staff. In a survey of more than 12,000 staff members, "5 percent of the survey's respondents indicated that they had not always been screened as required by the department's directive." A separate survey "identified multiple instances of thermometers malfunctioning during screenings. However, the screeners' survey responses did not indicate how they proceeded to conduct screenings when they could not accurately obtain temperatures"; in the absence of consistent instructions, it was "unclear whether they allowed entry to those individuals" or "allowed some staff and visitors entry without obtaining accurate temperature readings." The report found that many screeners apparently received no formal training at all concerning their prisons' screening processes, thus increasing the risk of allowing infected individuals to walk into prison facilities and expose others to the disease.

Much of the media reportage on CDCR's failures to properly act focused on issues of testing and cohorting, but consider the lessons of SCP: in a physical plant conducive—nay, *specifically designed*—to gate people and prevent them from escaping, screening is an especially effective preventative policy when appropriately employed. It was particularly important to emphasize screening given the testing gaps and delays (see below), as COVID-19–

positive employees would enter and exit prisons for several days before testing positive.

TESTING FAILURES

Well into the summer of 2020, COVID-19 testing in prisons was utterly dysfunctional, in terms of both capacity and speed. The AMEND physicians who visited San Quentin were dismayed by the significant delays—approximately six days—in obtaining results, which, combined with the prison's failure to cohort and isolate the prison population and the staff, rendered testing ineffectual.

The failure to properly test the prison population turned out to have been much graver than the physicians predicted in mid-June, and stemmed directly from CDCR's refusal of generous offers from the public and private sectors.[52] According to a *Nature* article published in early July, at least San Quentin was offered free, rapid COVID-19 testing as early as March—and declined:

> Fyodor Urnov, a scientific director at the Innovative Genomics Institute at Berkeley, offered free, philanthropy-supported COVID-19 testing services to San Quentin. "The reply was a polite, respectful 'Thank you, but we're all set for now,'" Urnov says. He wrote to San Quentin officials again when the outbreak emerged in June, and got a similar response.
>
> Researchers at another authorized testing lab, run by UCSF and the Chan Zuckerberg Biohub in San Francisco, also offered free tests to San Quentin officials in May and June, says a researcher at the lab who asked not to be named because they do not have permission to speak on behalf of the institutes. Those offers were not taken up until last week, when the prison sent them a batch of samples to process. "I'm frustrated and sad we couldn't have done more," says the researcher.[53]

As then president Trump was mocked for saying that "with smaller testing we would show fewer cases,"[54] CDCR seemed to take a page out of his pandemic policy playbook. Because testing was so unreliable and slow, CDCR's case reporting lagged behind the actual infection rate. According to the CDCR population tracker, testing at San Quentin picked up shortly after the transfer disaster was reported by the mainstream media, and, predictably, a high percentage of the tests were positive. Although cases were still rising, around July 3, testing came to a grinding halt—and the few returned tests were positive. The correlation we found at the time between cumulative testing and cumulative cases was 0.99. The correlation between new testing and new cases was 0.7. Any reported abatement in the number of infections, such as at Avenal and Chuckawalla in the summer of 2020, might have been merely an indicator of lower testing rates.

PATHOGENIC PHYSICAL ENVIRONMENT

Iatrogenic Plant: No Ventilation, No Solid Doors, Compromised Hygiene

The dilapidated and compromised condition of many correctional facilities in California, particularly the older ones, transformed into a trap during COVID-19 times. Incarcerated filmmaker Adamu Chan, who would be released from San Quentin in October 2020 and would subsequently join the #StopSanQuentinOutbreak coalition, wryly observed how visitors to the prison, prior to the pandemic, were shown the prison's new hospital, as it sat on the ruins of the dungeon ("a solemn memorial to San Quentin's bygone cruelty"). He would later have a chance to see how the archaic plant contributed to the contagion. The new hospital, he wrote, "provided little in the way of prevention or relief for the people incarcerated at San Quentin. Numerous incarcerated people have been sent to hospitals in neighboring communities to receive emergency care, access to ventilators, and ICU beds. So one is left to wonder, what is the function of the hospital if not to deliver medical care?" The archaic plant, of course, remained: "massive cell blocks packed with human beings confined in poorly ventilated, unsanitary, and squalid conditions have, by all accounts, accelerated and exacerbated the spread of the virus throughout the prison."[55]

The AMEND delegation to San Quentin made note of the facility's horrific condition[56] when it concluded that, within the physical plant, the only realistic prevention method would have been reducing the population by 50 percent, because it would "allow every cell in North and West blocks to be single-room occupancy and would allow leadership at San Quentin to prioritize which units to depopulate further including the high-risk reception center and gymnasium environments." The physicians, several of whom were geriatric experts, noted that they "spoke to a number of incarcerated people who were over the age of 60 and had a matter of weeks left on their sentences. It is inconceivable that they are still in this dangerous environment."[57]

Throughout the summer of 2020, as the virus ravaged prison populations and staff, basic functions of sanitation and provision ground to a halt. Incarcerated people were required to assume new responsibilities to provide these basic services. For example, the porters, who were responsible for basic cleaning and meal provisions, were now required to clean cells of people sick with COVID-19 who had been evacuated to hospitals.

In one case at San Quentin, the need to isolate and quarantine people led to the use of decrepit, filthy units, full of animal excrement and dust. A team was contracted to provide "deep cleaning," but the residents of that floor saw little difference before and after the procedure.[58]

Overcrowding and a Lazy Interpretation of Plata

As explained in chapter 1, the *Brown v. Plata* mandate upheld the order to reduce California's overall prison population to "only" 137.5 percent capacity. Because this benchmark applied to the system as a whole, many incarcerated people still resided in *Plata*-noncompliant facilities. In late 2017 data scientist Nick Jones designed an algorithm that pulled population data out of the CDCR weekly counts, which are provided in an inaccessible PDF format,[59] and found out that all prisons, except 2, were overcrowded, and 15 prisons exceeded the *Plata* mandate.[60]

Under these conditions, maintaining the advised social distance was, as many incarcerated people reported, impossible:

> The pandemic seems to be just overwhelming. There's—there's inmates dropping off like flies. Um—to the left of me, to the right of me, across from me. I mean, inmates sleep within three feet of me. They're fallin' off like flies um—10, 11 inmates in the last seven days. I have underlying conditions. I live in fear of my life every day.[61]

> We are supposed to be six feet apart from one another. How are we supposed to do that when someone like me is in cell living and have a cellmate. We can't be six feet apart in a cell that's the size of small restroom with two twin size beds in it with a desk.[62]

> CDCR has done nothing to quell the overcrowding, even after they claimed to be enforcing social distancing policies of six feet, but they're not doing anything to perpetuate that.[63]

> Then they said we are suppose to stay six feet away from one another hah! We sleep less than three feet away from each other. Twenty-four men to a very small dorm two showers, two sinks, two shitters.[64]

It was hard to be able to wear a mask. And it was uh, they harassed you, they didn't, the staff didn't wear a mask. It was um, you know as quick as we wanted to be able to wear a mask, they weren't letting us wear them, it wasn't until like a whole building tested positive, that they took it more seriously. . . .

UCI: Are they saying you can't wear it for identification purposes?

Caller: That's what they were saying in the beginning, and it was really ironic because they called me over by name, and told me that I couldn't wear a face covering because they couldn't identify who I was.[65]

Lack of Masks, Sanitizer, and Protective Equipment

In the early weeks of the pandemic, concerns about mask supply led to dissuading people from wearing them, so that first responders could be prioritized.[66] In May, however, this recommendation was reversed following the protestations of medical experts.[67] Nevertheless, for many months after this reversal, masks and other equipment in proper amount and condition were unavailable in many California facilities:

> And there was really no precautions here, you know, at the county jail until towards almost the middle of the pandemic when they started using face masks and all that, almost December.[68]

> Well, I mean, the only thing that they've given us here is, they've given us masks but we've had these masks now for, I want to say, about six months now probably. And it's the same masks all we do is just wash them in the sink and wear 'em again. So, yeah. I mean, all we do is we try to maintain our social distance. But, you know, it's, I don't know. I can't explain it. We go to yard and people, they play basketball, they, you know, they still, not everybody follows that social distancing.[69]

> Because at first they were giving us all of this cleaning stuff. But I'm actually a worker and I will be the one doing national cleaning. But lately, they haven't given us the right cleaning stuff to work. Everything's pretty much germed up.
>
> And the masks, I know we're supposed to be getting new masks, like every day because we're workers and each mask gets dirty and sweaty. And we're pretty much getting, I'm telling you, from like four to five days if that.[70]

> As for the first two to three months went by we fought first for masks. Then for adequate cleaning supplies in which it took two more months but, we received them. Earlier I spoke of the social distance aspect of our living arrangements, and I'll say it again.[71]

Hand sanitizer was considered contraband, because its alcohol content raised concerns that the prison population would drink it,[72] leading some incarcerated people to manufacture it on their own.[73]

Against these abundant and consistent reports, the prison engaged in dishonesty about the timing and amount of supplies. During the San Quentin litigation, the attorney general representatives repeatedly presented their (eventual) provisions of personal protective equipment (PPE) as evidence of mitigating harm to the prison population. The realities behind bars were very different:

> Before I got here, some of the other inmates, they told me they were caught lying on the news. The county jail told the news stations that they're providing a mask and bars of soap every two weeks. Apparently, they asked the COs about that, like, "Where's our soap? Where's our masks that you're supposed to be providing us?"
>
> The COs were just pushing it off, saying, "That's not true. We don't provide that." And what not.[74]

LAX ENFORCEMENT OF PANDEMIC PREVENTION MEASURES AMONG STAFF

On October 26, 2020, the OIG issued its second report,[75] which severely criticized CDCR for neglecting to address PPE protocols. The report observed that, at least for staff, the amount and quality of PPE, if appropriately worn, would have made a difference. CDCR "appeared to be successful in distributing the face coverings to staff and incarcerated persons." But actually inducing the custodial staff to wear the masks was a completely different story:

> [A]lthough the department distributed face coverings to its staff and incarcerated population, and the department issued memoranda communicating face covering and physical distancing requirements, we found that staff and incarcerated persons frequently failed to follow those requirements. As part of our customary monitoring activities that occurred between May 19, 2020, and July 29, 2020, our staff frequently reported observing departmental staff failing to comply with face covering guidelines during our staff's multiple visits to 23 of the department's 35 prisons. For example, during a visit to one prison, the Inspector General and Chief Deputy Inspector General observed multiple prison executives improperly wearing face coverings during a meeting that also included the prison's warden, who did not attempt to correct the noncompliance.

In a survey administered by OIG personnel, "31 percent reported they had observed staff or incarcerated persons failing to properly wear face coverings. Regarding physical distancing, 38 percent of the staff who responded to the survey stated they had observed staff or incarcerated persons not complying with physical distancing requirements."

This frequent noncompliance, the report observed, "was likely caused at least in part by the department's supervisors' and managers' lax enforcement of the requirements":

> Despite the department's then-Secretary's statements during a legislative hearing on July 1, 2020, asserting that the department was enforcing its face covering requirements, and despite a memorandum the department issued on the same day, stating that it was vital for staff to adhere to face covering directives, we found that the department's enforcement efforts have been very limited. In fact, based on records provided to us by five sampled prisons, prison supervisors and managers had taken just 29 actions—over a period spanning seven months—for noncompliance with the department's face covering or physical distancing requirements.
>
> One of the five prisons, California Institution for Men, provided no documentation of any disciplinary actions, and another of the five prisons, San Quentin State Prison, provided documentation of just one action. We found that almost all the actions that supervisors and managers took were instances of verbal counseling or written counseling, the lowest levels of the progressive discipline process. We also found that supervisors' and managers' failure to enforce COVID-19 requirements was not limited to the five prisons. Our staff reviewed every formal request for investigation and punitive action for the entire department since February 1, 2020, and we found that hiring authorities statewide only requested formal investigations or punitive actions for misconduct related to face covering or physical distancing requirements for seven of the department's more than 63,000 staff members. We find that number surprisingly low, given the prevalence of noncompliance observed by our staff and by the departmental staff we surveyed.

Paradoxically, the report found that "the department perplexingly loosened those requirements at the same time it reported increasing numbers of cases of COVID-19 among both its staff and incarcerated population":

> Despite the increasing cases of COVID-19 in its prisons, the department sent memoranda on June 11 and June 24 relaxing face covering requirements for staff and incarcerated persons, respectively. The updated requirements allowed staff and incarcerated persons to remove their face coverings when they were outside and were at least six feet away from other individuals.

Considering the volatile nature of a prison environment, the potential increased difficulty in enforcing the updated requirements, and the possibility that the virus could be spread even when people maintained a distance of six feet from others, the department's relaxed requirements appeared to unnecessarily increase the risk of COVID-19's spread among the staff and incarcerated population.

Many incarcerated people were stunned by the lackadaisical, and sometimes defiant, approach of the guards toward pandemic prevention:

I seen this one particular CO would not cover his mouth, he would wear it around his throat. And, when you would mention it he would snap on you "I ain't fucking sick."[76]

But the COs well mainly the sergeant that works third watch on D-yard who is just an a-hole got COs outside the chow hall patting people down. No social distancing, no changing gloves. They are there to spread and kill us because all we are are a number to them. They moved one inmate here that started this whole thing but they have kept it spreading and by closing the chow hall because that's how it spread last time.[77]

INCOMPETENCE AND MISMANAGEMENT OF THE PHYSICAL ENVIRONMENT

A Litany of Housing Issues

The prison system's confusion and discombobulation begat frantic, and often counterproductive, efforts to shift populations between and within prisons. Even after the medical community learned that COVID-19 positivity was not a binary situation, and people who tested positive could become sicker through continued exposure to other patients, prisons with no isolation space resorted to housing sick prisoners together.[78] Incarcerated journalist Juan Haines, who movingly and consistently reported about the pandemic experience, reported:

Richard "Rock" Lathan, 52, another plaintiff, has been incarcerated for more than 30 years. He testified that he contracted COVID-19 while working on a team that cleans up after medical emergencies. "I still do it, because I care about those still being affected by COVID, the long haulers and the sick," Lathan told me.

"These cells are originally built for one man. It's like living in a gas station bathroom with two people," he said. "Spend a night or a week in one of these so you can see for yourself what it's like and how the atmosphere is and how easily someone can get COVID again, even though we're vaccinated."[79]

The incompetence infusing the housing decisions was painfully obvious to the people who were being shuffled like game pieces:

> I think cause for a while they stopped moving inmates. And then once it started to calm down a little bit then they started putting inmates in gyms on different yards. They started putting inmates in different buildings on other yards.
>
> . . .
>
> And so, it just shows a lack of consistency and a lack of knowledge of what to do. And I understand they're trying to do as best they could but if they would truly look at what the CDC and the WHO were trying to do and how they were trying to stop the spread, they seem to be just you know lighting fire to the virus and letting it spread you know instead of trying to contain it within individual inmate groups you know and individual buildings.[80]

> I tested positive for COVID-19 on December 10, 2020. I was placed into isolation in the gymnasium that was eventually packed with over 107 prisoners (not including staff) mostly double bunked. Many people felt they did not have the virus and voiced their concerns but, went unheard. Some knew they had it.[81]

> Trying whatever, like they just had no clue what they were doing. At this point, they're not doing so much of the moving but we do have 14 tents sitting in the middle of our yard. On a couple of key—on one occasion, we had a Santa Ana windstorm and many of those tents blew away.
>
> So they had to evacuate the people from those tents. And they got sent to another yard. Well they had to rebuild the tent city because the tents had actually literally blown away.[82]

> On October 27, 2020 inmates that were infected at Old Folsom prison were transferred to Solano prison (where I currently reside). This was done after Governor Newsom told CDCR to stop with the transfers. One of those prisoners was moved right next to me and told me he tested positive for COVID at Old Folsom and went through their quarantine. Then was moved to Solano prison without being quarantined here.[83]

> I look at this place as a concentration camp where people come to die. My wishes is to remain where I am currently housed and do my schooling and drug classes. I've been moved three times and I only been here a year. Instead of containing the sickness they're spreading it by moving everyone around so much.[84]

Transgender people, in particular, reported that the careless COVID-19–era transfers resulted in placing them in cells with transphobic cellmates and exposing them to violence, which went untreated.[85] The already existing challenges in housing trans prisoners became even more convoluted: "COVID-19 precautions have slowed the transfers [to gender-matching prisons] and . . . officials could not estimate how long a transfer might take under normal circumstances, citing bed availability as a factor."[86]

Conflating Medical and Punitive Isolation

The need to quarantine and isolate people in overcrowded facilities with no dedicated physical space led some prisons to use solitary confinement space for medical isolation. This practice, which "rewarded" COVID-19–positive prisoners with a move to a space strongly associated with punishment, dissuaded prisoners from reporting their symptoms and getting tested—in addition to the exacerbation of mental health problems.[87] This profoundly misguided approach to what should have been treated, essentially, as a medical issue struck AMEND physicians as a grave mistake:

> Those requiring Quarantine (i.e., people with a credible exposure to COVID-19 who are asymptomatic) are in the Reception Area's Carson Unit. Those requiring Medical Isolation (who have tested positive for COVID-19 or who have symptoms suggestive of COVID-19 and are still awaiting testing) are in the Adjustment Center as this is the only unit at San Quentin that has single cells with solid doors. Per our notes, there are ~106 cells in the Adjustment Center, with ~80 occupied at the time of our visit. Urgent Concerns: 1. A massive outbreak at San Quentin will significantly and quickly overwhelm the availability of these 106 Adjustment Center cells, and there will quickly be nowhere for infectious cases to be moved. Further, we cannot emphasize enough the incredible fear that residents we spoke with expressed about being moved to cells typically used for administrative segregation/punishment or "death row"—potentially resulting in short- and long-term mental health consequences. Especially given that early identification of suspected COVID-19 cases depends on reporting of symptoms, quarantine strategies relying on the Adjustment Center or cells usually used for punishment may thwart efforts for outbreak containment as people may be reluctant to report their symptoms.

The folly of this isolation strategy, which was bound to reduce buy-in in the form of prisoners reporting symptoms and seeking testing, was obvious to prison authorities, whose management of the prison population had always relied on the designation and threat of adjustment center cells for the purpose of punishment.[88]

Resorting to Tents

Unable to put six feet of distance between the people in their care, and frustrated by the ramifications of hasty groupings and transfers, some prisons pioneered a new strategy in 2020: placing either the sick or the healthy in outdoor tents. These testimonies offer a flavor of the resulting living situation:

> Two huge circus tents were erected with porta-potties and shower units. They were erected and taken down way too early. I state that because the facility could have been used for the numerous outbreaks.[89]

> Like three in the morning I was moved out of my single cell and into a large 150 man dorm. A few weeks later many of us were rotated into tents outside on the yard, each tent held 10 to 12 people, mind you it was freezing cold outside at this time of the year. A few weeks later I was moved yet again, this time to a much smaller dorm, another 10 man dorm.[90]

> That's right back where I began only to be forced to live in a tent. There are 13 tents out here on the sports field. With portable toilets, sinks, and showers—which are mostly cold.
> I've been housed out here since August the 26th. On September the 26th, our tents were blown down from 50 to 60 mph winds. After having about eight to nine hours in the dining hall. Staff decided that we must allow them to move us back over to B yard . . . without our personal property—for only one night.
> Right. So 85 out of 86 men told staff that we would not go without one property. They did not like us standing up to them at all. So they gave us 30 minutes to pack up everything in the world that we own before they forcibly moved us over into cells with no power—electrical, or glass in the bars—so these cells are full of dirt and leaves; trash from miles away! My cell also had no working sink.
> Our one night turned into a four day and night stay. Once we were brought back to a new "tent city," the powers decided that since we demanded not to leave without everything we own in the world, that we must search for a missing extension cord—which is 25 feet long. So the officer who's searching my property is opening every box of soap, every toothpaste box, even letters I haven't answered yet. After 44 minutes of having all my food opened, like eight-ounce boxes of mackerel—every jar of coffee and creamer, etc., etc.[91]

The folly of housing hundreds of people in tents amid a hot summer (scorching days and cold nights in California's Central Valley) would be magnified many-fold by the horrific fires that devastated a million acres in the state during the summer of 2020. The fires engulfed the areas close to at least two prisons: the California Medical Facility (CMF) and Solano State Prison. CMF's population—aging and infirm people—were particularly vulnerable to the smoke, and both prisons were located within evacuation zones. Nevertheless, throughout the fires, the prisons were not evacuated, nor had preparations been made—not even bringing a bus nearby in case transportation was necessary. Incarcerated people and family members who spoke with the *Guardian*'s Sam Levin reported heavy smoke, ash, and an inability to escape toxic fumes: to their horror, they witnessed prison guards arriving in the facility covered in ash:

> "They are breathing in fire and smoke, and they have nowhere to run," said Sophia Murillo, 39, whose brother is incarcerated at CMF in Vacaville. "Everyone has evacuated but they were left there in prison. Are they going to wait until the last minute to get them out?"
>
> To increase social distancing and limit the spread of Covid, CMF had moved 80 people to sleep in outdoor tents instead of indoor cells, but with the fire approaching and air pollution rising, the prison moved them back indoors. Murillo said she now fears a major Covid outbreak inside the prison, and noted that mass evacuations could also spread the virus if people are packed in buses together.[92]

Other observers of this double threat had different concerns than Levin's. For the *New York Times*' Thomas Fuller, for example, the meager crumbs of compassion in the form of releases and quarantine were hurting the firefighting effort by depleting the ranks of incarcerated firefighters.[93] Fuller's interviewee Mike Hampton, a former corrections officer who worked at a fire camp, shamelessly explained: "The inmates should have been put on the fire lines, fighting fires . . . How do you justify releasing all these inmates in prime fire season with all these fires going on?" This perspective, of course, did not originate with the pandemic. In a 2014 legal process regarding the *Plata* population reduction benchmarks, the lawyer representing attorney general Kamala Harris wrote, "if forced to release these inmates early, prisons would lose an important labor pool." Those prisoners, the *Times* reported, earned wages that range from "8 cents to 37 cents per hour." In a September 30 filing in the case, signed by deputy attorney general Patrick McKinney but under Harris's name, the state argued, "Extending 2-for-1 credits to all minimum custody inmates at this time would severely impact fire camp participation—a dangerous outcome while California is in the middle of a difficult fire season and severe drought."[94]

Vindictive Approach to Resistance

Those who protested these absurd, counterproductive housing decisions found themselves penalized with disciplinary violations:

> One day last week, when prison staff tried to move a new man into an empty spot in Meyer's eight-man cell, he got nervous, he said in an interview via JPay, a prison email service. Days earlier, another man sleeping mere feet away from Meyer had developed COVID-19 symptoms and was removed by staff, and Meyer suspected that his new cellmate might also be infectious. Meyer approached the officers' station and complained, saying he didn't want to be housed with a potentially contagious person. That's when he was handcuffed, Meyer said.[95]

> At first, prisoners who showed symptoms or tested positive were sent to the Adjustment Center, the highest-security unit, where the cell doors are made of solid concrete. Others who needed to be quarantined were sent to Carson, a unit known as "the hole" and typically used to isolate prisoners awaiting disciplinary action. As a result, according to advocates, some prisoners have been refusing to take COVID-19 tests for fear of being put in solitary confinement. People on death row have reportedly refused tests because of concerns that nurses were not changing their gloves. Prisoners know that if they report symptoms, Rudd says, "they're going to be whisked away to the worst possible place in the universe that they can do their time."[96]

Plata litigators informed the court that their clients, who were arbitrarily ordered to change cells for no good reason (often against medical logic and common sense) and refused, received disciplinary write-ups for their obstinance, which were not removed later even though medical staff came to agree with them.[97] These practices, and others, eroded the trust of incarcerated people in the custodial and medical staff to the point that garnering cooperation became extremely challenging and, as we explain in chapter 4, raised concerns about the expected vaccine acceptance rates among the incarcerated population.[98]

Many health-care workers in California prisons during the pandemic were dedicated, consummate professionals, who attempted to provide the best and most compassionate care in impossible situations. That "only" 260 incarcerated people perished from COVID-19 is largely due to their selfless dedication. However, the abundant vacancies within the system and the mounting medical needs made it impossible to provide care not only to COVID-19 sufferers, but also to people suffering from a variety of related and unrelated conditions. These included worsened mental health stemming from the stress, and violence resulting from the frequent housing shifts.[99]

> Well, I suffer from bipolar disorder and depression. And one of the first things that happened after the outbreak here at San Quentin was they stopped all medical and mental health appointments that were non-emergency that were just routine checkups. They stopped those completely for several months. So, for a while I was not receiving any mental health care.[100]

> And for our a.m. meds we were not getting them sometimes until 10:30 a.m. and then they are combining our 5:00 p.m. with our bedtime meds. So sometimes I would get my meds at 8:45 p.m. and I am scheduled to take Seroquel at 8:00 p.m. Which they were giving to me at 5:00 p.m. and crushing it so I was knocked out before 6:00 p.m.
>   And if you had meds they could not give you back to back they would change your meds without even telling you. My Seroquel was at 8:00 p.m., they changed it to 5:00 p.m. without even asking me or telling me.[101]

> We can't even get proper or, in cases, any medical attention, and this is a "medical facility"? I've had no exaggeration about 20 medical appointments in the past 2 months and got seen only 1 time. They say if it's not important, don't bother. Due to the pandemic, they/medical is only receiving "emergencies." So that's another reality I live.[102]

> So, every morning I clean my floor with a wet towel, which is what every man, in every cell in the state uses to clean their floor with anyways. That is something I do everyday and have done since day one, and well, I had a hard time doing that.
>   I was breathing hard as hell as if I had worked out, when I stood up I lost my balance and was unsteady. I never felt like that. All I could think about was "why did the doctor, who well knew that, I had underlying health conditions still decided to send me out to get exposed?"[103]

And because I was taking blood pressure medication, the doctor told me that was a "cocktail for disaster. And that's why you passed out and we had to get you down so quick. Because you had a seizure like episode" and I never had seizures in my life. You know?[104]

I'm personally I'm a transgender inmate, so aside from dealing with the COVID situation, we're still dealing with a lot of this stuff that relate to being trans as well. And a lot of that being disregarded, especially treatment regarding trans individuals, medical treatment is being pushed to the backburner.

We don't get any sort of regular treatment or the ability to see our doctor to have anything done or any adjustments made regarding the medically necessary treatment that we are supposed to have. I had to beg, beg them to finally even want to see me so I could get my mammogram done, which I'm way, way, way, way past due, you know those types of things. So yeah, I'm sorry.[105]

People trying to challenge mistaken diagnoses encountered disbelief and delays:

And so after 14 days of being confined with no medical access, I seen a doctor that was going to clear me of COVID-19 no matter what I said. And sure enough, I was cleared of COVID-19 and sent back to a building with COVID-negative people.

And I still have not seen a doctor. So, yeah, it has not been good. I didn't get a printout or a pamphlet or anything of what to expect, what was gonna happen, what would happen if I got really bad sick, nothing. You know, It was nothing. So, that's pretty much my experience with COVID in prison.[106]

Fundamental Miscommunication between Custodial and Medical Staff

The hearing in *In re Hall*, as we explain in chapter 6, exposed profound miscommunications between custodial and medical stuff. Numerous first-person accounts described special medical needs going unmet because they were not communicated to the custodial side:

There are procedures in place to ensure that we are seen and evaluated by a medical professional. But they think that all inmates are out to con their way into getting high on drugs or getting something not normally provided. So we are forced to go on requesting medical attention for an extended [period], before our needs are looked into.

Sometimes we have to fake medical grievances, forcing the medical department to see the person requesting medical attention. I contacted COVID-19 right before Christmas. I lost taste, smell, and had back pains for about ten days. The entire housing unit I live [in] had caught it by the new year.[107]

I witnessed the guards influence medical personnel to implement absurd orders to justify their cause using medical as a crutch. I've been moved around several times and even put in medical isolation without any medical diagnosis, exposure, or positive COVID test results. I thank God, I haven't tested positive due to speaking up.[108]

Nowhere was this miscommunication more obvious than in the warden's testimony in *In re Hall*, and no one was more keenly aware of its consequences than incarcerated journalist Juan Haines, who wrote:

Broomfield told the court that he could not have refused the transfer of prisoners from Chino to San Quentin. He said that he had concerns about receiving prisoners from "an outbreak institution," but he testified that he "had no knowledge that prisoners were exposed to someone with confirmed cases of COVID-19." He acknowledged that the transfers from Chino were not immediately tested upon arrival.[109]

Aging and Infirm Prisoners: The Special Case of CMF

The tragedy of medical neglect played out in a particularly vile manner at CMF in Vacaville, a skilled nursing facility which, as explains above, houses aging and infirm people.[110] On December 11, 2020, there were only 2 COVID-19 cases at CMF; on December 12, the prison went under lockdown. Within five days, the number of cases had risen to 58. As of January 17, despite the lockdown, the number of positive cases on the tracker was 260 (about 13 percent of the population). At the height of CMF's outbreak, the total was 463. In all, 520 people (about 26 percent of the population) had been infected, and 7 died.

Before the outbreak began, reports from incarcerated people and their loved ones of correctional officers refusing to wear masks and the incarcerated population not having access to cleaning supplies had persisted for months. Additionally, some incarcerated people have said that they had not been given new masks when their old ones wore out to the point of being ineffective—until December 24, that is (a whole 12 days into the outbreak), when new masks were finally distributed.

The dorm used as triage/COVID-19–positive space had formerly been used for the prison's therapeutic dog program, Paws for Life; the dogs were removed shortly after the start of the pandemic, and the dorm was not cleaned prior to being used for quarantine. The few porters who were not stricken with COVID-19 were not provided adequate cleaning supplies, and dirty laundry was not picked up. Olivia Campbell, a visitor and volunteer at CMF, reported:

> The strain of covid that is moving through CMF is causing severe diarrhea. Several people have soiled themselves and do not have access to clean clothes. Each person is only being given one roll of toilet paper per week. This is nowhere near enough for those experiencing diarrhea.
>
> Nurses are refusing to go bed to bed to check on people. They expect sick and bedridden people to line up in the middle of the dorm to have their vitals taken, with the result that the people too ill to get up are being missed completely and not getting help when their conditions become life-threatening. Around the end of December, a man fainted and defecated on himself. When medical staff refused to respond to calls for help, other incarcerated people in the dorm, who were themselves ill, cleaned him up and carried him to his bed before he was finally taken to an outside hospital. In a similar incident, a man fainted and was refused medical attention for hours before finally being carried out on a stretcher. Staff are hesitant to call ambulances because they are concerned about how it will look with regard to the Plata litigation. Correctional officers tell the nurses to call for ambulances, and the nurses ignore them. They would rather refuse to get people the proper medical attention they need than make it look like they're incapable of caring for them at the prison.
>
> The incarcerated who are too sick to cook for themselves are still being given raw vegetables like onions, on top of the already deplorable food situation. Food amounts are proportionally small, not enough for an adult. Some correctional officers are not wearing masks or refusing to wear them properly. Many refuse to wear gloves. Some are moving around from positive to negative units, socializing with other COs. Many believe this is intentional for the purpose of spreading the virus around the prison. People who are sick are not being given access to over-the-counter medications, and only a select few are being given antibody treatments. The incarcerated have been moved from one area to another in hopes of containing the virus. This, apart from being completely ineffective, has presented additional problems of loss of property.
> . . .
> The disabled population at CMF, who are supposed to have assistance with various daily living tasks from other incarcerated people (people who are employed to do this specific job as their work assignment), have seen this help severely hampered by the outbreak. People with disabilities are required to be accommodated under the Americans with Disabilities Act, and no alternative accommodations for the disabled at CMF have been offered.

Many of the population at CMF are over 60, and many have medical conditions such as diabetes, AIDS, and high blood pressure—all of which put them at higher risk of serious complications if they were to be infected with covid. Some are already being held in a hospice unit due to terminal illnesses. Some have covid risk scores, as defined by California Correctional Health Care Services (the office responsible for healthcare in prisons after conditions were declared unconstitutional), as high as 16. Hospitals in some parts of California have already begun to turn away the incarcerated, and many are talking of rationing medical care. If they do, they will deny treatment to those they deem to be less likely to survive a covid diagnosis. This would be catastrophic for anyone from CMF in need of hospitalization. There is a dorm at CMF that holds 21 wheelchair users. There are not enough wheelchair-accessible single cells to facilitate the quarantine of these people, resulting in the spread of the virus through this dorm. Poor ventilation within the prison is also a facilitator of the spread.

Execution by COVID-19: The Special Case of San Quentin's Death Row

One of the cruelest ironies of the pandemic was the experience of COVID-19 on San Quentin's death row, which, given the complex history of capital punishment in California, is a dilapidated, poorly staffed and constructed long-term home to approximately 750 men. California's death penalty was abolished in 1972 after the state Supreme Court found it dehumanizing and violative of the California Constitution. A few months after that, the US Supreme Court decided *Furman v. Georgia* (1972), in which a majority of the court found serious procedural defects in the application of the death penalty. The outcome was a sentence commutation for 104 people, from death row to life with parole (life without parole was not yet in existence in California). The massive political backlash in California[111] led to a return of the state's capital punishment statute, found constitutional in 1978. But since then, only 13 people have been put to death in California, while more than 100 have died of natural causes.

The decades since the return of the death penalty saw the litigation avenues attacking it on Eighth Amendment grounds closing. Arguments of racial discrimination became difficult to pursue. Arguments of innocence were, more often than not, rejected. Finally, in 2013 an Orange County federal judge found that the delays in providing representation to death row inmates—an average of 16 years' wait for a postconviction attorney—were in themselves cruel and unusual punishment, only to be reversed by the Ninth

Circuit on a technical basis (courts may not create "new rules" in habeas corpus proceedings).

In 2019 Governor Gavin Newsom—influenced in no small part by the controversy surrounding death row inmate Kevin Cooper, largely believed to be innocent[112]—placed a moratorium on the death penalty.[113] The death chamber was dismantled, and even though prosecutors in several counties continued to ask for the death penalty, the effort lost considerable steam after California's most notorious and heinous criminal, the Golden State Killer, was caught— and sentenced to life without parole.[114] The result of the moratorium was a calcification of death row as a relic of the past, a living museum to a punishment no longer practiced, with 725 human beings as historical exhibits.

Because the death row population tends to be older and sicker than the general prison population, and because of the conditions on San Quentin's death row, the virus spread quickly among the prisoners. Prison authorities did what they could to obscure the outbreak's impact on death row, but the *San Francisco Chronicle*'s journalists uncovered it:

> A coronavirus outbreak exploding through San Quentin State Prison has reached Death Row, where more than 160 condemned prisoners are infected, sources told The Chronicle on Thursday.
>
> One condemned inmate, 71-year-old Richard Eugene Stitely, was found dead Wednesday night. Officials are determining the cause of death and checking to see whether he was infected.
>
> State prison officials declined to confirm that the virus has spread to Death Row, but three sources familiar with the details of the outbreak there provided The Chronicle with information on the condition they not be named, and in accordance with the paper's anonymous source policy. Two of the sources are San Quentin employees who are not authorized to speak publicly and feared losing their jobs.
>
> There are 725 condemned inmates at San Quentin, and of those who agreed to be tested for the coronavirus, 166 tested positive, the sources said.
> . . .
> It is unclear whether Stitely was infected with the coronavirus. He refused to be tested, according to the three sources with knowledge of the situation.[115]

By contrast to general population residents, whose identities were hidden from the public for medical privacy reasons, CDCR sent emails to interested parties about deaths of people on death row listing their name and full details. Through subtracting the named casualties from the total death toll, a horrifying truth emerged: more people died on death row from COVID-19 under Governor Newsom's moratorium than California had executed since the reestablishment of the death penalty in 1978.[116]

This outcome was deeply ironic, because even after the moratorium, California courts continued to be clogged with death penalty litigation concerning minutiae and technical detail,[117] revolving around whether various modes and aspects of the execution process are "cruel and unusual" even as the death penalty itself is "kind and usual." Flying in the face of this precious and expensive effort to sever the death penalty from any of its potentially cruel and unusual implications was an execution clearly not prescribed by the California Penal Code: death from a contagious pandemic compounded by incompetence and neglect.

Months of Solitary Confinement, with Resulting and Predictable Mental Health Implications

Scholarship[118] and first-person accounts of solitary confinement[119] consistently highlight its severely destructive psychological effects. As befitting a quintessentially quarantinist institution, CDCR's most impactful emergency move was to place numerous wings in numerous facilities under solitary confinement, sometimes for long months. This policy had a predictably corrosive effect on the prison population's mental health, particularly those with preexisting mental conditions:

> I was supposed to transfer to another prison due to a change in my level of care. I'm a patient inmate in the Mental Health Department System.
> I'm supposed to go to a hospital setting prison because this prison: CCI, isn't equipped to assist me being this isn't a hospital/prison.
> So I was to be moved ASAP but due to COVID-19 all transfers are to be stopped completely! Now I'm stuck here and I'm not getting the proper care I'm needing of. I am trying my best to cope under these unfortunate times but it has been very challenging![120]

> They stopped all transfers and cancelled visitation. Honestly nobody thought nothing of it until they kept prolonging the lockdown and because [it was] really stressful and a lot of individuals were becoming agitated with the system because nothing was going right. COVID-19 broke out in institutions all over the United States and we were now receiving modified programs, to where you can only socialize with a few people or sometimes none at a time.
> That honestly does a lot to a person's mind because there's already a lot of frustration built up, especially without the visitations from your family,

wives, etc. Plus trying to stay as clean as possible and sometimes that doesn't always work out because of the lockdown you're on. I haven't seen or touched my mother in a very long time and honestly couldn't wait to get back to prison to be able to do that.[121]

This HAS been the most difficult year I have spent in prison. I got incarcerated on [redacted] and never faced such a difficult time. At the beginning of this pandemic I believed that we will be "shut-down" for a couple of months. But two months turned to four, then to eight, and now exactly a year.

I found it at the beginning to be necessary being quarantined, but got fatigued 10 months into quarantine.[122]

Staffing Problems: Kitchen and Cleaning

Even before the virus, feeding the prison population has been a challenge; as Erika Camplin has written, "we as a nation are effectively feeding around 2 million mouths at least three times over each and every day."[123] But the pandemic led to a deterioration far beneath even the existing low baseline. Throughout the summer and the fall of 2020, kitchen workers—both staff and incarcerated people—fell prey to the virus, leading to deficits in the provision of food and basic hygiene. Seemingly asymptomatic people were ordered to clean cells of symptomatic people who had been hospitalized, and then rapidly succumbed to symptoms after completing such tasks.[124] Kitchen staff—professional and incarcerated—became ill, paralyzing kitchen activity and leading to inadequate food distribution. Those who refused to work, citing reasonable concerns about contracting COVID-19, received disciplinary write-ups:

> I work in the kitchen. And what happened was—is that they—they wrote me up because I refused to go in to work, and they wrote me a 115 for not coming into work. And they said I refused to work, but I never refused to work. It's I told them that I didn't want to put my life in danger because I'm a diabetic. And while that happened, it's—it's a lot of people that kept getting sick in the other buildings and they were working in the kitchen, too.
>
> So now we're—they have three buildings on this yard at this time, and one is already down, and those are kitchen workers that got sick. So right now, I'm trying to fight this 115 and they found me guilty on it because they said I refused to work. But I never refused to work. I only refused to put my life in danger.[125]

The outcome was a panoply of problems with food supply:

> For a while the inmates here at High Desert State Prison, have been getting mistreated. The food they was serving us as meals was never cooked. The portions that [they] give us on the food trays is not enough to feed a child, let alone grown men and women in the California prison systems.
>
> We have a store here on the prison grounds that they, the prison, call commissary. We are allowed to go to commissary once a month. All inmates are allowed to go to commissary, but for some strange reason, a lot of inmates have been denied to go to commissary for two months now. And the staff here don't care about that at all.[126]

At Pelican Bay, a staff member called Bryan Price emailed a Chad Parry, cc'ing associate warden David Barneburg:[127]

> Hey Chad how's your night going.
>
> Well as for here, it's not going to[o] good. The inmate are starting to act out over the food and I don't blame them. I thought when we cut one of their hot meals like dinner. In the past we have given them two lunches for dinner to make up for the calorie lost. Right now they got six crackers, two cookies, a small bag of pretzels, block of cheese and a drink mix. They also got 1 peanut butter, banana and a jalapeno. It is hard to believe that two of these lunches and the breakfast meal has the calories that is due to them. I[n] the memo it states they will be getting box lunches with fruit, milk and juice.
>
> So my question is, is this right because it does not seem right. The same lunch they saw this morning is the one they got for dinner. Hope there is something we can do. I think it's going to get really bad really fast around here.
>
> Any help in this matter would be greatly appreciated.

Chad Parry responded:

> Hey Bryan, that's the correct meal. They were supposed to get the extra stuff you mentioned . . . not sure what is planned for tomorrow.
>
> Kim, anything we can do to improve upon this meal? The fellas aren't enjoying it much . . .
>
> Thank you

When this correspondence was leaked on Twitter, several family members and friends of incarcerated people reported similar food shortages and deprivations. Several photos of prison meals were leaked (likely captured with the cameras of smuggled cell phones). These photos featured, incredibly, raw whole onions as the "vegetables" in the meals. One family member reported having received a letter from someone incarcerated at Valley State Prison, according to whom "they [we]re receiving 8 tablespoons of food per meal."

FEAR AND FEARMONGERING

Throughout the prison, coughing, crying for help, and the ubiquitous "Man down!" calls were heard.[128] People frequently saw their cellmates and neighbors being taken to the hospital, and sometimes dragged out after dying in their cells.[129] The appalling, undignified treatment of those who became seriously ill and were hospitalized also led to extreme anguish among the people left behind.

The anguish, stress, panic, misinformation, and maltreatment severely impacted incarcerated people. Many reported experiencing panic, anxiety, depression, heightened blood pressure, and cardiac symptoms because of living through the pandemic in prison.[130]

This was not helped by some staff members, whose animosity lowered morale among the incarcerated population:

> some of the medical staff have real negative attitudes and they kind of voice their negative attitudes around the inmates, which kind of creates a negative environment for the inmates in trusting the medical staff. So uh . . . basically it's uh . . . kinda a scary environment.[131]

Worse was the abundance of medical misinformation, provided by custodial staff. Staff members spreading rumors about COVID-19—claiming that it was a hoax, or that vaccination would be harmful—were not uncommon. As we show in chapter 4, among the "frequently asked questions" document prepared by AMEND was the question "I heard that some of the officers, warden or health care staff are refusing to get the vaccine, why should I?"[132] Some incarcerated people reported to their families that staff members mocked them for wearing (or asking for) protective equipment and ordered them to stand closer to each other as they waited in line for showers.[133]

> I just think there's some you know some added stress there. I mean with them already dealing with it out there and you know being locked down and see-ing-, and kinda seeing the inconsistency that's been going on in here. That's kinda just been kind of I think concerning.

You know when I talk to my parents or anybody in my family you know it just seems to you know that they don't understand it but at the same point you know there's not much you can do.

But I mean kind of just look out for and try to take your own personal precautions that you can by wearing your mask and trying if you know that an inmate maybe has tested positive or you know or there's a situation, there's something you can do to try to protect yourself and others you know trying to take that standpoint.

You know just to not be that spreader or be that person who you know affects somebody negatively. And just always kinda to reassure my parents too you know that I'm safe and you know I'm just trusting in what God's doing here and you know, knowing that he's in control of all things.[134]

Since I have been vaccinated with both Moderna shots. Now it's on the news about Moderna booster shot that is a vaccine that may ward off the variant. But the big but is in the question is when elderly high-risk medical prisoners going to receive this booster?[135]

The officers are the primary carriers that bring it into the prison and then refuse to wear their mask. Sometimes even opted not to get the vaccines.[136]

The overall effects of this environment are palpable in comments from incarcerated people who experienced them:

I felt hopeless, anxious, and really scared. There was absolutely no movement, meaning no phone calls, no dayroom or recreational time. With a staff member testing positive our quarantine time was extended, I was tested for COVID-19, no kidding at least 10 times in a month; Every time waiting for the results I had high anxiety.[137]

One month [after my friend was released, he] died. His body suffered from prolonged effects of COVID exposure, and compounded with other underlying health issues, just gave out. As I sit here write you, my heart flutters in pain because COVID robbed the world of my friend. COVID has taken four people from my family, and still my time here is the only guarantee in my life.[138]

SABOTAGE AND FRAUD

Financial Extraction and Fraud

During the pandemic, California newspapers reported a large-scale unemployment fraud, in which unemployment claims were filed, and paid, on behalf of prisoners.[139] According to the reporting, a handful of incarcerated people contacted friends and relatives on the outside, supplied them with Social Security numbers and other information, and persuaded them to file for pandemic relief on behalf of 30 different prisoners. The outsiders had the unemployment payments—in the form of Bank of America debit cards issued by EDD—mailed to them. The accomplices delivered their inside partners' share of the profit into their jail accounts, which could be used to buy extra toiletries or other items.

What went completely unreported was the parallel withholding of relief funds *from* the incarcerated population. Among its other relief provisions, the Coronavirus Aid, Relief and Economic Security (CARES) Act provided benefits to low-income individuals, including incarcerated individuals. The funds, however, were withheld by prison authorities, leading to a federal class-action lawsuit that culminated in an order issued by Judge Phyllis Hamilton on September 24, 2020. Even following the order, though, members of the #StopSanQuentinOutbreak coalition reported that several facilities had interfered with their population's ability to complete the claim forms. In one case, when the family member called the San Joaquin County Jail, they were told the jail would not accept any IRS checks, and that "they [jail staff] don't care what law was passed."

Rehabilitative Programming Shutdown

One of the adverse aspects of the recession-era correctional shrinkage was the reduction in rehabilitative offerings. Access to these programs is at a premium for people who must show evidence of rehabilitation in order to receive parole or early release. The pandemic drastically reduced the already paltry access to the programs, causing enormous anxiety and distress to people trying to compile a positive dossier for their parole hearing:

> I asked to come to California Rehabilitation Center, "CRC," to get help with my drug problem. I arrived in 2019. I asked at my initial review to be placed into whatever programs available to work on my addiction and help me help myself so I can get my life back on track!
> For several months I sat around with nothing to do because this prison was so full it was approaching at 160%. Way overcrowded. People have been on waiting lists for two and three years just to get into any programs, which also means our living conditions are inhuman! We live in dorms that are actually falling apart.[140]

Ostensibly due to concerns that people could contract COVID-19 through public phones, prisoners were denied access to the phones for weeks, hampering sanity-saving conversations with family members, as well as stopping the flow of information to lawyers and advocates on the outside.[141] This was one of the most heart-wrenching aspects of the COVID-19 experience:

UCI: What about not [being] able to see your family and loved ones?

Caller: Yeah, no. That's not, that's restricted to phone calls only. I don't want my family to come here anyways even if the restrictions were lifted and I told my family that I wouldn't want to see them because there's people coming from different cities from all over. And the probability of her catching COVID from somebody just to come see me would be really high. So, for me it's not worth the risk.[142]

The hardest thing about this has been our visits. I use to get visits every weekend from my family and loved ones. It is bad enough that we're limited to six hours of visit on Saturday and Sunday, but now to cut our only ties completely is devastating! Relationships, marriages, and companionships have ended due to no visits.

Some men here have lost their loved ones to COVID and wives that can no longer wait out the "no visit policy" and turn to addiction to find comfort or cope with the loss. I know that I personally have been stressed and at times feel defeated. Especially that my mother was diagnosed with stage III colon cancer during this pandemic and it puts her at high risk. Enclosed I have placed a photo of her and me to show that this story has real people.[143]

Visits have been cancelled. They are beginning to give them back to us but they are very restricted so that most guys don't even bother. This is a real source of anger and frustration among those who got their vaccines and have family members who are also vaccinated. I don't really get visits as most of my family died while I was in the SHU (Security Housing Unit). I can still empathize with my fellow prisoners but it's not an issue that affects me directly.[144]

So the only way to communicate with our families was through snail mail. Everyone was freaked out because no one knew how our families were. Mail here takes weeks.[145]

DEHUMANIZATION

Crass Treatment

Many incarcerated people were deeply affected by the crassness and animosity of their interactions with the custodial staff, some of whom exhibited breathtaking insensitivity even as people were grieving the deaths of cellmates and neighbors:

> How do we get treated while we're in here? In the beginning we're getting treated like we're fucking just, like, animals and shit stuck in a zoo. Like, look at these guys, you know, they're fucking—they're virus, they got a virus, you know, they're deadly, they're dangerous and ill. And then, like, it is kind of weird because if you had it and you're incarcerated, some people look at you like they're, like, better than you.
>
> And, like, oh, my god, like, they don't even want to get near you, but they still got to feed us, they got to bring us this, they got to do that. But, it was just weird, it was awkward. It was awkward last year, like, when it first hit. You know, it was like, oh, you got it, like, oh, my god, didn't even want to go near you.[146]

> So, for the most part, they only address it after the fact or after people die or after people really get sick or anything like that. Instead of taking the time to think it through and maybe consider, "hey", or they don't ev—they didn't even take the time to ask us, what could have been issues. They just do it after the fact and hopefully they don't get sued basically, is what they're trying to do.[147]

> No, I don't feel safe simply because of how officials and medical staff have responded to and are treating this COVID-19 epidemic. In the beginning most staff were treating us prisoners like we were the ones who could infect them. When in all reality if COVID-19 entered the prison system it would be from an officer, free staff and/or medical staff being infected and spreading it to the prison population. And this was the case at CTF Central.[148]

Cruelty to Families and Loved Ones

The staff's insensitive behavior extended beyond incarcerated people to their family and friends. Wrongful death lawsuits filed on behalf of prisoners who succumbed to COVID-19 revealed that their condition was kept secret from their families until shortly before they died.[149] And family members who lost incarcerated loved ones to COVID-19 would receive a further shock. As Jason Fagone reported for the *Chronicle*,[150] grieving families, who did not have a chance to say goodbye to their deceased loved ones, were immediately handed a $900 cremation bill:

> During a call with a mortuary service that contracts with the prison, Tracy learned that according to state policy, family members of those who die in prisons—of COVID-19 or any other cause—must pay out of their own pockets if they want to receive the remains of their children, spouses and parents. [Tracy's husband] Melford's cremation and the shipping of his ashes would cost nearly a grand. If Tracy didn't want the remains, the state would cover the expense, she was told, but then her husband would be considered "unclaimed," his ashes scattered at sea by strangers.
>
> Hearing that, "I cried my eyes out," recalled Henson, who is disabled and relies on Social Security disability benefits. "I don't have that kind of money sitting around."

Prison officials reported, in response, that they merely followed the state's penal code: if a family wishes to claim the body of a relative who died in state custody, all burial services—and costs—become the family's responsibility, without any reimbursement from the state. California pays only if the body is considered unclaimed.

CHALLENGES AND COUNTERARGUMENTS

"Prison and Healthcare Problems Are Inseparable"

This inventory of suffering might raise the inference that inadequate health care is simply part and parcel of the prison experience, and understandably so: at the #StopSanQuentinOutbreak press conference, infectious disease expert Peter Chin-Hong insightfully said, "prisons are incompatible with public health." Chin-Hong is not the only one to flag this thorny problem: the American Public Health Association has issued a declaration that indicts the entire system for its contribution to social ills.[151] But this grim descriptive assertion does not compel a normative conclusion that we must simply put up with such neglect, incompetence, and dehumanization. An alternative approach might be the one adopted in the *Plata* litigation: given the inability to provide minimal health care to the prison population under our current incarceration regime, this regime must change.

"Everybody Hurts"

Another possible challenge might that COVID-19 wrought worldwide, universal suffering, and that prisons were merely one more locus of suffering. But the facts defy this conclusion. Prison deaths soared almost 50 percent in the first year of the COVID-19 pandemic.[152] A study conducted by the UCLA Law COVID Behind Bars Data Project revealed that by June 6, 2020, there had been 42,107 cases of COVID-19 and 510 deaths among the United States' 1,295,285 prisoners, constituting a case rate of 3,251 per 100,000 prisoners. The COVID-19 case rate for prisoners was 5.5 times higher than the US population case rate of 587 per 100,000. The crude COVID-19 death rate in prisons was 39 deaths per 100,000 prisoners, which was higher than the US population rate of 29 deaths per 10,000. This outcome is even more stark when considering that individuals aged 65 years or older, who accounted for 81 percent of COVID-19 deaths in the US population, comprised a much lower share of the prison population than of the US population (3 percent vs. 16 percent, respectively). When adjusting for age, therefore, the death rate in the prison population was 3.0 times higher than would be expected if the age and sex distributions of the US and prison populations were equal.[153]

Contributory Guilt

Throughout the COVID-19 prison litigation, as we demonstrate in chapter 6, prison authorities argued that the prisoners themselves were at least partly responsible for their own plight. Again, the facts defy these claims. Prisoners were making what medical and behavioral decisions they could with little reliable information, understandably mistrusting the authorities that neglected and endangered them, and within a very limited range of self-preservation options. In keeping with the principles of situational crime prevention and the findings of carceral geography scholarship, people constrained by their environment made rational choices under the circumstances. As we have shown here, oftentimes, prisoners opposed transfers and housing decisions that, in hindsight, endangered them (and are still suffering the disciplinary consequences of their self-preserving choices).

The Ethos of Deservedness, or the Zero-Sum Game

The most stubborn aspect of resistance to the pains of imprisonment analysis is moral. As we argue throughout this book, the myth of prison impermeability led many policymakers, professionals, and members of the public to consider any benefit or relief to the prison population as a detriment to the general population. Not only is this approach legally misguided—the California Penal Code sentences no one to death from neglect, misinformation, and ineptitude, from a preventable viral infection—but, as we demonstrate in chapters 3, 4, and 5, it defies the basic realities of pandemic prevention: that including all aspects of a community, inside and out, in pandemic prevention planning is essential to public health.

THREE

Bottleneck

In those days there was no king in Israel: every man did that
which was right in his own eyes.

JUDGES 21:25

AS PUBLIC ATTENTION was drawn to the catastrophic prison outbreaks, similar medical disasters playing out in the country's numerous county jails received remained mostly out of the limelight. In these local facilities, the myth of impermeability took a peculiar shape: policymaking paralysis stemming from a mechanical understanding of jails as jurisdictional, administrative units belonging to the county and answering to different masters than state prisons, rather than an organic perspective that sees them as geographically embedded within counties that also include prisons, immigration detention facilities, and other entities. The mechanical-jurisdictional perception of jails plagued not only their role in mass incarceration, but also their inappropriate use as the solution for population overflows and health-care challenges in state prisons; in that respect, the remedy was, yet again, as misguided as the disease. The outcome of this misperception was the essence of the COVID-19 problem in jails: acting as bottlenecks for a population destined for prison or for the community, they sprouted outbreaks of their own, which were underreported, improperly addressed, and managed in a haphazard, decentralized fashion.

It is historically interesting that the linkage between incarceration and disease initiated from the context of jails, which preceded the emergence of modern prisons. While early jails varied dramatically in ownership, management, and size, they were generally not conceived as places of punishment.[1] Jail residents were a heterogeneous hodgepodge, residing there for multiple reasons—mental illness, awaiting trial or corporal punishment, learning a trade—but what they had in common was poverty, which meant malnourishment and ill health preceding incarceration.[2] Conditions within these unregulated, overcrowded facilities were abysmal: victimization of more vulnerable residents was common due to the mixed population, and no uniforms or food were provided, resulting in cold and hunger. The air was stale due to lack of ventilation; the facilities were never or seldom cleaned; and sometimes, raw sewage ran through the facilities.[3]

Consequently, disease ran rampant through jails. Recall Howard's aforementioned report of the Black Assize,[4] as well as several smaller outbreaks, which had occurred between the 1730s and 1750s in various locations, such as Taunton and Devonshire.[5] In Howard's time, foul air was thought to be the cause of various diseases, including yellow fever and gaol fever; Howard wrote of "guarding [him]self by smelling to vinegar, while I was in those places, and changing my apparel afterwards"; after these visits, his clothes were "so offensive, that in a post-chaise I could not bear the windows drawn up, and was therefore often obliged to travel on horseback. The leaves of my memorandum book were often so tainted that I could not use it till after spreading it an hour or two before the fire." Indeed, the jailers themselves, fearing infection, had "made excuses and did not go with me into the felons wards."[6]

The legacy of filth and disease left its impression on American prison reformers; as we explained above, Eastern State Penitentiary[7] and Walnut Street Jail[8] were explicitly designed to prevent the spread of disease. But as Jonathan Simon has noted,[9] the transition to larger, isolated institutions had adverse implications as to the perception of incarceration. One of them was the decreased visibility of the incarcerated population, locked away in sterile and distant facilities, which Simon argues led to seeing confinement "like a state" rather than "like a city."[10] These new carceral settings removed problems from the public eye and discouraged community-oriented solutions for overcrowding and health-care problems. By contrast, Simon argues, jails' closer association with the wider community can facilitate a more holistic perspective on reform.

Simon's perspective, which hailed jails as the hopeful site of criminal justice reform, reflected the sentiment of advocates statewide at a unique moment in California's correctional history: the Supreme Court's aforementioned decision in *Brown v. Plata*.[11] In addition to their more urban, community-related character, jails held a double promise: they could become the immediate solution to the prison overcrowding crisis, first through the Schwarzenegger-era prosecution of "wobbler" offenses as misdemeanors[12] and then as the Realignment-era place for the "non-non-nons,"[13] and they would be a prominent site of the recession era's characteristic transfer of prisoners to and fro based on financial considerations,[14] because in this manner, the sentencing county would internalize the costs of the imposed sentence.[15]

But alongside the great hope that jails would be a useful depressurizing valve, advocates and scholars expressed concerns that the problems in prisons could duplicate themselves in jails. Malcolm Feeley and Edward Rubin's analysis of judicial intervention in correctional management is rife with examples of poor jail conditions.[16] Perhaps the most prophetic commentator was Margo Schlanger, who warned that jails could sprout the same problems of neglect and dysfunction as prisons, and litigation against them would be encumbered by decentralization and lack of accountability.[17]

This chapter demonstrates that, tragically, Schlanger was right: settling on jails as a bottleneck for prisons with little accountability and supervision yielded wide variation in correctional strategies among counties, ranging from preemptive decarceration and diversion to the expansion and construction of more jails. During the pandemic, these proverbial chickens came home to roost: jails became wastelands of paucity and unreliability of data. In the face of recalcitrant sheriffs and the lack of leadership from the entity designed to supervise them, the Board of State and Community Corrections (BSCC), nonprofits, academic institutions, news agencies, and private individuals stepped up to fill the knowledge gap about COVID-19 in jails through exposés and independent data collection efforts. But these interventions could not cure the fundamental problems in jails—overcrowding, lack of protective equipment and sanitation, toxic approaches among staff members, and a shortage of medical staffing—which were compounded by a protective mechanism exercised by state prisons: shutting down transfers from jails. This, in turn, necessitated a domino effect of strategies, including an emergency zero-bail initiative to depopulate the jails and uphill battles to vaccinate, and litigate on behalf of, jail populations. To understand how this happened, we begin with an important theoretical distinction.

TWO PERSPECTIVES ON COUNTY JAILS

With an annual national admission of close to 12 million people[18] in more than 3,000 jails[19]—a million of them in California's[20] more than 160 facilities[21]—jails are an important component of correctional policy. As in most states,[22] California's jails are administered at the county level; most of the state's jails are administered by a single county, and a handful of jails serve multiple counties. Many jails are in the vicinity of other types of correctional institutions: state prisons, state and local juvenile facilities, federal prisons, and ICE detention facilities.[23] Before the COVID-19 crisis, California jails spent years near or above their total capacity of 79,093 beds. The use of release mechanisms led to a population drop; as of January 2020, California's jail population was 57,568. The jail population is heterogeneous: currently, 75 percent of it (43,148 people) consists of pretrial detainees.[24] The remaining people in jail are a mix of people sentenced locally for minor crimes, apprehended probation or parole violators, and state-sentenced people serving time on the county level to alleviate overcrowding in state prisons. Since the passage of Proposition 47, approximately 90 percent of the people in California jails are either sentenced or awaiting trial for felonies.[25]

The unique patterns and composition of jail populations can be understood through two complementary frameworks: a mechanical-jurisdictional perspective, which examines their budgeting and administration, and an organic-geographic perspective, which views them in relation to their surrounding communities.

The Mechanical-Jurisdictional Perspective

Jails are a perfect example of the fragmented reality of the carceral state.[26] While prisons are run and funded by the state, jails operate under the auspices and budget of counties. This distinction has several important implications. As a Vera Institute report[27] explains, the size of jail populations and the length of time spent cycling through jails are a function of a series of decisions made by largely autonomous system actors: the police who choose to arrest, release, or book people into jail; prosecutors who determine whether to charge or divert arrested persons; pretrial services program providers who make custody and release recommendations; judges, magistrates, or bail commissioners who decide whom to detain or release, and under what conditions; other court actors, from attorneys and judges to administrators, whose action or inaction can accelerate or delay pending cases; and community corrections agencies that choose how and when to respond to persons who violate their conditions of supervision in the community. Release and detention decisions may also depend on the existence of critical community services that can provide the supports needed to keep people charged with crimes out of custody. To these criteria we must add, especially in California, legislative actors who engage in jurisdictional gymnastics, such as creating new offenses or changing offense categories, with particular carceral destinations (jails or prisons) in mind.

The relative independence of these actors, and their diverse (and sometimes contradictory) goals, make it difficult to align their efforts to control the use of jails. Some of these actors may be more aware than others of the share of jails in the county budget and take it into account when managing jail intake and releases. Others yet may believe that jails are inappropriate for housing certain residents, such as people serving long stretches of time for serious offenses; these categories of people require long-term programming that is difficult to administer in facilities originally conceived as temporary housing for people on trial (or even for people who are booked for just a few days).

As explained in a National Institute of Corrections report,[28] the population dynamics of jails are a function of multiple questions: what the purpose of the jail is, who is in the jail, how people enter and exit it, and how long they remain at the jail. The entrance and exit doors are jurisdictional valves: some people enter jail upon arrest, from the community, while some enter after they are sentenced; some people spend a few days in jail, whereas some serve yearslong sentences there; some exit the jail directly into the community, while some shift to other jurisdictions, through a state prison sentence, an ICE hold, or a federal hold. The population's heterogeneity and the multiplicity of entrance and exit doors make predictive modeling difficult; this is compounded by the fact that individual counties cannot reliably plan intake and exit using aggregate data. Mass incarceration is regarded as a national problem and is analyzed at the national or the state level, but the structure of jails and their location in the administrative hierarchy means that they are "first responders" in the criminal process—an example of what public policy scholars have referred to as "disjointed federalism."[29]

The Organic-Geographic Perspective

By contrast to the jurisdictional perspective, an organic-geographic perspective examines the continuity between jails and surrounding communities. Even a superficial glance at the California map reveals that jails are an inexorable element of the carceral continuum: they are embedded in cities and rural communities, and often not that distant, geographically, from prisons and detention facilities. A bus transferring people from jail to prison is, technically, traversing jurisdictions, but at the same time, it creates a contin-uum of carceral power by smoothly transitioning people between geographic locations without a break in carcerality. More figuratively, the shift from the outside world into a jail is not as abrupt as the jurisdictional perspective sug-gests if one considers the carceral elements embedded in practices such as drug testing in workplaces,[30] meting out discipline in schools,[31] and surveillance of homes[32] and neighborhoods[33]—oft referred to through the apt metaphor of a "pipeline." As mentioned in the introduction, even technological tools operat-ing within the private sector, such as the use of software for predictive polic-ing;[34] the racialization of surveillance in employment, buying, and selling;[35] limitations on financial mobility through the creation of credit scores;[36] and the employment of surveillance tactics, offered by loss prevention corpora-tions, on employees in the retail industry,[37] serve as conduits of carceral power, creating a continuous stream between "the outside" and the jail space.

The importance of supplementing the jurisdictional perspective with the geographic one cannot be overstated. If one considers jails separately, framing the entrances and exits as valves in and out of separate, disjointed jurisdic-tions that can be open and closed at will, policymaking for one level of gov-ernment may completely overlook the other. By contrast, thinking of jails as one area in a smooth carceral continuum requires taking them into account when planning policies involving population control and management. As the next part shows, the Achilles' heel of the *Plata*/Realignment solution to the prison health-care crisis was that it focused exclusively on the jurisdic-tional aspect.

BOTTLENECK

The Correctional Free Lunch Problem and Its Solutions

Decades before the Criminal Justice Realignment relied on a jurisdictional shift to achieve population reduction in prisons, scholars pointed to a basic problem contributing to mass incarceration. Elegantly referred to by Franklin Zimring and Gordon Hawkins as the "correctional free lunch,"[38] it was essen-tially an argument about economic externalities: prosecutors charge felonies, and judges sentence people convicted of them, in county courts, whereas the sentence itself takes place in state prisons. This means that the county never "feels" the costs associated with the sentence and therefore does not take them into account when dishing out lengthy sentences.

Several solutions were proposed for the correctional free lunch problem. Zimring and Hawkins themselves advocated for homogenizing sentencing policies at the state level, through the work of a sentencing commission.[39] Other scholars have argued that judges should be informed of the cost of incarceration, and have offered empirical proof that, when they are informed, judges tend to sentence more leniently.[40]

As the health-care crisis in state prisons raged, another solution emerged: shifting the responsibility of incarceration to the counties who mete out the punishment. The Schwarzenegger administration's initiative to reconfigure nonviolent felonies as "wobblers"—offenses that can be prosecuted as felonies or as misdemeanors—was designed to offer prosecutors the option to dictate whether the sentence would be served in a state prison (for a felony) or in a county jail (for a misdemeanor). But prosecutorial discretion would prove insufficient to solve the problem of disease and neglect in prisons. The pressure to solve this problem was augmented by the advent of the 2008 financial crisis, which hurt state and local correctional budgets,[41] and by the growing sense that federal courts would intervene with a population reduction order. Indeed, a federal three-judge panel heard evidence according to which, every six days, a prisoner in California died of a preventable, and often iatrogenic, condition.

As Margo Schlanger recounts,[42] the Brown administration's response to this multifaceted state prison crisis—the enactment of A.B. 109—was for the most part a jurisdictional shift initiative. Under the Realignment, people convicted of nonserious, nonviolent, and nonsexual crimes (colloquially known as the "non-non-nons") would serve their sentences in county jails, granting sheriffs the authority to release them if necessary. In addition, most postsentence supervision, which used to be under the auspices of state parole authorities, shifted to county probation offices, and parole revocations also became a county matter.

Lest it appear that the jurisdictional shift was the product of calculated econometrics, Schlanger convincingly explains it as a last-resort strategy: jails had 10,000 available beds at the time and, given the population reduction order's approval by the Supreme Court, using them for state prisons was deemed the only palatable solution because, as the prisons' health-care federal receiver Clark Kelso explained, "politically, nobody could tolerate a straight release of inmates prior to serving their sentence." County authorities "went along with this approach, albeit reluctantly. As Orange County Sheriff Sandra Hutchens explain[ed to Schlanger], 'We had no choice. The

State had to deal with the three-judge panel and reduce population. The sheriffs were given the option of working with the State on a plan, or the State releasing tens of thousands of prisoners early, with no supervision.'"[43] However, overall, reformers and advocates hailed the jurisdictional shift as a method of deliverance from the deep failures of the state correctional apparatus. Some of the support for Realignment came from the perception that no health care provided by the counties could possibly be worse than the dysfunctional, neglectful health-care nightmare of the state prison system, which, at the time, had already been under federal receivership for five years.[44]

At the same time, some tried to inject econometric reason into the chaotic funding method of the plan, whose success, after all, would depend on the extent to which the counties would internalize the costs of their own appetites for incarceration. Under Realignment, over $1 billion annually of state sales tax revenue, phased in over several years, was shifted from the state to the counties, and $1.2 billion in jail construction bonds that had been authorized in 2007 was to be accelerated. This, as Schlanger notes, was known to be insufficient to fund the transition even at the time; the "sweetener" of the deal was that the counties would have absolute freedom in spending the money, which was to be awarded as a block grant. Counties could use the money as they saw fit: invest in diversion programs and treatment to prevent incarceration or increase jail capacity.

The problem with relying on this allocation technique as an incarceration appetite suppressant was the allocation technique, which relied on a formula using the number of offenders that each county had sent to state prison, the county's adult population, and prior grant funding. Counties that had invested in alternatives to incarceration prior to realignment complained that they were being penalized for their good work, while more punitive counties were rewarded for their punitiveness with a larger share of the pie. In a series of important papers,[45] W. David Ball proposed tweaking the formula in a way that would exercise a bit more control over the counties by incorporating a proxy for their need to rely on incarceration: violent crime rates in each county. Under this system, Ball proposed, "[l]ocalities would receive funds based on reported rates of violent crime and would be free to spend these monies on prison, diversion, jail, or anything else. The state would continue to administer prisons but would charge counties for every prisoner they sent." This plan would "end the correctional free lunch" by making the trade-offs obvious to county officials. Counties that would retain or even increase their incarceration rates would be free to do so, but they would have to fund it on their own; moreover, they would face political accountability for their choices, because "[t]he average person could more easily spot the linkage between increasing numbers of prisoners and, say, a decrease in the frequency of road repairs or a shorter public school year, allowing political checks on criminal justice to operate more effectively." Whether this strategy would work was still unknown; Joan Petersilia observed that "if it [did] not work, counties [would] be overwhelmed with diverted inmates, unable to operate needed programs, which ultimately results in continued criminality and jail (instead of prison) crowding."[46]

The Establishment of the Board of State and Community Corrections (BSCC) and the Effort to Share County Data

To provide some support for the counties' new Realignment-era responsibilities, the state established the BSCC. Its website identifies it as an "independent statutory agency that provides leadership to the adult and juvenile criminal justice systems, expertise on 'Public Safety Realignment issues, a data and information clearinghouse, and technical assistance on a wide range of community corrections issues" and also "promulgates regulations for adult and juvenile detention facilities, conducts regular inspections of those facilities, develops standards for the selection and training of local corrections and probation officers, and administers significant public safety-related grant funding."

The idea of the BSCC as a liaison mechanism between state and county stakeholders is evident in its composition. As of now, per its website, it consists of a chair, two CDCR officials (the secretary and the director of adult parole operations), two county sheriffs, two county chief probation officers, one retired judge, one chief of police, and three representatives of diversion and rehabilitation programs.[47]

The BSCC's role as information clearinghouse for the counties was especially important given the decentralized nature of county data. In 2016, at the request of the BSCC, the US Justice Department's Office of Justice Programs (OJP) Diagnostic Center evaluated the BSCC's data collection enterprise. This resulted in a self-evaluation checklist for California counties, designed to encourage data collection and information sharing. The checklist consisted of four principles: using national approaches for interagency information exchange and strategy development; using data to support informed justice and public-safety decision-making; developing responsible information-sharing policies, including by connecting existing networks and systems with strong identity, access, and discovery capabilities; and cross-boundary information-sharing and collaboration with input from all involved stakeholders.[48] Despite this initiative, information about jails would continue to be disseminated primarily through the respective sheriffs' departments, with a few notable exceptions, chief among which are the jail profile survey (administered since the 1970s, but now under the auspices of the BSCC),[49] the jail population dashboard,[50] and a few reports on inspection of local detention facilities.[51] In comparison to the detailed population reports and annual population data conducted by CDCR and provided on its website,[52] the BSCC database is underwhelming; specific functions, such as inmate locators, are accessible only at the individual county level,[53] and the respective websites for the different sheriffs' departments vary widely by style, quality, clarity, and amount of available information.[54]

Admittedly, county jails differ from state prisons in that transfers between counties are much rarer than transfers between state prisons, which at first blush obviates the need for a centralized inmate locator function. But transfers between jails and prisons are extremely common; most of the jail population consists of pretrial detainees, many of whom will eventually serve state sentences. Not only does BSCC's data dissemination quality pale by comparison to CDCR's, but there is virtually no interface between the respective websites of the two agencies, which presents an enormous obstacle to any effort to trace population movements across the state/county jurisdictional divide.

This is not to say that the BSCC has been entirely ineffectual; the agency has processed grants for county programs and offered supervision of county facilities.[55] The BSCC functions, but even in its express mission—the provision of information—it fails to provide anywhere near a full picture of how people move, in real life, between facilities. This is emblematic of the mechanical-jurisdictional understanding of counties and states as separate realms, rather than for the organic-geographic understanding that, for real people in real time and space, these facilities are located on a continuum of movement on both the individual and the aggregate levels.

The only effort to systematically harmonize state- and county-level data in California is the Multi-County Study (MSC), a joint venture between the BSCC and the Public Policy Institute of California (PPIC). Unfortunately, the only participating counties are Alameda, Contra Costa, Fresno, Humboldt, Kern, Los Angeles, Orange, Sacramento, San Bernardino, San

Francisco, Shasta, and Stanislaus—a problem somewhat mitigated by the fact that the aggregate population of these jails is two-thirds of the state's jail population.[56]

Jail Conditions in the Post-Plata Decade and the Prospect of the Hydra Problem

When Schlanger wrote about Realignment, shortly after its enactment, she found "deep dissensus among observers about the prospects for nonincarcerative county responses," with some commentators labeling the incentive structure "a liberal fantasy" and others welcoming the need to implement uncomfortable change. One of Schlanger's interviewees, sheriff's lobbyist Nick Warner, was remarkably prophetic: he observed that, in some counties, there were "a lot of good things going on," while in others, he predicted, "we'll have overcrowded local jails, and people will sue the pants off us."[57] Schlanger referred to the possible result of such variation, and resulting health-care failures at the county level, as a "potential hydra problem," after the famous mythological creature who, whenever her head was cut off, would sprout two heads in its place. The concern was that incarcerated people and their lawyers, rather than filing one lawsuit against the entire state apparatus, would find themselves fighting multiple legal battles against various county jails.

Indeed, as PPIC researchers found through the MSC data in 2015, realignment alone did not result in a concerted decarceration effort at the county level.[58] The immediate effect of realignment was a simultaneous population decline in state prisons and population increase in county jails. The jail population continued to rise at a steady pace until the November 2014 passage of Proposition 47, which reclassified several drug and property offenses as misdemeanors. Proposition 47 had a salutary effect on both state and county facilities. At the state level, in combination with building and renting additional prison beds, it helped CDCR finally reach the population reduction target required by *Brown v. Plata*. As shown in figure 2, at the county level, the passage of Proposition 47 resulted in an almost immediate population reduction, from 82,000 in October to 72,000 in November, bringing the jail population back under the statewide rated capacity of nearly 80,000 beds. This also resulted in 20 percent fewer releases due to housing constraints.

PPIC researchers expressed concerns that the relief for jail populations was temporary; data through March 2015 for Los Angeles County, for

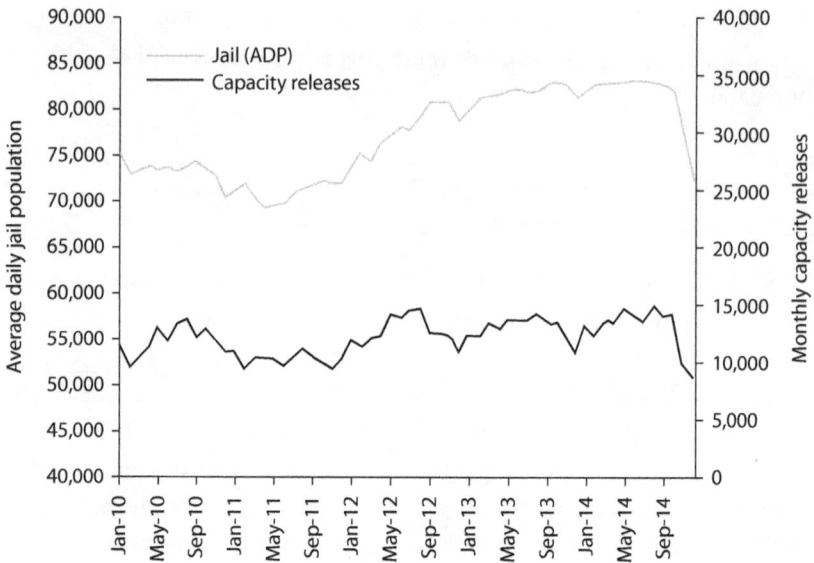

FIGURE 2. Adult jail population and capacity releases in California county jails, 2010–2014 (Public Policy Institute of California).

example, showed that the jail population dipped below 16,000 in December (down from more than 18,000 in October) but rose above 17,000 in January and stayed above 17,000 through March. But a retrospective view of the aggregate population changes on the BSCC population dashboard reveals that, overall, Proposition 47's effect was salutary and lasting. Figure 3 depicts jail population and releases due to housing constraints since the passage of Proposition 47, showing consistent bookings close to (but below) the aggregate capacity of county facilities, and a more or less consistent occupation relative to jail capacity.

Importantly, the trends reviewed above were observable on the aggregate level. On the individual jail level, counties differed dramatically in terms of their reliance on incarceration versus noncustodial alternatives. A comparative study of 12 counties conducted by RAND researchers in 2015 found considerable variation in policies, practices, jail admissions, and jail release patterns.[59] In San Francisco and Stanislaus Counties, jail populations did not rise after Realignment. Fresno, Kern, Los Angeles, Riverside, Sacramento, San Bernardino, San Diego, and Stanislaus Counties were using early releases, and each had one or more facilities under a court-ordered population cap. Some of these counties had been using early releases and noncustodial alterna-

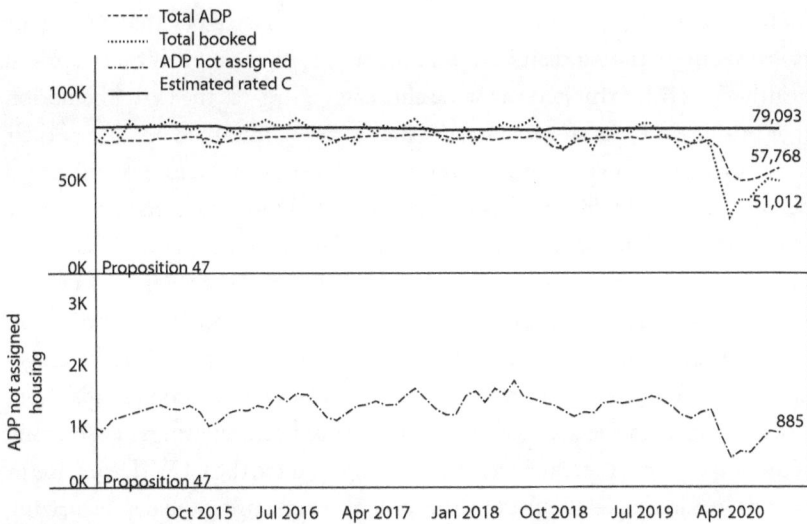

FIGURE 3. Average daily population, rated capacity, and bookings in California county jails, 2015–2021 (Board of State and Community Corrections).

tives before realignment to manage their populations. In interviews conducted by the researchers, different stakeholders expressed different concerns: while probation officers thought that their counties balanced incarceration and rehabilitation, sheriff's departments expressed strong concerns about jail crowding and the need to cope with people serving long sentences in county facilities by providing programming that was previously unnecessary. In some of these counties, such as Los Angeles and San Francisco, struggles erupted between county officials and local activists regarding plans to build new facilities or expand old ones to accommodate newcomers.

This new landscape in county jails would confirm Schlanger's concerns about the hydra problem even prior to the COVID-19 crisis. In addition to the aforementioned court-mandated population caps in several California counties, which preceded Realignment, Schlanger (who wrote her article in 2013) mentioned the filing of the Prison Law Office's first jail case, in Fresno, and the expansion of the ACLU of Southern California's work on conditions in Los Angeles County jails. She also observed that some ongoing prison litigation would encompass supervision of proceedings in jails as well.

This retelling of the *Plata* story, from the perspective of the counties, foreshadows the havoc that the pandemic would wreak on these facilities and, more specifically, the systemic weaknesses and oversights that would be revealed during the pandemic crisis. As we have seen, the remedy for the prison health-care crisis exhibited the same shortsightedness as the cure: the notion that prisons and jails are separate, distinct entities, disjointed because of their differing jurisdictional statuses, and that jails could therefore be used as a depressurizing valve for problems in prisons without much regard to how these solutions would impact the jails themselves. The decentralization of jails, the paucity of centralized information of high quality, and the absence of systematic interface between the prison and jail data systems would obscure important interactions between the facilities. Any efforts to help the jail's heterogeneous, transient population, through political advocacy or through legislation, would struggle in the absence of data, and would face challenges in securing counsel and providing timely relief. Most importantly, the COVID-19 crisis in prisons would exacerbate the crisis in jails, this time using the depressurizing valve to prevent intake, and pushing the jails to fend for themselves.

THE CHICKENS COME HOME TO ROOST: COVID-19 AND THE FAILURE OF THE JURISDICTIONAL APPROACH

Agnotology: The Paucity of Jail-Level Data as a Social Fact

Agnotology, a term coined by Robert Proctor and Iain Boal,[60] is the study of culturally induced ignorance or doubt, particularly the publication of inaccurate or misleading scientific data. In epistemological areas such as climate change[61] and vaccination,[62] attention to agnotology can reveal the political and cultural roots of mistaken opinions or information gaps and develop educational and persuasive countermeasures.

Agnotology plays an important role in understanding the production of knowledge (or lack thereof) about criminal justice and correctional topics. The prevalence of myths about racial crime rates[63] and sex crimes[64] is well documented in the literature. But agnotology also examines glaring information gaps, treating them not as coincidental but as social facts that are important in themselves. For example, in his book *When Police Kill*,[65] Franklin Zimring devotes considerable attention to the incompleteness of governmental statistics on police use of lethal force. Similarly, in her book *American Roulette*,[66] Sarah Beth Kaufman discusses the sociological meaning of a lack of any centralized database containing information about capital trials.

As in these examples, it is impossible to separate the effects of COVID-19 in jails from the glaring gaps in their documentation: the failure to collect data—enabled by the lack of accountability—is in itself indicative of the problem. Since the BSCC's inception, obtaining complete data in a usable format was always a challenge with county jails, and its efforts to centralize data collection resulted in a sparse, user-unfriendly database that did not interface with CDCR's database.

For almost five months, no official, centralized data collection on COVID-19 in county jails took place. CDCR began collecting data on the spread of COVID-19 at its institutions—state prisons—on March 10, 2020;[67] despite some delays in reporting deaths and some unclarity as to the categories used,[68] CDCR's tracker at least provided information on cumulative and active cases, deaths, and testing rates. No equivalent tool tracked cases in counties. For months, there was great variation in the amount and type of information reported by the counties, as well as the format in which it was offered. Some sheriffs' departments offered a web page with their COVID-19 readiness protocols (such as the cancellation of visitation). Others reported only on active cases. Even though, during this period, several serious outbreaks occurred in county jails, some involving hundreds of cases, public knowledge about these outbreaks came almost exclusively from local news.

Advocates and public health experts had warned, early in the course of the pandemic spread, that jails posed a bigger infection and transmissivity risk than prisons, due to the transience of their populations. At public meetings in which activists demanded statistics about COVID-19 spread in jails, BSCC leadership waffled about centralized data collection efforts; Linda Penner, the board's chair, said that this was an "unprecedented time" and that teams were being as responsive as possible, but that collecting and publishing data about jail outbreaks would not be a priority. The *Sacramento Bee* quoted Penner as saying, "We don't want to sound like bureaucrats, but we also have to be well aware of the magnitude of this across the state and the various other reporting requirements locals have. We try to balance that conundrum right now."[69]

In the absence of centralized data collection, the task of informing the public about serious county jail outbreaks—several of which occurred during the spring of 2020—was almost exclusively performed by newspaper exposés. On April 27, the *Los Angeles Times* reported the untimely death of 52-year-old Riverside County deputy sheriff Terell Young, who "for two weeks in early March . . . routinely drove inmates, one at a time . . . to a hospital for medical appointments" and was exposed, during those trips, "to several people, including inmates and a nurse, who would later test positive for the coronavirus infection."[70] As of late April, the jail had reported 136 cases and 2 deaths—one of a jail resident and one of another deputy. The article compared the sheriff's rebuke of jail releases as an essential emergency measure by comparing it to a serious outbreak at the Los Angeles jail complex (whose population numbered 11,866 at the time); by late April, 71 jail residents and 61 staff members had tested positive, and a nurse had died.[71] In June, the *Sacramento Bee* reported that Fresno County Jail had quarantined 1,200 residents, after 13 who had been transferred to a state prison tested positive. In Sacramento County, 5 jail residents tested positive for COVID-19—information that took the *Bee* 10 days to obtain from the sheriff's office. Officials were also slow to report an outbreak at the jail in Auburn, Placer County, where 17 residents and a correctional officer tested positive. The newspaper noted that none of those three counties regularly posted information about COVID-19 in their facilities. In the face of county sheriffs' resistance to release the data, BSCC's position was, again, astonishingly laissez-faire: Penner mentioned that she was having conversations about data tracking but that the board's hands were largely tied, and it was on local health and jail officials to decide how much information to share. She expressed concerns that "if [the data reporting was to be done] based on self-reporting COVID cases to us jail by jail, I think there's a concern that there would be issues with accuracy."[72]

By mid-July 2020, the paucity of data became a serious problem, and Penner finally wrote a memorandum to all county sheriffs, informing them that a centralized data collection effort would be underway and that their assistance would be necessary.[73] The letter required the sheriffs to report "the number of new positive COVID-19 tests for both residents and staff (reported separately), and deaths at each facility each week. We will also make a one-time request for your facilities' cumulative COVID-19 case information and deaths to date." In addition, Penner requested that each sheriff's department ensure that "your facility health care providers are immediately reporting detailed case-level COVID-19 data to your county public health COVID-19 Data Dashboard Page 2 agency. Every facility administrator should work with their health care providers to ensure that data are being reported timely and completely to your county public health department."

The resulting database, which went live in late July, was disappointingly sparse and unwieldy.[74] Not only was the data presented per individual facility, with no analysis or aggregate data functions, but it was bound to allow outbreaks to occur undetected; per Penner's request to the sheriffs, any number of infections below 11 would be reported and displayed as "{{lt}}11," with no information as to testing rates. Obviously, the database did not interface at all with CDCR's tracking tool, making it impossible to contact-trace across the jurisdictional divide.

But even after the BSCC data collection effort, massive outbreaks continued to occur undetected. On August 27, 2020, KQED journalists reported on a massive outbreak at the Fresno County Jail—at least 1,115 residents and 76 employees had tested positive, 21 of whom had been hospitalized—and sought an explanation from the California Department of Public Health (CDPH). The department's spokesperson replied that CDPH collected information on jails from county health officials but did not publish it because it was often "incomplete"; the spokesperson attributed the data quality problem to the high volume of cases and inadequate resources for counties to report them.[75]

In the absence of useful data through official channels, other actors stepped in to fill the gaps. Launched on March 24 by Sharon Dolovich and Aaron Littman,[76] the UCLA Law COVID Behind Bars Data Project[77] began collecting data on a national level, including federal, state, and local facilities. The project tracked infection rates, hospitalization, deaths, recoveries, transfers, testing, et cetera, for all correctional institutions, but found it difficult to obtain data on jails. On its web page, the project explained that data collection depends on data quality and availability, as "correctional authorities vary dramatically in what they report publicly" and "[t]here have been instances when the values reported by an agency changed over time in ways that were unexpected based on the description of the variable." The variation in reporting quality posed special difficulty in the context of testing, which "var[ies] widely by correctional agency. As a result, true case counts are likely higher than reported, and the extent of this underdetection is extremely variable." Another area of concern was the lack of reliable reporting on staff infections, as "[s]ome jurisdictions leave it to staff members' discretion whether to report positive test results they receive from community healthcare providers. As a result, the number of staff cases reported may be lower even than the number detected by testing."[78]

A glance at the project's California page reveals that, as late as February 28, 2021, they did not have reliable data for several California jails. The project did not rely on the BSCC database for its numbers; instead, it scraped data from the more informative databases for the individual sheriff's departments and relied on external, reliable sources for the rest.[79]

One such resource was a regional collection effort by the *Davis Vanguard*, which included an accessible database covering several counties.[80] The *Davis Vanguard* relied on websites maintained by the sheriff's departments in Alameda, San Francisco, Solano, Yolo, Los Angeles, Orange, Santa Clara, and Sacramento Counties; the *Vanguard* also reported BSCC numbers but stated that the BSCC database "remains incomplete as many facilities have refused to comply. Further, it does not contain historical data prior to July 20."[81] Importantly, the *Vanguard*'s reporting included information about quarantines of specific units in some of the jails, as well as about testing rates where available. Launching an independent statistical inquiry into COVID-19 in jails, statistician Aparna Komarla formed the COVID-in-Custody Project,[82] which carefully followed jail cases and vaccination rates. In several perceptive op-eds, Komarla highlighted that jails were not sharing their data and coping strategies even when they seemed to be doing fine. The massive outbreaks in so many jails, she wrote, "[made] the success of San Francisco jail all the more impressive. It also ma[de] it all the more critical to understand what it [was] doing right." Confounding the problem was the opaque way in which the data was reported. Komarla observed that the San Francisco Sheriff's Office's website "has data on the number of COVID cases staff-wide since March 2020. But without disaggregating that data to distinguish between jail and non-jail employees, the overall risk of jail staff introducing the virus to the incarcerated population cannot be quantified."

Another sore point, which became a major issue of concern after the advent of the vaccine, was the opaqueness of reporting on the vaccination rate of the staff: the sheriff's office, explained Komarla, "has provided one data point for 'custody sworn staff,' stating that 52% were self-reported as fully vaccinated as of July 2 [2021]. But this does not account for the 32 custody civilian staff, or other non-custody Sheriff's Office members who also work at the jail. Again, without accurate data on all the staff interacting with the jail population, few if any insights can be garnered." She added:

> Data regarding vaccinations among the incarcerated population is also sparse. Upon request, San Francisco stated that 59% of its jail population was fully vaccinated in June 2021, but given the transient nature of the jail, that number alone is not helpful. Subsequent public records requests for information for July and August were ignored.

The best shot we have at bringing down infection rates at correctional facilities across the state is by sharing best practices from those that are doing a good job at preventing outbreaks. Data transparency is the first step.[83]

Notably, these academic and journalistic efforts were supplemented by efforts by private individuals who pored over data from specific jails. For example, UC Berkeley law student Darby Aono maintained her own database of the Santa Rita Jail which, in addition to population, case numbers, and testing rates, included information on quarantines by housing unit.[84]

That a serious, rigorous actor such as the UCLA Law COVID Behind Bars Data Project preferred to avail itself of these alternative sources, rather than the incomplete BSCC data, is an important social fact. It resembles Franklin Zimring's aforementioned effort[85] to quantify lethal force exercised by law enforcement. Zimring compared the FBI database to those maintained by the *Washington Post* and the *Guardian*, finding that the official statistics left out about half of the lethal incidents, and relying for his analysis and recommendations on the journalistic databases. Such data collection gaps by governmental agencies are not unimportant: handling complicated, tragic phenomena requires careful study of their extent and distribution, and neglect in this area can cast doubt on the seriousness that is ascribed to these tragedies and the efficacy of the efforts to prevent and address them.

The COVID-19 Experience in County Jails

The prepandemic warnings to decarcerate correctional facilities included jails. In early March, when San Francisco saw only 13 cases, San Francisco public defender Mano Raju sent a letter to San Francisco sheriff Paul Miyamoto, expressing his "serious concern" that the 1,100 residents in San Francisco's jails were at risk. Raju warned Miyamoto about the specific risks to the pretrial detainee population, writing: "The constant flow of both staff and detainees in and out of the jails—where large numbers of people are housed in close proximity—means that a powerful virus like COVID-19 can take over quickly and easily."[86]

But as with Realignment, jails differed greatly in their COVID-19 prevention strategies. In early March, the *Sacramento Bee* reported that the Merced County Sheriff's Office planned to halt visitation at two county facilities as a temporary, "precautionary measure" and started conducting visitor screenings; by contrast, a Fresno County Sheriff's Office spokesman said the agency had no plans to halt visitation and was "constantly educating inmates, staff and visitors about the importance of good hygiene." Sacramento County reported it had not changed anything about its daily operations, intake screening, jail visitation or communicable disease practices because they were already "sufficient." Placer County, where a cruise ship passenger had died on March 4, said it would not answer basic questions regarding its jail policies except in response to a formal request under California's Public Records Act.[87] Remarkably, in late March, the *San Francisco Chronicle* reported that Solano County sheriff's deputies were driving to other county jails and picking up recently freed people on minor traffic offenses, then transporting them to their own jail.[88]

This variation, as well as the difficulties of coordinating a response to the closure of prisons to jail transfers, were at the root of the COVID-19 problem in jails. On March 24, in an effort to curb the contagion in prisons, Governor Newsom ordered CDCR to halt all transfers from jails.[89] The stoppage of jail intakes did not eliminate the risk to state prison residents; transfers between CDCR facilities continued, resulting in several outbreaks—notably, the infamous San Quentin outbreak.[90]

The closure of prisons created a bottleneck in jails, jamming the flow of residents in and out of county facilities. This resulted in serious overcrowding, which was documented in several lawsuits brought on behalf of jail populations. In late April, the American Civil Liberties Union (ACLU) filed lawsuits against Governor Newsom and Xavier Becerra, the attorney general, demanding that jail populations be reduced: "Outbreaks at local jails and juvenile facilities threaten to tax the broader community's health care system beyond capacity. This impending viral explosion—imminently likely to occur in most, if not all, of California's 58 counties—will directly impact all California residents, including correctional staff, their families, and their respective communities."[91]

The situation in Orange County, described by Justice Sonia Sotomayor in her dissent in *Barnes v. Ahlman*[92]—a class-action suit on behalf of the Orange County jail population—was emblematic of these problems. Relying on "dozens of inmate declarations," Justice Sotomayor summarized the situation as follows:

> Although the Jail had been warned that "social distancing is the cornerstone of reducing transmission of COVID-19," inmates described being transported back and forth to the jail in crammed buses, socializing in dayrooms

with no space to distance physically, lining up next to each other to wait for the phone, sleeping in bunk beds two to three feet apart, and even being ordered to stand closer than six feet apart when inmates tried to socially distance. Moreover, although the Jail told its inmates that they could "best protect" themselves by washing their hands with "soap and water throughout the day," numerous inmates reported receiving just one small, hotel-sized bar of soap per week. And after symptomatic inmates were removed from their units, other inmates were ordered to dispose of their belongings without gloves or other protective equipment. Finally, despite the Jail's stated policy to test and isolate individuals who reported or exhibited symptoms consistent with COVID–19, multiple symptomatic detainees described being denied tests, and others recounted sharing common spaces with infected or symptomatic inmates.

Two jail residents, José Armendariz and Lonnie Kocontes, described the conditions in an interview with CalMatters.[93] The two said that they had witnessed jail staff fail to follow cleaning protocols, particularly when distributing pills to residents from plastic pill bags or handling inhalers. They reported that the staff frequently did not wear masks, and that the residents' masks were made from torn-up bedsheets. They also reported that incarcerated workers used soiled rags to clean communal spaces after mealtimes; according to Armendariz, residents were required to buy their own rags to clean with from the jail's commissary, and that cleaning supplies were diluted to the point of uselessness. Armendariz and Kocontes also described the residents' response to the conditions—creating their own quarantine system:

> New arrivals are told not to touch anything—newspapers, communal surfaces, the phones attached to the wall—for 12 days after they arrive in the medical unit. There is one phone designated for new inmates.
> "We don't touch that one even if it's open. You just line up and wait for a different one," Armendariz said.[94]

Similar problems were reported in a class action lawsuit on behalf of the Tulare County jail population, filed in July 2020. The plaintiffs accused the sheriff of failing to implement state-mandated health protocols; ACLU attorney Kathleen Guneratne reported that jail residents "described 'alarming,' 'cramped,' and 'restrictive' conditions, including prolonged hours of confinement, where inmates are stuck in their cells for more than 23 hours per day." Jail residents reported that sick people were "neglected, denied medical attention, and ignored when they asked to be tested. Many were shuffled in and out of cells and around the facility, potentially exposing others to infection."[95]

Some of the neglect stemmed from staff shortages, a chronic problem plaguing both prisons and jails, particularly in distant, rural locations.[96] Other problems involved misallocation of funds intended for COVID-19 care relief; the Orange County Sheriff's Department, which received $90 million in federal coronavirus response money, spent the vast majority of the funds on staff salaries and benefits.[97] Yet more problems resulted from the jail architecture. According to a class-action lawsuit on behalf of the Los Angeles County jail population, the Los Angeles County jail population was crammed into open dormitories and two-person cells the size of parking spaces. They slept inches from one another, unable to socially distance. Officers did not always wear masks, and prisoners' masks were not regularly replaced.[98] The plight of one plaintiff was told in an op-ed in the *Los Angeles Times*: Teresa Gomez learned she was pregnant shortly after her arrest in August. After testing positive for COVID-19 in October, she was moved to a small, windowless, dirty solitary confinement cell and locked in for 23 hours a day—punitive conditions the CDC had warned would deter prisoners from reporting symptoms. A scheduled obstetric wellness exam was canceled because of her COVID-19 status. And her criminal case has come to a standstill; the courts had repeatedly canceled hearings due to COVID-19 risks.[99]

Zero Bail as a Depressurizing Valve

Handling COVID-19 in cramped, inappropriate facilities, without transfers to prisons, required another depressurizing valve—and the answer came from the courts. On April 6, the Judicial Council of California moved to set a statewide emergency bail schedule that reduced bail to $0 for most misdemeanor and some low-level felony offenses, for 90 days, starting April 15.[100] Because approximately 75 percent of the jail population consists of pretrial detainees, the emergency measure resulted in considerable population reduction. As reported by the Prison Policy Initiative[101] and elsewhere, by the end of May, jail populations in Los Angeles[102] and Sacramento Counties[103] had decreased by over 30 percent. Orange County's jail population dropped by almost 45 percent in the same period,[104] while other counties—including San Diego,[105] San Mateo,[106] and Stanislaus[107]—also released hundreds of pretrial detainees.

The results of the measure were mixed. Sheriff's departments in Alameda and Ventura Counties reported that the reduced number of residents allowed them to divide the population into cohorts, which slowed the spread of the pandemic;[108] nevertheless, outbreaks occurred at both locations, including the death of six residents in total in Ventura[109] and a serious outbreak in Alameda County's Santa Rita Jail.[110] The Santa Rita outbreak prompted the Alameda County public defender, Brendon Woods, to call for the emergency release of more than 100 people with less than six months left to serve; district attorney Nancy O'Malley declined, arguing that she could not "jeopardize the safety of victims or the community."[111]

In June 2021, during the phased reopening of the state, the Judicial Council voted to end the emergency zero-bail measure, leaving it up to the individual county courts "to continue to use the emergency COVID-19 bail schedule where necessary to protect the health of the community, the courts, and the incarcerated."[112] Thirty-one counties (collectively housing about 80 percent of California residents) elected to keep the emergency bail schedule in place. The outcome, again, reflected the atomized, jurisdictional nature of jail policies. A population tracking tool created by the Vera Institute of Justice shows wide variation in the population trends of various California counties.[113] The highest decreases were reported in Yuba (-48 percent), Orange (-39 percent), Marin (-31 percent), Santa Clara (-29 percent) and San Francisco (-26 percent) Counties. Tehama County increased its jail population by 28 percent, followed by Monterey (+7 percent) and Placer (+1 percent) Counties. Notably—again—the data evinces an agnotology problem: the tracking tool reported populations for only 16 counties.

The Hydra Rears Its Ugly Heads: Litigation

Soon enough, Schlanger's prediction that health-care litigation in the post-*Plata* era would sprout hydra heads had come true. In California, and nationwide, numerous lawsuits were filed on behalf of both prison and jail populations—some as consolidated habeas corpus petitions, some as class-action lawsuits, and some, tragically, as wrongful death grievances.

Litigation on behalf of the jail population puts the incarcerated petitioner simultaneously in better and worse positions vis-à-vis the prison population. On one hand, jails house mostly pretrial detainees, who, of course, are presumed innocent and therefore more deserving of sympathy; on the other, they sometimes require courts to pore into conditions in small facilities in remote locations, which can be labor intensive if supervision is necessary. In addition, the remedies sought in jail lawsuits run the gamut between improved health-care protocols and population reduction orders.

Of particular interest was the federal litigation involving COVID-19 protocols in the Orange County jail system. In late May 2020, District Court judge Jesus G. Bernal ordered the sheriff to enforce social distancing, administer regular testing, and distribute cleaning supplies and hand sanitizers.[114] The sheriff appealed the order all the way to the Supreme Court which, in a 5–4, stayed the lower court's preliminary injunction.

The decision was brief, with only Justice Sotomayor writing in dissent that the decision to stay the injunction was "extraordinary." Ordinarily, the conditions for granting a stay require (1) a "reasonable probability" that the Supreme Court will grant certiorari to hear the case; (2) a "fair prospect" that the Supreme Court will subsequently reverse the decision on the merits; and (3) "a likelihood that irreparable harm [will] result from the denial of a stay." None of these applied in the Orange County litigation: the Ninth Circuit ruled on clearly established law—it found ample proof of "deliberate indifference" because the jails were forewarned and knew the risks—and, even if the Eighth Amendment constituted insufficient grounds for relief, there would be an alternative claim under the Americans with Disabilities Act. The odds that the Supreme Court would grant certiorari and hear the case, therefore, were slim—and, worst of all, the "likelihood of irreparable harm" was obvious from the facts, which are quoted in a previous subsection.

The extent (and expense) to which the sheriff—who, according to the claims in *Ahlman*, did not provide PPE to jail residents—went to challenge the decision were remarkable, especially given that the remedy granted was not a mass release but merely a mandate regarding health protocols. But the Orange County mess would eventually result in a more dramatic remedy. Some jail residents filed habeas corpus writs with the Orange County Superior Court—which, on December 11, 2020, ordered the jail to reduce its population by 50 percent.[115]

In his decision, Judge Peter Wilson recounted a horrifying picture of the COVID-19 experience at the jail. Not only was it impossible, given the conditions, for residents to socially distance, staff behavior was not monitored when away from the facility. Staff members were not tested except by their request, even when displaying symptoms. The staff was provided PPE but not required to wear it. Housing decisions did not take medical vulnerability into account. None of these facts, which were backed by statements from medical experts and staff members, were contradicted by respondents with any evidence.

The decision was a straightforward application of *In re Von Staich*, a Court of Appeal decision regarding the San Quentin outbreak.[116] As we show in chapter 6, in *Von Staich*, the court applied the procedural standard from *People v. Duvall*,[117] according to which, on habeas corpus, the respondent (in this case, the correctional facility) must state facts in its return brief—and if respondent merely denies the petitioner's allegations, no evidentiary hearing is granted. Accordingly, the Court of Appeal agreed with the experts' estimate that proper social distancing could only be achieved through population reduction, and found nothing in respondent's briefs to contradict these findings.

In *Campbell*, Judge Wilson found that the Orange County sheriff took a page from the San Quentin warden's litigation strategy and limited his response to denying the jail residents' allegations. Consequently, Judge Wilson relied on the facts argued by the petitioners to find an Eighth Amendment violation—the sheriff's "deliberate indifference" to the health and safety of the jail population. Consequently, the court granted the *Campbell* petitioners immediate relief, in the form of release or transfer. For everyone else in the Orange County Jail, the court modeled its order after the *Von Staich* order, with some more specificity: it ordered population reductions of at least 50 percent in all dormitories—and, if this were to be insufficient to achieve proper distancing, even further reductions.

The district attorney criticized the decision,[118] arguing that the population reduction order "will release dangerous and violent criminals back into our neighborhoods to commit more crimes and victimize more people." The sheriff—mere days after declaring that his deputies would not enforce Governor Newsom's stay-at-home order[119]—issued a statement: "We are evaluating the order, its impacts and our options for appeal . . . If the order stands, it will result in the release of more than 1,800 inmates."[120]

These fearmongering statements echoed the aftermath of *Von Staich*. As we explain in chapter 6, *Von Staich* was reversed by the California Supreme Court,[121] remanded to the Marin Superior Court alongside hundreds of other cases for an evidentiary hearing on whether the San Quentin authorities engaged in remedial measures sufficient to counter the court's finding of deliberate indifference,[122] and ended in a pyrrhic victory for San Quentin's prisoners. For the jail population, which is more transient, any justice delayed by appeals was, effectively, justice denied.

There were some upsides to the Orange County litigation and other jail cases. Encouragingly, the transience of jail populations hindered neither class certification for the lawsuits nor excellent legal representation. In that respect, civil rights litigators have adapted well to the post-*Plata* world. But on a bigger scale, the COVID-19 jail crisis complemented the way the myth of impermeability played out in prisons. By viewing jails and prisons as jurisdictionally severable from each other, rather than part of the same continuum of people flowing through the system, the individual counties and their supervising agency failed to create an effective, cohesive plan. As is the case in many aspects of local government in California, the tendency to ignore and discount counties except as depressurizing mechanisms has resulted in a "hydra problem" of infections, human rights violations, haphazard release countermeasures, and a flurry of litigation with varying degrees of success.

FOUR

Elixir

For I will go through the land of Egypt in that night, and will strike all the firstborn in the land of Egypt, both man and animal. Against all the gods of Egypt I will execute judgments: I am Yahweh. The blood shall be to you for a token on the houses where you are: and when I see the blood, I will pass over you, and there shall no plague be on you to destroy you, when I strike the land of Egypt.

EXODUS 12:12–13

WHEN THE FIRST CASES of COVID-19 were diagnosed in California prisons, the global search for a vaccine was well underway. Chinese scientists isolated SARS-CoV-2, the virus that causes COVID-19, in late 2019.[1] On January 11, 2020, the WHO reported that their Chinese office had received the genetic sequences for the novel coronavirus from Chinese authorities,[2] a breakthrough that ushered in unprecedented international collaborations, spanning public authorities and pharmaceutical giants, and resulted in the development of vaccines at a record pace. In February 2020, WHO chief Adhanom Ghebreyesus opined that a vaccine should not be expected to be available in less than 18 months;[3] Rob Grenfell and Trevor Drew of the Commonwealth Scientific and Industrial Research Organisation (CSIRO), an Australian agency, explained that vaccine development, the product of necessary collaboration, would involve repeated testing on animals followed by rigorous human trials, onerous processes of regulatory approval, and the ongoing challenges of virus mutation.

The eventual development of multiple effective COVID-19 vaccines on a faster timeline was, therefore, a true scientific and technological triumph.[4] Four vaccine candidates entered the human evaluation stage as early as March 2020.[5] Among these was the first vaccine to be authorized for use in the United States, an mRNA vaccine developed by Pfizer-BioNTech; this vaccine, which required two doses in consecutive months, received an emergency use authorization (EUA) from the Food and Drug Administration

(FDA) on December 11, 2020, and final, full FDA approval on August 23, 2021.[6] A second mRNA vaccine, developed by Moderna and also requiring two doses, received an EUA on December 18, 2020.[7] On February 27, 2021, a third vaccine—the Janssen Biotech vaccine, developed by a subsidiary of Johnson & Johnson—received an EUA as well.[8]

Two important medical and regulatory aspects of these developments would later play a role in vaccine administration and acceptance in prisons. First, in the early months of 2021, when California authorities and health providers began offering the vaccine, all three vaccines—Pfizer, Moderna, and Johnson & Johnson—had not yet received full FDA approval, and were still on EUA status. And second, two of these vaccines—Pfizer and Moderna—differed from the Johnson & Johnson vaccine in three important ways: they were based on a different immunology mechanism, they required two consecutive shots, and they were found in clinical trials to be more effective than the Johnson & Johnson vaccine.

The good news about vaccine emergency approval was tempered by clunky administration proceedings and scant availability. As of January 2021, California had merely two million doses of COVID-19 vaccines and had vaccinated only 500,000 people. Anticipating a period of scarcity, and aware of the need to prioritize certain at-risk populations for vaccine delivery, the California Department of Public Health (CDPH) published a three-phase vaccination plan in October 2020.[9]

CDPH officials anticipated that, during phase 1, the state would have a limited supply of vaccines, and therefore they planned to prioritize the vaccination of critical populations in two subphases. Phase 1-A would see the vaccination of health-care personnel likely treating patients with COVID-19 and health-care personnel likely to be exposed to COVID-19. Phase 1-B would make the vaccine available to people at increased risk for severe illness or death from COVID-19 and to essential workers, whose obligations exposed them to COVID-19 infection risks. The memorandum established an Allocation Data Team, tasked with "identifying disadvantaged populations and communities that have been disproportionately impacted by COVID-19 in terms of higher rates of infection, hospitalization, and deaths." To combat these well-documented disparities, state health officials developed a health equity metric, which would factor in numerous demographic categories, including race and ethnicity. Importantly, for developing guidelines on comparative infection, mortality, and risk figures across populations, the CDPH Allocation Data Team was to review datasets from various community partners, one of which was CDCR.

This plan appeared to be in line with an understanding of contagion and public health that viewed the state as a geographic continuum. The report explained the necessity of communications between state officials, local governments, and thousands of health providers, and an extensive networking strategy employing field staff as liaisons between provider offices and local health departments, as well as "with first responder organizations, groups serving vulnerable populations and large employers throughout our state's diverse counties." Many local health departments embarked on "specific outreach, education and mitigation efforts" aimed at "communities most adversely affected by COVID-19 . . . establishing good relationships along that way that are paving the way for COVID-19 vaccine." Among CDPH's priorities was the need to provide clear guidance regarding the timing of vaccinating critical populations, as well as the definition of said populations.

While the state was still vaccinating people in phase 1A, which included people in long-term care facilities and some frontline medical workers, concerns emerged that incarcerated people were not going to be included on this list. Hadar wrote an op-ed for the *San Francisco Chronicle*, explaining why prison populations should be included in this early phase:

First, COVID-19 infection and mortality rates in prison are several times higher than in the general population. Prison staff (correctional officers and other prison workers) treat, and come in direct contact with, incarcerated COVID-19 patients just like health care personnel on the outside. Moreover, incarcerated people have not seen their families and loved ones since early March, when all visitation was halted because of the pandemic. Vaccinating them should be a priority.

Second, prisons must be prioritized because vaccinating behind bars protects everyone in the state. It is imperative to understand the role that prison outbreaks play in the overall COVID picture of the state. As of today, all but two CDCR facilities have COVID-19 outbreaks, and numerous prisons have suffered serious outbreaks with hundreds of cases. Months of analysis . . . show correlations between pandemic spikes in prison and in the surrounding and neighboring counties. Vaccinating people behind bars protects not only them, but also you and yours.

Third, CDPH's vaccination plan rightly emphasizes the need to factor equity in the distribution of vaccines, specifically through the prioritization of communities and race/class demographic groups who have borne the brunt of infections and deaths so far. It is hard to imagine a category of Californians who have, disproportionately, suffered more from COVID-19 than incarcerated people. Vaccinating them first is not only prudent and worthwhile—it is fair.[10]

Advocates were trying to combat disturbing news: kowtowing to public pressure not to prioritize prisoners, CDPH removed prison populations from tier 1B of vaccination.[11] This misguided zero-sum thinking—based, of course, on the myth of prison impermeability—reflected similarly worrisome developments nationwide. In Colorado, for example, the first draft of the vaccine distribution plan prioritized the prison population, but the governor later backtracked, "sa[ying] during a media briefing that prisoners would not get the vaccine before 'free people.'" His response caused public uproar and was reported in national media outlets.

Similarly, in Wisconsin, parroting the old law-and-order playbook, assemblymember Mark Born tweeted, "The committee that advises @GovEvers and his department tasked with leading during this pandemic is recommending allowing prisoners to receive the vaccine before 65 year old grandma?"[12]

And, in Tennessee, health officials placed the state's prison population last in line, because a state advisory panel tasked with vaccine prioritization, which acknowledged that prison populations were high-risk, concluded that prioritizing them could be a "public relations nightmare." Documents reported that the panel understood the problem: "If we get hit hard in jails it affects the whole community. Disease leaves corrections facilities and reenters general society as inmates cycle out of their sentencing," the document read, adding that when inmates get the disease, "it is the taxpayers that have to absorb the bill for treatment." But while corrections workers were bumped up to one of the earliest slots, incarcerated people—including those who met the state's age qualifications for earlier vaccinations—were relegated to the last eligible group.[13]

But a small number of vaccines was made available to CDCR in December (for the futile judicial efforts to persuade the governor to allocate more in late 2020 and early 2021, see chapter 6). CDCR secretary Kathleen Allison and the receiver, Clark Kelso, communicated the good news to the family members and advocates on December 18. In a letter addressed "To All Loved Ones of Incarcerated Individuals and Valued External Stakeholders," Allison and Kelso announced that CDCR was working on a vaccination plan, whose "initial focus would be on people at high risk of becoming infected or severely ill from COVID-19, as well as frontline workers." They communicated the following expectation: "We encourage everyone to accept the vaccine once they are eligible to receive it, and in accordance with the phased distribution approach. These collective efforts will set us on the path to recovery, and will allow us to reduce the risk of COVID-19 in our institutions, and safely reopen to in-person visiting, group programming, volunteering, and other opportunities." Because of vaccine shortages, as of early January 2021, systemwide vaccinations at CDCR were still not planned. This meant limiting vaccinations to skilled-nursing facilities housing a higher proportion of aging and infirm people, such as the Central California Women's Facility (CCWF) in Chowchilla, the California Health Care Facility (CHCF) in Stockton, and the California Medical Facility (CMF) in Vacaville.[14] As Ann Hinga Klein explained in the *New York Times*, this decision targeted individuals who were more frail, but

> none so far at the 25 prisons that have been most overwhelmed by infections, including San Quentin, Avenal State Prison and the California Institution for Men.
>
> Elizabeth Gransee, a spokeswoman for J. Clark Kelso, a court-appointed official who oversees prison health care in California, said on Wednesday that the prison system had decided to concentrate its vaccination efforts at facilities where "people are at significant risk of becoming infected or severely ill from the coronavirus."
>
> But the facilities chosen . . . have had far fewer infections and deaths than most other state prisons.
>
> Ms. Gransee would not provide the specific date of when vaccinations started at the three facilities. She also declined to provide other details about the state prison's vaccination program in response to written questions.[15]

The relentless civil rights advocacy on behalf of incarcerated individuals paid off. In late January, the state posted the phase 1A, tier 2 vaccine eligibility list, which now included all incarcerated people. In response, CDCR formulated a prioritization plan, which was disclosed to lawyers from the Prison Law Office during the *Plata v. Newsom* litigation (which we discuss in chapter 6). The vaccination plan prioritized the quickly diminishing category of "COVID-naïve" people—those who had not contracted COVID-19 in the last 90 days. Within this category, prioritization was based on a complicated COVID-19 risk algorithm, which allocated points to individual members of the prison population based on the risks they faced due to age, preexisting conditions, or both.[16]

The lawyers and advocates faced another difficulty: serious concerns about vaccine acceptance. The need for public buy-in is a serious consideration whenever designing a public health response to a crisis, certainly on a massive scale; in the context of COVID-19,[17] prevention measures depended, in large part, on an enormous amount of groundwork to foster compliance, including virtual community building, fostering solidarity between high-risk and low-risk groups, and trust building between decision-makers, health-care workers, and the public. Vaccine controversies in the United States were instructive of the dangers of government that not only fails to make this effort but actively stokes the opposite sentiments through misinformation and divisiveness. Even against this already contentious backdrop, there were unique concerns about compliance from the incarcerated population. Law and public health scholar Osagie Obasogie recounts the ugly history of medical experimentation in prisons, which can explain vaccine and health-care hesitation behind bars:

> As early as 1906, Dr. Richard P. Strong—director of the Biological Laboratory of the Philippine Bureau of Science who later became a professor of tropical medicine at Harvard—gave a cholera vaccine to twenty-four Filipino inmates without their consent in order to learn about the disease; thirteen died ... Twelve inmates from Mississippi's Rankin Farm prison became test subjects in 1915 to study pellagra—a disfiguring and deadly disease characterized by skin rashes and diarrhea. Though common wisdom at the time suggested that pellagra was a disease caused by germs, Dr. Joseph Goldberger—a physician in the federal government's Hygienic Laboratory, predecessor to the National Institutes of Health—thought it was linked to malnutrition characteristic of Southern rural poverty. After Mississippi Governor Earl Brewer promised pardons to all participants—an inducement to participate in research that would be intolerable today–Goldberger tried to prove his theory that poor diet caused pellagra by subjecting inmates to what many called a "hellish experiment": eating exclusively high-starch foods such as "corn bread, mush, collards, sweet potatoes, grits and rice" that caused considerable pain, lethargy, and dizziness. Despite their pleadings to end the study, prisoners were not allowed to withdraw. And, in an early 1920s experiment that was as bizarre as it was gratuitous, 500 inmates at California's San Quentin prison had testicular glands from rams, boars, and goats implanted into their scrotums to see if their lost sexual potency could be rejuvenated.[18]

For California's prison population, there were very recent reminders that their health-care providers did not, to say the least, have their best interests in mind. One of the grimmest episodes of prison medical scandals was the recent practice of sterilizing incarcerated women, documented in Erika Cohn's documentary *Belly of the Beast*.[19] Echoing horrific antebellum racialized and eugenic practices, a 2013 report from the California State Auditor report found, during eight years, that 144 sterilizations were performed on women housed in CDCR facilities. Shockingly, we noted that 39 inmates were sterilized following deficiencies in the informed consent process. For 27 of the 39 inmates, the physician performing the procedure or an alternate physician failed to sign the inmate's consent form certifying that the inmate appeared mentally competent and understood the lasting effects of the procedure. For 18 of the 39 inmates, we noted potential violations of the waiting period between when the inmate consented to the procedure and when the sterilization surgery actually took place. Finally, among these 39 inmates were six who were sterilized following violations of both these requirements. Although neither Corrections nor the Receiver's Office's employees actually performed the sterilization procedures, we concluded that they had a responsibility to ensure that the informed consent requirements were followed in those instances in which their employees obtained inmates' consent, which was the case for at least 19 of the 39 inmates. Our audit also noted that prison medical staff infrequently requested approval to sterilize inmates, and when they did so, it was not always clear that these requests were approved. However, since January 2010, medical claims data from the Receiver's Office show that the number of female inmates who have undergone bilateral tubal ligations and other medical procedures that may result in sterilization has greatly decreased.[20]

In her 2020 review of Cohn's film, the *Guardian*'s Shilpa Jindia makes the appalling historical roots of the practice explicit:

> The eugenics movement casts a long shadow through the persistent discrimination within the healthcare system against women of color, and the state's control over women's bodies. "You can call [forced sterilizations] state violence," said Hafsah al-Amin of the CCWP [California Coalition of Women Prisoners]. "The neglect in the system enables, if not sends a message to people that it is OK to do to this particular group of people."
>
> "What's going on with covid is the same," she argued.
>
> "When you take many thousands upon thousands of women of color, Black women of reproductive age, and you put them in prison during that period of their reproductive age and then you slowly kill them due to the problems of inadequate healthcare, then that's also a eugenics program," echoed [Diana] Block [of CCWP].

Despite a 2012 law[21] prohibiting the use of federal funds for sterilization as a means of birth control in prisons, California continued to pay doctors a total of almost $150,000 to sterilize women. One doctor who spoke with Jindia remarked that this amount paled in comparison to "what you save in welfare."

This disturbing history, some of it very recent, would suggest that CDCR invest considerable efforts to engender vaccine compliance and build trust.

Instead, given the harrowing experiences described in chapters 2 and 3, the prison population arrived at the vaccine moment with a fundamental mistrust of prison authorities. It was clear from the litigation briefs at the time that prison authorities, either obtusely or intentionally, completely missed the point. In one brief, they stated, "the physical plant is not conducive to compliance"—identifying the physical, but not the psychological, aspect of the problem. The most glaring breach of trust, of course, had been the botched transfer from CIM to San Quentin and Corcoran, and the prison's disingenuous refusal to take any responsibility, which rose to the level of writing, in one of the attorney general's briefs for the prison, "petitioners' attempts to suggest prisoner transfers of any kind are not safe or effective is not well taken."

But the transfer issue was merely one among many. By the end of 2020, when vaccine rollout was contemplated, prison and jail populations had already witnessed multiple forms of suffering due to neglect, incompetence, and explicit cruelty on the part of staff, the spreading of rumors and misinformation suggesting antiscientific approaches, and other issues. In addition, at that point, the prison and jail litigation efforts were already well underway, and state lawyers at these hearings exhibited grandstanding, performative protestations about public safety, and staunch resistance to the idea of releases. In the face of such behavior, why would prisoners be expected to comply with PPE-wearing requirements when they saw guards frequently and openly flouting these requirements with no consequences? Why would people be expected to rush to report symptoms and get tested when the consequence would be being assigned to cells that they had associated, for decades, with punishment and deprivation? Most importantly, given the history of using prisoners as experiment subjects, how could CDCR and CCHCS possibly lay some trust groundwork when rolling out a vaccine, so that people would not suspect them, understandably, of subjecting them to untested, unreliable treatments?

There were already disturbing indications that the break in trust could result in noncompliance. The AMEND report about conditions in San Quentin, published in June,[22] reported that the men incarcerated at San Quentin expressed fear of getting tested or reporting symptoms, lest they be placed in isolation in a death row or solitary confinement cell.

Thankfully, these grim predictions did not come to pass: vaccine acceptance rate by incarcerated people in all correctional facilities—almost 70 percent as of July 2021[23]—surpassed the rate in California's general population at the time. The credit for this phenomenal success goes primarily to the incarcerated people themselves, who overcame their understandable bitterness and mistrust to obtain reliable medical information on their own (often on smuggled cell phones). Family members on the outside, while understanding their loved ones' reluctance, urged them to get vaccinated.

Some of the credit for the high vaccine acceptance rate also rests with several formerly incarcerated men, who still had many friends and acquaintances inside and recorded short videos that could be easily viewed on smuggled cell phones, urging their friends to get the vaccine. Ken Hartman, a recently released freelance writer and the advocacy coordinator for the Transformative In-Prison Workgroup, said:

> I was in prison for 38 years, I've been out about 3 years now, just got off parole about 2 weeks ago, I'm just doing this right now because I'm hoping that folks inside will see it, I know there's a lot of rumors out there, I want you to know I strongly encourage you please get the vaccine when it's available to you, I know that when it's available to me I definitely will take it, I have a lot of friends in the medical world out here, they're all taking it, I know there's a lot of these rumors, I know what it's like when you're inside, it's hard to know what to believe and who to trust, I honestly believe it's the right thing to do and I strongly encourage you to take the vaccine when you get the chance. This thing is real and it's killing people and, you know, I don't want this to happen to any of you all. This is with love, and please take the vaccine when you can.[24]

Arnold Treviño said:

> I wanna talk to you guys about the COVID-19 vaccine. My name is Arnold, I'm a former lifer, I spent 25 years in the pen. As of today, January 11, 2021, there had been no known death, no one has died as a result of taking the COVID-19 vaccine. Nobody, zero, zip. Nada. No one has died as a result of that. On the other hand, over 380,000 loved ones have died who did not take the vaccine. They were not given the opportunity to take it. The choice is yours. Good luck.[25]

Rasheed Lockheart, a formerly incarcerated firefighter, said:

> What's up, everyone—my name is Rasheed. I am a formerly incarcerated person who spent, since the age of 15, my entire life incarcerated, literally, every year since I was 15 incarcerated, I'm now 43 years old. Most recently, I just did an 18-year term starting off in level 4 and working my way out and making a commitment to myself that I was going to do something better, something

better in a way not just for myself, but in a way that would have an impact for my community of currently incarcerated people that I just left behind. And so, for the last two years I was an engineer firefighter at San Quentin, where I did CPR over 50 times. And the reason why I did that is because you guys are part of an aging, dying population. I can't even begin to tell you how many people died from flus, from overdoses, from old age. So now we're faced with the coronavirus. I'm now advocating and trying to draw attention to what's happening inside of our prisons with this coronavirus outbreak and trying to get people to understand that, one, we need to release people, we need to get you guys out. It's not safe, and it's not safe because of what we see on TV, with the violence and all that, it's not safe because it's inhumane. You guys are living amongst the worst virus outbreak this country's ever known. Right now, there's a vaccine going around for you guys. You men, women, however you identify, there's a vaccine for you, and now's the opportunity to be proactive. Because people out here and in there are dying at all-time highs and now there's relief with this vaccine. Today there's been no known deaths with this vaccine. There are some side effects, but that's with anything, any flu shot that you take, there's going to be people who have side effects. Your chances of survival are much higher with this vaccine. I'm getting it and I would hope you're getting it, too, because until we break those walls and get everybody out, the best thing you can do is protect yourselves. Please.[26]

Much of the credit also goes to the members of AMEND who, as explained in chapter 2, had been doing important, lifesaving work in prisons from the early stages of the pandemic. AMEND members issued two special FAQ documents about the vaccine geared specifically toward incarcerated populations, including efforts to correct misinformation:

I heard that some of the officers, warden or health care staff are refusing to get the vaccine, why should I?

Reasons that people don't get the vaccine include not knowing how safe and effective they are, a lack of understanding about COVID-19 itself, mistrust of the medical system, and more. We encourage you to empower yourself by learning as much as you can about the COVID-19 vaccines and make your own decision about getting the vaccine based on facts.

Will the COVID-19 vaccine harm my fertility?

No. There is no evidence that the vaccine affects the fertility. There is also no evidence of infertility caused by COVID-19.

The Pfizer and Moderna COVID-19 vaccines are mRNA vaccines. Does that mean they change your DNA (your genetic code)?

The Pfizer and Moderna vaccines both use "messenger RNA" (also called mRNA) to teach the cells in your body to recognize the outside part of the COVID-19 virus (called the spike protein) and create antibodies against the virus. That way, if you are exposed to the virus, your immune system will attack the virus and stop it from making you sick. The COVID-19 vaccine does not change your DNA. mRNA cannot combine with your DNA.

Do the vaccines contain fetal tissue?

None of the vaccines contain fetal tissue.[27]

The videos, as well as the AMEND FAQ, offer meaningful clues to the second vaccination problem, which proved much thornier than the first: vaccine suspicion and reluctance among the custodial staff.

As explained in chapter 2, misinformation and fearmongering among the prison population often originated with staff members. These approaches to COVID-19 would later impact vaccination rates among custodial staff.

Many people who work in prison are not part of the custodial hierarchical ladder. As explained in chapter 1, correctional health care is run by the federal receivership (CCHCS), rather than by state prisons. Caring for the ailing prison population put enormous strains on the medical staff, particularly the nurses: amid serious nursing shortages, existing staff was necessary not only to administer the vaccines and care for COVID-19 patients but also to check vitals for thousands of isolated people twice a day. Dr. Shereef Aref, the chief executive officer of the receivership, explained CCHCS's "zero tolerance" policy toward COVID insubordination among the medical staff:[28]

"A refusal to a mandate is insubordination," Dr. Shereef Aref wrote. "It is not acceptable and it will not be tolerated."

First refusals will result in a write-up, Aref wrote. "A second refusal will be referred, as a request for Adverse Action, to the Hiring Authority."

One prison medical worker, who spoke anonymously out of fear of losing her job, said the stress was intense.

"Nursing staff [have] children out of school; to be away 16 hours not including walk time to the parking lot and drive time home could add up to 18 hours a day," she said. In many cases, both spouses work at the prison. "It's stressful. There is no such thing as 'social distancing' in prison.

"Also, the office staff have masks, but if you go on a housing unit, very few have masks because of the scarcity . . . . We are confused as to why they seem to have masks for administrative posts."

She added, "Oh, and an inmate committed suicide yesterday. And two officers committed suicide in March."

This situation, complete with insufficient protective equipment and lack of social distancing, affected other prison workers as well. On July 28, 2020, at the height of the first COVID-19 wave, SEIU Local 1000, a union representing health-care workers, clerical staff, custodians and other prison employees, filed a wide-ranging grievance against CDCR and CCHCS in all 35 California prisons for employing them, throughout the state, in unsafe conditions.[29] The grievance cited multiple failures to protect the workers, including inadequate supply of PPE and disinfecting materials, faulty hygiene, absence of appropriate training regarding the state's COVID-19 guidelines, lack of notice that a coworker was infected, physical inability to maintain social distancing, lax discipline regarding masking, failure to properly test the staff and population, and failure to maintain adequate internal command and provide responsible safety protocols. The grievance listed much of the suffering that affected the prison population (see chapter 2) as affecting the staff as well. SEIU demanded that prison authorities correct these problems immediately.

Employees at San Quentin also reported numerous instances in which health and safety were compromised by inadequate action to California's Division of Occupational Safety and Health (Cal/OSHA), which investigated the complaints. San Quentin's administration was fined for failing to report the infection and illness of numerous staff members, as well as for requiring that staff transport nonambulatory COVID-19 patients on the stairs and through unsafe corridors and pathways.[30]

By contrast to these efforts to enforce occupational safety, the COVID-19 approach espoused by the custodial staff and their union left much to be desired. As we have already seen, the guards' lax adherence to COVID-19 prevention and the misinformation they spread throughout the facility caused much suffering among the prison population. The second of three reports by California's Office of the Inspector General (OIG) flagged flagrant and frequent noncompliance with PPE wearing by the guards,[31] including "multiple occasions . . . at prisons statewide [in which] OIG staff directly observed departmental staff's failure to follow the department's face covering and physical distancing requirements."[32] In response to the report, in November 2020, the California Assembly held a hearing on CDCR's handling of the COVID-19 crisis, which already flagged vaccine suspicion, lax enforcement of PPE wearing, and other staff shortcomings.[33] Assemblymember Phil Ting was polite but firm, and consistently held CDCR secretary Kathleen Allison to account for the problems at the various facilities. Allison was defensive throughout, arguing that the department had been doing a good job overall monitoring COVID-19 prevention protocols. Ting, unconvinced, pointed out numerous ways in which Allison could monitor compliance. He drew the obvious comparison to nursing homes, explaining that the homes were audited through surprise visits. "When I show up for inspection," he explained, "everyone's on their best behavior." When Allison insisted that there was no systemic problem at CDCR, Ting responded:

> The reason we're having the hearing is . . . far and away, institutionally, these two types of institutions [prisons and nursing homes] created a disproportionate number of COVID cases. Obviously, there's a lot going against all the prison facilities, because of how people are housed, the crowding, etc., etc., but that's why we are so concerned. There are things out of your control, such as the physical plant, but there are things that are in your control and that's what we're concerned about. There were things that could have mitigated, could have reduced the situation, it was not done, and was not done in a systemic fashion. The fact that there's enough data to show significant inconsistency between institutions shows some systematic failure, in my opinion. I asked the same of the IG, but is this under your purview or under the receiver's? You both signed the memorandum.

When a doctor employed by the receivership testified about the difficulties of engendering staff cooperation, Ting became testy and asked, "You have people dying in facilities in pretty high numbers. Why do you think they wouldn't have taken that as a cue to take this seriously?" The doctor replied: "I think what we see in our system mirrors what we see in our country, people in doubt, people in confusion whether masks are helpful or harmful. As you know, this has been a topic of conversation in our political system for some time. What we're seeing in our institutions is a reflection of the political conversation." Ting became impatient: "You don't run a hospital, you run a department where freedom was taken away. You characterized as 'unclear.' I see it as crystal clear. These are all state employees—why were state employees allowed to ignore what the governor and the secretary ordered everyone to do?"

Emphasizing that he did not want to be misunderstood as doubting the efficacy of masks, the doctor explained that noncompliance could be attributed to the fact that they were "thick, hot, hard to breathe." He explains that we should "extrapolate" what it was like for people on the outside to wear them for part of the day to people who "are expected to wear them 24/7, 365, because they cannot get away by themselves in a closed room with no one else. It's a heavy lift. The overwhelming majority of patients and staff are doing a good job—they are not being perfect, they are fallible. Our physical plant is not conducive to people complying."

Finally, the doctor admitted that the missing piece was the "disciplinary component of what we'll do with folks who are just not willing to comply. That component is being strengthened and it will improve even more." Ting wondered why this had not been done previously: "You work for Mr. Kelso, and he has fairly broad authority in this realm. Why didn't you use your authority to ensure everyone was wearing a mask?" The doctor insisted that wearing a mask was "not a choice" and that there was a "firm consistent message from secretary and receiver about our expectations about face coverings. I've personally been to 14 facilities since July and reminded staff and patients. There's been a really clear expectation. The part that was not there was a progressive disciplinary process. I guess we hoped that people would do the right thing."

This reply, unsurprisingly, led to a scolding by Assemblymember Cooper: "Everyone has been indoctrinated on how we do it, not just for ourselves but for other people. It's a leadership issue, it starts at the top. Progressive discipline starts at the lower level. That should've been going on at the [outset]. It's sad but it's a failed leadership."

Some of the initiatives of the prison guards' union, the California Correctional Peace Officers Association (CCPOA), during this period defy credulity. With the COVID-19 vaccine on the horizon, and in the face of thousands of sick staff members and 12 staff dead, including 2 in December, CCPOA leadership began planning their annual board meeting excursion to . . . Las Vegas. Wes Venteicher's *Sacramento Bee* article about these plans reported that the gathering would include representatives of all 35 prisons, some parole agents, and some retired chapter members. While plans for this gathering were in the making, wrote Venteicher, "[a] dozen state prisons have reported more than 200 new COVID-19 infections among inmates in the last two weeks, and another six have reported more than 100 new infections. More than 2,500 prison employees have reported new infections in the last two weeks and about 13,000 out of 55,000 have contracted the virus since the start of the pandemic." In response to Venteicher's query, CCPOA spokeswoman Nichol Gomez emailed that "[t]hese meetings are important to the association and its members as it relates to many topics including COVID-19 inside prisons" and that "the group would follow all Nevada and California state protocols and is "constantly evaluating the situation and will make decisions accordingly. . . . Gomez did not respond to questions about how many of the members who have been invited plan to attend, nor did she say whether the members plan to get tested or quarantine before or after the trip."

The union's decision that early 2021 would be the right time to party was especially notable given that these quarterly meetings were typically held in Sacramento. While the Las Vegas party would subsequently be canceled, CCPOA's cavalier approach to COVID-19 would come to characterize their approach toward vaccination as well. In August 2021 the UCLA Law COVID Behind Bars Data Project published a sobering report titled "Prison Staff Are Refusing Vaccines. Incarcerated People Are Paying the Price." They found a deeply disturbing national trend:

> We estimate that, to date, just 47% of prison staff have received at least one dose of a vaccine, based on data from the 21 agencies that have recently reported this information. By comparison, more than 71% of all adults in the U.S.—and 64% of incarcerated people—have been vaccinated so far.
>
> In several states, staff vaccination rates are much lower than the national average. In Alabama, Pennsylvania, and Georgia, fewer than 25% of prison staff report being vaccinated. In these states, more officers have tested positive for COVID-19 over the course of the pandemic than have reported getting a vaccine. In nearly all states that report data, staff vaccination rates lag behind the overall rate among adults by a considerable margin.

At that point, the vaccination rate among California's incarcerated population was 79 percent. The corresponding rate among the custodial staff was 57 percent.[34]

As we explain in chapter 6, the litigation in *Plata v. Newsom*, which started off with a demand to release more people to allow for social distancing, coalesced, within a few months, around a more modest goal: requiring mandatory vaccination for guards (which, as we will see, was not accomplished). Throughout the remainder of the crisis, as well as the litigation, CCPOA's leadership was reluctant to enforce or encourage masking.

It is not entirely clear whether this reluctance to accept vaccination is the product of top-down union messaging or of COVID-19 denialism among the rank-and-file members. The latter assumption is untestable, as there are no reliable surveys of the politics of correctional officers (though anecdotal evidence of support for Trump among law enforcement definitely exists). But there is certainly support for the former assumption. In his work on the CCPOA, Josh Page documents the union's transition from a run-of-the-mill organization advocating for better work conditions for their employees to a high-powered political player in California.[35] CCPOA's behavior throughout the pandemic certainly bears this history out. In late 2020, when the rational interests of their members would require CCPOA leadership to advocate for decarceration, PPE, and COVID-19 safety—and as custodial staff were ailing from COVID-19 themselves—the organization busied itself not only purchasing political ads featuring bull's-eye graphics on Democratic candidates[36] but also investing $4 million in supporting punitive voter initiatives on the ballot:

> The prison guards' union, through its political committees, spent $1 million to support incumbent Los Angeles County District Attorney Jackie Lacey, but she lost to progressive criminal justice reform advocate George Gascon, a former San Francisco district attorney.
>
> It gave $2 million to support Proposition 20, which would have stiffened prison sentences and restricted parole, but the measure is failing by a 24% margin.
>
> And the union spent at least $1 million to support Efren Martinez, a Los Angeles businessman who lost his race against incumbent Democratic Assemblyman Reggie Jones-Sawyer, chairman of the Assembly Public Safety Committee.
>
> The union also backed some winners, potentially including Dave Min, a Democrat who defeated Republican state Sen. John Moorlach of Orange County.[37]

CCPOA's president, Glen Stailey, was undeterred by the union's humiliating and expensive campaign losses, declining an interview request but stating via email: "We're only getting started . . . We want to build our profile as an active participant in policymaking in California, and working on campaigns is one small piece of it."

Vaccination refusals among custodial staff were an even more serious problem in the counties, where vaccine acceptance among the jail population was considerably lower than in the prisons. This was predictable and understandable: people's jail stays, whether before conviction or as punishment, tend to be considerably briefer than state prison sentences, oftentimes lasting no more than a few days. Under these circumstances, it is much more difficult to appeal to consensus and a sense of community in a vaccine policy. Nevertheless, some jails made considerable efforts to persuade the population to get vaccinated. Mary Izadi, the constitutional policing advisor to the

Orange County Sheriff's Department, wrote to BSCC, asking for their intervention on behalf of the jail population:

I am writing you about the critically important and time sensitive issue of COVID-19 inoculations for incarcerated persons. OCSD is aware of discussion at the state level about modifying the prioritization of COVID-19 vaccines to a purely age-based model. Does BSCC plan to formally take a position on this issue as county jails have a disproportionately younger, yet medically vulnerable, population?

Here at OCSD we are concerned about immunization disparities including differences in vaccination rates by age, socioeconomic status, race and ethnicity, in addition to the constitutional duty to provide for the health and safety of those in our care. Under current CDC guidance for correctional and detention facilities, "[j]urisdictions are encouraged to vaccinate staff and incarcerated/detained persons of correctional or detention facilities at the same time because of their shared increased risk of disease." Additional CDC Guidance states: "Individual-level factors that may be helpful for vaccination sub-prioritization include older age, high-risk medical conditions, recent COVID-19 in the past 90 days, and risk of exposure to other incarcerated/detained persons who have COVID-19."

The Board of State and Community Corrections is uniquely situated to provide leadership and expertise to the State on a critically important issue impacting all California county jails. I am happy to assist BSCC in any way to achieve our mutual goal of continued improvement in local corrections.

In an effort to refute the myth of jail impermeability, Izadi also appealed to the common sense of Orange County's COVID-19 Vaccination Task Force concerning "the urgent need to vaccinate the Orange County Jail Population":

It is essential to protect the health of residents in Orange County, and that necessarily includes incarcerated persons in a county jail who are not in an isolated and enclosed environment, but actually, just the opposite. Those housed in Orange County Jails interact daily with members of the community, including medical staff (inside and outside the jails), corrections employees, contractors, and volunteers. Unfortunately, that is just the tip of the iceberg; county jails are a revolving door of incarcerated persons. Individuals housed in Orange County Jails are not "locked away" without significant risk to the community at large. Orange County Jails only house about 50% of those who are booked. The transitory nature of the incarcerated population creates a substantial risk to the community for further spread of COVID-19 and has a high likelihood of burdening local hospitals and ICU capacities.

Undeterred by the lack of response to her entreaties, Izadi produced a persuasive video to encourage the jail population to take the vaccine, which featured the aforementioned clips featuring Lockheart, Treviño, and Hartman. She thought that the unique features of the Johnson & Johnson vaccine—the fact that it was a more traditional vaccine rather than an mRNA vaccine, and thus easier to explain to skeptics, and that it required only one shot—made it ideal for jail vaccination. In the clip, she explained that people incarcerated in jail need not exert themselves to procure the vaccine—it would be offered to them at no cost; a custodial sergeant appearing in the video tried to appeal to a sense of community by explaining that vaccination of the overall jail population was a "group effort" and would allow the jail to reopen programming.

The success of this effort, and other well-intentioned initiatives, was modest. The COVID-in-Custody Project, spearheaded by Aparna Komarla, collected data on jail vaccine intake from six counties: Alameda, Sacramento, Fresno, San Francisco, Santa Clara, and Yolo.[38] As we explained in chapter 3, a big hurdle in understanding and addressing COVID-19 in jails is the absence of data, and, glaringly, the only data available on staff intake is about medical, rather than custodial, staff in Santa Rita. Despite the absence of data, there is anecdotal evidence to suggest that vaccine refusal among sheriff's employees was as serious a problem as it was among CCPOA members. In February 2021, at a conference, Sheriff Dean Growdon of Lassen County expressed serious concerns about his staff's predicted vaccine acceptance, stating that he was considering financial inducements.[39] And as late as August 2021, when San Francisco instituted a citywide vaccine mandate for public employees, sheriff's deputies threatened en masse resignations in protest, with their union, the Deputy Sheriff's Association, ventriloquizing CCPOA:

Mandated vaccines "will result in law enforcement officers and firefighters retiring early and seeking employment elsewhere," the union wrote on its Facebook page Thursday.

"Public safety of San Francisco has turned into the Wild West and will get worse when officers quit due to the vaccine mandate."

Union President Ken Lomba said he's heard threats of resigning or retiring early because of the mandatory vaccine policy "from a large group within our membership."[40]

As we explain in chapter 6, CDCR's custodial staff and their union emerged victorious in their fight not to get vaccinated, holding in hand the ultimate threat—resignation—and consequently, rendering California prisons unmanageable. We will never know whether this threat was real or empty. The importance of CCPOA's grandstanding, however, is twofold. First, as we showed in this chapter, prisoners and their advocates overcame immense odds—prejudice, optics problems, vaccine unavailability, misinformation— not only to obtain the vaccine in the first place but also to accept it in large numbers. This protection would prove essential given that the people entrusted with their care fell significantly behind their wards in vaccine acceptance and, in fact, continue to endanger the prison population to this day. Second, as prison staff enter and exit the facilities on a daily basis, the threat of transmissivity they carry applies not only to the incarcerated population but also to their own home communities. This argument flies in the face of the myth of impermeability, which would have us believe that COVID-19 is a zero-sum game: if you will, in the words of the Tennessee legislature, "prisoners vs. grandma." As the next chapter demonstrates through primary and secondary data analysis, the opposite is true: when people in prison become sick, largely through the vector of unvaccinated guards, everyone, inside and outside the prison, suffers.

FIVE

Incubator

Moses said, "This is what Yahweh says: 'About midnight I will
go out into the midst of Egypt, and all the firstborn in the land
of Egypt shall die, from the firstborn of Pharaoh who sits on his
throne, even to the firstborn of the female servant who is behind
the mill; and all the firstborn of livestock. There shall be a great
cry throughout all the land of Egypt, such as there has not been,
nor shall be any more. But against any of the children of Israel a
dog won't even bark or move its tongue, against man or animal;
that you may know that Yahweh makes a distinction between
the Egyptians and Israel.'"

EXODUS 11: 4–7

OUR NARRATIVE, SO FAR, features a common theme: despite dire warnings of catastrophe, reports of untold suffering, and the promise of a vaccine
that could alleviate their plight, incarcerated people faced a tough uphill
battle to garner public support. Much of this phenomenon is in step with the
classic literature on the punitive turn in the United States, which documents
the political framing of criminal justice as a zero-sum game: what is good for
offenders is bad for victims and for the general public.[1] The inflection point
for this sentiment, some argue, was Richard Nixon's presidential campaign,
which ascribed rising crime rates to permissive laws and constitutional pro-
tections,[2] though others find evidence of punitive animus before the 1970s.[3]
For the last few decades, politicians of all stripes have espoused "tough on
crime" policies to satisfy the public's perceived punitive appetite, and there is
persuasive evidence that public opinion does impact criminal justice system
outcomes, particularly under conservative governments.[4] But are people truly
so uncaring about prison conditions?

The answer, it turns out, is complicated. In public opinion surveys, respondents register support for rehabilitation alongside public safety.[5] These surveys reveal a bifurcated approach to crime:[6] people convicted of serious crime require incarceration for the protection of others,[7] while people perceived as nonviolent offenders merit second chances.[8] For the latter category, respondents often support alternatives to incarceration, registering cynicism about the rehabilitative value of incarceration.[9] Notably, the better informed respondents were about the realities of the criminal justice system, including the availability of alternatives to incarceration, the more likely they were to support these alternatives.[10]

Several studies offer an insight into this complexity. It turns out that the zero-sum game logic works both in favor of and against punitiveness. Respondents who report sentiments of economic insecurity—anxiety about their future, combined with fear that others are receiving unfair advantages and benefits—hold significantly more punitive views.[11] Simultaneously, when people are aware of the costly implications of mass incarceration for themselves—the taxpayers—they support significantly cheaper and less punitive alternatives.[12] Consequently, the idea that decarceration, prison closures, and support for noncarceral alternatives can be framed not as bleeding-heart progressive compassion for offenders but rather as austerity and prudence was a big driver of the "cheap-on-crime" wave of criminal justice reforms following the 2008 financial crisis.[13]

But while the cost of incarceration can dissuade the public from supporting its *scale,* it does not have similar purchase for prison *conditions.* While well-funded prisons are not necessarily safe, healthy, and rehabilitative environments, prison cuts can yield what Hadar referred to elsewhere as "tough 'n' cheap" incarceration.[14] In some US states, correctional systems take pride in their thrifty and tough prison systems.[15] The idea of a no-frills prison experience enjoys considerable public support.[16] Politicians and the media capitalize on public sentiments against the resort-like "Club Fed" and other perceived prison luxuries.[17] Indeed, one of the sentiments fueling public punitivism is that the prison experience is "easy."[18] Participants in focus groups resent prison access to televisions and exercise equipment[19] (recall Justice Scalia's reference, in his *Plata* dissent, to the "fine physical specimens . . . pumping iron in the prison gym").

There is a strong zero-sum undertone to these sentiments: taxpayer concerns that hardworking, law-abiding Americans are paying for nonessential comforts behind bars.[20] Kevin Wozniak's careful public opinion survey[21] reveals that the perception of prisons as insufficiently harsh correlates not only with essentialist views on criminality (the idea that people are predisposed to commit crime) but also with the perception that minorities enjoy undue advantages, presumably at the expense of the law-abiding respondents. We have a direct experience with zero-sum thinking about prison conditions: at Hadar's public lectures, audience members frequently ask why prisoners receive "free health care" while they do not.

That the morality of this calculus is questionable at best should be obvious from the suffering described in the previous chapters. But it is misguided for yet another reason: to the extent that so-called prison amenities, frills, and comforts include decent health care and disease prevention, viewing them through a zero-sum lens is public health idiocy. Stuart Kinner explains:

> COVID-19 outbreaks in custodial settings are of importance for public health, for at least two reasons: first, that explosive outbreaks in these settings have the potential to overwhelm prison health-care services and place additional demands on overburdened specialist facilities in the community; and second, that, with an estimated 30 million people released from custody each year globally, prisons are a vector for community transmission that will disproportionately impact marginalised communities.[22]

This logic was unpersuasive to prison authorities. In June 2020, as COVID-19 spikes ravaged Lassen County, local politicians Brian and Megan Dahle (the former would later run as a Republican gubernatorial candidate against Newsom) wrote a letter to CDCR secretary Ralph Diaz, asking him "to provide answers on questionable protocols that have led to a surge of inmate #COVID19 cases in Lassen County." Despite some posturing about the county's lack of jurisdiction over a state correctional facility, "in the past two days the Lassen County Public Health Department and our local prisons worked together to test more than 2,000 inmates and approximately 180 employees for the virus according to a Friday, June 26 statement from the Lassen COVID-19 Incident Command." They expressed dismay at the prison's rebuff of county concerns, encapsulated in a letter informing them that "[t]he state is not an entity under local health officers' jurisdictions, and thus local health officer orders are not valid against the state."[23]

Our counterfactual transmissivity model, which we present below, shows how disastrous this approach was not only for California's prisons but also for the entire state population. By examining the interaction between prisons and their surrounding communities, we show that allowing disease to run rampant through prison hurts everyone—from incarcerated people to the correctional staff to the people who reside throughout the state.

THE BURNING RANCH AND THE CHALLENGES OF BIDIRECTIONAL CAUSALITY

Imagine a ranch in the American West, at the peak of a hot, dry summer. The ranch is covered mostly with grassland, but atop the property is a large pile of dry leaves and branches, surrounded by a firebreak of bare earth. A cinder from a distant fire is blown onto the ranch. There are two possible scenarios, either of which ends with the ranch engulfed in flames:

1. *The spark falls into the grass, igniting a grass fire. After burning for some time, the fire causes the brush pile to ignite.*
2. *The spark falls into the brush pile, igniting a large fire that quickly spreads to the grassland.*

The ranch exemplifies a system with mutual, or bidirectional, causality. In such a system, the statements "A causes B" and "B causes A" are simultaneously true: an external threat affects both A and B, but the interconnectedness of A and B means that we cannot rule out either causal direction of the fire. The arrows in figure 4 illustrate the direction of the fire threat.

This model relies on separating populations, preferably across a boundary that has relatively low levels of transmission. This analysis considers two such mutual causality systems. In the wildfire analogy, the grassland is labeled Population A, and the more flammable brush pile is labeled Population B. Each arrow represents the direction a spark could travel. In our case study, at the local level, a county (such as Marin) is labeled Population A, whereas the prison it houses (San Quentin) is Population B; at the state level, the state population is Population A and CDCR's population is Population B.

Within the state's counties and communities are hundreds of correctional institutions, only some of which (the ones under CDCR's supervision) are

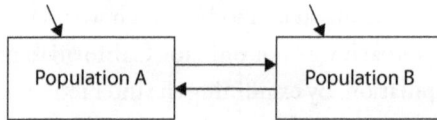

FIGURE 4. Mutual causality system.

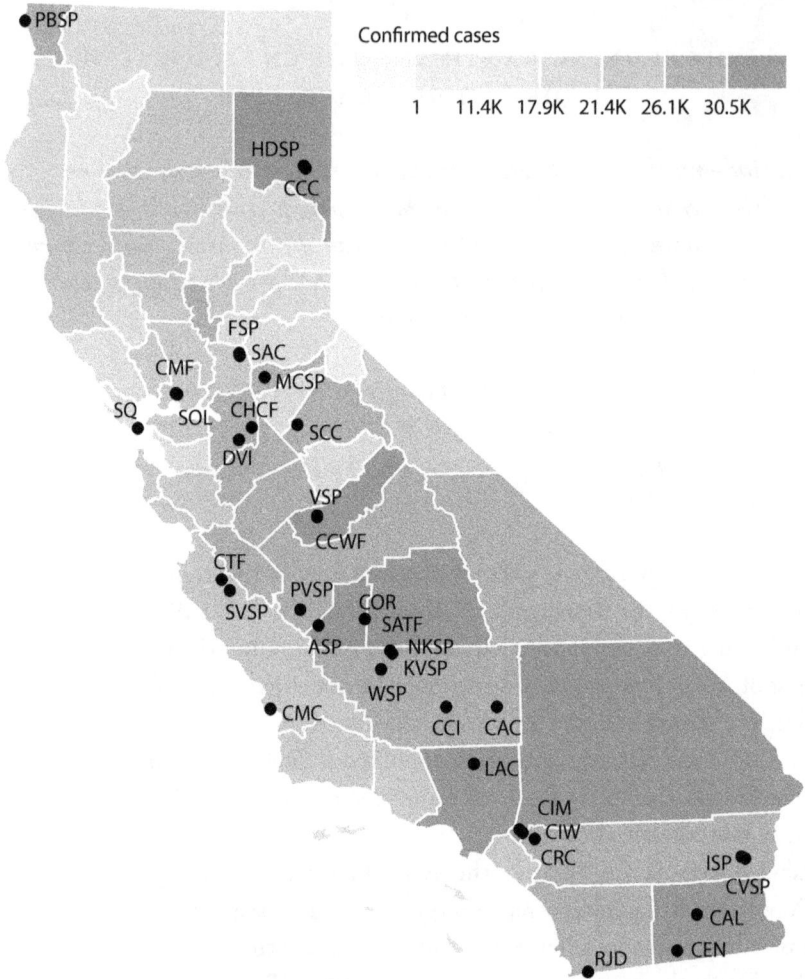

FIGURE 5. Map of correctional institutions in California, superimposed on California counties, color-coded by number of cases. Sources: *Los Angeles Times;* CDCR website.

depicted in figure 5. We picked CDCR institutions for this analysis because they provided relevant data of sufficient quality. Regardless of the jurisdictional designation of correctional facilities—federal, state, or county—each represents a population that has limited, but by no means nonexistent, contact with the outside population, and that is held in close quarters, making infection and transmissivity within the facility more likely.

The wildfire example illustrates the challenge of accurately portraying the interrelationships in mutual causality systems. In the first scenario (fire in the grassland), careful observation of the fire will reveal the amount of heat steadily increasing in the grassland, then suddenly spiking in the much more flammable brush pile. By contrast, in the second scenario (fire in the brush), observing the fire will reveal a fast spike of heat in the brush pile preceding the steady fire spread in the grassland. By analogy, if we had the ability to isolate the pandemic spread to a single epidemiological episode, we would be able to see whether rising cases in the community then yield a spike within the associated prisons or vice versa by measuring delay estimates between the respective spikes.

Unfortunately, when many such scenarios occur simultaneously, any correlation analysis between the two loci of the infection will provide varying estimates of delay, the average of which will result in mutual cancellation between the two scenarios: a delay estimate close to zero. Such an analysis, without more information, will often fail to find the bidirectional causal link; all we would be able to say about pandemic spread would be that both infection spikes, in the prison and in the surrounding county, were caused by extraneous cases. Because, as all amateur statisticians like to recite, correlation does not equal causation, a purely correlational model would not suffice for showing the interplay between the internal components of the system: the prison and its immediate surroundings.

In some epidemiological inquiries, it is possible to overcome this problem with careful case tracking, but such data was, of course, not available in California or in its prisons. Rarely was the beginning of a prison outbreak traceable to a single dramatic event, with two important exceptions: the Chino transfer to San Quentin and the North Kern outbreak, which reportedly originated with a particular staff member.[24] Even in those cases, by the time infections mounted and testing times lagged, case tracking was impossible. To overcome this problem, we rely on a widely accepted set of epidemiological criteria for determining causality.

Established in 1965,[25] the Bradford Hill criteria are nine principles that can assist in inferring causality. When statistical correlation is found between a presumed cause and an observed effect, the following can support a conclusion that the relationship is causal:

Analogy: a well-accepted scenario maps to the system being studied

Strength of association: assesses the strength of the correlation between two events

Biological gradient: an increase of the strength of the cause results in an increase in the strength of the effect

Temporality: the cause occurs before the effect, generally by a characteristic delay period

Consistency: similar scenarios show similar results

Plausibility: the scenario can be simulated by a model

Coherence: the effect matches what would be expected by other evidence

Specificity: disease can be traced to specific exposures

Experiment: a controlled situation where the effect can be predicted by controlling exposure to the cause

Over the years, the Bradford Hill criteria were adapted to innovations in epidemiology.[26] One such adaptation was the frequent addition of a counterfactual analysis: an estimation of how a change in conditions would influence the ultimate outcome.[27] We proceed to examine the available evidence about the prison-community interaction using these factors.

Our analysis focuses on the time period prior to widespread vaccination. We use July 2021 as a cutoff date for data analysis because that is the date when the COVID-19 vaccination rate among California residents exceeded 50 percent. Due to the protective effects of the vaccination, this period accounts for most COVID-19 deaths in California.

For the incarcerated population, we use data provided by CDCR, obtained from the *Los Angeles Times* COVID-19 database[28] and verified with numbers we coded directly from the CDCR tracker.[29] For California data, we used the California Department of Public Health database.[30] Our hypothesis is that COVID-19 outbreaks within CDCR institutions contributed to infection rates outside of the institutions. We rely on the Bradford Hill criteria to support this hypothesis.

Having undertaken the first step—analogy—with our wildfire story, we turn to the remaining factors. The only factor left unexplored, the controlled experiment, would not be possible without CDCR's cooperation, and the counterfactual analysis we provide in its place estimates the impact that high infection rates in California prisons had on the rest of the state.

Strength of Association, Biological Gradient, and Temporality:
CDCR and State Data

Superspreading events are events in which an infectious disease spreads significantly more than usual. The basic reproduction number, $R°$, of COVID-19 is estimated to be between 2 and 2.5.[31] In other words, an event at which one person infects four or more people in one place and time is considered a superspreading event. A perusal of the superspreading database,[32] a list of superspreading events throughout the state, is revealing. Although the list is not exhaustive, superspreading events in prisons dominate the list: out of 39,571 cases attributed to superspreading events, 32,254 of them, or over 81 percent of them, occurred inside prisons. Table 1 lists superspreading events in California by their location.

What stands out is the scale of superspreading events in prisons: the average number of infections among carceral superspreading events within California is 1,008, whereas the average number of cases in superspreading events outside of CDCR is below 185. This database is incomplete and likely biased toward larger superspreading events, but even given this caveat, correctional institutions are clearly associated with the state's largest superspreading events. Superspreading events are indicated to be primary drivers of the spread of the virus. Miller et al. find[33] that small numbers of individuals account for the bulk of the infections, concluding: "We further report high levels of transmission heterogeneity in SARS-CoV-2 spread, with between 2–10% of infected individuals resulting in 80% of secondary infections." They further recommend: "focused measures to reduce contacts of select individuals/social events could mitigate viral spread." It was a lost opportunity that this recommendation, which was implemented for nursing homes, medical centers, and religious halls, was neglected in carceral institutions.

TABLE 1 COVID-19 superspreading events in California by location, March 31, 2021

	Number of Cases	Average Number of Cases per Event	Superspreading Cases (%)
Prison	32,254	1,008.0	81.5
Nursing home	1,831	83.2	4.6
Medical	4,776	86.8	12.1
Ship	63	63.0	0.2
Religious	77	38.5	0.2
Shelter	207	103.5	0.5
Labor	359	184.5	0.9

Superspreading events are important sources of overall spread, but it is widely and incorrectly assumed that their effects are limited to the institutions where they occur. First, we must establish that there is a higher rate of COVID-19 infection inside institutions. We focus on CDCR facilities both because we are best informed about their population and COVID-19 rates (as we explained in chapter 3) and because they are responsible for most incarcerated people within the state.[34]

CDCR's population had an infection rate of 42.7 percent on March 21, 2021, while at the same time, only 9 percent of the California population had been infected. A time history of daily infection rate, depicted in figure 6, shows that incidence of COVID-19 was consistently and substantially higher than that of the state through the first year of the pandemic.

Prior to March 20, 2020, the infection had not yet been detected in CDCR institutions. However, once COVID-19 entered the prison gates, it quickly spread through several institutions in CDCR, and by April 8 the rate within CDCR surpassed the rate within the state and did not drop below the statewide rate until March 5, 2021. The initial surge of infections was geographically restricted to the Central Valley, but by January 2021, it had spread throughout all CDCR facilities. This massive surge accounted for most cases and deaths within CDCR and immediately preceded the deadly wave of infections that spread throughout California in late 2020 and early 2021.

The elevated infection rates were not limited to CDCR institutions. The following analysis provides evidence for strength of association. Counties containing CDCR institutions showed significantly higher rates of COVID-19 infections as compared to counties without CDCR institutions. In figure 7,

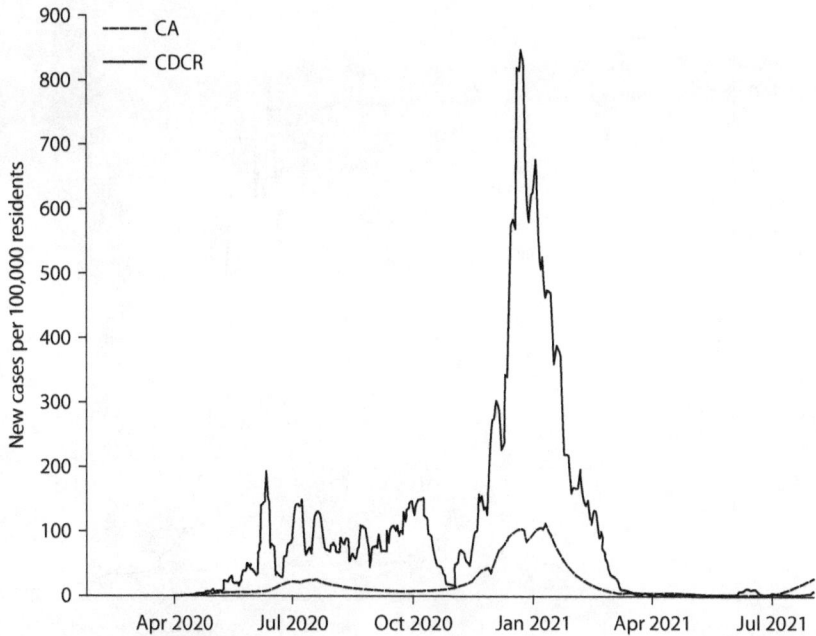

FIGURE 6. Time history of seven-day average of new cases per 100,000 people in CDCR and in the state of California as a whole.

we portray the time history of case rates in counties according to their distance from CDCR facilities. Zone 1 consists of counties that contain CDCR institutions, Zone 2 consists of counties that share a border with Zone 1 counties, and Zone 3 consists of counties distant from CDCR institutions. As figure 7 shows, residents living in a county containing at least one CDCR institution faced a 60 percent higher rate of COVID-19 infection.

This strength of association can be further tested to look for a biological gradient: this section examines whether infection rates increased with the number of CDCR institutions in the county. CDCR institutions are not spread evenly across the state: the number of prisons per county varies from zero to five, and they have roughly comparable populations. Figure 8 depicts the correlation between the number of facilities in a county and that county's infection rate. The linear regression on the left shows a trend of increasing case rates in counties with increased numbers of CDCR facilities ($f(x) = 7025.99 + 1770.37$ x, $R^2 = 0.330$). The linear regression on the right shows a trend of increasing case rates in counties with increased proportion of incarcerated population ($f(x) = 7537.71 + 0.42345$ x, $R^2 = 0.237$).

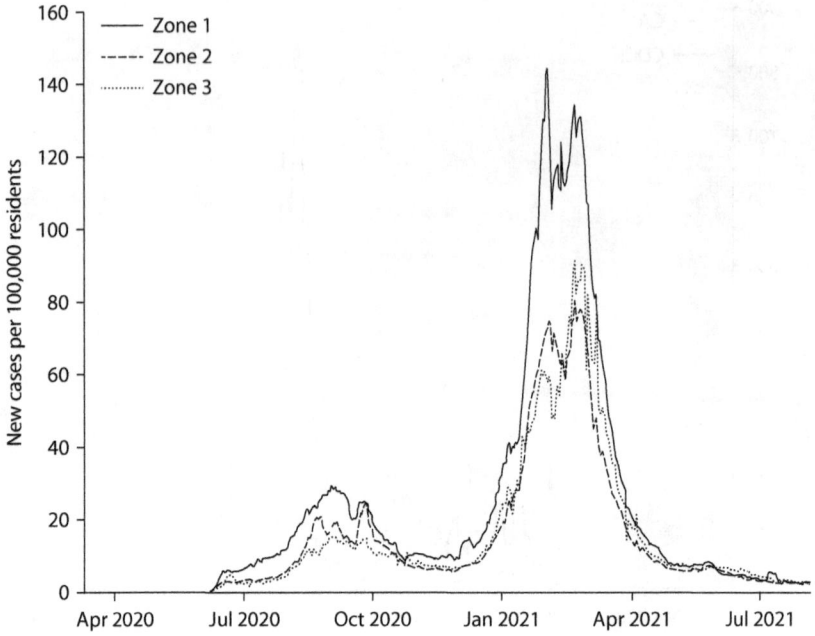

FIGURE 7. Time history of total cases per 100,000 people in surrounding, neighboring, and remote counties.

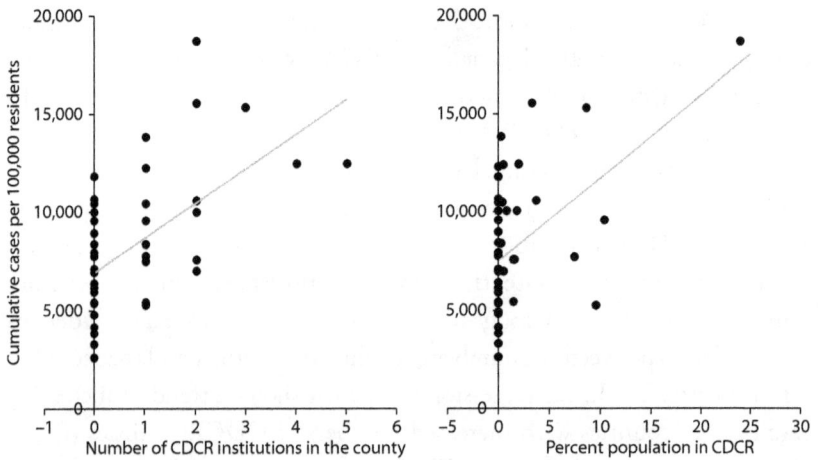

FIGURE 8. Correlation between number of CDCR facilities in the county and county case rates (*left*); correlation between proportion of incarcerated population within the county and county case rates (*right*).

The regression analysis shows that the infection rate increases with the number of CDCR institutions in the county, with a 26 percent increase for each institution added. This is consistent with a Prison Policy Initiative report[35] that executed a nationwide county-level analysis. As Gregory Hooks and Wendy Sawyer discovered, nationwide community spread in both metropolitan and nonmetropolitan counties increased with density of incarcerated people per square mile.

We investigated the strength of this analysis further by incorporating yet another dimension of interrelation: the distance from the nearest CDCR institution. We classified all California counties based on their distance from CDCR institutions: primary counties contain at least one CDCR institution within their border; secondary counties are located within 20 miles of a CDCR institution in a neighboring county; and tertiary counties are located more than 20 miles away from any CDCR institution. As shown in figures 7 and 8, counties labeled as primary have consistently higher rates of COVID-19 than counties labeled secondary or tertiary.

We used lagged correlation as an estimator for lag between the rate of new cases in CDCR and the rate of new cases in California as a whole. In this method, the correlation coefficient between the CDCR new case rate and the California new case rate is calculated at a variety of time shift values, in days. In this case, the shifted correlation was inconclusive. While the two datasets are highly correlated with a correlation coefficient of 0.935, the coefficient peaks when CDCR data is one day ahead of state data. Furthermore, the correlation coefficient is not sensitive to changes in lag values, reducing confidence in the lag estimate. What's more, the lag delay switches sign after July 2021. This could be interpreted that prior to vaccination, CDCR superspreading events drove the rate of infection in California, but after vaccination, California drove the infection rate inside CDCR. This can be explained by herd immunity inside CDCR: it is estimated that the majority of CDCR residents contracted COVID-19 in the winter of 2020, and furthermore, vaccination rates among CDCR residents exceeded the statewide rate. This provided CDCR a high level of immune protection against outbreaks in the following year.

Consistency

This section demonstrates consistency, both geographically and historically. The association of higher COVID-19 infection rates holds across the entire state and is not limited to any geographic region. CDCR institutions have had 1.5 to 11.1 times the rate of infection as compared to their host county, with an average of 3.9 times the county rate. The highest ratio occurs for San Quentin, which has had over 11 times the rate of infection in its host county, Marin County. This demonstrates that infection rates are consistently substantially higher inside CDCR institutions as compared to their surroundings.

Incarcerated populations are associated with higher COVID-19 infection rates and death rates throughout the country. A report from the Prison Policy Initiative shows a significant correlation of increased infection rates with number of incarcerated people per square mile within the United States.[36] COVID-19 infection and death rates inside 32 state prison systems were many times higher than overall infection and death rates in the states,[37] with many states having an even higher ratio of infection rates inside prisons and jails than in California. They further show that mass testing, as was accomplished by CDCR, was successful in mitigating the highest death rates that occurred in states without mass testing.

The influenza pandemic of 1918–20 showed some notable similarities to the COVID-19 pandemic. The pandemic in San Francisco[38] peaked in late October of 1918 with 1,800 cases per 100,000, while the October 1918 peak in San Quentin prison[39] had incidence estimated at 3,700 per 100,000.

Plausibility, Coherence, and Specificity

Plausibility and coherence are addressed by epidemiological models that have already been published, including those that model COVID-19. Many epidemiological models of COVID-19 outbreaks have been published since 2020. For instance, a simulation approach[40] fitted a susceptible-exposed-infectious-removed (SEIR) model to data from Northern Italy early in the pandemic. The modeling approach most suitable for this situation is a virtual dispersal model,[41] which uses susceptible-infected-susceptible (SIS) and susceptible-infected-removed (SIR) simulations with multiple populations, where a proportion of the population moves between the multiple populations. This approach was applied to SEIR with the multipatch framework with an arbitrary number of populations.[42] Preliminary fitting of the data shows that pure SEIR frameworks don't fully capture the subexponential form of the data from California—this is likely because they do not incorporate social distancing. A social distancing model such as the one that was fitted to data from the 1918 pandemic in England[43] is needed to fully capture the data.

The population is divided into two patches, with limited movement between them as well as inputs from external regions (such as the United States as a whole). The resulting model has a large number of parameters, from 20 to 40. This large parameter count gives a high risk of overfitting the data, which is a known problem in epidemiological modeling. Because both multipatch framework and social distancing models are relatively new in the field of epidemiology, the task of fitting an appropriate SEIR model to the two populations while also fitting a social distancing model was deemed to be beyond the scope of this analysis.

However, Bichara et al.[44] propose general methods to calculate effective reproduction number of the overall population, as well as examples of two-patch models with different reproduction numbers and strengths of connection between the patches. They find that stronger connections result in the high-risk region having lower prevalence and the low-risk region having higher prevalence. But as strengths of connection decrease, the two regions act more like independent regions. This model constitutes the theoretical basis for the counterfactual analysis, which uses linear combinations of various populations' incidence rates to estimate the impact of the high-risk region on the low-risk one. This work in particular provides a plausible and coherent model of risk over two or more populations.

Specificity can be tested by comparing correlations of infection rates versus CDCR facilities with correlations with other plausible sources of infection. Table 1 lists prisons, nursing homes, and medical facilities as the most significant sites of outbreaks. Newspapers in 2020 warned that regions of high population density were at risk. We used correlation analysis to determine which of these factors was most important. In this analysis, a value of 1 represents perfect correlation, a value of 0 represents no correlation, and a value of -1 represents perfect negative correlation (i.e., increasing variable A results in a decrease in variable B). Table 2 gives the results of this analysis for a county-by-county accounting of various variables, such as population density, and their correlation with cumulative rates of COVID-19 cases detected and deaths. The numbers of hospital beds and nursing facilities per county were downloaded from the California Department of Health Care Services and California Health and Human Services websites.

Variables for incarcerated population stand out well above any of the other factors. Exceptions include county area and death rates for skilled-nursing facility density. While it makes sense that counties with high numbers of skilled-nursing facility residents had higher death rates, the correlation of

	Cases / 100k	Deaths / 100k
Population / square mile	-0.15	-0.04
County area	**0.39**	**0.38**
Skilled-nursing facility occupants / 100k	0.05	0.24
Hospital beds / 100k	-0.07	0.02
CDCR population per 100k	**0.48**	0.05
CDCR facilities	**0.57**	**0.39**
CDCR population	**0.59**	**0.36**
Cases vs. deaths	**0.66**	
County area vs. CDCR population	**0.30**	
CDCR facilities vs. CDCR population	**0.39**	

NOTE: Variables with "/ 100k" are normalized by county population. Correlation values greater than 0.25 are marked in a bold typeface.

COVID rates with county area was initially puzzling. Three more correlations are shown at the bottom of table 2 to give more context. County area is correlated with CDCR population: larger counties tend to have more CDCR facilities and, so by association, have higher COVID-19 rates. The dominance of CDCR correlations is striking.

Counterfactual Analysis

Our counterfactual analysis, offered in lieu of experimental data, is designed to address the impact of the high incidence of COVID-19 inside CDCR facilities on the surrounding communities. To estimate this prison-on-community impact, we geographically allocated the infection data to concentric rings with no overlapping populations, as shown in figure 9. The inner ring includes San Quentin's population of 3,511. The intermediate ring includes Marin County's population of 257,289, after subtracting San Quentin's population. The outer ring consists of the surrounding counties: Contra Costa, San Francisco, Solano, and Alameda, home to 4,182,520 people.

As explained above, we obtained data for San Quentin, as well as for individual counties, from the *Los Angeles Times*. Note that the county count of COVID-19 cases includes the cases within the CDCR facility—dividing the data into nonoverlapping regions required subtracting CDCR counts from

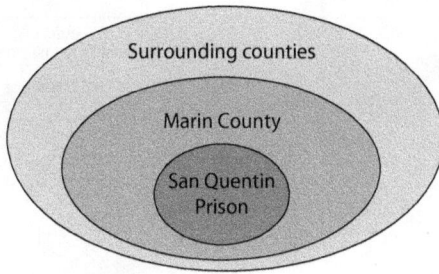

FIGURE 9. Concentric rings surrounding San Quentin Prison.

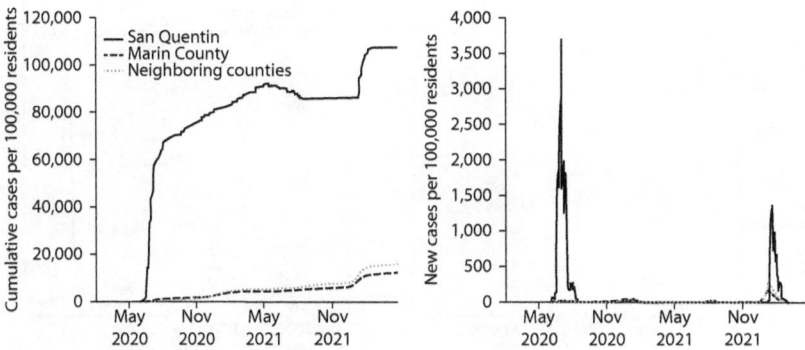

FIGURE 10. Cumulative cases per 100,000 residents (*left*) and new cases per 100,000 residents (*right*) for San Quentin, Marin County, and the neighboring counties.

Marin County counts. In a similar manner, the Marin County counts were excluded from the region count. For each of these concentric rings, daily and cumulative infection and death rates were calculated. Time series of these counts are shown in figure 10. Since San Quentin's population fluctuated significantly during this period, the total cumulative cases per 100,000 decreased as population decreased.

As in the rest of California, figure 10 shows that infection rates inside San Quentin were orders of magnitude higher than in the surrounding county and surrounding region. These are the datasets that are used as bases for the counterfactual analysis.

For this analysis, the time series for Marin County minus San Quentin is estimated from the time series for connected regions. Two hypotheses are considered. The first hypothesis, or null hypothesis, assumes that infection rates in the county are predicted solely by the rate in the surrounding

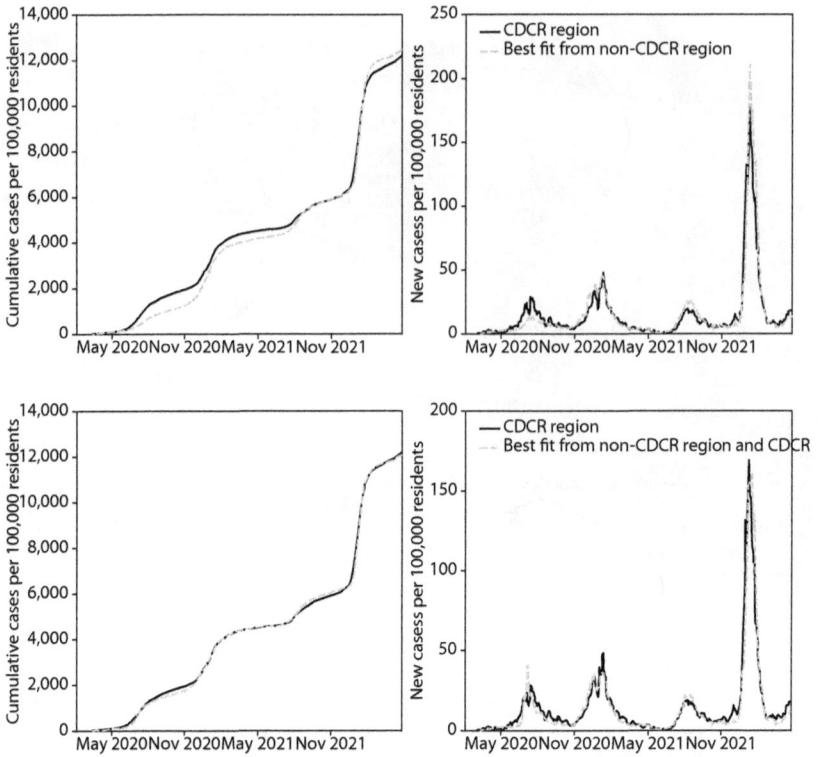

FIGURE 11. Best fit for Marin County based on hypothesis 1: a linear transform of neighboring county rates (*top*), and on hypothesis 2: a linear combination of neighboring counties and San Quentin Prison (*bottom*).

counties, and that the prison has no influence. The second hypothesis assumes that a combination of rates in the surrounding counties and the prison predicts the rates inside the county.

Hypothesis 1: Marin County rates are predicted by surrounding region rates alone

Hypothesis 2: Marin County rates are predicted by a combination of surrounding region rates and San Quentin rates

The curve fits are accomplished using the least squares method, where one time series is a fit of a linear combination of other time series. The least squares method minimizes the root mean square error (RMSE) of the fitted time series as compared to the actual time series. In this case, the minimization problem is solved by an interior point Monte Carlo optimization method. Care was taken to avoid overfitting. For the single curve fit, there are only two parameters: σ_{Region} and τ_{Region}. For the linear combination fit, there are four parameters: σ_{Region}, τ_{Region}, σ_{SQ}, and τ_{SQ}. The parameter count is intentionally kept low to avoid overfitting.

Figure 11 shows the result of the least squares fit for both hypotheses. The fit for hypothesis 1 shows a large error in the region of 100 to 200 days following February 1, 2020, when the San Quentin Prison superspreading event occurred. The fit for hypothesis 2 is significantly better than the fit for hypothesis 1, with about half the error. The actual fit for hypothesis 2 can be expressed by the following formula:

$$\text{Hypothesis 1:} f_{Marin}[t] = \sigma_{Region} f_{Region}[t - \tau_{Region}]$$

$$\text{Hypothesis 2:} f_{Marin}[t] = \sigma_{Region} f_{Region}[t - \tau_{Region}] + \sigma_{SQ} f_{SQ}[t - \tau_{SQ}]$$

The complete list of best fit parameters is given in table 3. There is a high level of agreement between scenarios. For instance, RMSE score for hypothesis 1 is approximately double that of hypothesis 2 for all four scenarios. Delays were found to be small, with most values equal to zero, and San Quentin leading Marin County by three days. Since all the data sets show a strong seven-day cycle, it is difficult to resolve delays less than one week.

The scale parameter for San Quentin is much smaller than the scale parameter for surrounding counties. This is to be expected, because San Quentin has a much smaller population and many fewer opportunities for mixing with the Marin County population as compared to the neighboring counties. The following counterfactual allows the influence of San Quentin to be separated by that of the surrounding counties: from the hypothesis 2 fit, set the SQ scale term to 0. The results of this counterfactual are shown in figure 12 and in table 4.

Together, these show that due to the extraordinarily high prevalence of COVID-19 cases inside CDCR facilities, particularly during the year 2020, these facilities had a large influence on their regions, far more than their relatively small population and isolation would suggest. Note the difference between the total casualties in Marin County with and without the counterfactual—58 deaths, 22 percent of the COVID-19 deaths in Marin for this period—and the difference between the total casualties in California without CDCR facilities—11,974 deaths, or 18.5 percent of the COVID-19 deaths in California for this period. Furthermore, the outbreaks in San Quentin

TABLE 3 Fitted parameters for transmissivity models between San Quentin, Marin County, and Marin neighboring counties and between CDCR institutions, surrounding counties, and remote counties

	Inner Region	Middle Region	Outer Region	H	Scale outer	Delay outer	RMSE	H	Scale inner	Delay inner	Scale outer	Delay outer	RMSE (%)
Cases	San Quentin	Marin County	Marin region	1	0.785	0	9.63%	2	0.009	3	0.699	0	4.94
Deaths	San Quentin	Marin County	Marin region	1	1.058	0	18.05%	2	0.023	0	0.747	0	9.46
Cases	CDCR	CDCR region	Non-CDCR region	1	1.419	0	4.79%	2	0.030	0	1.256	0	2.77
Deaths	CDCR	CDCR region	Non-CDCR region	1	1.709	0	5.27%	2	0.185	0	1.332	1	2.63

NOTE: Column H denotes each hypothesis.

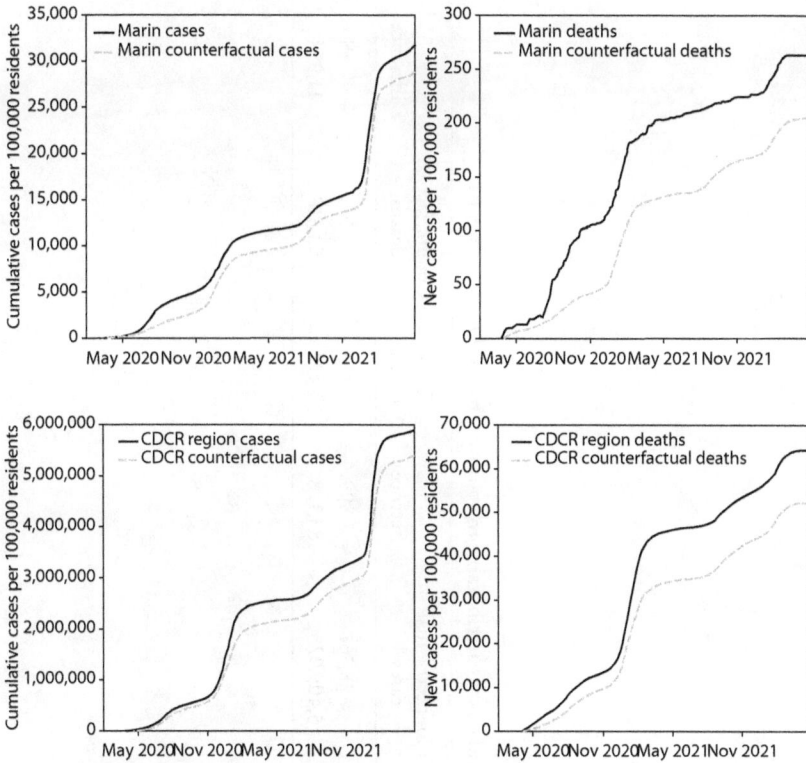

FIGURE 12. Counterfactual cases and deaths estimated by zeroing the scale coefficient for San Quentin Prison (*top*) and all CDCR facilities (*bottom*).

and CDCR occurred before vaccinations were publicly available and before effective treatments for COVID-19 were developed, making them particularly high impact on mortality.

Should Californians have exhibited more solidarity toward the state's prison population, demanding relief and vaccine priority for their incarcerated neighbors, given that prison outbreaks endangered them and their loved ones? Even without correlations and models, the notion that pathogens entering the prison can exit via the same means was surely not unimaginable. Public apathy could be a product of the stress, anxiety, and empathy deficit that characterized much of the pandemic atmosphere; however, given public awareness of the risks posed by contagion in other congregated facilities, such as nursing homes and cruise ships, it attests at least partly to the myth of prison impermeability, and to the degree to which the public habituation to

TABLE 4 Counterfactual estimates of cases and deaths attributable to spillover from CDCR outbreaks

Region	Population	Total cases	Counterfactual cases	Difference	Total deaths	Counterfactual deaths	Difference
Marin County minus San Quentin	258,160	31,660	28,761	2,899	263	205	58
CDCR region minus CDCR facilities	24,620,188	5,892,201	5,409,023	483,178	64,492	52,518	11,974

zero-sum criminal justice thinking overrode commonsense public health considerations. However, the silence and inaction were not only inexplicable but also inexcusable, among those who had the authority and the opportunity to take bold preventive steps: the judges presiding over COVID-19 litigation, the lawyers representing the state and responsible to all Californians, and everyone in the governor's administration who was responsible for spearheading pandemic response.

SIX

The House Always Wins

Yahweh hardened the heart of Pharaoh, and he didn't listen to
them, as Yahweh had spoken to Moses.

EXODUS 9:12

WITH RISING CASES AND ADMINISTRATIVE indifference to their
plight, prisoners and their advocates recurred to courts for relief. But nationwide, the hope that litigation would deliver incarcerated people from
COVID-19 proved hollow. Brandon Garrett and Lee Kovarsky examined the
national landscape of COVID-19 litigation on behalf of incarcerated people,
reading hundreds of custody cases, and concluded:

> [O]ur analysis defines the decision-making by reference to three attributes:
> the substantive right asserted, the form of detention at issue, and the remedy
> sought. Several patterns emerged. Judges avoided constitutional holdings
> whenever they could, rejected requests for ongoing supervision, and resisted
> collective discharge—limiting such relief to vulnerable subpopulations. The
> most successful litigants were detainees in custody pending immigration pro-
> ceedings, and the least successful were those convicted of crimes.[1]

Garrett and Kovarsky's findings are striking. Universal vulnerability to a
dangerous contagion should have produced increased empathy across demographic lines, but the findings reveal the opposite trend: a pathological reluctance to reduce custodial populations and a decision-making pattern that
reveals considerations of deservedness, or perceived virtue, rather than public
health.

Are these disappointing outcomes the product of legal doctrine hostile to
population reduction, or of a deeper, entrenched animus against humanitarian support for incarcerated people? The answer is not dichotomous. As
Margo Schlanger explains,[2] the Prison Litigation Reform Act of 1996
(PLRA),[3] which greatly undermines the ability of incarcerated people to litigate, and prevail, against correctional facilities, came about for precisely that

purpose: it was part and parcel of the Newt Gingrich era's "Contract with America," passed for the express purpose of hindering prison litigation. Not all of this alignment with prison authorities against institutional actors comes from statutory constraints, though: as Sharon Dolovich explains,[4] despite presumed checks and balances, "the relevant institutional actors" (including courts) "align themselves with the officials they are supposed to regulate, leaving people in custody unprotected and vulnerable to abuse by the very actors sworn to keep them safe."[5] Dolovich ascribes this to a prevalent animus, deeper than the constitutional or legal provisions: "This pattern is no accident. It reflects a palpable normative hostility and contempt toward the incarcerated, an attitude with deep roots in the virulent race hatred endemic to the American carceral project from its earliest days."[6]

This chapter examines the interplay between the legislative barriers to effective humanitarian litigation, as portrayed by Schlanger and others,[7] and the fear-and-loathing animus permeating the entire litigation process, as portrayed by Dolovich and others.[8] While not exhaustive, this chapter focuses on the two major California COVID-19 cases: *Plata v. Newsom*,[9] a federal class action involving the entire prison system, and *In re Hall*,[10] a cluster of consolidated habeas corpus writs brought in state court by residents of San Quentin State Prison. Both cases resulted in an effective denial of meaningful relief to the prison population, and despite this fact, both cases—astoundingly—were appealed *by the government,* resulting in an effective defeat of the prisoners and their advocates.

While both cases revolve around the question of whether prison conditions wrought by COVID-19 mismanagement constitute a constitutional violation (in *Plata*, the US constitutional prohibition against "cruel and unusual punishments";[11] in *Hall*, the California constitutional prohibition against "cruel or unusual punishment"[12]), the two cases differ both jurisdictionally and procedurally. *Plata*, a civil-rights class action, was brought and pursued by the legal teams that litigated health-care conditions in California prisons for the last three decades; as a federal case, it was, and remains, subject to the limitations set in the PLRA. By contrast, *Hall* consists of hundreds of individual habeas petitions brought in state court, where the PLRA has no jurisdictional foothold.

Doctrinally speaking, the mechanisms for denying relief to the prisoners varied considerably. In *Plata,* the initial hesitation to provide relief in the form of population reduction ostensibly resulted from the PLRA's high threshold for relief, and the eventual, much more modest remedy (currently under appeal) skirted the issue of releases or ongoing danger. In *Hall*, the hesitation stemmed from a judicial finding that the advent of the COVID-19 vaccine supposedly rendered relief moot despite the constitutional violations. The bottom-line comparison we undertake here looks not only at the legal decision—the final product—but also at the process by which the courts arrived at these decisions, suggesting that the fear-and-loathing animus has a protean, shape-shifting quality: it contorts itself into the shape of legal limitations and avoidance maneuvers available, respectively, in federal and state litigation. Despite the jurisdictional differences, we show several striking similarities between the two proceedings: a sense that, in prison cases, special caution must be exercised with the facts, and deference must be given to correctional authorities; a heightened tolerance for dishonesty and bad behavior on the part of government litigants and lawyers; overwhelming preference for, and idealization of, consensus between custodians and incarcerated people in the face of clear evidence of its impossibility; and a misapprehension of urgency and timeliness, resulting in justice denied on account of being delayed. Our analysis shows how these factors played out in federal and state courts, and suggests that reforming these respective procedures will not improve prison litigation outcomes.

The chapter begins with *Plata*, documenting the gradual diminution of the plaintiffs' proposed remedy, from systemwide population reduction, through the vaccination of incarcerated people, to a final, much more modest, request: a vaccination mandate for prison staff. During each step, we demonstrate the court's efforts to placate government actors, judicial tolerance toward bad-faith arguments and positions, and the judge's perceived inability to issue orders or even find Eighth Amendment violations. This part ends with the Ninth Circuit's reversal of the guards' vaccine mandate, a decision emblematic of the pathology of prison health-care litigation.

We then move on to *Hall* and its Court of Appeal sequel, *In re Von Staich*.[13] Here, we show how the bulk of habeas petitions were halted in the Marin Superior Court, while one petitioner's case made it to the Court of Appeal; we explain the struggle surrounding the appropriate jurisdiction for these cases (rife with bad-faith behavior on the part of government representatives) as well as the struggle to determine whether an evidentiary hearing is needed under California law; we then follow the case, through the landmark decision at the Court of Appeal, to its reversal by the California Supreme Court, the attorney general's efforts to unpublish (!) the decision, and finally, the evidentiary hearing at the Marin Superior Court. We then describe the final determination, denying the petitioners relief despite a finding of constitutional violations, and end with the government's misbegotten appeal.

We then compare the two lawsuits, showing that, in both cases, judicial caution regarding factual findings of prison conditions worked in favor of prison authorities. We identify the common litigation tricks employed by the government, including jurisdictional evasive maneuvers, internal finger-pointing and splintering, and wasteful appellate endeavors, demonstrating the judicial tolerance for these behaviors. We conclude by critiquing judicial fetishization of consensus, which results, in both cases, in the pursuit of goals that are anything but common to all litigants, and in a fear of giving orders to prison authorities.

PLATA V. NEWSOM

Phase I: Tears and Slideshows—The PLRA and the Failure of Population Reduction Remedies

Plata v. Newsom, a continuation of the original *Plata* litigation, was spearheaded by the same litigation teams: the *Plata* team, addressing medical issues and consisting of attorneys from the Prison Law Office, and the *Coleman* team, addressing mostly mental health issues and consisting of the complex-litigation firm Rosen, Bien, Galvan and Grunfeld. The class certification sought and granted consisted of "all prisoners who are now, or will in the future be, under the custody of the [California Department of Corrections]."[14]

Judge Jon Tigar, a former complex-litigation specialist and public defender and an Obama appointee,[15] presided over the case. Judge Tigar held case management conferences (CMCs) every two to three weeks via Zoom,[16] each of which was preceded by a joint memo from the parties detailing the situation in the prisons. The conferences largely followed the submitted memos. While the conferences in April and May focused on the entire system, in the summer, the focus became San Quentin, then the epicenter of prison outbreaks. At the July 16 CMC, the lawyers for the plaintiffs bluntly stated, "San Quentin is a disaster, given the number of patients infected, the number who so far have died, the current number hospitalized . . . , the establishment of a large 'Alternate Care Site,' a kind of skilled nursing facility, equipped and staffed by a contractor at presumably enormous cost to the State . . . , and the profound disruption to prison operations including incarcerated people being unable to get outdoors for exercise or even make phone calls."[17] The AMEND memo was mentioned, with plaintiffs observing that the physicians' concerns had "c[o]me to pass: patients with active COVID-19 at San Quentin . . . continue[d] to be housed in the same facilities [and sometimes in the same cell] with others known to be negative."[18]

The attorney general representatives reported that CDCR had taken several steps to address the outbreak at San Quentin and was cooperating with the federal receiver to implement additional measures; among these measures was an effort to cohort the staff, so that they would not move freely within the prison and cross-contaminate units. As of July 14, the lawyers for the prison noted, all staff was required to wear N95 masks (this was optional for inmates at that point); dozens of patients were referred to the alternative care site, and the prison was constructing outdoor tents, with room for 10 patients each (which would become uninhabitable during the 2020 summer fires).[19]

By late October, when the virus had already ravaged San Quentin, Judge Tigar was vocally critical of CDCR's handling of the crisis.[20] However, he remained skeptical of making demands—a strategy that he referred to as a "sledgehammer approach"—and preferred gentle suasion methods. For this purpose, Judge Tigar recounted, he had consulted with Elizabeth Linos of the UC Berkeley Goldman School of Public Policy. Judge Tigar encouraged the state's representatives to ask their clients to address the crisis through leadership and role modeling, going as far as expressing doubt that the new CDCR policy to ensure testing compliance—and any measures taken by CCPOA, the prison guards union—went far enough, given the existence of significant "pockets" of noncompliance among the staff. Judge Tigar became visibly emotional as he discussed his visits to the California Medical Facility in Vacaville, which housed aging and infirm people; he told of several people he had met behind bars, including a man in his 90s and a man who had been eligible for parole since 1993. He then showed a slideshow on Zoom, which displayed pictures of several people who had died of COVID-19 behind bars. Judge Tigar spoke at length about two of them: Eric Warner, 57, an amputee, reformed Christian, and volunteer, and Sergeant Gilbert Polanco, 55. When speaking of Warner's passing, Judge Tigar had to stop to wipe his tears.

Judge Tigar then made a lengthy and forceful plea to CDCR secretary Kathleen Allison to consider releases, stating that the time had come for that remedy and giving Governor Newsom his support in this effort. Notably, Judge Tigar used the term of art "deliberate indifference"—a term indicating a finding of Eighth Amendment violation—several times; he stressed that the threshold had not technically been met but explicitly said that CDCR's behavior would fuel further lawsuits.

The upshot of the hearing was an order requiring the parties to brief Judge Tigar on the feasibility of quarantine and social distancing (including, for example, the existence of solid doors), as well as on relevant changes in pandemic-prevention guidelines. The petitioners' plea for releases on a larger scale would remain unanswered even at that stage, when vaccines were not yet available.

Phase II: "Couch Money"—The Efforts to Prioritize Vaccination for the Incarcerated Population

In December 2020 and January 2021, the petitioners' litigation team changed tack. The reasons were twofold: the advent of COVID-19 vaccines and Judge Tigar's ongoing reluctance to order releases. As we explained in chapter 4, the vaccines ushered heated debates and controversies about the appropriate vaccination priorities. Even as residents of congregate facilities such as nursing homes and educational institutions received priority, state administrators dawdled on vaccination for prisoners.[21] Petitioners moved for an order that would prioritize vaccinations, even as there were genuine doubts about vaccine acceptance in the incarcerated population given the serious erosion of trust caused by the pandemic experience. Finally, vaccination became available in prison, and the CMC in January 2021 opened with news on vaccination progress from the receiver.[22] Given the paucity of vaccine doses, the prison opted for vaccinating only people residing in skilled-nursing facilities; the high vaccine acceptance rates (close to 90 percent) were hailed as a pleasant surprise and yielded close to 80 percent vaccine coverage in those institutions.

Judge Tigar's next questions were an effort to find out how far CDCR and CCHCS were from vaccinating the entire COVID-19–naive population behind bars, assuming that appropriate vaccine dosage would be available. Kelso explained that the next step would be to offer the vaccine to everyone aged 65 and older (2,000 people, excluding those who had already been infected). After that, the next priority would be people under 65 who had not been infected with COVID-19 with risk scores of three and above (based on a CDCR risk assessment scale relying on preexisting conditions). Kelso estimated that this group—approximately 5,200 people—could be vaccinated in about seven days. The next step would be to tackle 42,000 people—the remaining people in CDCR custody who had not been infected—which would realistically take about four weeks, given the severe nursing shortage.

It quickly became clear that, contrary to the bleak predictions, the problem was not buy-in from incarcerated people. Within the skilled-nursing facilities—the only settings in which vaccinations were administered at the time—staff buy-in was also very high (perhaps due to the prevalence of medical staff). Looming on the horizon, however, was predicted staff noncompliance, and even though no one at the hearing provided a breakdown, it was widely assumed (with good reason) that the problem would be to persuade the custodial staff—who had already been flagged as noncompliant with masking and distancing requirements as well as spreading false rumors about the pandemic—to get vaccinated.

At that point, Judge Tigar talked about the elephant in the room: the institutional unwillingness to take the obvious best step, which would be releases. "I have sometimes become emotional when . . . discuss[ing] this," he said, referencing his slideshow from October.[23] Apparently believing that it was not within his authority, under the PLRA, to order releases, Judge Tigar reported that he had

> cajoled, begged, and pleaded with the Governor . . . to release a very significantly higher number of inmates beyond their current release efforts . . . so we can avoid unnecessary sickness and death . . . .
>
> So far these requests have—again, with all appreciation for the efforts that have been made, . . . fallen on deaf ears.
>
> The consequence of that is now becoming more apparent. COVID has spread more easily than it had to. And we'll never know the number, but I believe there is some unknown number of prison residents who got sick or died that didn't have to.[24]

Judge Tigar highlighted the importance of granting people the good time credits they were unable to earn because of the lockdowns, saying that "we're making over incarceration worse at precisely the time we need it to get better."[25] He also pointed out that he "[could] not emphasize strongly enough the need to release elderly medically-vulnerable inmates. We have started to see a heartbreaking increase in fatalities" (56 since the previous CMC) "[a]nd releases are a way to make sure . . . [it] does not continue. I take this case personally. So I asked CDCR to send me the records of all the inmates from CMF or CHCF who died from COVID. Most of them died since the last

CMC. . . . The vast majority of them were elderly."[26] Judge Tigar was visibly emotional when describing incarcerated people who have to use commode chairs when going to the bathroom—and "when the virus hit, they were defenseless and then they died."[27]

Judge Tigar then pressed CDCR counsel Paul Mello on whether the "primary reason" for the alarming infection rates was the prisoners' refusal to move to safer housing.[28] Mello replied that "in some instances people are not moved quickly enough, but [refusal] appears to be the primary reason."[29] Judge Tigar urged that education be increased, so that people "can accept the efforts [being made] to protect them."[30] This, again, led to the discussion of the thorny problem of the staff: refusals to wear masks and get tested. Judge Tigar probed as to what the reasons might be, getting very little input from the parties.[31]

Even in the face of all this, Judge Tigar insisted that he had not yet felt authorized by the PLRA to release people pursuant to a finding of "deliberate indifference." "If I could let people out . . . I would do it today," he said, but "[m]y view of the law is that I'm not allowed to do that."[32] The plaintiffs, of course, disagreed, but Tigar insisted that, legally speaking, his hands were tied, which he claimed was a "source of incredible frustration" to him. Judge Tigar stressed that he did not rule out a future finding of deliberate indifference but said, "we just haven't gotten there yet."[33]

Even though Judge Tigar explained his reluctance to order releases in formalist terms—the notion that the PLRA tied his hands—it was evident from his management of the CMC that his judicial psychology was a factor. Repeatedly stating that he did not want to give orders, Judge Tigar explained that "litigation is not the way to go with this . . . communication is the [right] way . . . ."[34] At the heart of this effort to create consensus was his continuous outreach to the CCPOA representatives, which evinced earnest efforts to get everyone on board: "Nobody . . . like[s] low staff testing rates," he said. "We need to get [them] as high as possible. . . . [W]hy [are] they . . . where they are to begin with[?]"[35]

At this point, he turned to the CCPOA's union lawyers, David Sanders and Gregg Adam, in an effort to get the union's collaboration at "[a] moment when CCPOA could become an invaluable partner, if they want to, in keeping their own brothers and sisters safe. . . ."[36] Judge Tigar hammered home the need for complete buy-in from the leadership: "If the captains say, you have to wear a mask, . . . [then] you have to wear a mask. . . . There are no exceptions. . . . [I]f they make that the policy, . . . that is how this is going to work."[37] The back-and-forth between the judge and union counsel offered another insight into Judge Tigar's cooperative psychology: he told them that the benefit would be that compliance orders from above "create[d] an environment where you can publicly take the position that you ... wear one ... because [you] don't have a choice. If leadership is uniform, it creates an environment where it's much easier for staff ... to be uniform." He added:

> ... It has to happen off the job, too. ... I have been hoping that CDCR or CCHCS ... would create videos for staff ... using staff.
> I asked and I asked and I asked. More than you will ever know. ... And then I gave up. And then they did it and they are great. I just saw them yesterday. Your staff will see them. ... And they make this point:
> You can't be in the car with your friends driving to work or going to someone's backyard and think, oh, I know these guys. ... COVID doesn't care who your friends are.
> The need to wear the mask is the same ... on the job, off the job. [I]t has to be at that level. [High command] order[s custodial staff] to do this on the job, [and] expect[s compliance] off the job.[38]

One of Judge Tigar's ideas was to solicit a volunteer in each prison who would be "down with the goal" to report to a member of Kelso's staff who "comes from custody [and] speaks the language."[39] He also continued to consult with suasion experts, this time Amy Lerman of the Goldman School, regarding correctional culture and fostering compliance. Happily, Adam also seemed to have respect for Lerman and also mentioned that they were planning to speak to Linos (whom Tigar referred to as the "persuasion guru") about compliance strategy.[40] At that point, CCPOA counsel Sanders offered a highly revisionist history of CCPOA's involvement in prison conditions litigation, presenting CCPOA as the great champions of the original *Plata* release order, both because of the safety of their own employees and because they apparently thought that it was "morally and professionally wrong what was happening in our prisons ... warehousing human beings, and literally seeing them die because of the medical conditions."[41] Ironically, a few months before the CMC, while their members were ailing and dying from COVID-19, the CCPOA had invested $4 million in support of punitive voter initiatives that failed at the ballot[42] and had planned an in-person jaunt to Las Vegas for a board meeting[43]—issues that went unmentioned by Judge Tigar. CCPOA representatives also balked at the idea of modeling good conduct through prison staff hierarchy, explaining that "we don't actually represent captains" and that "sergeants and lieutenants do not have collective bargaining rights ...."[44]

At this point, the hearing turned to the petitioners' change of strategy—from asking for releases and decarceration to a petition for vaccinations. The latter request was, of course, far more modest, but the prison authorities found it objectionable. In his argument against procuring vaccines for all incarcerated people, Mello resorted to legalese: not only did the respondents receive the request too late, he said, "we believe an order would be unnecessary ... and it would constitute ... undue intrusion on executive authority."[45] There would also be practical hurdles, he explained, and CDCR was not out of line by adhering to current CDC health directives. Finally, Mello opined that the plaintiffs faced an uphill battle showing deliberate indifference with expert testimony, which would stand in the way of even the modest request for vaccinations.

While Judge Tigar remained calm—and seemingly agreed with Mello about the legal point—he clearly found the resort to legalese somewhat tasteless. "I think about [this] in such a simple way, simplistic even," he said.

> I heard Mr. Kelso say he needs 40,000 doses ... to get the job done....
> [T]wo and a half million doses ... have already rolled into the State....
> 40,000 doses is like couch cushion-money.
> ... Do we think that the governor can shake 40,000 doses loose? ... [I]f the issue gets litigated ... by the time [the litigation] resolves, it will be a dead issue.... [T]here are things I can do to expedite it.
> [But] I have a much simpler question: Do we think the Governor could shake loose whatever the number is, ... 40,000 doses, to protect a population that he has already recognized is defenseless, deeply in need, and whose vaccination, because of the roles prisons play [in the larger infection story] will greatly affect public health in a positive way? Do you think he would shake loose those doses if I asked him to?[46]

Sara Norman of the Prison Law Office responded with a moral call to action. "[T]his is not litigation about vaccination," she explained, "[it's] about quarantine.... [H]undreds or thousands of people are being ... quarantine[d] ... with shared air, ... [which] has resulted in significant illness and death."[47] The solution, she said, "has been within Defendant's grasp from the beginning"; releasing people "is their choice and they have continued to place our clients, their patients[,] at significant[,] serious[, and] profound risk of harm.... We are now saying there's another solution."[48] Vaccination of incarcerated people—mandated by virtue of their classification as 1.B.2. in the priority list—is "within [CDCR's] reach.... They can do it."[49] Norman ended by quoting Yoda: "Do or do not; there is no try. It is up to them to do it."[50]

Phase III: Persuasion—The Efforts to Require Staff Vaccination

As detailed in chapter 4 above, the initial apprehension about vaccine acceptance among the prison population quickly gave way to a more realistic concern: vaccine reluctance among the staff. After months of no progress on the staff vaccination front, a development occurred: the receiver, Clark Kelso, broke lines with respondents, imploring Judge Tigar to issue a vaccine mandate. On September 27, 2021, Judge Tigar issued an order requiring a mandate.[51] The order relied heavily on Kelso's position:

> Facing these facts, the Receiver has recommended, based on his review of the medical and public health science, that a mandatory COVID-19 vaccination policy be implemented for workers entering CDCR institutions and incarcerated persons who choose to work outside of an institution or accept in-person visitation. Now before the Court is an order to show cause as to why the Receiver's recommendations should not be adopted.[52]

Indeed, the advent and availability of the vaccine, as well as the fact that incarcerated people, on their own initiative, accepted it in high rates, played an explicit role in ushering in Judge Tigar's order. That the dispute (including the requested remedy) was now narrowed to the modest and clearly delineated question of staff vaccination—something, he reasoned, that even the defendants could easily understand and support—was a factor in his decision:

> [N]o one disputes that the risks to the incarcerated population extend to the vaccinated as well as the unvaccinated. All agree that a mandatory staff vaccination policy would lower the risk of preventable death and serious medical consequences among incarcerated persons. And no one has identified any remedy that will produce anything close to the same benefit.[53]

Judge Tigar was also explicit in explaining how the advent of the vaccine facilitated his finding of deliberate indifference:

> A finding that Defendants were not deliberately indifferent based on a toolbox without a vaccine has little relevance when the same toolbox now includes a vaccine that everyone agrees is one of the most important tools, if not the most important one, in the fight against COVID-19.[54]

The order was immediately met with derision from the CCPOA. In response to a query from CalMatters, CCPOA president Glen Stailey texted, "We've undertaken an aggressive, voluntary vaccination program and we still believe the voluntary approach is the best way forward . . . . We are looking into our legal options to address this order."[55]

Phase IV: The Appeal

And address it they did. Immediately following Judge Tigar's order, CDCR published a three-page plan for implementation,[56] which excluded many people from the vaccine requirement, while at the same time filing a notice of appeal.[57] The attorney general representatives immediately moved to stay the vaccination order, a motion Judge Tigar denied. The state immediately appealed to the Ninth Circuit, which stayed the decision, citing "irreparable harm" to the guards should the remedy be implemented before the hearing.[58]

Far from an inconsequential interim decision, the "irreparable harm" would, arguably, all be borne by the other side to the litigation: shortly after the order, the Omicron variant swept through California prisons, infecting thousands of incarcerated people as well as thousands of staff members.

The Ninth Circuit reasoned that antivaccination sentiments were running rampant among prison guards and assumed that, in the face of vaccine mandates, many might quit their well-paying jobs, leaving prisons understaffed. This scenario was feared, but did not come to pass, in many other employment sectors with mandates, where vocal protestations and threats of resignation gave way to vaccine compliance. But even had the threat been real, the underlying question avoided by judicial decision-makers was whether incarceration at this scale was even possible if hiring and retaining sensible, caring staff was impossible.

The Ninth Circuit's evasion of this question, and protectionism of the prison's internal logics, was in full display again in the final decision on the appeal.[59] Reversing Judge Tigar's mandate, the appellate judges considered CDCR's efforts in

> making vaccines and booster doses available to prisoners and correctional staff, enacting policies to encourage and facilitate staff and prisoner vaccination, requiring staff to wear personal protective equipment, and ensuring unvaccinated staff members regularly test for COVID-19. Defendants also employed . . . symptom screening for all individuals entering the prisons; enhanced cleaning in the facilities; adopting an outbreak action plan; upgrading ventilation; establishing quarantine protocols for medically vulnerable patients; and testing, masking, and physical distancing among inmates.[60]

These steps, in the court's view, were sufficiently ameliorative to lower the level of misbehavior beneath the Eighth Amendment threshold.[61] Were these steps the best plan under the circumstances? This, said the court, did not matter, because "[a] decision to adopt an approach that is not the most medically efficacious does not itself establish deliberate indifference."[62]

The Ninth Circuit's decision is a textbook example of the inherent inadequacy of prison litigation as a solution for dynamic health-care situations. It reflects familiar attributes of the deferent standard in prison law: a perverse overfocus on the uniqueness of the prison setting,[63] a contortion of the Eighth Amendment to defend prison administration,[64] and an underlying assumption that lives lived behind bars are "second rate" to the point that efficiency and competence expectations from the free world become irrelevant.[65] The decision also reflects the pathology of the interagency game of "chicken" that stalemates efforts to provide relief in real time: optimally, during such a crisis, intervention and relief should emanate from the governor's mansion and the prison administration itself, but since neither has an incentive to step in, courts apply a clunky, time-consuming process to address changing situations.

IN RE HALL

Phase I: Stuck in Superior Court

By contrast to the litigation in *Plata*, the San Quentin litigation began as a grassroots effort by incarcerated men, who composed individual habeas corpus writs by themselves and later using a template offered by Legal Services for Prisoners with Children. By June 2020 hundreds of men had submitted petitions; many continued to join the litigation well into August and September, to the point that Judge Geoffrey Howard had to sort petitioners into groups based on the timing of their petitions. Other categorization would prove difficult, because the petitioners varied greatly by age, length of sentence, health conditions, and crime of commitment.

One such petitioner was Ivan Von Staich, at the time a 64-year-old man incarcerated at San Quentin on several charges, including second-degree murder. Since his incarceration in 1986, Von Staich has served time at California State Prison, Corcoran; California State Prison, Sacramento; California Institution for Men; Pleasant Valley State Prison; Soledad State Prison; and California Men's Colony.[66] Suffering from multiple health conditions, including chronic obstructive pulmonary disease (COPD)—a risk factor for COVID-19—and bronchitis, Von Staich was confined to a cell in West Block that he shared with his cellmate for 24 hours a day. At the time that Von Staich filed his appeal in the California Court of Appeal, he possessed only one cloth mask, issued to him two months earlier, which he washed regularly. In mid-July, Von Staich and his cellmate, Donald Jagiolka, tested positive for COVID-19; Jagiolka became symptomatic, and both were kept in their cell. Von Staich's attorneys, Richard Braucher and Brad O'Connell of the First District Appellate Project (FDAP), described what they termed his "daily nightmare" in their brief:

> Petitioner reports that staff try to talk inmates with COVID-19 symptoms out of medical treatment. They are told that hospitals in the area are overwhelmed and that they have to "kick it" on their own. Petitioner believes that prison authorities believe that everyone in West Block is going to somehow build up immunity to the coronavirus. He observed that when the virus first broke out in West Block and a prisoner came down with symptoms, a prisoner's cellmate would alert staff, yelling "man down," and prison staff would come and render aid. Now, petitioner says, prison staff leave the inmate in the cell.
>
> Petitioner reports that many inmates who are sick from COVID-19 avoid seeking medical treatment anyway, if it means being taken out of their cell. They have no confidence that the prison can do anything for them. Also, if inmates request treatment, they will be sent to a tent without access to any of their property. At least in their cells, inmates might have a radio or a TV.
>
> Petitioner reports that he and his fellow inmates are very frightened. Those who have not been tested or have tested negative for the virus, are afraid of contracting it. Those who have tested positive—whether or not experiencing symptoms—are afraid of serious harm or dying from COVID-19. Having received a positive test result and having experienced no symptoms, petitioner lives with the fear that it was a false positive or, if not a false positive, that, given the infectious environment he lives in, he could contract COVID-19 again and die.[67]

It was happenstance that Von Staich's case, one of the earliest habeas petitions, resulted in an appeal; after his case was denied by the Marin Superior Court, the FDAP took over his representation and appealed.[68] When the case was scheduled to be heard before a panel that would include Justice Anthony Kline, a veteran judge with an established reputation as a civil rights champion and criminal justice reformer,[69] petitioners' spirits were buoyed. Judge Howard paused the proceedings in all other pending cases, awaiting the Court of Appeal's resolution of Von Staich's case.

Phase II: "We Must Act Hastily"—
Von Staich *at the Court of Appeal*

On September 8, 2020, the First District Court of Appeal heard oral argument in *Von Staich*.[70] The hearing opened with a debate on evidence-law doctrine in California—namely, whether the respondents, who disputed all the declarations and reports made by AMEND physicians about the conditions at San Quentin, should have provided actual evidence to refute these reports. CDCR representative Kathleen Walton argued that the habeas rules did not require her to provide these facts and pressed the court for an evidentiary hearing; O'Connell, for the petitioner, argued that CDCR made no attempt to plead the facts or meet them at all. Justice Kline characterized the prison's response as "conclusionary statements, not facts," and rejected CDCR's argument that the issues they briefed (whether CDCR provided adequate cleaning, sanitizing, masks, continuation of holding petitioner Von Staich with other inmates, whether COVID-19 is still spreading at the prison, etc.) were the focus of the case. "What we believe this case is about," said Justice Kline, "is whether there is persuasive evidence that the court must do what the *Plata* court cannot do, which is to reduce population of San Quentin to a level that can permit the administration of social distancing within that prison."

After confirming that CDCR could release people serving life with parole through various mechanisms (including the governor's emergency authority to release), discussion shifted to the happenings at San Quentin. Walton intimated that some of the prison's vigorous efforts to contain COVID-19 spread at San Quentin were hindered by "inmates refusing to cooperate," including testing and reporting symptoms. Justice Kline countered with the possibility that people were disincentivized from cooperating because the prison relied on spaces with a punitive connotation (solitary confinement cells) for medical isolation (a problem pointed out in the AMEND report).

Justice Kline then pointed out the most obvious demographic for release: aging people serving long sentences for violent crime. Walton responded that Von Staich himself—a 64-year-old, chronically ill man incarcerated since the 1980s—was considered "moderate risk."

The hearing shifted to the respondents' claim that the *Von Staich* appeal was an inappropriate forum in that it was "duplicative" of the systemwide litigation in *Plata*. Justice Kline explained: "You keep making arguments that assume we have the same interests as the federal court. We are not being asked to evaluate the quality of care and attention to COVID they are providing. [The federal courts] are looking into that." Walton then presented Judge Tigar's *Plata* stance as "he didn't find an Eighth Amendment violation." Justice Kline immediately retorted that, as a matter of public knowledge, Judge Tigar had urged state courts to do something because he believed that, as a federal judge, his hands were tied by the PLRA. In short, said Justice Kline, the COVID-19 crisis at San Quentin was a state problem, happening at a state department of corrections, which made it the business of state courts. Justice Stewart proceeded to chide Walton for arguing "inappropriate forum" in each of the courts in which the state was battling prison conditions claims; Walton, in response, presented the attorney general's position as a hierarchy of litigation: the appellate court would have to defer to the superior court, which was handling hundreds of similar habeas petitions; both state courts would have to defer to the *Plata* court, which was handling the systemwide claims; and all courts would have to defer to the wisdom of prison administrators, as the answer to complicated health-care and prison-management policy issues lay with CDCR rather than with courts.

While the oral argument boded well for Von Staich, the court did press his representatives on the appropriate remedy. Issuing an order to release 50 percent of the prisoners per the AMEND "Urgent Memo," said Justice Kline, is "something I'm not sure I'm willing to do ... not confident that my court has the ability." Indeed, the role of the appellate court, he reasoned, might be limited to assessing whether the current conditions at San Quentin allowed the social distancing necessary to stop the spread in that facility, and ordering particular precautions. Justice Kline also commented that the lawsuit had already resulted in a benefit to Von Staich himself, who was now in isolation. When asked by the court "what would you have us say?," Richard Braucher (for the petitioner) replied that, in the absence of a vaccine or a cure, the only ways to effectively address COVID-19 at San Quentin were releases or transfers.

The court, however, expressed the need to restrain its interference with prison business. To show that the state was making an effort, the court cited a July 10 plan issued by Governor Newsom, which would result in the release of fewer than 8,000 people systemwide, most of them people on the verge of release (we discuss this plan and its implementation in chapter 7). In response to the question of how petitioner's counsel would determine release priorities, Braucher replied that the two linchpins should be age and medical condition (both present in Von Staich's case).

The discussion of Newsom's order opened the door to Walton's argument that there was "no need to act hastily." Walton explained that AMEND's "Urgent Memo," which called for a 50 percent population reduction, was composed before the prison implemented various ameliorative measures, including a new program for sanitation and distribution of protective equipment. At this, Justice Kline exploded: "Yes there is. Yes there is. There is a need to act hastily." People have gotten sick and died, he said, and we must ensure that no more of this happens.

In October, the Court of Appeal issued its decision: Von Staich had won.[71] The court wrote: "We agree that respondents—the Warden and CDCR—have acted with deliberate indifference and relief is warranted."[72]

The decision began by stating the magnitude of the catastrophe. Even against the horrific history of prison epidemics—including three separate spikes of the Spanish flu in 1918—San Quentin's COVID-19 outbreak was "the worst epidemiological disaster in California correctional history."[73] The court then highlighted the physicians' recommendation to reduce the prison population by 50 percent.[74] CDCR's response fell far short of this: between March and August 2020, they achieved a mere 23 percent reduction, "accomplished, in part, by suspending intake at San Quentin from county jails, which has increased the presence of COVID-19 in those local facilities, and is not likely sustainable."[75]

The court then rejected the evasive maneuvers employed by the Office of the Attorney General, which had urged deference to the *Plata* litigation. First, the court wrote, San Quentin was an antiquated prison with endemic problems, beyond the more general concerns of the federal litigation.[76] Second, these habeas cases sought temporary relief, rather than the more systematic remedies sought in *Plata*.[77] Third, state courts were not limited and bound by the PLRA, as federal courts were.[78] And fourth—remarkable considering the general perception of federal courts as the only resort in prison conditions cases—state courts "have the duty and competence to vindicate rights" under the US Constitution as well as the California Constitution[79] (which, like the US Constitution, forbids cruel and unusual punishment—albeit in slightly different wording).[80]

The court also rejected the attorney general's petition for an evidentiary hearing. The state's contentions that the AMEND physicians exaggerated the necessity of population reduction, the court reasoned, were "conclusions the Attorney General has failed to support with any factual allegations contradicting petitioner's allegations"—even with testimony from the state's own prison physicians.[81] Therefore, "the issue before us is simply whether respondents' disregard of the experts' conclusion that a 50 percent population reduction is essential constitutes the 'deliberate indifference' necessary to sustain petitioner's constitutional claim. The issue is one of law, not fact."[82]

On the merits, the court found that the prison authorities' failure to act satisfied the "deliberate indifference" standard; prison authorities conceded they knew the risk, and they recklessly failed to take the necessary steps physicians recommended, with no factual justification.[83] The continued congregated, dense housing plan was "not merely negligent [but] reckless"—and "the recklessness [was] aggravated by respondents' refusal to consider the expedited release, or transfer, of prisoners who are serving time for violent offenses but have aged out of a propensity for violence . . . ."[84]

The court addressed CDCR's pandemic response—establishing a central command, erecting tents, repurposing nonpunitive spaces for isolation, providing protective equipment to the population and staff, and releasing 922 people as part of Governor Newsom's plan—and found it inadequate.[85] The decision quoted Dr. Beyrer, one of the petitioners' experts: "[h]ad San Quentin done nothing, the rates of infection there would have been roughly the same."[86] The prison's ameliorative steps, while commendable, were insufficient without resorting to population reduction.[87]

The *Von Staich* court did, indeed, order a population reduction but left the means vague. On one hand, the court felt comfortable criticizing CDCR's release policies, particularly the prison's boast that it had reduced San Quentin's population to slightly more than 100 percent of design capacity.[88] In a facility like San Quentin, the court wrote, full occupancy could not facilitate the social distancing needed to fight the pandemic.[89] The decision quoted extensively from the AMEND memo, which detailed conditions in specific areas of the prison, notably North Block and West Block, showing that the combination of crowding and high-risk people was unsustainable.[90]

The court also criticized the prison's reluctance to release anyone incarcerated for "a violent crime as defined by law" when such people were approximately 30 percent of the prison population.[91] From a medical standpoint, the decision read, "[e]xclusion of lifers and other older prisoners who have committed violent offenses and served lengthy prison terms is also difficult to defend, given their low risk for future violence and high risk of infection and serious illness from the virus."[92] The decision cited robust legal, sociological, and medical materials to show the folly of excluding lifers and "strikers"— people serving lengthy sentences due to California's habitual-offender laws—

from release programs, including literature on life-course criminology, which consistently finds age a significant factor in desistance.[93] The court also opined that the decision to exclude aging people who had committed violent crimes "render[s] it doubtful whether a 50 percent reduction in San Quentin's population could soon take place . . . ."[94]

While finding that the habeas corpus process allowed the court to extend relief to people similarly situated to Von Staich (whom the court ordered to be immediately released or transferred from San Quentin),[95] the decision held that "it would be inappropriate and unwise to order the release of prisoners we considered vulnerable even if we thought we had the power to do so in this proceeding."[96] The court raised three concerns in this respect: one, that medical vulnerability was a question of "scientific facts, not law"; two, that it was unsure whether it could extend relief to people who had not filed a habeas petition; and three, that social distancing could be created not only by transferring vulnerable prisoners out of San Quentin but also by releasing other people in sufficient numbers to facilitate social distancing for the remaining prisoners.[97]

"Nevertheless," held the decision, "we are not without means to expedite the release or transfer from San Quentin of more inmates than are now deemed eligible for release."[98] These means were provided by §1484 of the California Penal Code, which allowed the court to take such a course of action.[99] The court cited numerous California cases that involved injunctive relief through habeas.[100] By this authority, the court ordered CDCR to bring the San Quentin population down to 50 percent—"no more than 1,775 inmates."[101] The court left the method to CDCR's discretion, though the decision provided some clues as to the proper approach: "expanding eligibility for the two expedited release programs currently limited to inmates not serving sentences for violent offenses to inmates like petitioner, who are over age 60 and completed minimum terms of at least 25 years."[102]

The *Von Staich* order wreaked panic amid prison authorities and their advocates. The attorney general immediately appealed the order to the California Supreme Court, arguing that an evidentiary hearing should have been held, awarding the prison the opportunity to refute the facts presented by the petitioners. Relying on *People v. Duvall*,[103] the California Supreme Court held that "it appears that there are significant disputes about the efficacy of the measures officials have already taken to abate the risk of serious harm to petitioner and other prisoners, as well as the appropriate health and safety measures they should take in light of present conditions. For this reason, we return the case to the Court of Appeal with instructions to consider whether to order an evidentiary hearing to investigate these matters before judgment is pronounced."[104] This reversal did not satisfy the attorney general, who went so far as to petition that the *Von Staich* decision be depublished (!),[105] as if to obliterate any trace of constitutional violations having been found. The California Supreme Court, to its credit, denied the request for depublication without dignifying it with an explanation.[106]

Von Staich himself was not particularly fortunate in the aftermath of the landmark decision in his case. In late October and early November, shortly before his transfer to Corcoran, Von Staich told a reporter that, following the decision, he was targeted by staff. He reported that a captain told him: "I don't give a fuck about a court order . . . . We can do what we want to you. You're destroying our whole prison . . . . You think you're going to get money out of this . . . . You got to live to get paid."[107] In early December, Von Staich was released from California custody only to find himself in federal custody due to a parole hold that predated his original 1986 trial.

Phase III: "Packed Like Sardines"—The Evidentiary Hearing at the Superior Court

The remand of the habeas cases to the Marin Superior Court for an evidentiary hearing spurred Judge Howard into action. By the time *Hall* was due to be heard, the factual landscape had been transformed beyond recognition. When *Von Staich* was filed, San Quentin was the epicenter of contagion, with thousands of cases and dozens of deaths; recall that, as late as September, Justice Kline bristled at the suggestion that there was "no need to act hastily." But at the opening of the evidentiary hearing in the spring of 2021, San Quentin had only four active cases—not because prison administrators won their battle against the virus, but because the virus had won and had run out of people to infect. By then, well over 50 percent of CDCR inmates had already been infected, and nearly all CDCR facilities had had outbreaks.

The dynamic shift in the landscape of contagion raised the question of whether the vagueness of the *Von Staich* remedy—which strongly urged CDCR to release aging and infirm people but explicitly accepted transfers as a viable path to compliance—coupled with the moral paralysis at the governor's office and at CDCR had led to a situation in which the "relief" that CDCR was willing to provide (i.e., transfers from San Quentin to other prisons) would now be worse than no relief at all. Between the *Von Staich* decision and the evidentiary hearing, many petitioners contacted their attorneys, asking to withdraw their petitions for fear of retaliation in the form of transfers.

These petitioners found themselves facing an unconscionable dilemma: stay at San Quentin and fight for release from a decrepit facility that could fall prey to a second COVID-19 wave, or move to other prisons and lose the rich, volunteer-led programming unavailable anywhere else in CDCR (and essential for compiling an impressive parole dossier). There were also concerns that hasty transfers would relocate people to facilities in which they would face animosity merely because they arrived from "the COVID prison." These dilemmas were pithily addressed by the attorney general representative, Denise Yates, thusly: "Petitioners can't have it both ways." The remaining petitioners were represented by a legal team consisting of private attorneys at Keker, Van Nest & Peters, LLP; seasoned solo practitioners in the prison space, such as Charles Carbone; and several public defenders from San Francisco and Marin Counties.

The evidentiary hearing was held via Zoom and broadcast at San Quentin Prison.[108] Incarcerated witnesses testified remotely from a room in the prison. The hearing lasted 11 days.

In his opening statement, Khari Tillery explained that, even before the pandemic, San Quentin residents were housed in an overcrowded facility "ripe for the spread of communicable disease," with no pandemic response plan despite continuous warnings, offers to help, and a special plan for prisons from the CDC. He recounted the fateful transfer from Chino, relying on the evidence unearthed in the Office of the Inspector General's report: "Even when [prison authorities] discovered some of [the transferees] were sick, they did not isolate or test them," nor did they listen to experts. The results were "predictably devastating."

Tillery explained the deliberate-indifference standard, highlighting the absurdity of the hearing: CDCR's triumphant bid for an evidentiary hearing would now allow petitioners to prove and bolster their claims about the horrors they experienced through live testimony from inside. He promised that the testimony would encompass the collateral consequences of the pandemic: double-celling with mixed COVID statuses, lockdown, no cooked food for days, a terrifying rumor mill, and close contact with potentially infected people.

Anticipating CDCR's argument about the ameliorative steps, Tillery preemptively warned the court that they should not be allowed to spin the end of the pandemic as a success story. Such claims, he said, would be belied by the actual results: an infection rate sevenfold the rate on the outside and 28 people dead. This, he explained, was a consequence of "nibbl[ing] at the edges of the problem" rather than taking the necessary and practical steps advised by experts: population reduction that prioritized aging, infirm people.

On behalf of CDCR, Paula Gibson argued that petitioners misrepresented the legal standard. Rather than rehashing the past, said Gibson, habeas cases could only address each petitioner's current condition at San Quentin, which, in the twilight of the outbreak, was no longer a risk meriting release.

The evidentiary hearing opened with testimony from John Mattox, one of the transferees from CIM. Mattox was tested (and found negative) on May 12, 2020, and housed in a dorm, alongside 120 others, sleeping in double bunks spaced three feet apart. While still at CIM, he observed sick people and was in close proximity to 2 people who tested positive. His neighbor, Francis Douglas, "ha[d] a high temperature, sweating, didn't want to get out of bed," and Mattox helped him get to the health-care services. Mattox himself started feeling sick in late May. Before the transfer, he informed health-care personnel three times of his symptoms but was ordered to transfer nonetheless. Subsequently, he recounted, "we were cramped like sardines," sitting shoulder to shoulder "in a holding tank before transfer with no ventilation, no movement, for 3–5 hours. It was so hot and cramped that a lot of inmates were agitated and took their masks off when talking to others—the only time to get up was to use the bathroom." Mattox again complained about his symptoms, but a nurse found his temperature normal and chided him for lying to avoid a transfer. The transferees were then loaded onto the bus—dressed in paper jumpsuits, their legs in shackles and their wrists bound—and instructed to sit in pairs on four-foot benches and don cloth masks.

The bus was packed shoulder to shoulder and unventilated for the entire 11-hour ride to San Quentin. While on the bus, Mattox witnessed people coughing and removing their masks, leaning their heads back to try to sleep.

Upon arrival, the transferees were deboarded. They were not screened in any way and were housed in groups of five. Mattox again told a health-care professional that he was unwell and was instructed to "let medical know when you're set up in a cell."

The transfer occurred on Saturday, and the transferees were housed in pairs in the Badger Unit; on Monday, Mattox was finally swabbed and placed in a filthy, isolated cell. The officer took a bottle of bleach, sprayed it on the mattress and walls, and left without giving Mattox a rag to wipe it off.

Four or five days later, Mattox received his diagnosis: he was the first COVID-19 case at San Quentin.

On cross examination, John Walters of the attorney general's office chose a questioning tack that would repeat itself for all incarcerated witnesses: he asked Mattox whether he was vaccinated (he was). This strategy would support CDCR's position in two ways: vaccinated people were sufficiently protected, and unvaccinated people were to blame for their own plight. Mattox was also asked about mitigation strategies and programming at San Quentin, to support the idea that the prison's ameliorative steps sufficed to dispel the deliberate indifference finding. Walters pursued this strategy by getting Mattox to admit that there was "no chow hall, meals were brought to you." Mattox replied: "yes, by inmates." Walters then posited, "and you saw that the population was being reduced." Mattox insisted that he had not experienced any difference.

The next witness, Larry Williams, was a building porter at San Quentin, responsible for food distribution and maintenance at the time of the outbreak. Williams testified about the horrific hygiene; only in April did he receive training on sanitation, and the special cleaning appliances he was promised never materialized. Williams said that the men socially distanced "to the best of their ability" and explained, "if you're standing down and he's standing down, it's impossible to be apart ... the showers are a foot apart. Even if you turn off a shower head in between, you're not six feet apart."

Williams said that the men received cloth masks only in late April, and N95 masks in late July. Staff members wore their masks where they could be observed by their superior officers, but inside their units, they never wore them.

When Williams and five others were ordered to handle the property of the Chino transferees, he feared contracting COVID-19. After finishing the job, Williams took a shower, after which his skin felt flushed, sticky, and warm. He immediately called his wife, informing her that he might have become infected.

Despite reporting his symptoms to the nurse in the evening, Williams was not tested for COVID-19. The nurse scanned his vitals and told him he did not have COVID-19 symptoms. Williams's effort to report his symptoms the next day received no sympathy, and he was ordered to continue working, which involved handling food trays. During this day, he came in contact with 300 men; he was tested that afternoon. He continued to work, while displaying symptoms, for the following four days, and it was only then that he was notified that he had tested positive.

Subsequently, Williams was moved to the adjustment center (a euphemism for solitary confinement), which he described as a terrifying, filthy place. He was unable to launder his clothes and linen, so he washed them himself in the sink while ill. The COVID-19 bout exacerbated his preexisting hypertension, and he was moved back to his unit while still experiencing symptoms. His cellmate passed away from COVID-19, and he heard on the radio reports of dead people being removed from the prison. "It was hard to go to sleep," he said. "I was afraid I wouldn't wake up."

On cross-examination, Walters pressed Williams on his refusal to get tested for COVID-19 after his recovery; Williams said that he and many others refused testing because of the abundance of false positives and because of the consequences they faced once they tested positive.

The next witness, Travis Vales, told of being moved in May 2020 to another unit and subsequently testing positive. He described witnessing people falling ill all around him: complaining of aches, nausea, loss of taste, and calling out, "Man down!"—a distress call to the staff—multiple times a day.

Vales's testimony was followed by that of Michael Williams, who described similar experiences—"a lot of man down calls"—and a revolving door of cellmates switched when they fell ill, culminating in him and his cellmate becoming COVID-19 symptomatic. During his 39-day quarantine, Williams explained, sometimes staff members came by twice a day, but on other days, they would not come at all.

The stream of incarcerated witnesses was paused for the testimony of Dr. John Grant, who had practiced medicine at San Quentin for 15 years. Grant, intimately familiar with San Quentin's layout, testified that only the adjustment center (consisting of 100 cells) had solid doors; the remainder of the prison had bars on the doors.

Grant testified about an op-ed he coauthored with colleague Haiyan Ramirez Batlle for the *Los Angeles Times*,[109] in which he wrote: "we have to further reduce the population in overcrowded prisons and jails to below capacity. This could be done safely by minimizing new incarcerations, releasing those within months of parole or imprisoned on technical charges, and expanding the use of compassionate release for people who are frail and at high medical risk."

Grant also offered a window into the working conditions of the healthcare professionals during the pandemic: the doctors, he said, worked 80-hour weeks for the duration of the outbreak and saw 80 percent of their June 2020 patients test positive.

Mark Stanley, the next witness, was incarcerated in San Quentin's North Block and employed in assisting mobility-impaired prisoners. He testified that, despite the posting of a form that required use of a surgical mask, gown, and gloves, he was not provided any protective equipment except for the cloth mask and gloves he already had. After weeks of working in close quarters with the people he assisted, he began experiencing symptoms but was required to continue working for five days, interacting with at least two people with disabilities who were also symptomatic. Predictably, Stanley's cellmate also tested positive, at which point the two of them were put in a two-and-a-half-month lockdown with no access to showers, clean linens, or cleaning implements.

The last witness on this momentous day was incarcerated journalist Juan Moreno Haines, who authored several op-eds about COVID-19 at San Quentin.[110] Haines, a senior editor for the *San Quentin News*, predicted as early as February that the pandemic would spread. His explanation—he had witnessed other contagions in prison, such as staph infections, influenza, and Legionnaires' disease—was stricken from the record.

Haines described his cell in North Block: the unventilated building contained 415 cells on five tiers, 18 inches apart, each shared by two people (it has never been less populated than at 135 percent of design capacity). The fan merely recirculated existing air, and there were mesh-covered openings between the cells. During the COVID-19 outbreak, four people were allowed to simultaneously use the communal showers. The surrounding fence catwalk was filthy and cleaned every other year of dust, trash, and animal carcasses. In July 2020 a private contractor was hired to "deep clean" that space, which consisted of walking along the tiers with spray bottles and wiping down the rails.

Haines described the fear and despair during the lockdown. He was desperate to get fresh air, shower, and use the phone to inform his friends on the outside what was happening. He described hearing people cough at night and hearing "man down" calls: "that was just par for the course, a daily occurrence."

When Haines tested positive and was quarantined in Badger Unit, he was housed with someone recovering from COVID-19. His cellmate had not packed his property or cleaned the cell, so it was grimy and dusty. The mesh was so filthy that grime was covering parts of it. There was no power in the cell, and they couldn't even make tea or soup. At first, Haines did not even realize his own shortness of breath until he tried to carry his property to the third tier.

Tom McMahon, of the Marin Public Defender's Office, asked Haines: "Is it fair to say Respondent left you there to die?" Haines replied: "Yes." Walters interrupted: "Objection, argumentative."

The following days proceeded in the same vein. The emerging picture was much worse than the description in the *Von Staich* briefs. The cross-examination, if anything, seemed to support the petitioners' case. The state's representatives' goal at the hearing was to demonstrate the use of ameliorative steps that mitigated the harm wrought by the Chino transfer (whose causal contribution to the crisis could no longer be denied), as well as to shift some of the accountability onto the witnesses who refused testing and vaccination. But some of these questions backfired spectacularly. When Walters repeatedly asked the witnesses whether—and why—they had declined testing, he opened the door to one of the main horrors of the pandemic: the fact that CDCR had lost credibility to such a degree that asking for help was putting oneself at a disadvantage.

Petitioners' later witnesses supported this factual picture. Matthew Willis, the director of public health in Marin County, had an opportunity to tell how his request to test and isolate the Chino transferees was rebuffed. Fyodor Urnov, a UC Berkeley epidemiologist, testified about his offer to help speed up prison testing, which was rebuffed. The prison medical experts, Joseph Bick and Alison Pachynski, testified about the medical ameliorative steps, explaining that they had not been involved in the transfer decision.

The disconnect between the medical and the custodial staff became evident during the testimony of the warden, Ron Broomfield, on days four and five. Under cross-examination, Broomfield admitted that he had no knowledge of any CDCR recommendation to cohort staff members and that San Quentin did not comply with that policy. He also admitted that there was no policy in place to cohort incarcerated people, address a pandemic surge, or distribute N95 masks. He was also unable to recount whether any staff members had been reprimanded for mask-wearing violations. Broomfield stressed that the medical aspect of the prison was run exclusively by the receiver's staff.

The petitioners presented expert testimony by epidemiologist Alison Morris, who supported the causal link between the botched transfer and the outbreak and explained that, short of population reduction, the prison's ameliorative steps did very little to curb the spread of COVID-19. Terry Kupers, an expert on mental health in prison, testified about the lack of control incarcerated people exercise on their environment and the deleterious effect that pandemic conditions had on their mental health.

On November 16, 2021, Judge Howard issued his tentative ruling in *Hall*. The 116-page ruling provides a comprehensive historical narrative of the outbreak at San Quentin, starting with the fateful transfer from CIM and complete with the testimonies of incarcerated and expert witnesses.[111] Judge Howard discussed the ineptitude and mismanagement at San Quentin, from the warden to the custodial and medical staff; he relayed the many rejected offers for help. The opinion extensively relayed the impact of the crisis on mental health and morale (through the testimony of Kupers and several incarcerated witnesses).[112] Judge Howard also discussed the collateral punitive aspects of the prison's response to COVID-19, which amounted to months-long solitary confinement.[113]

While the decision commended CDCR for the mitigating strategies they adopted, ultimately it relied on evidence from both petitioners and respondent to show that, had they done nothing, the rate of infection, disease, and death would have been the same.[114]

The bottom line, however, was a disappointment to petitioners: Judge Howard accepted CDCR's argument that, for the purposes of relief, he needed to examine the conditions at present. The advent of vaccines, he wrote, "changed the game" and rendered relief in the case moot:

> With a nearly 80 percent inmate vaccination rate, COVID-19 has all but disappeared from inside the prison. Although COVID-19 remains a risk within San Quentin, . . . it [is] no more a risk at present than the risk faced by the community at large.
>
> But even if COVID-19 continues to pose a substantial risk of serious harm, the combination of substantial population reduction, mitigation measures, and vaccine rollout to every inmate in the prison shows that Respondent does not "knowingly and unreasonably" disregard an objectively intolerable risk of harm. By offering the vaccine to all inmates, Respondent has responded reasonably and effectively with the best tool available to mitigate the harm. This situation differs from the scenario presented to the *In re Von Staich* court, where "[a]bsent a vaccine or an effective treatment, the best way to slow and prevent spread of the virus is through social or physical distancing, which involves avoiding human contact, and staying at least six feet away from others." Here, the vaccine, combined with other measures, allows less physical distance. Petitioners did not carry their burden to show that Respondent continues to unreasonably disregard a known serious risk by failing to take further measures such as further reducing the prison population.[115]

Despite denying relief, Judge Howard wrote that for "a question of general public interest which is likely to recur," habeas petitioners may seek a declaration of rights, "including where the court may have difficulty ruling on the issue while the controversy is alive, and where it presents important issues of liberty and social interest."[116] This, he wrote, was just such an issue. And so, the last five pages of the decision lambasted CDCR and the receivership in general, and San Quentin officials in particular, for their ongoing neglect and for the pathogenic conditions of the prison:

1. *Respondent caused "the worst epidemiological disaster in California correctional history."* . . . In doing so, Respondent recklessly ignored what it knew then and concedes now—that COVID-19 posed a "substantial risk of serious harm to the health and safety of petitioners."

2. Respondent's conduct that resulted in 75 percent of the San Quentin inmates contracting COVID-19, and 28 deaths, implicates "matters of clear statewide importance" relating to the "efficacy of the measures officials have already taken to abate the risk of serious harm to petitioner and other prisoners, as well as the appropriate health and safety measures they should take in light of present conditions."

3. During the 2020 COVID-19 outbreak at San Quentin, Respondent violated Petitioners' rights under the Eighth Amendment to the United States Constitution and article I, section 17 of the California Constitution to be free of cruel and unusual punishment. Respondent exhibited deliberate indifference to the admitted risk posed by COVID-19, by (a) violating its own rules and procedures when it transferred the CIM inmates to San Quentin, knowing that those inmates posed a risk of introducing COVID-19 into San Quentin; (b) violating its own rules and procedures during the intake and processing of the newly-arrived CIM inmates, in particular by ignoring obvious COVID-19 symptoms, failing to quarantine the transferees, failing adequately to screen them, and failing to test them until after they had already begun to infect the existing San Quentin population; (c) ignoring advice from its own medical professionals and CDC guidance by failing to provide adequate PPE, mixing sick and well inmates, failing to cohort inmates adequately, failing to enforce social distancing, and failing to provide adequate or timely testing; and (d) ignoring Willis/MDPH's recommendations without any basis other than that MDPH purportedly had no authority over Respondent.

4. As in *Plata*, "[n]umerous experts testified that crowding is the primary cause of the constitutional violations." The evidence shows that compliance with the Urgent Memo's population reduction recommendation in a timely fashion substantially would have reduced the scope and severity of the COVID-19 outbreak at San Quentin. Respondent knew about the Urgent Memo. It further knew that population reduction could effectively combat viral spread (as evidenced by its own population reduction efforts). Respondent failed to comply with the Urgent Memo recommendation or

engage any expert of its own. Without adequate investigation or the benefit of any alternative expert opinion, ignoring the Urgent Memo's population reduction recommendation constituted further deliberate indifference. Indeed, Respondent had the means at its disposal quickly to comply with the Urgent Memo's recommendation; instead, it chose to litigate the matter while people died.

Respondent has offered no valid argument why it could not have complied with the Urgent Memo's recommendation. In *Plata*, in addition to the criteria imposed by the PLRA, the state had to consider an order involving the entire California prison system. The state could not comply with that order simply by moving inmates. It had to either release them or build more space. Here, by contrast, the problem involves only one, antiquated prison, with architectural characteristics not shared by many other prisons in the state system. Respondent contends it would violate "contemporary standards of decency" to release Petitioners prior to the end of their sentences. (Respondent Opp. at pp. 23, 57.) But it could have reduced the population through means other than outright release. Indeed, the remedy ordered by the Court of Appeal in the October 2020 *In re Von Staich* Order did not necessarily involve releasing any inmates. . . Instead, the Court of Appeal left to Respondent the most efficient and effective means of reducing the population, considering the variety of factors prison officials must consider. While release is certainly one option to reduce the population at San Quentin, prison officials had several other options available to them. For example, they could have transferred inmates to a different prison (following all safety protocols). The failure to do so, or at least to make good faith efforts to do so, unreasonably exposed inmates, staff, and the surrounding community to a substantial risk of serious harm.

5. The failure to reduce the population resulted in other constitutional deprivations of liberty. Because Respondent did not reduce the population as recommended, it effectively consigned hundreds of inmates to unwarranted, unnecessary, solitary confinement. And not just for a day or two. Where Respondent had the ability to move inmates to other facilities or release them, the court can conceive of no argument to support forcing inmates to remain in a cell smaller than 50 square feet, with two bunks, and a cellmate, for virtually 24 hours a day, seven days a week, for months on end. Doing so enhanced the inmates' exposure to COVID-19. For the duration it lasted, it also amounted to solitary confinement in violation of common standards of decency, with all the physical and mental health effects that result. . . Respondent knows about these effects. Its mental health team prepared for them, reported them, and treated them. Simply put, confinement for that long, with another person, in a space so small and foul, implicates "nothing less than the dignity of" humans.

6. Isolating COVID-positive inmates in the AC contributed to the spread of COVID-19 because inmates fear the AC. Using the AC as an isolation unit

disincentivizes candid reporting of symptoms, an essential component of any effective COVID-19 mitigation strategy.[117]

Judge Howard added:

[I]f Respondent insists on continuing to operate an obsolete and dangerous prison that, whenever an airborne pathogen arises, threatens the health and safety of the prison population, not to mention the surrounding community, then Respondent will leave the courts with no choice but to intervene . . .

No one knows how COVID-19 will behave in the future. No one knows what effect Respondent's efforts to vaccinate the entire inmate population will have in combating any future outbreak. Petitioners have not—at this time—carried their burden to show current deliberate indifference warranting injunctive relief. However, the record raises serious questions about whether Respondent has learned the right lessons from the 2020 COVID-19 debacle at San Quentin. It continues to operate a prison uniquely situated to allow the spread of any airborne pathogen, including COVID-19, in a manner seemingly indifferent to the specific characteristics that resulted in such extensive illness and death just last year. For example, Respondent continues to double cell prisoners in multi-tiered units with open barred doors, a living environment that enhances the risk of disease transmission. Respondent also appears intent on relying on the same population spread—as opposed to population reduction—strategy it employed in 2020. It plans to lockdown double-celled inmates, when necessary to quarantine them, in the cells measuring 49 square feet that make up the tiered housing units. Depending on the circumstances, including the severity of any future outbreak, the findings above should cast significant doubt on the wisdom of those strategies.[118]

Phase IV: The Appeal

The denial of relief rendered Judge Howard's declaration, while symbolically valuable, practically useless to the petitioners. This was particularly poignant because, as of its publication day, relief was not moot: there were already rising cases in other prisons. Within a few weeks, as the Omicron variant spread, 21 prisons had significant outbreaks, many of them consisting of hundreds of cases, and San Quentin saw a rise in cases as well. At its peak, this third wave of infections consisted of more than 6,000 cases among incarcerated people and more than 4,000 among the staff.

Under these circumstances, petitioners' representatives debated whether to appeal the decision and finally decided against it. Much to their surprise, Judge Howard's decision was appealed by the Office of the Attorney General. This astounding use of taxpayer money to combat a decision that offered the opposite side no material remedy remains unexplained as of the writing of this manuscript. After several months, the attorney general withdrew the appeal.

CONCLUSION: STATE AND FEDERAL LITIGATION COMMONALITIES

The two proceedings—*Von Staich/Hall* and *Plata*—varied greatly along procedural lines: a class action in federal court, in which a judge felt bound by the PLRA, and a cluster of habeas corpus cases in state courts, in which a judge felt that the facts did not merit a remedy despite a finding of constitutional violations. Nevertheless, dig underneath the procedural surface, and you'll find a similar animus, which suggests the patterns and mechanisms through which prison litigation invariably defers to the state.

Tolerating Bad Behavior

The most notable common characteristic was the plethora of examples of judicial tolerance for bad behavior. The most striking similarity was the use of circular and evasive jurisdictional maneuvers. Before Justice Kline in the Court of Appeal, the attorney general's representatives argued that the appropriate forum for addressing Von Staich's writ was the Marin Superior Court, where the remaining habeas cases were pending; before Judge Howard in the Superior Court, they argued that the appropriate forum for addressing all the writs was the all-encompassing federal litigation in *Plata*; and before Judge Tigar in the District Court in *Plata*, they argued that the appropriate thing would be to stop litigating altogether and defer to the prison's management of the pandemic.

Another common example of bad behavior was the cynical allocation of risk and blame, tasking incarcerated people with responsibilities for their own well-being. The attorney general representatives argued, with a straight face, that exempting prison guards—the people moving freely within, into, and out of the prison—from vaccination made sense, because unvaccinated prisoners could accept the vaccine and protect themselves. Elsewhere, they argued that prisoners shared some responsibility for their own condition in that they refused (often sensibly) to be moved to different cells. When CDCR's cynical and vindictive implementation of Justice Kline's order put the petitioners in an impossible situation, they portrayed themselves as trying to help and petitioners as kneecapping their own well-being.

This perverse behavior was bolstered by the expectation that it would be not only tolerated but also rewarded on appeal. That the attorney general's staff spent taxpayer money not only appealing the decisions but also attempting to *obliterate* them, even when they had no practical implications, was breathtaking. In *Von Staich*, this manifested itself in the unheard-of request to *depublish* the decision after it had already been reversed; in *re Hall*, it was a declarative decision offering no operative relief for the prisoners. It is as if the very whisper of an Eighth Amendment violation in writing was anathema to the state.

The government's position was rife with hypocrisy. Governor Newsom's support of the prison guards' appeal against the vaccine mandate flew in the face of his position on vaccination in other congregate settings, including schools.[119] In his public appearances while the appeal was pending, Newsom extolled vaccine mandates as a shining example of his "science forward" approach.[120] The bitter fruit of this inconsistency was predictable: antimasker protesters asked Newsom why, if he did not require people working with criminals to become vaccinated, he required it of their children.[121]

It is tempting, and not difficult, to speculate about the reason for this inconsistency. In November 2021, shortly after Judge Tigar's vaccination order in *Plata*, Newsom withstood—and survived—a recall challenge. His campaign was partly funded by $1.75 million in contributions from the CCPOA.[122]

The attorney general's hypocrisy was also in plain view. As an assemblymember from San Mateo, Rob Bonta urged Governor Newsom to provide relief; a year and a half later, Bonta, now California's attorney general, appealed both the state and the federal cases. When pressed on his hypocrisy by CalMatters journalists, he explained that his role as public official (presumably to urge vaccinations and protect Californians) differed from his role as advocate, telling the journalist, "I have a client."[123]

This approach raises serious questions about the attorney general's professional and ethical obligations. Can, and should, the attorney general wear two separate hats when supporting legislation and in litigation, as a government agency's attorney? Bonta's behavior recalls a previous attorney general, Kamala Harris, who declined to defend Proposition 8, an amendment to the Constitution of California passed by voter initiative, because the amendment forbade same-sex marriage.[124] Harris explained that Proposition

8 "violate[d] the Constitution. The Supreme Court has described marriage as a fundamental right 14 times since 1888. The time has come for this right to be afforded to every citizen." In the face of modest, legally sound, and practically advisable legal decisions, Bonta chose to defend the indefensible by pursuing appeals that not only display a shocking moral eclipse but are also wasteful and impractical: Judge Tigar's guard vaccination order was extremely narrow, and Judge Howard's decision did not even offer the petitioners relief. Government lawyers who pursued these legal avenues knew full well that their behavior would be tolerated, and that appellate courts stood guard to reverse decisions that offered even a faint threat to the correctional status quo.

Fetishizing Consensus

Another important common factor was the judicial psychology that characterized most of the proceedings (excluding Justice Kline's impatience with the state's dawdling at the Court of Appeal). Judge Tigar's ongoing management of the *Plata* CMCs might have been a masterful exercise in consensus building, had there been any chance of it. In the face of poor behavior, obfuscation, and unacceptable support for indefensible staff behavior, he continued treating the staff's representatives in a kind, welcoming manner, perhaps hoping that his civility would garner cooperation; he indulged their staunch opposition to vaccine mandates by faithfully and continuously pursuing gentle suasion methods long after their futility was obvious. Judge Tigar's constant explanations that orders were a poor way to manage complex litigation (likely true in other contexts) were continuously refuted by reality: anything except orders had been tried and found unsuccessful.

Similarly, Judge Howard ran the evidentiary hearing with flexibility and deference to the schedule of prison officials, including the warden—a condemnable practice in many other scenarios, but not in a situation that involved live testimony from busy experts, medical professionals, and incarcerated people.

Justice Delayed Is Justice Denied

Finally, both cases illustrate the perverse effects of the passage of time. All the judges were shocked by the tragedies they were exposed to, and surely all of them realized that urgency was the only way to save lives (recall Justice

Kline's sentiment that "[w]e must act hastily!"). But the litigation structure was not conducive to emergency management. In both cases, the lengthy delays worked cruelly in favor of the state and against incarcerated people. In *Plata*, the two turning points—the advent of vaccination and the high vaccine acceptance rate among incarcerated people—significantly narrowed the scope of the proceeding, to the state's benefit. In *Von Staich* and *Hall*, the delays allowed the virus to ravage the prison, ironically helping the state's case because population reductions could not address damage that had already occurred. Far from innocent bystanders, the state's representatives knowingly exploited these delays by allowing CDCR to engage in vindictive, perverse tactics (such as the threat of forced transfers) and exploiting the new factual situations to absolve their clients from accountability. After the fact, the state was content to pursue appellate proceedings, depublication requests, and order stays, purely to serve CDCR's organizational vanity.

Against the macro-level backdrop of Garrett, Kovarsky, Schlanger, and Dolovich's works, the stories of *Plata* and *Hall* demonstrate how the broad trends they identified played out in specific locations, underscoring that the real problem is not statutory scaffolding but rather the punitive animus and zero-sum thinking that underlies it. Perhaps, paraphrasing Tolstoy, each unhappy correctional system is unhappy in its own unique way, but the commonalities between the federal and the state procedures suggest that the hostility transcends jurisdictional boundaries. It is striking that well-intentioned, ethical, and conscientious federal and state judges—all of whom were openly shocked and grieved by the horrors of the COVID-19 catastrophe—can be swept and manipulated by correctional agencies and their legal representatives, thwarting their compassion when it was so sorely needed.

SEVEN

———

Fear and Loathing

Afterward Moses and Aaron came, and said to Pharaoh, "This is what Yahweh, the God of Israel, says, 'Let my people go, that they may hold a feast to me in the wilderness.'"

Pharaoh said, "Who is Yahweh, that I should listen to his voice to let Israel go? I don't know Yahweh, and moreover I will not let Israel go."

They said, "The God of the Hebrews has met with us. Please let us go three days' journey into the wilderness, and sacrifice to Yahweh, our God, lest he fall on us with pestilence, or with the sword."

The king of Egypt said to them, "Why do you, Moses and Aaron, take the people from their work? Get back to your burdens!"

EXODUS 5:1–4

ONE BY ONE, THE RECTANGLES on the Zoom screen lit up. Chill lounge music played in the background as the newcomers greeted each other in the chat window. A few dark rectangles represented people calling in from their cars, from their jobs, as they walked and ran errands. At 10:30 a.m., Isa Borgeson, smiling warmly, greeted the participants. "Hi, everyone. We're gonna wait a few more minutes. Meanwhile you can check in by drawing an emoji of how you feel today." Most of the participants took Isa up on the suggestion, drawing smileys or frowning faces on pieces of paper and holding them up to the screen. Elliot Hosman volunteered to take notes.

James King was ready for this conversation. The state campaigner for the Ella Baker Center for Human Rights, he had friends inside; moreover, his memories of his own long incarceration period were vivid. It hadn't been COVID-19 then, but rather other contagions: valley fever, Legionnaires' disease, bad colds and flus that spread like wildfire across the prison. Su, from UnCommon Law, was ready as well; the uphill battle that would be waged in the following months was familiar to her, because her organization, led by experienced attorney Keith Wattley, focused on helping parole hopefuls prevail at their hearings. Many others on the call had experienced health care in prison either firsthand or through their loved ones—husbands, boyfriends, sons, some in general population and some on death row. They were determined to save lives; when Isa asked, "What is your goal?," many replied, "To free them all."

#FreeThemAll would become the rallying cry of the #StopSanQuentinOutbreak coalition. They would be facing inertia, concerns about political optics, the despair of loved ones inside, and mostly an ethos of fear and loathing, hostile to the idea of releases—stemming from a paradoxical triangle of aging, violence, and risk.

Readers of the previous chapter might be forgiven for focusing their outrage and frustration on the courts. However, as the history of prison conditions struggles demonstrates, courts are not the sole (or even optimal) address for remedying such harms. Sharon Dolovich has observed that the governmental tendency to capitulate to the interests of correctional institutions is far from limited to the judiciary.[1] Indeed, the gubernatorial prison-release strategies of the pandemic era were characterized by the same type of capitulation, hypocrisy, and dawdling.

In previous work, Hadar attributed the paralysis characterizing the reluctance to parole, pardon, or administratively release a considerable percentage of the prison population to deep misunderstandings of the nature of the relationship between age and violence.[2] Aging and frail inmates—previously an ignored demographic—have recently drawn interest because of the heightened costs of their incarceration[3] and their low reoffending risks. Life-course criminologists consistently find that people age out of violent crime, though the trajectory of desistance varies.[4] This high-cost/low-risk equation poses a strong argument against lengthy incarceration of elderly and frail inmates; while this argument is partly humanitarian,[5] it also reflects concerns about prison health-care expenses,[6] exacerbated by the growth of the elderly and infirm prison population.[7]

Aging people are the fastest-growing demographic in US prisons. Between 1999 and 2008, the number of prisoners aged 55 and older increased by 76 percent (from 43,300 to 76,400), while the entire prison population increased by only 18 percent.[8] Despite state efforts to ameliorate this trend, it persisted throughout the recession.[9] The graying of the prison population is a function of two factors: the rising numbers of inmates entering prison at older ages[10] and, more influentially, the advent of tough sentencing laws and harsh parole revocation policies. Twenty percent of prisoners between the ages of 61 and

70 are serving sentences of more than 20 years (not including life sentences), compared to 11.4 percent of prisoners aged 31 to 40.[11] State lifers' numbers between 1984 and 2008 ballooned from 34,000 to 140,610, to the point that one in 10 to 11 people in a state prison is serving a life sentence. Federally, the number of lifers grew from 410 in 1998 to 4,222 in 2009.[12] Of federal prisoners aged 51 or older, Human Rights Watch[13] estimates that 11 percent are serving sentences ranging from 30 years to life. The long prison sentences are mostly correlated with violent offenses. A higher percentage of older prisoners (by contrast to younger offenders) were serving state sentences for violent crimes (65.3 percent vs. 49.6 percent), reflecting a "stacking phenomenon": people enter the system but do not leave it at nearly the same rates.[14]

Studies in prison gerontology identify a pattern of ignorance and neglect. Despite the decline in overall prison population in the recession's aftermath, the share of people requiring costly health care has risen to nearly 10 percent of the prison population.[15] Quality health care is unavailable, not only in prison but also upon release. Ignorance about this problem is prevalent: a survey of criminal justice professionals—judges, prosecutors, defense attorneys, and court-affiliated social workers—revealed knowledge deficits regarding age-related health, identification of cognitive impairment, assessment of safety risk, and optimization of services upon release from jail.[16] These problems, compounded with people's fragility and the unsuitability of prison facilities, inhibit the provision of health care, be it pain alleviation[17] or palliative care.[18]

The graying prison population is reflected not only in prison entry but also at the exit door—in terms of parole denials and parole revocations. Since the 1970s, political winds and legislative changes have effectively transformed parole in most US states from an instrument of hope to an almost unattainable goal, blurring the difference between life with and without parole.[19] California's modern parole process reflects a shift away from professional, clinical assessments of rehabilitation and risk, focused mostly on the applicant's postrelease prospects, to a populistic, emotional, victim-driven focus on the crime of commitment. The shift, which occurred between the late 1970s and the 1990s, was a function of the decline of rehabilitation as a correctional ideal,[20] the encroachment of determinate sentencing policies and the resulting rise in prosecutorial influence on all stages of the criminal process,[21] the rise of the victims' rights movement as a punitive moral entrepreneur,[22] and the cautionary tales of violent, heinous crimes with high emotional valence.[23] This shift, and subsequent changes in California sentencing and prison composition,[24] have limited the Board of Parole Hearings' authority[25] mostly to people serving life sentences for serious crimes[26] such as homicide or kidnapping[27]—an "island" of indeterminate sentencing within the overall determinate sentencing scheme.[28] Therefore, parole commissioners—political appointees, almost all former law enforcement officers[29]—retain control over the fate of a large population: according to CDCR's annual report, in 2019 there were 27,115 people serving a life-with-parole sentence and 6,817 serving a life sentence pursuant to the Three Strikes Law, amounting together to 27 percent of the entire prison population.[30]

The connection between aging and parole flows directly from this political turn. Lifers become eligible for parole consideration within a year of their minimum eligible parole date (MEPD),[31] which, for people who committed their crime before November 8, 1978, is 7 years, and for people who committed later crimes, 25 and 15 years, respectively, for first-degree and second-degree murder.[32] The rate of denial is very high: over 1,800 people appear before the board annually, and approximately 80 percent are denied parole.[33] The CDCR website explicitly states that "these inmates are sentenced to the possibility of parole, not the assurance of it, recognizing that their maximum potential sentence is life."[34] Additionally, following the passage of a 2008 voter initiative known as Marsy's Law, any parole denial carries a presumptive wait of 15 years before the next hearing unless the board finds by clear and convincing evidence that public safety can be served by a shorter deferral period[35] of 3, 5, 7, or 10 years.[36] Sometimes, when the applicant expects a parole denial, the wise choice is to defer the hearing and invest in preparing a strong record for a future date.[37] Finally, even applicants whom the board recommends for parole might be denied parole via a gubernatorial veto.[38] Consequentially, the time spent behind bars before parole has increased dramatically, from an average of 12 years in 1980 to 28 years in 2012—and even this data point is misleading, because the statistics factor in only people who were ultimately released.[39]

Title 15 of the California Code of Regulations requires the board to grant parole unless "consideration of the public safety requires a lengthier period of incarceration."[40] For this purpose, "all relevant, reliable information available to the panel shall be considered in determining suitability for parole."[41] Such information includes

[c]ircumstances of the prisoner's social history; past and present mental state; past criminal history, including involvement in other criminal misconduct

which is reliably documented; the base and other commitment offenses, including behavior before, during, and after the crime; past and present attitude toward the crime; any conditions of treatment or control, including the use of special conditions under which the prisoner may safely be released to the community; and any other information which bears on the prisoner's suitability for release.[42]

Within this rudimentary statutory framework, the board is vested with ample discretion.[43] Title 15 lists some circumstances "tending" to show unsuitability,[44] including a crime of commitment perpetrated in a "heinous, atrocious or cruel" manner. Per the California Supreme Court's 2008 decision *In re Lawrence*,[45] the heinousness of the crime is not sufficient ground for parole denial; there must be actual evidence of "current dangerousness."[46] In a companion decision, *In re Shaputis*,[47] the court clarified that the crime of commitment could still be one consideration among several. It is therefore permissible to deny parole to those who, in addition to the "cruel and heinous" nature of their crime, do not show sufficient "insight" into why they committed the crime.

The "insight" inquiry—vague and subjective—is a central consideration at parole hearings and generally encompasses a coherent account of the crime, a genuine expression of remorse, and a personal transformation. The malleability of insight authorizes the board to deduce sincerity, authenticity, and transformation from the applicant's words, deeds, or even body language, without having to provide falsifiable evidence as to this determination. Moreover, the vagueness of "insight" liberates the board from the constraints of consistency and opens the possibility that the determination of insight, or lack thereof, will reflect implicit prejudices and biases, cultural or otherwise. Most importantly for our purposes, the flexibility of "insight" traverses past, present, and future, protecting the board from judicial review if they deduce its absence from the crime of commitment.

These parole logics, juxtaposed with the graying of the prison population, exemplify the age-violence-risk triangle at its most problematic. At the point when parole applicants appear before the board, they have already served lengthy prison sentences, which, of course, are meted for serious, violent crimes. These violent crimes fit the "heinous and cruel" rubric (what homicide is not "heinous and cruel"?) and can therefore demonstrate "lack of insight." Simultaneously, due to the same long sentences and unsuccessful hearings, parole hopefuls behind bars age more rapidly than their cohort on the outside. Older parole applicants pose an extremely low risk of reoffending: a robust body of literature in life-course criminology demonstrates that people age out of violent crime in their mid-20s and hardly ever recidivate in their 50s.[48]

The deep reluctance to release aging, infirm people who pose little to no recidivism risk was, to some extent, retrenched by the recession-era tendency to settle for milquetoast, publicly acceptable reforms.[49] As we explained above, these reforms—including, of course, Realignment—targeted people convicted of low-level crimes.[50] This bifurcated reform approach[51] reflected two separate but related logics: the idea that "violent offenders"—viewed as a monolith[52]—deserve whatever they get, by contrast to "nonviolent offenders," and the mistaken equation of the violence/nonviolence of the crime of conviction with risk of future criminal activity.[53]

This philosophy was, in part, the fruit of recession-era bipartisanism, which included libertarian concerns about overenforcement, the costs of incarceration, and the excesses of criminalizing minutiae.[54] But bifurcation is the exclusive creation of centrists and libertarians: it was fueled by popular progressive commentators, whose main concern was the racial effect of the war on drugs.[55] It was only years later, as critics of the bifurcation approach pointed out that mass incarceration is not solely, or even predominantly, drug-related incarceration,[56] that the progressive tune changed to encompass people convicted of violent crime.[57]

The age-violence-risk triangle would come to characterize the Newsom administration's pandemic relief approach. As we saw, in litigation, the state resisted not only releases but also far more modest requests: vaccine prioritization and vaccine mandates for staff. The same animus would emanate from the executive branch.

On July 9, 2020, as the outbreak in San Quentin encompassed more than a thousand cases and claimed dozens of lives, the #StopSanQuentinOutbreak coalition held a press conference outside the prison gate.[58] The event was emceed by Adnan Khan, director of the nonprofit Re:Store Justice, the driving force behind California's felony murder reform while he was still behind bars. Epidemiologist Peter Chin-Hong, a regular media commentator on COVID-19, spoke first; to applause from doctors and medical students, many of them from White Coats for Black Lives, he stated simply, "prisons are incompatible with health." San Francisco's progressive district attorney, Chesa Boudin (who would later be recalled), spoke, as did public defenders Mano Raju and Brendon Woods. Several legislators attended and spoke: Marc Levine, Ash Kalra, Scott Weiner, and Rob Bonta, then a progressive

FIGURE 13. #StopSanQuentinOutbreak press conference. *From left:* Scott Weiner, Chesa Boudin, Hadar Aviram, Marc Levine, Rob Bonta (courtesy of Brooke Anderson).

assemblymember from San Mateo County. Bonta, who would later be appointed as California's attorney general and would staunchly support prison administration and the prison guards' union, spoke so movingly that he was quoted by the *Guardian*:

> "We are in the middle of a humanitarian crisis that was created and wholly avoidable," said the California assembly member Rob Bonta at a press conference in front of San Quentin state prison on Thursday.
>
> "We need [to] act with urgency fueled by compassion," he added. "We missed the opportunity to prevent, so now we have to make things right."[59]

James King, Adnan Khan, and Eddie Zheng, all of whom had considerable experience behind bars, spoke about the pathogenic conditions and about previous epidemics; they had many friends behind bars and read aloud heart-wrenching letters received from inside. Among the speakers were also family members of those behind bars. Shawanda Scott spoke of the loving home waiting for her son, in an effort to shatter the perception that released people would have nowhere to go. James King, too, emphasized: "the minute they are released . . . tens of thousands of families will be here at the gate to welcome them with open arms." Marion Wickerd reported about prison conditions as experienced by her husband, Tommy: lack of protective equipment, sluggish testing schedule, senseless transfers.

Newsom, who had been invited to attend and urged by several speakers to tour the prisons and see the conditions for himself, was absent. Notably, speakers with loved ones inside did not express spite or rancor toward the governor. They all stressed that they were not interested in blame, only in saving their loved ones from illness and death.

The coalition authored a letter to Newsom,[60] detailing numerous strategies that would enable him to considerably reduce the prison population. The letter asked Newsom to stop all ICE transfers from prisons and jails and to grant pardons to recently released people at risk of deportation (as of May 2020, 9,512 people in CDCR custody were subjected to ICE holds). It also invited Newsom to "strengthen the Death Penalty moratorium by ending LWOP—a living death sentence—and commuting all LWOP and Death Penalty sentences to life sentences with immediate eligibility for parole review," a move that would affect 706 death row residents and 5,200 lifers. Another proposal was to review for commutation all cases of survivors of intimate partner violence.

The letter also urged Newsom to expedite the release of people who had already been found suitable for parole (1,000 people in total) and to reconsider the cases of a few hundred people whose parole he either vetoed or referred to court for an en banc review. In addition, the coalition proposed expediting the release of people who were medically vulnerable to COVID-19 and eligible for medical and elderly parole (50,000 with at least one risk factor for severe complications and death from the COVID-19 virus; 25 percent of the prison population, who are aged 50 years or older; and 1,400 people eligible for medical and/or elderly parole in 2019, whose number was significantly expanded by policy reforms in 2020).

The letter identified additional attractive candidates for release: people eligible for early parole under California's Proposition 57 and youth offender parole hearings (10,000 and 6,000, respectively); people with homecoming dates within a year who were serving "enhancement time" (at least 25,000); 52 percent of the prison population deemed "low risk" by CDCR's own standards; and the 10,000 people serving time for parole violations.

At the height of the San Quentin outbreak, *San Francisco Chronicle* journalist Jason Fagone, a member of the team that reported about the botched CIM-to-San-Quentin transfer, was inundated with phone calls from prison, as well as from family members and loved ones. He set out to examine the practical feasibility of the coalition's suggestions and concluded:

The state has the power. The main obstacle is political: Three-fourths of all prisoners have been convicted of violent acts. This means that decarcerating the state system by 50% would require the release of large numbers of people convicted of violent crimes. Is it possible to do that safely? A wealth of evidence suggests that the answer, again, is yes. All it would require is a fresh look at the data. And some political courage.[61]

A plan was, indeed, forthcoming from the governor's mansion, but political courage would be in short supply. The day after the coalition's press conference at the San Quentin gate, Newsom's office announced plans to release 8,000 people,[62] mostly by pushing out people whose release was imminent anyway: 4,800 release candidates had merely 180 days left on their sentences. The plan excluded anyone serving a sentence for violence or domestic violence or registered as a sex offender. A further undetermined number of people with a year left on their sentence and a nonviolent, nonsexual conviction would be released if serving their sentence at a prison identified at the time as a pandemic epicenter. Those aged 30 and over would be immediately eligible; younger people would be reviewed case by case by the parole board, which was entrusted with the execution of Newsom's program.

In addition, the plan would hasten the release of anyone not on death row or serving life without parole with a clean disciplinary record since March 1, 2020 (when, as explained in chapter 2, many people incurred disciplinary write-ups for merely trying to socially distance or refusing life-threatening cell transfers) by granting them a 12-week programming credit. "Serious rules violations" would encompass anything from murder to possession of a smuggled cell phone. This category encompassed 108,000 people, 2,100 of whom would be eligible for release in the summer of 2020.

One of the most surprising aspects of the plan was its modesty regarding populations that, medically speaking, should have been the easiest and most plausible cases for release: people over 65 years old with a chronic medical condition or with respiratory illnesses. Out of this population, those assessed as low risk for violence who were not on death row, serving life without parole, or high-risk sex offenders would be assessed for release on an individual basis. CDCR also would assess for release people in hospice or pregnant, and expedite release for people who have been granted parole.

The total number of projected releases under this plan, 8,000, was a mere drop in the bucket—no more than 6 percent of the prison population in summer 2020, and much fewer than the 50 percent population reduction recommended by the AMEND physicians in their report on conditions in San

Quentin. Systemwide, the July 8, 2020, population count put 26 facilities—24 for men, 2 for women—at beyond design capacity, with 9 of them morbidly overpopulated (above the 137.5 percent *Plata* standard) and 10 of them more than 120 percent overcrowded. Releasing 8,000 people would not come close to enabling the social distancing necessary to halt pandemic spread.

The plan was also proposed far too late and was too reactive. Given the warnings and forecasts described in chapter 1, case-by-case parole reviews might have been useful in early March 2020, but by the summer, the prison system did not have the luxury of time for individualized consideration. Moreover, the list of pandemic epicenters was dated at its inception: on the day it was published, new outbreaks occurred in several facilities. The plan was based on COVID-19 test results, which did not truly reflect pandemic rates, as several prisons that reported apparent abatement in infections had brought their testing programs to a grinding halt.

Most importantly, the governor's program was overly sensitive to public backlash and featured the classic hallmarks of the age-violence-risk paradox. Bifurcation—applying early releases and good time credits only to nonserious, nonviolent, nonsexual offenses—was in evidence in every category in the plan, despite the lack of correlation between the crime of commitment and the risk to public safety.

At first blush, such kowtowing to public outcry would seem uncharacteristic of Newsom, whose political path, from his early days as mayor of San Francisco, featured bold, high-profile moves to advance progressive values, which he presented as doing the right thing no matter the backlash. His leadership in legalizing same-sex marriage in California—the subject of ferocious litigation that culminated in a Supreme Court victory—was wrongly predicted by some, at the time, to be political suicide.[63] Similarly, his moratorium on the death penalty was criticized for not reflecting the wish of a small but consistent majority of Californians.[64] In both cases, Newsom correctly read the political winds, and his predictions proved true; his self-styled image as an idealistic pioneer was boosted by the fact that his executive decisions preceded wider societal shifts. But Newsom's reluctance to release people convicted of violent crime reflected age-old wisdom in California politics that, even in the bluest of counties, it is not a wise political move to flout entrenched fears of violent crime. Reflective of the justifiability of this concern was a disparaging story in the *Los Angeles Times* about Newsom's plan titled "California Is Releasing Some Murderers due to COVID-19. Some Say It Should Free More."[65] After a barrage of phone calls from coalition

Prisoners released early for COVID reasons

A total of 7,483 prisoners have had their release expedited by the California state prison system for COVID reasons since July 1.

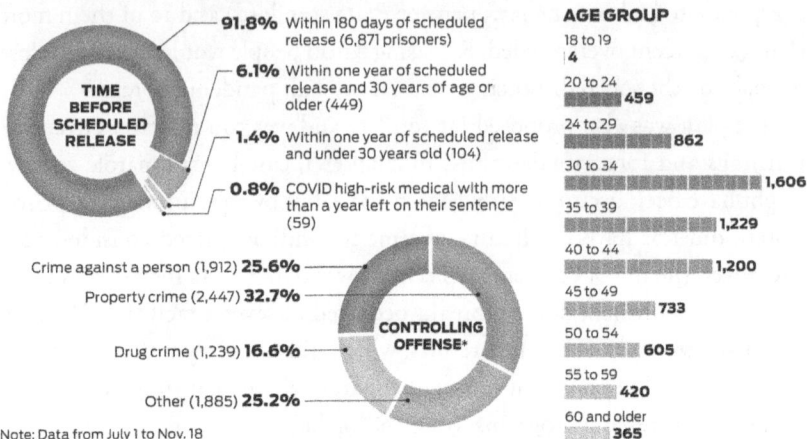

TIME BEFORE SCHEDULED RELEASE

- **91.8%** Within 180 days of scheduled release (6,871 prisoners)
- **6.1%** Within one year of scheduled release and 30 years of age or older (449)
- **1.4%** Within one year of scheduled release and under 30 years old (104)
- **0.8%** COVID high-risk medical with more than a year left on their sentence (59)

CONTROLLING OFFENSE*

- Crime against a person (1,912) **25.6%**
- Property crime (2,447) **32.7%**
- Drug crime (1,239) **16.6%**
- Other (1,885) **25.2%**

AGE GROUP

Age	Count
18 to 19	4
20 to 24	459
24 to 29	862
30 to 34	1,606
35 to 39	1,229
40 to 44	1,200
45 to 49	733
50 to 54	605
55 to 59	420
60 and older	365

Note: Data from July 1 to Nov. 18
* Crime for which any sentencing court imposed the longest term of imprisonment
Source: California Department of Corrections and Rehabilitation

Todd Trumbull / The Chronicle

FIGURE 14. Prisoners released early for COVID-19 reasons (courtesy of *San Francisco Chronicle*).

members, the newspaper changed the headline, but the content, which rehearsed tired tough-on-crime tropes from the Reagan administration days, remained unaltered: the writers chose to interview crime victims who, while entitled to their personal opinions, were neither the statewide curators of victims' perspectives nor qualified to be the ultimate arbiters of emergency health-care policies. They also mentioned, without a shred of irony, Willie Horton.

As of mid-September 2020, the promised releases had not brought the hoped-for relief. The prison population was reduced to 96,827, but more than half of CDCR institutions were still overcrowded, with others hovering at or near 100 percent capacity. Only in mid-November did *San Francisco Chronicle* journalist Nora Mishanec succeed in obtaining a demographic breakdown of the thousands of people who were released under Newsom's plan.

Between July 1 and November 18, CDCR claimed to have released 7,483 people. The population counts revealed that the population was reduced from 113,292 in July[66] to 97,891 in mid-November.[67] The difference (15,401) was partly due to the summer release plan, and partly due to the cessation of transfers from county jails (which, as explained in chapter 3, caused countless COVID-19 problems on the county level). More importantly, the numbers reflected the weakness of Newsom's plan. Most people who had been released had only months left on their sentence back in early July and, by December, would have been released anyway. Only 0.8 percent of the people who were released were deemed "COVID high-risk medical," when a full quarter of the population on the eve of the pandemic were aged 50 and over. This outcome, absurd from a medical standpoint, was due to the principle that guided Newsom's entire plan: people aged 50 and older are disproportionately serving sentences for violent crimes, and thus, as we saw, were explicitly excluded.[68]

Three stories of such aging, low-risk people exemplify the role that optics and public perception played in the Newsom administration's calculus. Twice during the pandemic, the parole board recommended parole for Leslie Van Houten, born in 1950 and housed at the California Institution for Women (CIW). Van Houten had been consistently recommended for parole since 2017, but governors—first Brown, now Newsom—kept reversing the recommendation for what appeared to be, considering her exemplary prison record, pure political spite. Throughout her incarceration, Van Houten maintained a clean disciplinary record, participated in a variety of laudable programs, and incessantly excavated her psyche to show "insight" to the board. She participated in the Manson murders when she was 19 years old, manipulated and sexually exploited in a setting that, with today's #MeToo sensibilities, might have shed a completely different light on her involvement.[69]

As Hadar has explained elsewhere,[70] the Manson family cases shine a light on the question of redeemability, featuring people who have clearly done their utmost to undergo, live, and exude transformation but whose notoriety stands in their way. But Van Houten's two last hearings featured an additional consideration: the parole hopeful was over 70 years old, and CIW, where she was housed, was experiencing an outbreak just as she was denied parole. It was only in 2023 that Van Houten was finally granted parole, an outcome obtained through litigation that reversed Newsom's veto. Newsom took the trouble to publicly criticize the decision.[71]

Another notorious member of the "Class of '72"—the 107 people condemned to death whose sentences were commuted to life with parole after *People v. Anderson*[72]—was Sirhan Sirhan, who had assassinated Robert Kennedy. At the time of his COVID parole hearing, Sirhan was 77 years old. The *Chronicle*'s Bob Egelko forecasted his parole bid:[73]

"Anybody that has ever walked into my office, you have to walk by photographs of Bobby Kennedy's funeral procession, those famous train photos," the governor said, according to a transcript provided by his office. "The first photograph, the only photograph you will see in my office is a photo of my father and Bobby Kennedy just days before Bobby Kennedy was murdered."

At the time of Sirhan's parole bid, Newsom was facing a recall election in which he had everything to lose, and absolutely nothing to gain, from releasing Sirhan. As Egelko explained, Newsom's leading opponents in the recall, all of whom were well to his right politically, would seem equally unlikely to approve Sirhan's parole. Moreover, any decision to release Kennedy's murderer would surely become a flash point in the 2022 gubernatorial election. Predictably, Newsom vetoed Sirhan's parole and, perhaps hoping to win political points while facing a recall election, took the trouble to pen an op-ed about it in the *Los Angeles Times*:[74]

> Kennedy's assassination not only changed the course of this nation and robbed the world of a promising young leader, it also left his 11 children without a father and his wife without a husband. Kennedy's family bears his loss every day. Millions of Americans lost a unifier in a time of national turmoil and grief, just nine weeks after the assassination of the Rev. Martin Luther King, Jr., and four-and-a-half years after the murder of Kennedy's brother, President John F. Kennedy.
>
> Yet, after decades in prison, Sirhan still lacks the insight that would prevent him from making the kind of dangerous and destructive decisions he made in the past. The most glaring proof of Sirhan's deficient insight is his shifting narrative about his assassination of Kennedy, and his current refusal to accept responsibility for it.

The language in Newsom's op-ed echoes the aforementioned concept of "insight," which parole researchers broadly agree is a deliberately opaque, vague term used to justify denials based on the now-prohibited consideration of the heinousness of the original crime.[75]

But the absurdities in Van Houten's and Sirhan's cases pale in comparison with the continued incarceration of Gerald Albert Oates, who, at the age of 94, is the oldest living person incarcerated at CDCR. After a parole denial in 2018 because, unbelievably, Oates is still categorized as "high risk" by CDCR,[76] he remained incarcerated throughout the COVID-19 crisis, apparently surviving the Newsom administration's project to identify priorities for release. Oates's case highlights the extent to which the calcification of fear and loathing of people convicted of violent crime stood in the way of making sound parole decisions during the pandemic.

Finally, any modicum of release provided by Newsom's plan would be short-lived. Figure 15 depicts the CDCR population throughout 2021. As of

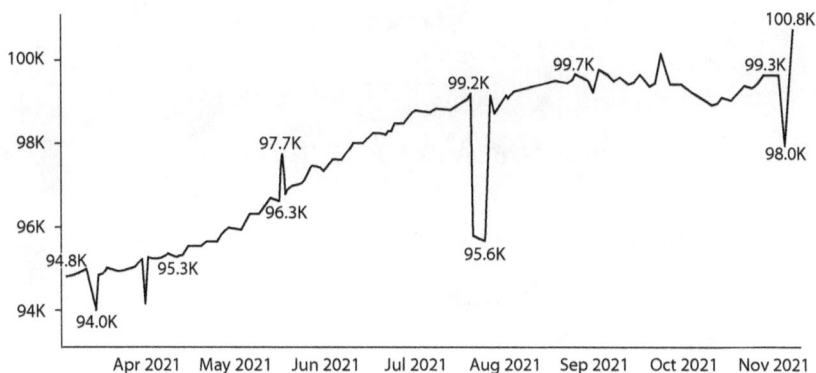

FIGURE 15. CDCR population, April–November 2021 (CDCR).

late 2021, the population again exceeded 100,000 people, likely due to incoming people from county facilities and completely eclipsing the 2020 releases.

Entrusting two entities—the governor and the parole board—with releases during a medical emergency would seem to be a good idea given how slow and ineffective litigation channels had been in providing relief; recall that the attorney general representatives argued as much in *Plata* as well as in *Hall*. But this perspective fails to consider how habituated these two entities are to their roles as gatekeepers and deniers of freedom. Expecting them to act differently in the face of serious threats to life and health was a pipe dream.

These disappointing solutions in the face of a dangerous pandemic, which sickened more than half of the prison population and killed 260 incarcerated people, suggest that *Plata* and *Hall* are not anomalies. These judges and political officials are not comic book villains; they are caught in a habitual thought pattern that regards the prospect of population reduction as a threat to the system's very existence, leading courts to coddle and defer to prison authorities even when lives are at stake. They fail to see the geographic continuum between prisons and surrounding communities because years of exclusion have made it unimaginable for incarcerated people to actually be part of these communities. On both the litigation and executive action fronts, this is a tragically missed opportunity to learn from the virus about our common humanity and foster true solidarity among people on the inside and the outside of the prison gate.

EIGHT

The Next Plague

When Israel was in Egypt's land,
Let my people go!
Oppressed so hard they could not stand,
Let my people go!

Go down, Moses,
Way down in Egypt's land;
Tell old Pharaoh
To let my people go!

ANONYMOUS, ADAPTED FROM EXODUS 5:1

ON AUGUST 5, 2022, the *San Francisco Chronicle* reported the first case of mpox, previously known as monkeypox, within the county jails.[1] This report was a grim reminder that the question of pandemic protection within California's correctional facilities is indeed, as Judge Howard predicted in *Hall,* "a question of general public interest which is likely to recur." We have seen that, under pressure to act swiftly, neither the courts nor the executive actors took the necessary steps to save lives; as we recover from the devastation of COVID-19, it is time to take stock and consider in advance how to prevent the next plague from spreading like wildfire.

At the root of the pandemic prevention failure lies the myth of prison impermeability. Politicians, courts, prison administrators, and the public have operated under the assumption that prisons can be effectively cordoned off from the outside community. This book attests that nothing can be further from the truth. We saw the futility of sealing off prisons from surrounding counties precisely when a joint preventative strategy, treating the entire region as a geographic continuum, would have benefited everyone, on the inside and on the outside. We saw the chain reaction of outbreaks caused by jurisdictionally separating prisons from jails. Even when prison wings, or entire prisons, are placed under lockdown to prevent outbreaks, quarantinism results in other forms of pathology: anxiety, terror, and mental health setbacks for incarcerated people, not to mention the impact on their families.

Obtuseness to prison permeability may be a product of the United States' national culture: in other countries, the gates of the prison are more readily acknowledged, if not embraced (sometimes in a sinister way: Gary Moore, commenting on the destructive impact of home visits and easy prison escapes on Mexican cartel activity, refers to the local prisons as "Swiss cheese"[2]). But the sobering outcomes of the crisis compel, in our opinion, a crucial revision of some of the field's most established metaphors. Erving Goffman's "total institutions" concept was pioneering in the 1950s, when ethnographic research in prisons opened windows into the unique features of these types of institutions;[3] research conducted during that era drew attention to the unique acclimation to prison culture,[4] the endemic forms of suffering associated with the loss of liberty,[5] the rigid constraints of inmate-staff relationships, complete with role-playing,[6] and the formation of the prison economy.[7] The immense value of these contributions is not diminished by the acknowledgment that many of these observed phenomena essentially map normal, rational (within bounds) human behavior and adaptation mechanisms—and that an analysis of human behavior in prison can no longer be conducted through an isolative framework.

Similarly in need of spatial/geographic revision is Michel Foucault's concept of the "carceral archipelago,"[8] as well as many important works that were inspired by it. Ironically, Foucault tried to communicate the extent to which shifting the locus of discipline and control from centralized authorities' savagery of the body to the decentralized self-surveillance of the soul turns all of us—not just those whose physical confinement is most extreme—to targets of our own normalizing gaze.[9] This is not an "archipelago," where carceral islands are surrounded by water, but rather a continuous geographical landscape, where coercion and control vary only by degrees (albeit greatly sometimes). Similarly, the concept of prison permeability refines Malcolm Feeley and Jonathan Simon's "New Penology,"[10] in highlighting that sites of "selective incapacitation" are not impermeable silos but more akin to traffic lanes in which cars travel at different speeds, with frequent lane transitions and not-infrequent rest stops.

Revisiting the isolated, enclosed metaphors of the prison can benefit us in many important ways. In her critique of Goffman's paradigm, Rachel Ellis draws on her study of religion in a women's prison. She highlights a process she refers to as "institutional infusion": the extent to which the external concepts and resources of religious principles and life can be interpreted and implemented by people on the inside.[11] Coralynn V. Davis and Carol Wayne

White offer a reminder of the beneficial possibilities of prison education that brings together incarcerated and nonincarcerated college students.[12] Megan Comfort's work on family members of incarcerated people shows the impact that prison has on loved ones outside.[13] The entire field of reentry studies is premised on the notion that the vast majority of people behind bars will, eventually, come home and that a continuum of care and support is necessary.[14]

Sykes's famous "pains of imprisonment" and their many adaptations continue to matter in 21st-century prisons and must incorporate the spatial aspects of these pains as they unfold. The next plagues will produce more suffering along the lines we identified in chapter 2, and, at the very least, the loss of health and health care must be a cornerstone for any further analysis along those lines.

If prison scholars, who generally approach prison research with curiosity and open-mindedness, need an invitation to infuse more of their thinking with geography, certainly policymakers and the public do—but that requires a serious examination of social values, not just geographic literacy. As we have shown here, the myth of prison permeability is the offspring of ignorance infused with a sense that improved prison conditions somehow disadvantage people outside—yielding the tragic, but not unpredictable, formation of "pandemic policies of the self" and "pandemic policies of the other" that we mentioned in the introduction. It is essential to root out this poisonous moral approach by showing the many ways in which incorporating prison policy (conditions, population control, reentry considerations) as seamlessly as possible into overall governmental policy on the state and local level benefits everyone—not just those behind bars.

We follow up with practical policy suggestions, many of which have been made not only by prison scholars but also by community advocates and activists; these range from drastic cuts to the entire prison system—which, we believe, will not significantly erode public safety on the outside—to a variety of policy, administration, and litigation proposals.

CUT 50

Our most important and pressing recommendation is to immediately—before the next pandemic—reduce California's prison population to 50 percent of its current size. This is not an abolitionist fantasy; it is a practical,

8 WAYS TO STOP AN OUTBREAK

Governor Newsom must release people for the safety of all. Who can go home now?

50,000 PEOPLE HAVE 1+ HIGH RISK FACTOR FOR COVID

And there are thousands who have more than 4 risk factors for COVID. We must recognize that people facing severe health issues are not a threat to public safety and must be compassionately released to community.

60,000 PEOPLE HAVE "LOW RISK" SCORES & ARE READY FOR RELEASE ON PAROLE

50%

Why should we as a society spend $80,000/year to keep people in overcrowded and cruel congregate settings when they are fully prepared to reenter the community?

31,000 PEOPLE ARE WITHIN 1 YEAR OF RELEASE

It has never been more urgent that we avoid unnecessary delays in order to usher people to safety who have come to the end of their sentence and have received parole grants.

OVER 5,000 PEOPLE ARE OVER THE AGE OF 65

Our elderly loved ones lead our families and communities from inside. They've never been just a number to us. We are ready to receive them home, and to find homes through our network for anyone in need.

#CARENOTCAGES   #LETTHEMGO
#STOPSANQUENTINOUTBREAK
Read more at bit.ly/StopSanQuentinOutbreakDemands

8 WAYS TO STOP AN OUTBREAK

Governor Newsom must release people for the safety of all. Who can go home now?

2,000 PEOPLE ARE ELIGIBLE FOR RELEASE UNDER SB 1437

After decades of injustice - the "Felony Murder" rule has been repealed. It's time to acknowledge people who are serving unjust sentences should be released.

OVER 6,000 PEOPLE WERE UNDER THE AGE OF 26 WHEN THEY WENT IN

Science shows us that people's brains don't fully develop until the age of 25. While many people are excluded from Youth Offender Parole eligibility, everyone ages out of crime, and people change from the youth that they were.

10,000 PEOPLE SHOULD ALREADY BE HOME DUE TO PROPOSITION 57

For years, CDCR has delayed justice by creating criteria repeatedly struck down by the CA Supreme Court, and keeping people locked inside without real hearings and without logical grounds for the denials.

COMMUTE 6,000 PEOPLE WITH LWOP & DEATH SENTENCES TO PAROLE ELIGIBLE

We need mass releases without categorical exclusions, including for our community members on Death Row and who are serving Life Without Parole sentences. They are our elders, our leaders, our family. They have been dedicated to healing and change for decades despite their sentence. We love them and we will support a safe reentry for all.

#CARENOTCAGES   #LETTHEMGO
#STOPSANQUENTINOUTBREAK
Read more at bit.ly/StopSanQuentinOutbreakDemands

FIGURE 16. 8 Ways to Stop an Outbreak (courtesy of Elliot Hosman for the #StopSanQuentinOutbreak coalition).

eminently realistic strategy for saving lives on the inside and on the outside. Our propositions for accomplishing this in a relatively short period of time build on prison demographics, are shared by many people in the field with both personal and professional experience,[15] and draw on proposals made by the #StopSanQuentinOutbreak coalition, depicted in figure 16.

The main hurdle to accomplishing a large-scale population reduction is the politically expedient distinction between so-called violent and nonviolent offenders. One of the great successes of the Obama-era criminal justice advocacy was to bring the war on drugs to the forefront of the reform struggle; Michelle Alexander's popular book *The New Jim Crow*[16] focused on the ills of drug criminalization and prosecution because of their racially discriminatory origins and implications. But targeting people convicted of drug offenses for release while retrenching our approach toward people convicted of violent offenses will not make a dent in our prison population,[17] because most people in California prisons are serving time for a violent offense (see figure 18 below).

The relative proportions of violent crimes to drug crimes of conviction in the prison population are largely attributable to the reforms already accomplished in the aftermath of *Plata*. In 2020, before the pandemic, CDCR predicted a continuing but more modest population decline (see figure 17). If more significant impact is sought, there is no choice but to tackle the untapped, less politically expedient population: people serving long sentences for violent crime.

Releasing people convicted of violent crime should not result in significant rises in crime. Because of the political challenge of "selling" these categories of release, it is important to combat the public misperception that people convicted of violent offenses are inherently more dangerous than those convicted of less violent ones—which is provable with careful, proper use of risk assessment tools. As Susan Turner and Julie Gerlinger have shown, risk of reoffending is not correlated with the crime of commitment.[18] These findings suggest that, had we been willing to release people convicted of violent offenses, we may have been able to meet, and easily exceed, the *Plata* benchmarks through our three major population-reduction efforts—Realignment, Proposition 47, and Proposition 57—without compromising public safety.

How is this possible? Consider the low clearance rate of homicides in California (65,864 out of 112,762, or 58.41 percent).[19] A person's crime of commitment does not necessarily indicate their underlying criminal activity. Moreover, there are important intervening variables that influence risk con-

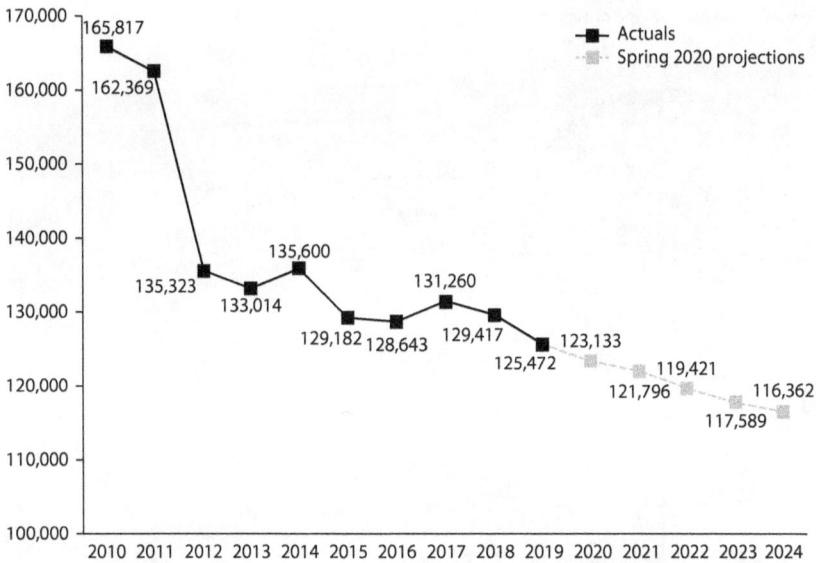

FIGURE 17. Population reductions—actual and projected (as of spring 2020) (CDCR).

siderably more than the crime of commitment: the person's age and the time that has passed since the commission of the crime. As we explained in chapter 7, a robust body of research in life-course criminology confirms that people largely age out of violent crime by their mid- to late 20s, and at 50 they pose a negligible risk to public safety. Emphasizing true criminogenic factors over false, political ones creates opportunities for releasing people who, while not risky release prospects themselves, *face* risks from contagion and illness behind bars.

Having addressed the violent/nonviolent bifurcation head on, a reasonable proposal for population reductions will tackle three partly overlapping populations: people designated "low risk" by CDCR's own admission, people who have already served extremely lengthy sentences, and people aged 50 or more. The first of these categories constitutes about half of CDCR's population, and even this may be a conservative estimate: the Legislative Analyst's Office (LAO) has found CDCR's risk classification method in dire need of an overhaul.[20] According to the LAO analysis, CDCR officials use their classification mostly for housing decisions, and their "low risk" category is too restrictive, unnecessarily relying on the crime of commitment as a factor. Again, the intervening variable that should be at the forefront of these decisions is age. Figure 18 tells a useful story about the gradual emergence of a large graying, low-risk contingent

Inmate population by type of offense

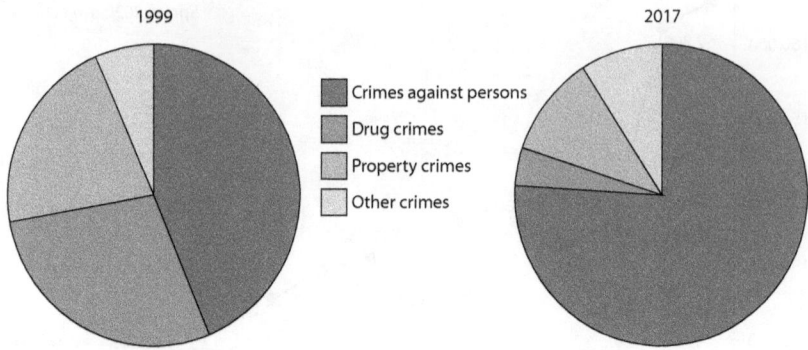

1999

2017

Crimes against persons
Drug crimes
Property crimes
Other crimes

Inmate population by age

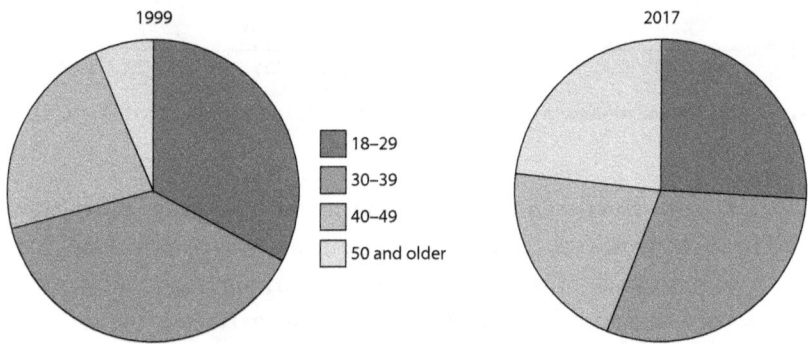

1999

2017

18–29
30–39
40–49
50 and older

FIGURE 18. Prison population demographics by type of offense and by age, 1999 and 2017 (Legislative Analyst's Office).

in California prisons: most of our prison population were convicted for violent crime, and a quarter of this population are 50 and older. Given the length of sentences for violent crimes, and the fact that a quarter of California prisoners have spent decades behind bars through one of the "extreme punishment trifecta" of sentences (death, life without parole, or life with parole),[21] it is not difficult to figure out where the older, lower-risk people fit in.

Releasing people over 50 would also make sense financially. According to the Public Policy Institute of California and Pew Center data they cite, in 2015 the state spent $19,796 per incarcerated person on health care—more than thrice the national average.[22]

These populations considerably overlap with yet another demographic meriting release: people who have already served very long sentences. This is the time to question the marginal utility of serving a few more years after being in prison for decades. According to the Public Policy Institute of California, about 33,000 incarcerated people are "second strikers," about 9,000 of whom are released annually after serving about 3.5 years. Another 7,000 are "third strikers," fewer than 100 of whom are released annually after serving about 17 years. Approximately 33,000 people currently serve sentences of life or life without parole. Fewer than 1,000 of these are released every year, typically after spending two or more decades behind bars.

To this group we can add a few smaller populations, numbering a few thousand each, including people on death row—whose chances of execution, with the death chamber dismantled, are nil, but whose expensive capital punishment litigation continues to siphon state funds—and people on life without parole, whose lengthy incarcerations might have already been ended if a serious inquiry into the risk they pose had been carried out.

ELECT PUBLIC OFFICIALS WITH THE COURAGE TO ACT IN AN EMERGENCY

There are executive powers that allow quick decarcerations in emergency times—if public officials have the courage to exercise them. In a letter to the governor, Keith Wattley, director of parole representation nonprofit UnCommon Law, identifies multiple such release valves, including early releases, commutations, and parole.[23] Section 8 of Article V of the California Constitution authorizes the governor to "grant a reprieve, pardon, and commutation, after sentence, except in case of impeachment."

Likewise, Sections 4800–4813 of the California Penal Code elaborate and explain this process, as well as the division of labor between the governor and the Board of Prison Terms, which "may report to the Governor, from time to time, the names of any and all persons imprisoned in any state prison who, in its judgment, ought to have a commutation of sentence or be pardoned and set at liberty on account of good conduct, or unusual term of sentence, or any other cause, including evidence of intimate partner battering and its effects." Direct applications to the governor are referred to the Board of Prison Terms for a recommendation. Per section 4812, the governor may request that the board "investigate and report on all applications for reprieves, pardons and commutation of sentence and shall make such recommendations to the Governor with reference thereto as to it may seem advisable."

The extent to which the Board of Prison Terms exercises independent diligence in flagging potential candidates for release depends, of course, on the appointees to the board. Elsewhere, Hadar has recommended the professional diversification of the Board of Parole Hearings beyond former law enforcement officers,[24] and while a proposed bill to do so has failed to make it out of committee,[25] we still believe that the courage to appoint people with diverse experience to these roles is an essential gubernatorial quality. The support of people from therapeutic, community organizing, and other areas of expertise will be essential if the governor feels that mass clemencies are called for.

In addition to these mechanisms, Section 8658 of the California Government Code creates an emergency release valve that seems to have been drafted precisely for a pandemic situation:

> In any case in which an emergency endangering the lives of inmates of a state, county, or city penal or correctional institution has occurred or is imminent, the person in charge of the institution may remove the inmates from the institution. He shall, if possible, remove them to a safe and convenient place and there confine them as long as may be necessary to avoid the danger, or, if that is not possible, may release them.[26]

CREATE A SUCCESSFUL, GOVERNMENT-SPONSORED REENTRY CONTINUUM

The idea of a geographic continuum between the prison and its surroundings requires a smooth transition from prison to the outside. During the summer of 2020, the #StopSanQuentinOutbreak coalition developed a series of recommendations for safe and effective reentry, reproduced in figure 19. Many of these recommendations apply beyond an active pandemic situation. Notably, one important recommendation is to train returning citizens on the use of smartphones, online resources, digital billing, and public transit, and the use of apps and social media to promote small businesses.

As Alessandro De Giorgi showed in his ethnography of reentering people in Oakland, the most pressing need upon release is help with basic survival: housing and employment.[27] As much as possible, California must improve reentry success through realistic rehabilitative programming and eliminating barriers to vocation.

A classic example is Assembly Bill 2147, which eliminates barriers to employing incarcerated firefighters in their skilled profession upon release by

10 WAYS TO SUCCESSFULLY REENTER

Our community is committed to providing our incarcerated loved ones with the resources and holistic care they need upon reentry. They have homes with us, and we keep us safe.

#CARENOTCAGES #LETTHEMGO #STOPSANQUENTINOUTBREAK

RIDE HOME

We can commit to providing our loved ones with a safe ride home upon release from prison.

HOUSING FOR ALL

Many of our people in reentry have family and community members already equipped to provide safe housing for their loved ones upon release. Additionally, we can assist in coordinating immediate housing needs through shelter programs, transitional housing, and emergency hotel rooms to isolate.

FOOD

Our community commits to providing meals and groceries to people coming home while they get back on their feet. We have local food banks, community gardens—where new neighbors can meet and contribute to a community resource of free food, and support networks that will keep our loved ones fed.

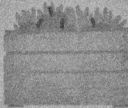

EMPLOYMENT OPPORTUNITIES

Many of our loved ones have job offers waiting for them when they come home. Through community mutual aid funds, we will raise funds to provide direct-cash support to newly released folks. Additionally, we will share opportunities for education, training, and employment.

IMMEDIATE COVID-19 TESTING

We will coordinate with local community health clinics to provide people in reentry with coronavirus testing upon release.

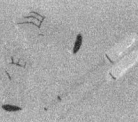

PPE

Upon release, we will support our community members by providing them with personal protective equipment necessary during this global pandemic, including sanitizer, masks, gloves, and hygiene products.

COMMUNITY SUPPORT NETWORKS

It is essential for people in reentry to have their own "pod" of community members, dedicated to supporting them emotionally and materially. We will work with people in reentry to develop their own "Support Network" contacts, as well as a relapse prevention plan and accountability systems within their community. This prioritizes the safety, health, and self-determination of our loved ones. We commit to NOT calling the police, as we know the police is a violent, anti-Black, racist institution whose presence increases violence in our communities.

ACCESS TO MEDICAL SERVICES

We will provide a list of local primary care community health clinics, resources for urgent care, and places to refill prescriptions. We will also offer guidance for applying for health insurance.

ACCESS TO MENTAL HEALTH RESOURCES & SUBSTANCE USE SUPPORT

We will provide a list of local community health clinics, crisis lines, and mental health services and resources, as well as a list of local treatment programs that can be accessed during COVID-19. Additionally, community support networks or "pods" can act as AA/NA sponsors and emotional support systems.

CELL PHONE

A cell phone is necessary to call for community resources, a job, and reconnecting with family and establishing life-saving support networks. We will provide our community members with cell phones upon release.

FIGURE 19. 10 Ways to Successfully Reenter (courtesy of Shruthi Venkata for the #StopSanQuentin Outbreak coalition).

allowing them to have their records expunged. Rewarding heroism with respectable, well-paying employment prospects is an excellent example of overcoming the impermeability myth and zero-sum-game thinking. Everyone in California wins when experienced people enlist in emergency services.

Given the zero-sum-game mentality, it is important to confront and address public concerns about the expense involved in developing robust reentry programming. While reentry programming for thousands of people can be costly, it is a fraction of what the state currently spends on incarceration: In the 2021–22 fiscal year, the LAO estimated that the average cost to incarcerate one person in California for a year was $106,131—more than a $50,000 increase since our recession-era prison population reduction in 2010–11.[28] There is reliable evidence-based information on the success rates of alternatives to incarceration;[29] even the costs of transitional housing would not scratch the surface of incarceration costs.

INTRODUCE SPATIAL FLEXIBILITY AND CONTINUITY TO LOCAL GOVERNMENT

Several of the pandemic prevention problems we identified in this work, particularly in chapter 3, are related to a rigid and dogmatic perception of the ambit of responsibility and chain of command across jurisdictions, the thorniest of which was the state-county divide. It is time to revise the *Plata* prediction that, given the horrors of state incarceration, counties could not possibly do worse; they can, and some of them do. The Board of State and Community Corrections should be restructured and offered more authority over county sheriffs, and more cooperation between CDCR and the county jails must be induced through legal reporting requirements. Rather than viewing jails as the release valve for prisons, these entities must be seen as interrelated, and any population reduction or control must be exercised at all levels.

It may also be necessary, in times of pandemic emergency, to place prisons under the authority of the health officials in the counties where they reside. These health officials were among the few prescient people who sounded the alarm about the prison-community continuum, and we must assure that their commonsense efforts to protect their county's population are not rebuffed through jurisdictional posturing.

Chapters 2 and 6 exposed alarming mismatches between the custodial and the medical sides of prison administration during the pandemic. We ascribe at least some of the problem to the historical animosity between the state prison apparatus and the federal receiver, and flagged several instances when these two authorities were at odds. The chain of command—including emergency situations in which the last word must be given to medical professionals—must be clarified before the next plague.

It is essential to avoid penalizing incarcerated people for doing what they can to protect themselves, and any grievances accrued through resistance to prison regulations that later turn out to have been life-endangering must be removed from the prisoners' C-files.

The need to respond to medical emergencies professionally and humanely in prison must be at front and center of correctional officer selection, the hiring process, and training. Chapters 2, 3, 4, and 6 teach us that one principle must not be compromised: anyone caring for people who are involuntarily held in confinement must be willing to do what it takes to protect said population from disastrous health outcomes, and this includes submitting to reasonable medical expectations, such as donning protective equipment and getting vaccinated. Rather than hiding behind the fear that insubordinate guards will resign en masse, it must be understood and implemented that, if recruitment tools do not supply the state with a sufficient number of guards to care for the incarcerated population at the standard that the constitution demands, we must incarcerate fewer people.

On a related note, pains must be taken to minimize, or eliminate completely, the political capture of the California Correctional Peace Officers Association (CCPOA). Proposals for accomplishing this are beyond the framework of our book, though the CCPOA's maneuvers throughout this crisis are a microcosm of many of the defects of California's electoral system. Publicly funded elections with stricter campaign contribution controls and limited contributions for voter initiatives might rein in overly enthusiastic and political organizations, and perhaps redirect the union's efforts toward protecting the rational interests of its members. If the rank-and-file members do not pressure the union to prioritize their health and safety over political posturing, it is the duty of California's attorney general to disavow the union as a pseudoclient.

As many prison law scholars have concluded, the existing doctrine, which buffers prison administrations from effective judicial review, is extremely challenging for prison litigators.[30] Prison litigation is an especially poor fit for emergency litigation, where the need to exhaust ineffective and hostile internal grievance systems can jam the wheels of the judicial machine[31] and life-saving solutions delivered in time are in short supply.[32]

One possible way forward addresses our concerns about the myth of prison permeability: Littman proposes applying frameworks from regulatory law in the free world to resolving problems and challenges within the prison.[33] Littman explains how applying regulatory frameworks, when possible, broke the impasse of prison law to deliver real COVID-19 relief in federal facilities:

> Transcontextual regulatory law is much better equipped than the constitutional law of punishment to take account of th[e prison-community] interrelatedness—and, critically, to assess and weigh the adverse impacts of carceral conditions on society writ large. Telecommunications and financial-services regulators can not only compare prison and jail pricing to pricing offered on the free market, but can also consider the impacts of high prices (entrenched poverty and severed family ties) on loved ones in the free world. These are individuals who lack standing to sue and are irrelevant to constitutional analyses. Similarly, labor and workplace safety regulators can consider the impacts of incarcerated people's work on the broader market; paying incarcerated people higher wages both affords them fairer compensation and decreases their competitive threat to free-world workers in the same industries.
>
> The public-health context is replete with other examples. During the pandemic, state public-health regulators in some jurisdictions prioritized prisoners for vaccination both because they were at extremely high risk of infection and death, and because outbreaks propagated inside a prison or jail leaked out into the surrounding community and gravely ill prisoners occupied scarce ICU beds at free-world hospitals. In other instances, regulators failed to apprehend the interconnectedness of a prison and its surrounding community, such as when the California Department of Public Health agreed to exclude infections reported during a devastating outbreak at Lompoc federal prison in determining when to permit Santa Barbara County's lockdown to ease, reducing local public-health officials' incentive to get involved in mitigation efforts at the facility.[34]

The problem, as Littman explains, is that "even when courts do consider free-world regulations in constitutional analyses, they generally make clear that regulatory standards are relevant but not determinative, and that no more than substantial compliance is necessary":

> Recently, for example, courts excused prison and jail officials' (sometimes admitted) failures to comply with aspects of the Centers for Disease Control and Prevention's (CDC) guidance for managing the COVID pandemic in correctional institutions, concluding that because officials had taken some measures, they had not acted with deliberate indifference. This leniency is all the more striking because the CDC guidelines were both "general" and "precatory" and "light touch," while the toll of illness and death was grave: huge outbreaks led to the infection of over a fifth of all incarcerated people and age-adjusted mortality rates multiple times higher than in the community. At the same time, regulatory standards acted as a ceiling on constitutional liability, leaving carceral institutions that did comply "inoculated against coercive relief." As Margo Schlanger observed in 2015, when the Supreme Court appeared much more favorably disposed to prisoner claims than it currently does: "Litigation has receded as an oversight method in American corrections. It is vital that something take its place." One as-yet-underexplored possibility for that "something": the same regulatory processes that protect the wellbeing of people who are not imprisoned.[35]

One more lesson from California's COVID-19 litigation has to do with the persistent problem of bad faith on the part of state representatives. Chapter 6 highlights the jarring juxtaposition of the attorney general's position on policy mandates for California, such as mandatory vaccination in schools, and his position when representing a client. We propose amending California legislation to clarify the role of the attorney general, who must at all times represent his constituents—all California residents—rather than just representing the narrow interests of the prison guards' union or preserving the egos of California prison officials.

ADVICE TO ACTIVISTS

Among the many activism and advocacy groups in the Bay Area, the #StopSanQuentinOutbreak coalition stood out to us as a positive, supportive, uplifting group, where the efforts of people from all walks of life were celebrated and appreciated. Especially during times of crisis and strife, it is crucial to overcome professional and personal disagreements and support those who face the most extreme danger and suffering (in this case, incarcerated people and their families). People recently released from prison are often invited to contribute their time and experience to movements and organizations precisely when they should be able to devote their efforts to rebuilding their lives and caring for themselves. The coalition was a uniformly positive experience of division of labor and a mature balance between contributions and self-care.

Advocating for change in the criminal process often creates thorny dilemmas of how to spend limited time and energy. One example, highlighted in chapter 4, was the challenge of pivoting to an emphasis on vaccination. On one hand, vaccinations were essential to save lives; on the other, as many experienced activists predicted, the struggle for vaccination drained much-needed energy from the struggle for releases; this raised serious concerns among the activists, who wanted to continue advocating for releases. The lawyers, by contrast, saw the release quest as a dead end, given the prison system's reliance on vaccinations. The court was, of course, happy to pivot in the direction of the lower-hanging fruit, and vaccines, not releases, quickly came to dominate the legal conversation. Activists must cultivate the ability to fight for, and accomplish, short-term goals that can immediately improve lives, while also tending the fires of the long-term struggle to shrink the correctional colossus.

Above all, in the face of despair and rage, it is crucially important never to give up. Politics fluctuate, and even saving a few lives through short-term advocacy and compromise is worthwhile. Where there is life, there is hope.

NOTES

INTRODUCTION

1. This perspective was inspired by Idan Ben Barak, *Why Aren't We Dead Yet? The Survivor's Guide to the Immune System* (Brunswick, Victoria, Australia: Scribe, 2016).

2. Erving Goffman, *Asylums: Essays on the Social Situation of Mental Patients and Other Inmates* (1961; New York: Routledge, 2017); Christie Davies, "Goffman's Concept of the Total Institution: Criticisms and Revisions," *Human Studies* 12, no. 1/2 (June 1989): 77–95.

3. Thomas Gift, "Trump's Mismanagement of the US Covid-19 Response May Have Eroded His International Reputation—Not That He Cares," *USApp—American Politics and Policy Blog*, July 11, 2020, https://blogs.lse.ac.uk/usappblog /2020/07/11/trumps-mismanagement-of-the-us-covid-19-response-may-have-eroded-his-international-reputation-not-that-he-cares/.

4. Paul E. Rutledge, "Trump, COVID-19, and the War on Expertise," American Review of Public Administration 50, no. 6–7 (2020): 505–11.

5. John Agnew, "Dying from Ideology: The Spatial Paradox of Trump's 'Populism' in the Time of Covid-19," *Semestrale di Studi e Ricerche di Geografia* 2 (2020): 9–21.

6. "Coronavirus in the U.S.: Latest Map and Case Count," *New York Times*, 2020–23, https://www.nytimes.com/interactive/2021/us/covid-cases.html.

7. Ibid.

8. Rakesh Kochnar, "Unemployment Rose Higher in Three Months of COVID-19 Than It Did in Two Years of the Great Recession," Pew Research Center, June 11, 2020, https://www.pewresearch.org/fact-tank/2020/06/11/unemployment-rose-higher-in-three-months-of-covid-19-than-it-did-in-two-years-of-the-great-recession/#:~:text=Unemployment%20rose%20higher%20in%20three,years%20 of%20the%20Great%20Recession&text=The%20COVID%2D19%20outbreak% 20and,20.5%20million%20in%20May%202020.

9. Bay Area News Group, "Worst Coronavirus Outbreak in U.S.: A Timeline of How San Quentin Earned That Infamous Distinction," *San Jose Mercury News*,

August 4, 2020, https://www.mercurynews.com/2020/08/04/timeline-san-quentin-overtakes-ohio-prison-for-most-coronavirus-cases-in-u-s/.

10. UCLA Law COVID Behind Bars Data Project, https://uclacovidbehind bars.org/.

11. Brandon Saloner, Kalind Parish, Julia A. Ward, Grace DiLaura, and Sharon Dolovich, "COVID-19 Cases and Deaths in Federal and State Prisons," *JAMA* 324, no. 6 (2020): 602–3.

12. Megan Cassidy and Jason Fagone, "200 Chino Inmates Transferred to San Quentin, Corcoran. Why Weren't They Tested First?," *San Francisco Chronicle*, June 8, 2020, https://www.sfchronicle.com/crime/article/Coronavirus-and-prisons-Prisoners-went-weeks-15325787.php.

13. Megan Cassidy, "San Quentin Officials Ignored Coronavirus Guidance from Top Marin County Health Officer, Letter Says," *San Francisco Chronicle*, August 11, 2020, https://www.sfchronicle.com/crime/article/San-Quentin-officials-ignored-coronavirus-15476647.php.

14. Office of the San Francisco Public Defender, "Petitioners Allege CDCR Purposefully Ignored Marin County Health Official Warnings about Dangers at San Quentin; Over 400 Pages of Evidence Presented," August 17, 2020, https://sfpublicdefender.org/news/2020/08/petitioners-allege-cdcr-purposefully-ignored-marin-county-health-official-warnings-about-dangers-at-san-quentin-over-400-pages-of-evidence-presented/.

15. Goffman, *Asylums*, 11.

16. Donald Clemmer, "Prisonization," in *The Sociology of Punishment and Correction*, ed. Norman Johnston, Leonard Savitz, and Marvin Wolfgang (New York: John Wiley & Sons, 1970).

17. Goffman, *Asylums*.

18. In Gresham Sykes's classic book on prison, these were referred to as the pains of imprisonment. Sykes, *The Society of Captives: A Study of a Maximum Security Prison* (1958; Princeton, NJ: Princeton University Press, 2007).

19. Peter W. Greenwood with Allan Abrahamse, *Selective Incapacitation*, RAND Corporation, Report for the National Institute of Justice, 1982, https://www.rand.org/content/dam/rand/pubs/reports/2007/R2815.pdf.

20. Keith Farrington, "The Modern Prison as Total Institution? Public Perception versus Objective Reality," *Crime & Delinquency* 38, no. 1 (1992): 6–26, 6. See also Tea Fredriksson, *The Horror-Storied Prison: A Narrative Study of Prison as an Abject and Uncanny Institution* (Stockholm: Stockholm University, 2021), 181–82.

21. Dominique Moran, *Carceral Geography: Spaces and Practices of Incarceration* (New York: Routledge, 2018), 88.

22. Michel Foucault, *Discipline and Punish: The Birth of the Prison* (1979; London: Penguin, 2017).

23. Malcolm Feeley and Jonathan Simon, "The New Penology: Notes on the Emerging Strategy of Corrections and Its Implications," *Criminology* 30, no. 4 (1992): 449–74.

24. Also see Jonathan Simon, Nicholas Temple, and Renée Tobe, eds., *Architecture and Justice: Judicial Meanings in the Public Realm* (New York: Routledge, 2013), which is organized by "escalating increments of scale," "from the prison cell ... to the social realm" (1).

25. Giorgio Agamben, *Homo Sacer: Sovereign Power and Bare Life* (Stanford, CA: Stanford University Press, 1992).

26. Loïc Wacquant, *Punishing the Poor: The Neoliberal Government of Social Insecurity* (Durham, NC: Duke University Press, 2009).

27. Ashley Rubin and Michelle Phelps, "Fracturing the Penal State: State Actors and the Role of Conflict in Penal Change," *Theoretical Criminology* 21 (2017): 422–40.

28. Dominique Moran and Anna K. Schliehe, *Carceral Spatiality: Dialogues between Geography and Criminology* (New York: Palgrave, 2017); Karen Morin, *Carceral Space, Prisoners and Animals*, Routledge Human-Animal Studies Series (New York: Taylor and Francis, 2018).

29. Moran, *Carceral Geography*, 2.

30. Dominique Moran and Yvonne Jewkes, "Linking the Carceral and the Punitive State: A Review of Research on Prison Architecture, Design, Technology and the Lived Experience of Carceral Space," *Annales de Géographie* 2–3, no. 702–3 (2015): 163–84.

31. Richard Wener, *The Environmental Psychology of Prisons and Jails: Creating Humane Spaces in Secure Settings* (Cambridge: Cambridge University Press, 2012).

32. Moran, *Carceral Geography*, 122.

33. Yvonne Jewkes, "Men Behind Bars: 'Doing' Masculinity as an Adaptation to Imprisonment," *Men and Masculinities* 8, no. 1 (2005): 44–63; Olivier Milhaud and Dominique Moran, "Penal Space and Privacy in French and Russian Prisons," in *Carceral Spaces: Mobility and Agency in Imprisonment and Migrant Detention*, ed. Nick Gill and Dominique Moran (New York: Routledge, 2013).

34. Deirdre Caputo-Levine, "The Yard Face: The Contributions of Inmate Interpersonal Violence to the Carceral Habitus," *Ethnography* 14, no. 2 (2013): 165–85.

35. Moran, *Carceral Geography*, chap. 10.

36. Caputo-Levine, "The Yard Face"; Jennifer Sloan, "'You Can See Your Face in My Floor': Examining the Function of Cleanliness in an Adult Male Prison," *Howard Journal of Criminal Justice* 51, no. 4 (2012): 400–410.

37. Moran, *Carceral Geography*, 36.

38. Ibid., 78.

39. Lauren Martin and Matthew Mitchelson, "Geographies of Detention and Imprisonment: Interrogating Spatial Practices of Confinement, Discipline, Law, and State Power," *Geography Compass* 3 (2009): 459–77.

40. Nick Gill, Deidre Conlon, Dominique Moran, and Andrew Burridge, "Carceral Circuitry," *Progress in Human Geography* 42 (2018): 183–204.

41. Moran, *Carceral Geography*, 60.

42. Dale Sechrest, "Locating Prisons: Open versus Closed Approaches to Siting," *Crime & Delinquency* 38, no. 1 (1992): 88–104.

43. Ibid. Also see K. S. Abrams and W. Lyons, "Impact of Correctional Facilities on Land Values and Public Policy," *NCJRS* (1987), https://www.ojp.gov/ncjrs/virtual-library/abstracts/impact-correctional-facilities-land-values-and-public-policy.

44. Sechrest, "Locating Prisons."

45. Susan Blankenship and Ernest Yanarella, "Prison Recruitment as a Policy Tool of Local Economic Development: A Critical Evaluation," *Contemporary Justice Review* 7, no. 2 (2004): 183–98.

46. Abrams and Lyons, "Impact of Correctional Facilities."

47. Matthew D. Vanden Bosch, "Rural Prison Siting: Problems and Promises," *Mid-Southern Journal of Criminal Justice* 19, no. 1 (2020): 1–21; Tracy Huling, "Building a Prison Economy in Rural America," in *Invisible Punishment: The Collateral Consequences of Mass Imprisonment*, ed. Marc Mauer and Meda Chesney-Lind (New York: The New Press, 2002); Shaun Genter, Gregory Hooks, and Clayton Mosher, "Prisons, Jobs and Privatization: The Impact of Prisons on Employment Growth in Rural U.S. Counties, 1997–2004," *Social Science Research* 42, no. 3 (2013): 596–610.

48. John Eason, *Big House on the Prairie: Rise of the Rural Ghetto and Penal Proliferation* (Chicago: University of Chicago Press, 2017).

49. *Prison Town, USA* (Katie Galloway and Po Kutchins, dirs., 2007).

50. Ruth Wilson Gilmore, *Golden Gulag: Prisons, Surplus, Crisis, and Opposition in Globalizing California* (Berkeley: University of California Press, 2006).

51. Huling, "Building a Prison Economy."

52. Joelle Fraser, "American Seduction: Portrait of a Prison Town," *Michigan Quarterly Review* 39, no. 4 (2000), https://quod.lib.umich.edu/cgi/t/text/text-idx?cc=mqr;c=mqr;c=mqrarchive;idno=act2080.0039.415;view=text;rgn=main;xc=1;g=mqrg.

53. Morin, *Carceral Space, Prisoners and Animals.*

54. Brett Story, *Prison Land: Mapping Carceral Power across Neoliberal America* (Minneapolis: University of Minnesota Press, 2019).

55. *The Prison in Twelve Landscapes* (Brett Story, dir., 2016). Also see Caleb Smith, "Spaces of Punitive Violence," review of *Prisons of Poverty*, by Loïc Wacquant, *Criticism* 55, no. 1 (2013): 161–68.

56. Jonathan Simon, *Governing through Crime: How the War on Crime Transformed American Democracy and Created a Culture of Fear* (New York: Oxford University Press, 2007).

57. Victor M. Rios, *Human Target: Schools, Police, and the Criminalization of Latino Youth* (Chicago: University of Chicago Press, 2017).

58. Debra Satz, *Why Some Things Should Not Be for Sale: The Moral Limits of Markets* (New York: Oxford University Press, 2010).

59. Jeannie Suk, "Criminal Law Comes Home," *Yale Law Journal* 116, no. 2 (2006): 2–70.

60. Wacquant, *Punishing the Poor.*

61. Angela Davis, *Are Prisons Obsolete?* (New York: Seven Sisters Press, 2003); also see Jordan Camp, *Incarcerating the Crisis: Freedom Struggles and the Rise of the Neoliberal State* (Oakland: University of California Press, 2016).

62. Ruha Benjamin, ed., *Captivating Technology: Race, Carceral Technoscience, and Liberatory Imagination in Everyday Life* (Durham, NC: Duke University Press, 2019).

63. Andrea Miller, "Shadows of War, Traces of Policing: The Weaponization of Space and the Sensible in Preemption," in Benjamin, *Captivating Technology*, 85–106, 87; R. Joshua Scannell, "This Is Not Minority Report: Predictive Policing and Population Racism," in Benjamin, *Captivating Technology*, 107–29; Walter L. Perry, Brian McInnis, Cart C. Price, Susan C. Smith, and John S. Hollywood, *Predictive Policing: The Role of Crime Forecasting in Law Enforcement Operations* (Santa Monica, CA: RAND Corporation, 2013).

64. Winifred R. Poster, "Racialized Surveillance in the Digital Service Economy," in Benjamin, *Captivating Technology*, 133–69, 138.

65. Tamara K. Nopper, "Digital Character in 'The Scored Society': FICO, Social Networks, and Competing Measurements of Creditworthiness," in Benjamin, *Captivating Technology*, 170–87.

66. Madison Van Oort, "Employing the Carceral Imaginary: An Ethnography of Worker Surveillance in the Retail Industry," in Benjamin, *Captivating Technology*, 209–23, 213.

67. Morin, *Carceral Space, Prisoners and Animals.*

68. Wacquant, *Punishing the Poor.*

69. Gilmore, *Golden Gulag.*

70. David Weisburd, "Reorienting Crime Prevention Research and Policy: From the Causes of Criminality to the Context of Crime" (paper presented at the 1996 Conference on Criminal Justice Research and Evaluation, National Institute of Justice), https://books.google.com/books?hl=en&lr=&id=09fwqBcAKA4C&oi=fnd&pg=PA1&dq=david+weisburd+situational+crime+prevention&ots=WZgaEJQzzD&sig=3ys0HV-ygygS6f84zuFghgpxGE8#v=onepage&q=david%20weisburd%20situational%20crime%20prevention&f=false.

71. David Garland, *The Culture of Control: Crime and Social Order in Contemporary Society* (Chicago: University of Chicago Press, 2001).

72. For a critique of the social spaces that are generated by these perspectives, see Thomas Raymen, "Designing-in Crime by Designing-out the Social? Situational Crime Prevention and the Intensification of Harmful Subjectivities," *British Journal of Criminology* 56, no. 3 (2016): 497–514.

73. Thomas A. Loughran, Ray Paternoster, Aaron Chalfin, and Theodore Wilson, "Can Rational Choice Theory BE Considered a General Theory of Crime?," *Criminology* 54, no. 1 (2016): 86–112.

74. Marcus Felson and Lawrence Cohen, "Human Ecology and Crime: A Routine Activity Approach," *Human Ecology* 8 (1980): 389–406.

75. Ronald Clarke, "Situational Crime Prevention: Its Theoretical Basis and Practical Scope," *Crime and Justice* 4 (1983): 225–56.

76. Read Hayes, "Shop Theft: An Analysis of Shoplifter Perceptions and Situational Factors," *Security Journal* 12 (2020): 7–18.

77. Robert Rosenberger, "On Hostile Design: Theoretical and Empirical Prospects," *Urban Planning* 57, no. 4 (2020): 883–93.

78. Paul Michael Cozens, "Urban Planning and Environmental Criminology: Towards a New Perspective for Safer Cities," *Planning Practice and Research* 26, no. 4 (2011): 481–508.

79. Geoff Manaugh, *A Burglar's Guide to the City* (New York: FSG Originals, 2014).

80. See the communication methods between hunger strikers at Pelican State Prison's solitary confinement cells: Keramet Reiter, "The Pelican Bay Hunger Strike: Resistance within the Structural Constraints of a US Supermax Prison," *South Atlantic Quarterly* 113, no. 3 (2014): 579–611. But what is defined as resistance and what is mere adaptation is a subject of some contention: Ashley Rubin, "Resistance or Friction: Understanding the Significance of Prisoners' Secondary Adjustments," *Theoretical Criminology* 19, no. 1 (2015): 23–42.

81. Morin, *Carceral Space, Prisoners and Animals*, 15.

82. Agamben, *Homo Sacer*.

83. Jonathan Simon, *Mass Incarceration on Trial: A Remarkable Court Decision and the Future of Prisons in America* (New York: The New Press, 2014).

84. John Witt, *American Contagions: Epidemics and the Law from Smallpox to COVID-19* (New Haven, CT: Yale University Press, 2020).

85. Ibid., 12.

86. John Howard, *The State of the Prisons in England and Wales, with Preliminary Observation and an Account of Some Foreign Prisons* (London: William Eyres, and sold by T. Cadell in the Strand, and N. Conant in Fleet Street, 1777).

87. Robert R. Sullivan, "The Birth of the Prison: The Case of Benjamin Rush," *Eighteenth-Century Studies* 31, no. 3 (1998): 333–44.

88. Ashley Rubin, "Prisons and Jails Are Coronavirus Epicenters—But They Were Once Designed to Prevent Disease Outbreaks," *The Conversation*, April 15, 2020, https://theconversation.com/prisons-and-jails-are-coronavirus-epicenters-but-they-were-once-designed-to-prevent-disease-outbreaks-136036.

89. Jonathan Simon, "The New Gaol: Seeing Incarceration Like a City," *Annals of the American Academy of Political and Social Science* 664, no. 1 (2016): 280–301.

90. Michael Meranze, *Laboratories of Virtue: Punishment, Revolution, and Authority in Philadelphia, 1760–1835*, 2nd ed. (Chapel Hill: University of North Carolina Press, 1996), 185.

91. Witt, *American Contagions*, 16–17.

92. Ibid., 31.

93. José Cid, "Is Imprisonment Criminogenic? A Comparative Study of Recidivism Rates between Prison and Suspended Prison Sanctions," *European Journal of Criminology* 6, no. 6 (2009): 459–80.

94. Grant Duwe and Valerie Clark, "The Rehabilitative Ideal versus the Criminogenic Reality: The Consequences of Warehousing Prisoners," *Corrections* 2, no. 1

(2017): 41–69; Gerald Gaes and Scott Camp, "Unintended Consequences: Experimental Evidence for the Criminogenic Effect of Prison Security Level Placement on Post-Release Recidivism," *Journal of Experimental Criminology* 5 (2009): 139–62; Scott Camp and Gerald Gaes, "Criminogenic Effects of the Prison Environment on Inmate Behavior: Some Experimental Evidence," *Crime & Delinquency* 51, no. 3 (2005): 425–42.

95. Amy Wilson, Karen Ishler, Robert Morgan, Jonathan Phillips, Jeff Draine, and Kathleen Farkas, "Examining Criminogenic Risk Levels among People with Mental Illness Incarcerated in US Jails and Prisons," *Journal of Behavioral Health Services Research*, November 5, 2020, https://pubmed.ncbi.nlm.nih.gov/33155072/.

96. Ernest Drucker, *A Plague of Prisons: The Epidemiology of Mass Incarceration in America* (New York: The New Press, 2011).

97. Vanessa Barker, *The Politics of Imprisonment: How the Democratic Process Shapes the Way America Punishes Offenders* (New York: Oxford University Press, 2009).

98. Hadar Aviram, *Yesterday's Monsters: The Manson Family Cases and the Illusion of Parole* (Oakland: University of California Press, 2020).

99. Gilmore, *Golden Gulag*, 2006.

100. Margo Schlanger, "Plata v. Brown and Realignment: Jails, Prisons, Courts, and Politics," *Harvard Civil Rights–Civil Liberties Law Review* 48, no. 1 (2013): 165–215.

101. *Brown v. Plata*, 563 U.S. 493 (2011).

102. Assembly Bill 109 (Criminal Justice Alignment). Approved by governor April 4, 2011. Filed with secretary of state April 4, 2011.

103. Christopher Seeds, "Bifurcation Nation: American Penal Policy in Late Mass Incarceration," *Punishment and Society* 19 (2016): 590–610.

104. Soleil Ho, "You Have Very Legit, Totally OK Reasons for Attending a Big French Laundry Dinner Party Right Now," *San Francisco Chronicle*, December 2, 2020, https://www.sfchronicle.com/restaurants/article/You-have-very-good-totally-okay-reasons-to-15767743.php.

105. *Turner v. Safley*, 482 U.S. 78 (1987).

106. https://prisonpandemic.uci.edu/.

107. https://hadaraviram.com.

108. https://docs.google.com/spreadsheets/d/1UfboC8-cRf10glzfnN-mi_hrE1jfdvDYg4KkIuc-VB8/edit#gid=1142961037.

109. https://www.cdcr.ca.gov/covid19/population-status-tracking/.

110. https://www.latimes.com/projects/california-coronavirus-cases-tracking-outbreak/.

1. TRIGGERS AND VULNERABILITIES

1. Chairman Ben S. Bernanke, "Some Reflections on the Crisis and the Policy Response," Federal Reserve, April 13, 2012, https://www.federalreserve.gov/newsevents/speech/bernanke20120413a.htm.

2. Andrea Cipriano, "Global Covid-19 Impact 'Heavily Felt' on Prisoners: UN Expert," United Nations, March 9, 2021, https://news.un.org/en/story/2021/03/1086802.

3. Dom Phillips, "'Come Back Monday, OK?' Hundreds of Prisoners Escape in Brazil amid Covid-19 Anger," *Guardian*, March 16, 2020, https://www.theguardian.com/world/2020/mar/17/come-back-monday-ok-hundreds-of-prisoners-escape-in-brazil-amid-covid-19-anger.

4. Adam Payne, "Iran Has Released 85,000 Prisoners in an Emergency Bid to Stop the Spread of the Coronavirus," *Business Insider Nederland*, March 18, 2020, https://www.businessinsider.nl/coronavirus-covid-19-iran-releases-eighty-five-thousand-prisoners-2020-3?international=true&r=US.

5. Chase Burton, "COVID-19: Prisons as Public Health Risks," Leiden University Law Blog, May 28, 2020, https://www.leidenlawblog.nl/articles/covid-19-prisons-as-public-health-risks.

6. Joan Didion, *Slouching toward Bethlehem* (1968; reis., New York: Zola Books, 2013), 128.

7. Suzanne Guldimann, "Remembering Joan Didion," *Topanga New Times*, January 14, 2022, https://topanganewtimes.com/2022/01/14/remembering-joan-didion/.

8. Vanessa Barker, *The Politics of Imprisonment: How the Democratic Process Shapes the Way America Punishes Offenders* (New York: Oxford University Press, 2009).

9. California's culture can also be seen as somewhat overlapping the punitive politics of what Mona Lynch refers to as the "sunbelt." Lynch, *Sunbelt Justice: Arizona and the Transformation of American Punishment* (Stanford, CA: Stanford University Press, 2009). It also shares some characteristics with Florida's culture; see Heather Schoenfeld, *Building the Prison State: Race and the Politics of Mass Incarceration* (Chicago: University of Chicago Press, 2018).

10. Hadar Aviram, *Yesterday's Monsters: The Manson Family Cases and the Illusion of Parole* (Oakland: University of California Press, 2020).

11. Joshua Page, *The Toughest Beat: Politics, Punishment, and the Prison Officers Union in California* (New York: Oxford University Press, 2011).

12. Lynch, *Sunbelt Justice*.

13. Robert Perkinson, *Texas Tough: The Rise of America's Prison Empire* (London: Picador, 2010).

14. L. L. Stanley, "Influenza at San Quentin Prison," *Public Health Reports* 34, no. 19 (1919): 996–1008, 998.

15. Ibid., 1005–6.

16. Ibid., 1008.

17. Jonathan Simon, *Mass Incarceration on Trial: A Remarkable Court Decision and the Future of Prisons in America* (New York: The New Press, 2014).

18. *Plata v. Schwarzenegger*, 2005 U.S. Dist. LEXIS 8878, at *7 (N.D. Cal. May 10, 2005).

19. *Plata v. Schwarzenegger*, No. C01-1351TEH, 2005 U.S. Dist. LEXIS 43796, at *15 (N.D. Cal. October 3, 2005).

20. *Plata*, 2005 U.S. Dist. LEXIS 43796, at *20.

21. Aaron Rappaport, "Litigation over Prison Medical Services," *Hastings Race & Poverty Law Journal* 7, no. 1 (2010): 261–83.

22. *Plata*, 2005 U.S. Dist. LEXIS 8878, at *8.

23. *Plata*, 2005 U.S. Dist. LEXIS 43796, at *9–10, *41–42.

24. Id. at *3.

25. *Coleman v. Schwarzenegger*, No. CIV S-90-0520 LKK JFM P, 2009 U.S. Dist. LEXIS 67943, at *37 (E.D. Cal. August 4, 2009) (citing Little Hoover Commission, *Solving California's Corrections Crisis: Time Is Running Out* [Sacramento: Little Hoover Commission, 2007]).

26. "One in 100: Behind Bars in America 2008," Pew Charitable Trusts, February 28, 2008, https://www.pewtrusts.org/en/research-and-analysis/reports/2008/02/28/one-in-100-behind-bars-in-america-2008 (reporting the prison population in January 2008 as 171,444 inmates).

27. Franklin E. Zimring and Gordon Hawkins, "The Growth of Imprisonment in California," *British Journal of Criminology* 34 (1991): 83; Adam Liptak, "Inmate Count in U.S. Dwarfs Other Nations'," *New York Times*, April 23, 2008, www.nytimes.com/2008/04/23/us/23prison.

28. Design capacity refers to the number of inmates prisons were originally meant to hold.

29. Laura Sullivan, "San Quentin Gym Becomes One Massive Cell," NPR, July 7, 2008, https://www.npr.org/templates/story/story.php?storyId=92296114.

30. Bob Egelko, "Governor Approves New San Quentin Death Row," *SFGATE*, July 30, 2009, www.sfgate.com/cgi-bin/article.cgi?f-/c/a/2009/07/30/BAD219OL4J.DTL.

31. Ruth Wilson Gilmore, *Golden Gulag: Prisons, Surplus, Crisis, and Opposition in Globalizing California* (Berkeley: University of California Press, 2006).

32. Emily Widra, "Incarceration Shortens Life Expectancy," *Prison Policy Initiative*, June 26, 2017, https://www.prisonpolicy.org/blog/2017/06/26/life_expectancy/.

33. Hadar Aviram, "A Table before Me in the Presence of My Enemies: Susan Atkins and the Spectacle of Aging and Frailty on Parole," *International Criminal Law Review* 22, no. 1–2 (2022): 279–307, https://doi.org/10.1163/15718123-bja10096; Ernest K. Chavez, "From the Warehouse to the Deathbed: Challenging the Conditions of Mass Death in Prison," *Themis* 3, no. 1 (2015): 1–27.

34. Adam Liptak, "Justices, 5-4, Tell California to Cut Prisoner Population," *New York Times*, May 23, 2011, https://www.nytimes.com/2011/05/24/us/24scotus.html#:~:text=A%20lower%20court%20in%20the,Plata%2C%20No.

35. Simon, *Mass Incarceration on Trial*.

36. Rappaport, "Litigation over Prison Medical Services."

37. *Coleman v. Schwarzenegger*, No. CIV S-90-0520 LKK JFM P, 2009 U.S. Dist. LEXIS 67943, at *73-74 (quoting *Coleman*, 912 F. Supp. at 1306).

38. *Coleman*, 2009 U.S. Dist. LEXIS 67943, at *73 (quoting *Coleman*, 912 F. Supp. at 1309).

39. Id. at *75 (quoting Coleman, 912 F. Supp. at 1307).

40. Id. at *74 (quoting Coleman, 912 F. Supp. at 1314).

41. Ibid.

42. Ibid.

43. For a history of federal courts' laissez-faire position on prisons, see Malcolm Feeley and Edward Rubin, *Judicial Policy Making and the Modern State: How the Courts Reformed America's Prisons* (Cambridge: Cambridge University Press, 2000); for efforts to unpack courts' tendency to defer to security considerations, see Emma Kaufman and Justin Driver, "The Incoherence of Prison Law," *Harvard Law Review* 135, no. 515 (December 2021), https://harvardlawreview.org/2021/12/the-incoherence-of-prison-law/; Sharon Dolovich, "The Coherence of Prison Law," *Harvard Law Review* 135, no. 302 (April 2022), https://harvardlawreview.org/2021/12/the-incoherence-of-prison-law/.

44. *Coleman*, 2009 U.S. Dist. LEXIS 67943, at *26.

45. Judge Lawrence Karlton, "Keynote Remarks on *Plata/Coleman*" (presentation, California Correctional Crisis Conference, San Francisco, CA, March 19, 2009).

46. Donald Specter, presentation at the California Correctional Crisis Conference, March 19, 2009. Aaron Rappaport, reviewing the proceedings of the conference, notes: "In his luncheon speech at the California Correctional Crisis Conference, Judge Karlton was much more restrained, simply noting that 'just recently, I held a hearing dealing with the failure of the state to have a viable "bed plan" for members of the Coleman class needing beds separate from the general population.'" Rappaport, "Litigation over Prison Medical Services."

47. *Plata*, 2005 U.S. Dist. LEXIS 43796, at *4.

48. Id. at *5.

49. *Coleman*, 2009 U.S. Dist. LEXIS 67943, at *51.

50. *Plata*, 2005 U.S. Dist. LEXIS 8878, at *5.

51. Id. (quoting July 16, 2004, Report [part 2] at *1).

52. *Coleman*, 2009 U.S. Dist. LEXIS 67943, at *54 (quoting April 8, 2005, Medical Experts' Report on San Quentin, at *13 [filed in *Plata* on May 10, 2005]).

53. Id. at *66 (quoting *Plata v. Schwarzenegger*, No. C01-1351TEH, 2005 U.S. Dist. LEXIS 43796, at *91).

54. Thelton Henderson, "Confronting the Crisis of California Prisons Symposium Keynote Address: Confronting the Crisis of California Prisons," *USF Law Review* 43 (2008): 1–2.

55. Rappaport, "Litigation over Prison Medical Services," 269.

56. "Achieving a Constitutional Level of Medical Care in California's Prisons: The Federal Receiver's Turnaround Plan of Action," California Correctional Health Care Services, June 6, 2008, https://cchcs.ca.gov/wp-content/uploads/sites/60/2017/08/ReceiverTurnaroundPlan_060608.pdf.

57. "Federal Receiver's Prison Health Care Construction Program," Legislative Analyst's Office, https://lao.ca.gov/analysis_2009/crim_justice/cj_anl09004002.aspx.

58. Jon Ortiz, "Keep Your Chin Up," *Sacramento Bee State Worker*, July 25, 2008, www.sacbee.com/static/weblogs/the-state- worker/2008/07/kelso-keep-your-chin-up.htm.

59. Charles Piller, "Prison Medical Plan May Far Exceed Need," *Sacramento Bee*, March 15, 2009. ("[Sillen] began the colossal reclamation project with vigor and toughness. Sillen once threatened to back up a Brink's truck to state coffers to collect what the Receivership was owed. That confrontational posture was widely regarded as his undoing.")

60. Michael Rothfeld, "State Prison Health Czar Is Fired," *Los Angeles Times*, January 24, 2008, https://www.latimes.com/archives/la-xpm-2008-jan-24-me-prisons24-story.html.

61. AP, "Report: Ex-California Prison Receiver Sillen Overpaid in Benefits, Expenses," *Mercury News*, February 27, 2018, https://www.mercurynews.com/2008/02/27/report-ex-california-prison-Receiver-sillen-overpaid-in-benefits-expenses/.

62. *Plata v. Schwarzenegger*, 560 F.3d 976, 980 (9th Cir. 2009). The district court ultimately ordered the state to turn over $250 million to the receiver.

63. Id.

64. *Plata v. Schwarzenegger*, No. COI-1351 TEH, 2009 U.S. Dist. LEXIS 23683, at *12 (N.D. Cal. March 24, 2009). The motion was denied.

65. "Achieving a Constitutional Level of Medical Care."

66. Michael Rothfeld, "Officials Urge End to Prison Oversight," *Los Angeles Times*, January 28, 2009, https://www.latimes.com/archives/la-xpm-2009-jan-28-me-prisons28-story.html. The receiver, for his part, fired back: "In a jab at Brown, who is exploring a run for governor, Kelso wrote that 'public officials who choose to run their political campaigns for higher office' by trying to block judges' orders 'actively promote disrespect for the courts.'" Id. Kelso also "took a swipe at Schwarzenegger for reneging on pledges of cooperation, writing that 'court orders are not Hollywood contracts ... where promises are cheaply given and then ignored when convenient.'"

67. Don Thompson, "Judge Sets Deadline for California Prison Decision," *Ventura County Star*, June 16, 2009. The cut was not quite as dramatic as it first appeared. The original $8 billion plan was to be spent over 10 years. The compromise proposal was to cover anticipated health-care needs for the next 4 years. See, for example, Bob Egelko, "Governor Dumps Plan to Build Prison Hospitals," *San Francisco Chronicle*, June 26, 2009.

68. Thompson, "Judge Sets Deadline."

69. Anthony York, "Legislative Analyst Rips Schwarzenegger Proposal Linking State Funds for Prisons, Universities," *Los Angeles Times*, January 26, 2010, https://www.latimes.com/archives/blogs/politi-cal/story/2010-01-26/legislative-analyst-rips-schwarzenegger-proposal-linking-state-funds-for-prisons-universities.

70. *Hines v. Youseff*, 914 F.3d 1218, 1224-25 (9th Cir. 2019).

71. Hines, 914 F.3d at 1224-25.

72. Hadar Aviram, *Cheap on Crime: Recession-Era Politics and the Transformation of American Punishment* (Oakland: University of California Press, 2015).

73. David Dagan and Steven M. Teles, *Prison Break: Why Conservatives Turned against Mass Incarceration* (New York: Oxford University Press, 2016).

74. Barack Obama, "The President's Role in Advancing Criminal Justice Reform," *Harvard Law Review* 130, no. 3 (2017): 811, https://harvardlawreview.org/2017/01/the-presidents-role-in-advancing-criminal-justice-reform/.

75. Dagan and Teles, *Prison Break*.

76. Michelle Alexander, *The New Jim Crow: Mass Incarceration in the Age of Colorblindness* (New York: The New Press, 2010). For a critique of Alexander's excessive focus on drug crimes, see James Forman, "Racial Critiques of Mass Incarceration: Beyond the New Jim Crow," *New York University Law Review* 87 (2012): 101–50.

77. *Coleman v. Schwarzenegger*, No. CIV S-90-0520 LKK JFM P; *Plata v. Schwarzenegger*, No. C01-1351, Three Judge Court Opinion and Order (2009), http://cdn.ca9.uscourts.gov/datastore/general/2009/08/04/Opinion%20&%20Order%20FINAL.pdf.

78. This was not so much out of a principled resistance to private entrepreneurs, but due to fierce objection on the part of California's prison guards' union, which protested against a prison built by a private company on speculation: Joshua Page, *The Toughest Beat: Politics, Punishment, and the Prison Officers Union in California* (New York: Oxford University Press, 2013). In 2013 the state did, however, enter a contract to operate this speculative prison, the California City Correctional Center. Christine Bedell, "Cal City Prison to House State Inmates," Bakersfield.com, October 25, 2013, https://www.bakersfield.com/news/cal-city-prison-to-house-state-inmates/article_41af12cd-3acf-5a21-9485-30b7ce8af4cb.html.

79. Joan Petersilia, "A Retrospective View of Corrections Reform in the Schwarzenegger Administration," *Federal Sentencing Reporter* 22, no. 3 (2010): 148–53.

80. Senate Bill 109, 2011 Leg., Gen. Assemb., Reg. Sess. (Cal. 2011).

81. Franklin Zimring and Gordon Hawkins, *The Scale of Imprisonment* (Chicago: University of Chicago Press, 1991), 211; W. David Ball, "Defunding State Prisons," *Criminal Law Bulletin* 50 (2014): 1060–89.

82. Charis Kubrin and Caroll Seron, eds., "The Great Experiment: Realigning Criminal Justice in California and Beyond," *Annals of the American Academy of Political and Social Science* 664, no. 1 (2016).

83. Jonathan Simon, "The Second Coming of Dignity," in *The New Criminal Justice Thinking*, ed. Sharon Dolovich and Alexandra Natapoff (New York: New York University Press, 2017), 275–307.

84. Editorial, "Justice Kennedy on Prisons," *New York Times*, February 15, 2010, https://www.nytimes.com/2010/02/16/opinion/16tue3.html.

85. *Brown v. Plata*, 563 U.S. 493, 548-49 (2011).

86. *Brown v. Plata*, 22.

87. *Buck v. Bell*, 274 U.S. 200, 207 (1927).

88. Margo Schlanger, "*Plata v. Brown* and Realignment: Jails, Prisons, Courts, and Politics," *Harvard Civil Rights–Civil Liberties Law Review* 481 (2013): 165–215.

89. Alex Emslie, Julie Small, and Lisa Pickoff-White, "Realignment 5 Years On: Counties Build Jails for Inmates with Mental Illness," KQED, *California Report*, September 29, 2016, https://www.kqed.org/news/11107949/realignment-5-years-on-counties-build-jails-for-inmates-with-mental-illness#:~:text=Realignment%20 aimed%20to%20satisfy%20a,nonviolent%20or%20non%2Dsex%20offenses.&text= It's%20been%20about%20a%20%242.5%.

90. Michael Carona, "Pay-to-Stay Programs in California Jails," *Michigan Law Review First Impressions* 106, no. 1 (2007), https://repository.law.umich.edu/mlr_fi /vol106/iss1/.

91. Magnus Lofstrom and Brandon Martin, *Public Safety Realignment: Impacts So Far* (San Francisco: Public Policy Institute of California, 2015), https://www .ppic.org/publication/public-safety-realignment-impacts-so-far/.

92. David Ball, "Tough on Crime (on the State's Dime): How Violent Crime Does Not Drive California Counties' Incarceration Rates—And Why It Should," *Georgia State Law Review* 28 (2012): 987–1084.

93. John Pfaff, *Locked In: The True Causes of Mass Incarceration and How to Achieve Real Reform* (New York: Basic Books, 2017). The only setting in which this is not true is the federal prison population, which is approximately one-tenth of the national prison population.

94. "Offender Data Points: Offender Demographics for the 24-Month Period Ending December 2018," California Department of Corrections and Rehabilitation, https://www.cdcr.ca.gov/research/wp-content/uploads/sites/174/2020/01 /201812_DataPoints.pdf.

95. Susan Turner, "Moving California Corrections from an Offense- to Risk-Based System," *UC Irvine Law Review* 8 (2018): 97–120.

96. Hadar Aviram, *Yesterday's Monsters: The Manson Family Cases and the Illusion of Parole* (Oakland: University of California Press, 2018), 38.

97. Joseph Hayes, Justin Goss, et al., "California's Prison Population," Public Policy Institute of California, July 2019, https://www.ppic.org/wp-content /uploads/jtf-prison-population-jtf.pdf.

98. The relationship between age and crime is one of the most stable findings of life-course criminology and is reviewed in greater detail in chapter 7. For a useful summary, see Marc Mauer, "Long-Term Sentences: Time to Reconsider the Scale of Punishment," The Sentencing Project, November 15, 2018, https://www .sentencingproject.org/publications/long-term-sentences-time-reconsider-scale-punishment/.

99. Barker, *Politics of Imprisonment*.

100. Holly Cartner, *Prison Conditions in Romania* (New York: Human Rights Watch, 1992), 8; Eric Goldstein, *Prison Conditions in Israel and in the Occupied Territories* (New York: Human Rights Watch, 1991), 29.

101. World Health Organization, *Preparedness, Prevention and Control of COVID-19 in Prisons and Other Places of Detention: Interim Guidance* (Copenhagen: WHO Regional Office for Europe, 2021).

102. Ibid., 3–4.

103. Megan Wallace, Mariel Marlow, et al., "Public Health Response to COVID-19 Cases in Correctional and Detention Facilities—Louisiana, March–April 2020," *Morbidity and Mortality Weekly Report* 69 (May 2020): 594–98.

104. Premal Dharia, "The Coronavirus Could Spark a Humanitarian Disaster in Jails and Prisons," *Slate*, March 11, 2020, https://slate.com/news-and-politics /2020/03/coronavirus-civil-rights-jails-and-prisons.html.

105. Amanda Klonsky, "An Epicenter of the Pandemic Will Be Jails and Prisons, if Inaction Continues," *New York Times,* March 16, 2020, https://www.nytimes .com/2020/03/16/opinion/coronavirus-in-jails.html.

106. Brandon Garrett and Lauren Brinkley-Rubinstein, "We Must Act Now to Prevent an Epidemic in North Carolina's Prisons and Jails," March 23, 2020, https:// ncpolicywatch.com/2020/03/23/we-must-act-now-to-prevent-an-epidemic-in-north-carolinas-prisons-and-jails/.

107. Margo Schlanger and Sonja Starr, "Four Things Every Prison System Must Do Today," *Slate*, March 27, 2020, https://slate.com/news-and-politics/2020/03 /four-steps-prevent-coronavirus-prison-system-catastrophe.html.

108. Amena Kheshtchin-Kamel, "COVID-19 & Prisons," *Legal-Ease Podcast*, April 13, 2020, https://podcasts.apple.com/us/podcast/covid-19-prisons /id1532616623?i=1000491819705.

109. Sharon Dolovich, "Every Public Official with the Power to Decarcerate Must Exercise That Power Now," *The Appeal*, April 20, 2020, https://theappeal.org /every-public-official-with-the-power-to-decarcerate-must-exercise-that-power-now/.

110. Editorial Board, "No One Deserves to Die of Covid-19 in Jail," *New York Times*, April 23, 2020, https://www.nytimes.com/2020/04/23/opinion/coronavirus-prisons.html.

111. Andrea Armstrong, Bruce Reilly, et al., "Coping with Covid: Guidance for Prisons, Jails, and People Post-Release," May 29, 2020, https://irleaders.org/2020/05 /coping-with-covid/.

2. PETRI DISH

1. James King and Danica Rodarmel, "Gov. Newsom Must Release More People from Prisons to Protect Californians and Save Lives," *Sacramento Bee*, July 11, 2020, https://www.sacbee.com/opinion/california-forum/article244143422.html# storylink=cpy.

2. Amendment VIII, U.S. Const.

3. U.S. Const., Amendment VIII; *Farmer v. Brennan,* 511 U.S. 825 (1994).

4. *Brock v. Wright*, 315 F.3d 158, 162 (2d Cir. 2003).

5. *Hill v. DeKalb Reg'l Youth Detention Ctr.*, 40 F.3d 1176, 1187 (11th Cir. 1994).

6. Hadar Aviram, *Cheap on Crime: Recession-Era Politics and the Transformation of American Punishment* (Oakland: University of California Press, 2015); Joe Soss et al., *Disciplining the Poor: Neoliberal Paternalism and the Persistent Power of*

Race (Chicago: University of Chicago Press, 2011); Ruth Wilson Gilmore, *Golden Gulag: Prisons, Surplus, Crisis, and Opposition in Globalizing California* (Berkeley: University of California Press, 2006); Loïc Wacquant, *Punishing the Poor: The Neoliberal Government of Social Insecurity* (Durham, NC: Duke University Press, 2009).

7. Vanessa Barker, *The Politics of Imprisonment: How the Democratic Process Shapes the Way America Punishes Offenders* (New York: Oxford University Press, 2009).

8. *Gregg v. Georgia*, 428 U.S. 153 (1967).

9. Austin Sarat, *When the State Kills* (Princeton, NJ: Princeton University Press, 2002); Austin Sarat, *Gruesome Spectacles: Botched Executions and America's Death Penalty* (Stanford, CA: Stanford University Press, 2014); Hadar Aviram and Ryan Newby, "Death Row Economics: The Rise of Fiscally Prudent Anti Death Penalty Activism," *Criminal Justice* 28 (2013): 33–40.

10. Erving Goffman, *Asylums: Essays on the Social Situation of Mental Patients and Other Inmates* (New York: Anchor Books, 1961).

11. Keramet Reiter, "Making Windows in Walls: Strategies for Prison Research," *Qualitative Inquiry* 20, no. 4 (2014): 417–28. The increasing limitations on research in prisons may explain the declining numbers of prison ethnographies; see Ashley Rubin, "The 'Curious Eclipse' of Carceral Ethnography in International Context: Trends across the U.S., Canada, and the U.K.," Scottish Centre for Crime and Justice Research, December 8, 2021, https://www.sccjr.ac.uk/video/the-curious-eclipse-of-carceral-ethnography-in-international-comparison-trends-across-the-us-canada-and-the-uk/.

12. Norman Bruce Johnston et al., *The Sociology of Punishment and Correction* (Hoboken, NJ: John Wiley & Sons, 1970).

13. Donald Clemmer, *The Prison Community* (New York: Rinehart, 1958).

14. Gresham M. Sykes, *The Society of Captives: A Study of a Maximum Security Prison* (Princeton, NJ: Princeton University Press, 2007).

15. Victor L. Shammas, "Pains of Imprisonment," *The Encyclopedia of Corrections* (2017), https://onlinelibrary.wiley.com/doi/pdf/10.1002/9781118845387.wbeoc020.

16. Laura E. Gibson and Christopher Hensley, "The Social Construction of Sexuality in Prison," *Prison Journal* 93, no. 3 (2013): 355–70.

17. Benjamin Fleury-Steiner and Jamie G. Longazel, *The Pains of Mass Imprisonment* (Abingdon, UK: Routledge, 2013), 2.

18. Ibid., 8–9.

19. Benjamin Fleury-Steiner, "The Pains of Immigrant Imprisonment," *Sociology Compass* 10, no. 11 (2016): 989–98.

20. Ronald H. Aday, "Aging Prisoners," in *Handbook of Social Work in Health and Aging,* ed. Barbara Berkman and Sarah D'Ambruoso (Oxford: Oxford University Press, 2006), 231–44.

21. Ronald H. Aday et al., "The Effect of Health and Penal Harm on Aging Female Prisoners' Views of Dying in Prison," *Omega - Journal of Death and Dying* 60, no. 1 (2010): 51–70.

22. Benjamin Fleury-Steiner and Carla Crowder, *Dying Inside: The HIV/AIDS Ward at Limestone Prison* (Ann Arbor: University of Michigan Press, 2009).

23. Rabia Belt, "The Fat Prisoners' Dilemma: Slow Violence, Intersectionality, and a Disability Rights Framework for the Future," *Georgetown Law Journal* 110, no. 4 (2022): 785.

24. John Fabian Witt, *American Contagions: Epidemics and the Law from Smallpox to Covid-19* (New Haven, CT: Yale University Press, 2020).

25. Jonathan Simon, "From the Big House to the Warehouse: Rethinking Prisons and State Government in the 20th Century," *Punishment & Society* 2, no. 2 (2000): 213–34.

26. "About," UC Irvine Prison Pandemic, https://staging.prisonpandemic.uci.edu/about/.

27. All information is available at the CDCR's Population COVID-19 Tracking website. "Population Covid-19 Tracking: CDCR Patients: Covid-19 Cases and Outcomes," California Department of Corrections and Rehabilitation, last visited May 25, 2022, https://www.cdcr.ca.gov/covid19/population-status-tracking/; "CDCR/CCHCS COVID-19 Employee Status," California Department of Corrections and Rehabilitation, last visited May 20, 2022, https://www.cdcr.ca.gov/covid19/cdcr-cchcs-covid-19-status/.

28. Kerry Klein, "Lessons from California Prison Where Covid 'Spread Like Wildfire,'" *California Healthline*, February 23, 2021, https://californiahealthline.org/news/article/lessons-from-california-prison-where-covid-spread-like-wildfire/; Stephen Stock et al., "San Quentin Faces New COVID Outbreak, Sparking Fears of 2020 All Over Again," NBC Bay Area, January 14, 2022, https://www.nbcbayarea.com/investigations/san-quentin-prison-faces-new-covid-outbreak-sparking-fears-of-2020-all-over-again/2777726/.

29. Kenneth Lamott, *Chronicles of San Quentin: The Biography of a Prison* (Hassell Street Press, 1961), 8–9.

30. Jason Fagone and Megan Cassidy, "UC Health Experts: San Quentin Coronavirus Outbreak Could Pose Threat to Entire Bay Area," *San Francisco Chronicle*, June 25, 2020, https://www.sfchronicle.com/local-politics/article/UC-health-experts-San-Quentin-coronavirus-15364257.php.

31. Aviram, *Cheap on Crime*, 150.

32. Ibid., 150–52.

33. "California Governor Gavin Newsom Orders Dismantling of State's Death Row," Death Penalty Information Center, February 1, 2022, https://deathpenaltyinfo.org/news/california-governor-gavin-newsom-orders-dismantling-of-californias-death-row.

34. Paige St. John and Maloy Moore, "These Are the 737 Inmates on California's Death Row," *Los Angeles Times*, March 13, 2019, https://www.latimes.com/projects/la-me-death-row/.

35. "Inmates Executed 1978 to Present: California Executions since 1978," California Department of Corrections and Rehabilitation, last visited March 28, 2022, https://www.cdcr.ca.gov/capital-punishment/inmates-executed-1978-to-present/.

36. Hadar Aviram, "Death Penalty in Limbo," hadaraviram.com, June 8, 2013, https://www.hadaraviram.com/2013/06/08/death-penalty-in-limbo/.

37. Maintaining the death penalty costs California taxpayers $184 million per annum, most of which is litigation costs: the California Constitution awards each death row inmate two free attorneys for postconviction litigation. Carol J. Williams, "Death Penalty Costs California $184 Million a Year, Study Says," *Los Angeles Times,* June 20, 2011, https://www.latimes.com/archives/la-xpm-2011-jun-20-la-me-adv-death-penalty-costs-20110620-story.html.

38. Mary Harris, "California's Carelessness Spurred a New COVID Outbreak," *Slate,* July 7, 2020, https://slate.com/news-and-politics/2020/07/covid-california-san-quentin-outbreak.html.

39. Roy W. Wesley and Bryan B. Beyer, "COVID-19 Review Series, Part Three: California Correctional Health Care Services and the California Department of Corrections and Rehabilitation Caused a Public Health Disaster at San Quentin State Prison When They Transferred Medically Vulnerable Incarcerated Persons From the California Institution for Men without Taking Proper Safeguards," Office of the Inspector General State of California, February 1, 2021, 1–2, https://www.oig .ca.gov/wp-content/uploads/2021/02/OIG-COVID-19-Review-Series-Part-3-%E2%80%93-Transfer-of-Patients-from-CIM.pdf.

40. See infra, part III(C) (discussing the evidentiary hearing).

41. "Monthly Report of Population as of Midnight June 30, 2020," California Department of Corrections and Rehabilitation, July 1, 2020, 2, https://www.cdcr .ca.gov/research/wp-content/uploads/sites/174/2020/07/Tpop1d2006.pdf.

42. Daniel Montes, "Trial over COVID-19 Outbreak at San Quentin State Prison That Left 29 Dead to Begin Thursday," *Bay City News,* May 20, 2021, https:// localnewsmatters.org/2021/05/20/trial-over-covid-19-outbreak-at-san-quentin-state-prison-that-left-29-dead-to-begin-thursday/.

43. Which was, incidentally, also tied to the decrepit plant. Hamed Aleaziz, "San Quentin Prison Legionnaires' Outbreak Traced to Cooling Towers," *SFGATE,* October 1, 2015, https://www.sfgate.com/bayarea/article/San-Quentin-prison-Legionnaires-outbreak-6544114.php#:~:text=A%20Legionnaires'%20disease%20 outbreak%20at,state%20prison%20system's%20medical%20care.

44. Sandra McCoy et al., "Urgent Memo: COVID-19 Outbreak: San Quentin Prison," AMEND, June 15, 2020, https://amend.us/wp-content/uploads/2020/06 /COVID19-Outbreak-SQ-Prison-6.15.2020.pdf.

45. Ibid., 3.

46. Ibid., 6 (emphasis omitted).

47. See California Department of Corrections and Rehabilitation, CDCR Transfer Data, last visited April 3, 2022, https://docs.google.com /spreadsheets/d/1DKInH8SBb46vMQLEEbPaCht4_z9quChAEB5CYxJG7Ts /edit#gid=0.

48. Lauren Brinkley-Rubinstein et al., "Association between Intersystem Prison Transfers and COVID-19 Incidence in a State Prison System," *PLoS ONE* 16, no. 8 (2021), https://journals.plos.org/plosone/article?id=10.1371/journal.pone.0256185.

49. Danielle Wallace et al., "Is There a Temporal Relationship between COVID-19 Infections among Prison Staff, Incarcerated Persons and Larger Community in the United States?," *International Journal of Environmental Research and Public Health* 18, no. 13 (2021), https://www.mdpi.com/1660-4601/18/13/6873/htm.

50. Salinas Valley, 04/22/2021, https://staging.prisonpandemic.uci.edu/stories /the-fastest-way/.

51. "COVID-19 Review Series, Part One: Inconsistent Screening Practices May Have Increased the Risk of COVID-19 within California's Prison System," Office of the Inspector General State of California, August 2020, 15, https://www.oig .ca.gov/wp-content/uploads/2020/08/OIG-COVID-19-Review-Series-Part-1-Screening.pdf.

52. Brooks Jarosz, "Prison Officials Turned Down Free COVID-19 Testing for San Quentin," KTVU, July 22, 2020, https://www.ktvu.com/news/prison-officials-turned-down-free-covid-19-testing-for-san-quentin; Amy Maxmen, "San Quentin Prison Turned Down Free Coronavirus Tests and Urgent Advice before Its Massive Outbreak," *Nature* 583 (2020): 339, https://www.nature.com/articles/d41586-020-02042-9.

53. Maxmen, "San Quentin Prison."

54. Morgan Chalfant, "Trump: 'With Smaller Testing We Would Show Fewer Cases,'" *The Hill*, June 23, 2020, https://thehill.com/homenews/administration /504026-trump-with-smaller-testing-we-would-show-fewer-cases/.

55. Adamu Chan, "Trapped in the Dungeon," *Slate*, February 5, 2021, https:// slate.com/human-interest/2021/02/san-quentin-dungeon-covid-tour.html.

56. McCoy et al., "Urgent Memo: COVID-19."

57. Ibid.

58. *In re Hall*, evidentiary hearing, Marin Superior Court. See chapter 6.

59. Nick Jones, "CDCR Population Data," Github, https://github.com /nrjones8/cdcr-population-data/blob/master/data/monthly_cdcr_population.csv.

60. Hadar Aviram, "Are California Prisons Really Less Crowded?," hadaraviram.com, January 17, 2018, https://www.hadaraviram.com/2018/01/17/are-ca-prisons-really-less-crowded/.

61. Vacaville, January 11, 2021, https://staging.prisonpandemic.uci.edu/stories /dropping-like-flies-2/.

62. Orange County, April 19, 2021, https://staging.prisonpandemic.uci.edu /stories/letter-from-orange-county-theo-lacy-jail-april-19-2021-395/.

63. San Quentin, November 13, 2020, https://staging.prisonpandemic.uci.edu /stories/crowded-in-here-2/.

64. Susanville, April 26, 2021, https://staging.prisonpandemic.uci.edu/stories /less-than-three-feet-2/.

65. Avenal, October 30, 2020, https://staging.prisonpandemic.uci.edu/stories /harassed-you-2/.

66. Kelly Servick, "Would Everyone Wearing Face Masks Help Us Slow the Pandemic?," *Science*, March 28, 2020, https://www.science.org/content/article /would-everyone-wearing-face-masks-help-us-slow-pandemic.

67. Abby Goodnough and Knvul Sheikh, "C.D.C. Weighs Advising Everyone to Wear a Mask," *New York Times*, March 31, 2020, updated May 7, 2020, https://www.nytimes.com/2020/03/31/health/cdc-masks-coronavirus.html

68. ICE Detention Facility, August 11, 2021, https://staging.prisonpandemic.uci.edu/stories/bleach-on-the-floor/.

69. Tehachapi, January 19, 2021, https://staging.prisonpandemic.uci.edu/stories/the-same-masks/.

70. Corcoran, January 5, 2021, https://staging.prisonpandemic.uci.edu/stories/dirty-masks-2/.

71. Chino, December 1, 2020, https://staging.prisonpandemic.uci.edu/stories/fought-for-masks-2/.

72. Casey Tolan, "Hand Sanitizer Is Still Considered Contraband in Some Prisons around the Country," CNN, May 5, 2020, https://www.cnn.com/2020/05/05/us/coronavirus-prison-hand-sanitizer-contraband-invs/index.html.

73. Antonia Noori Farzan, "Inmates Are Manufacturing Hand Sanitizer to Help Fight Coronavirus. But Will They Be Allowed to Use It?," *Washington Post*, March 10, 2020, https://www.washingtonpost.com/nation/2020/03/10/hand-sanitizer-prison-labor/.

74. Fresno County, September 10, 2021, https://staging.prisonpandemic.uci.edu/stories/wheres-our-soap/.

75. Roy W. Wesley and Bryan B. Beyer, "COVID-19 Review Series Part Two: The California Department of Corrections and Rehabilitation Distributed and Mandated the Use of Personal Protective Equipment and Cloth Face Coverings; However, Its Lax Enforcement Led to Inadequate Adherence to Basic Safety Protocols," October 26, 2020, 22–24, https://www.oig.ca.gov/wp-content/uploads/2020/10/OIG-COVID-19-Review-Series-Part-2-%E2%80%93-Face-Coverings-and-PPE.pdf.

76. Donovan, April 27, 2021, https://staging.prisonpandemic.uci.edu/stories/being-eaten-alive-2/.

77. Chino, December 14, 2020, https://staging.prisonpandemic.uci.edu/stories/are-a-number-to-them-2/.

78. *In re Von Staich*, Supplemental Brief.

79. Juan Haines, "We Pleaded for Social Distancing Here in San Quentin. The State Refused, and Now COVID Is Raging," op-ed, *Los Angeles Times*, January 28, 2022, https://www.latimes.com/opinion/story/2022-01-28/covid-prison-san-quentin-ruling.

80. Avenal, November 5, 2020, https://staging.prisonpandemic.uci.edu/stories/less-understanding-2/.

81. Solano, March 12, 2021, https://staging.prisonpandemic.uci.edu/stories/letter-from-solano-march-12-2021-4717/.

82. Chino, December 8, 2020, https://staging.prisonpandemic.uci.edu/stories/were-scared/.

83. Solano, March 12, 2021, https://staging.prisonpandemic.uci.edu/stories/letter-from-solano-march-12-2021-4717/.

84. Fire Camp, March 17, 2021, https://staging.prisonpandemic.uci.edu/stories/concentration-camp-2/.

85. Jasmine Brown, "Transgender Gender-Variant & Intersex Justice Project" (California Correctional Crisis: Mass Incarceration, Healthcare, and the COVID-19 Outbreak, UC Hastings College of the Law, February 12, 2021).

86. Leila Miller, "California Prisons Grapple with Hundreds of Transgender Inmates Requesting New Housing," *Los Angeles Times*, April 5, 2021, https://www.latimes.com/california/story/2021-04-05/california-prisons-consider-gender-identity-housing-requests (https://perma.cc/3D3K-HJT6).

87. Katja Ridderbusch, "COVID Precautions Put More Prisoners in Isolation. It Can Mean Long-Term Health Woes," NPR, October 4, 2021, https://www.npr.org/sections/health-shots/2021/10/04/1043058599/rising-amid-covid-solitary-confinement-inflicts-lasting-harm-to-prisoner-health; Brian Osgood, "Weeks without a Shower: Neglect Defines Covid-19 Containment in California Jails," *Intercept*, May 9, 2021, https://theintercept.com/2021/05/09/covid-california-jails-neglect/.

88. Keramet Reiter, *23/7: Pelican Bay Prison and the Rise of Long-Term Solitary Confinement* (New Haven, CT: Yale University Press, 2016).

89. CMC, February 11, 2021, https://staging.prisonpandemic.uci.edu/stories/huge-circus-tents-2/.

90. Vacaville, April 28, 2021, https://staging.prisonpandemic.uci.edu/stories/letter-from-vacaville-april-28-2021-8432/.

91. Chino, April 30, 2020, https://staging.prisonpandemic.uci.edu/stories/tent-city/.

92. Sam Levin, "'Severe Inhumanity': California Prisons Overwhelmed by Covid Outbreaks and Approaching Fires," *Guardian*, August 21, 2020, https://www.theguardian.com/us-news/2020/aug/21/california-fires-prisons-covid-outbreaks.

93. Thomas Fuller, "Coronavirus Limits California's Efforts to Fight Fires with Prison Labor," *New York Times*, August 24, 2020, https://www.nytimes.com/2020/08/22/us/california-wildfires-prisoners.html?referringSource=articleShare.

94. Adam Serwer, "California AG 'Shocked' to Learn Her Office Wanted to Keep Eligible Parolees in Jail to Work," *BuzzFeed News*, November 18, 2014, https://www.buzzfeednews.com/article/adamserwer/some-lawyers-just-want-to-see-the-world-burn.

95. Jason Fagone, "Inmate at State's Largest Prison Says He Was Cuffed after Stating Concerns about COVID-19 Protocols," *San Francisco Chronicle*, December 4, 2020, https://www.sfchronicle.com/health/article/Inmate-at-state-s-largest-prison-says-he-was-15774637.php.

96. Madison Pauly, "'It's Like a Horror Movie': Trapped inside San Quentin during an Explosion of COVID-19," *Mother Jones*, July 8, 2020, https://www.motherjones.com/crime-justice/2020/07/san-quentin-prison-coronavirus-california/?fbclid=IwAR13asThcBOoeimucxtZogBWQIzoACjlifDg9s4KgDcxyGGzqzs8BhagyH8.

97. Field notes from case management conference (on file with author).

98. Nationwide, vaccine hesitancy in prison is largely attributable to distrust and suspicion of health care in prison. See Emily Widra, "The Prison Context Itself Undermines Public Health and Vaccination Efforts," *Prison Policy Initiative*, March 9, 2022, https://www.prisonpolicy.org/blog/2022/03/09/vaccinehesitancy/.

99. Trans people, in particular, reported that the careless COVID-19–era transfers resulted in placing them in cells with transphobic cellmates and exposing them to violence, which went untreated. Brown, "Transgender Gender-Variant"; Miller, "California Prisons Grapple" (noting "that COVID-19 precautions have slowed the transfers [to gender-matching prisons] and that officials could not estimate how long a transfer might take under normal circumstances, citing bed availability as a factor").

100. San Quentin, November 13, 2020, https://staging.prisonpandemic.uci.edu /stories/telehealth/.

101. CIW, December 1, 2020, https://staging.prisonpandemic.uci.edu /stories/i-am-not-doing-well-2/.

102. Donovan, April 26, 2021, https://staging.prisonpandemic.uci.edu/stories /we-go-hungry-2/.

103. "Not Out of the Woods," UC Irvine Prison Pandemic, https://staging .prisonpandemic.uci.edu/stories/not-out-of-the-woods-2/.

104. Chuckawalla, December 11, 2020, https://staging.prisonpandemic.uci.edu /stories/popped-up-positive-2/.

105. Chino, December 8, 2020, https://staging.prisonpandemic.uci.edu/stories /way-past-due/.

106. Mule Creek, December 29, 2020, https://staging.prisonpandemic.uci.edu /stories/no-access-to-doctor-2/.

107. Kern Valley, April 20, 2021, https://staging.prisonpandemic.uci.edu /stories/no-inmate-is-safe-2/.

108. Centinela, February 23, 2021, https://staging.prisonpandemic.uci.edu /stories/absurd-orders-2/.

109. Juan Moreno Haines, "I Got COVID in San Quentin and Watched as Hundreds More Were Infected and 29 Died. Here's Our Story," *San Francisco Chronicle*, October 9, 2021, https://www.sfchronicle.com/opinion/openforum /article/I-got-COVID-in-San-Quentin-and-watched-as-16519424.php.

110. Olivia Campbell, "COVID Ignites Long Fight for Health Care in California Prisons," *Convergence*, July 20, 2022, https://convergencemag.com/articles /covid-ignites-long-fight-for-health-care-in-california-prisons/; email exchange with Olivia Campbell, December 28, 2021 (on file with authors).

111. Hadar Aviram, *Yesterday's Monsters: The Manson Family Cases and the Illusion of Parole* (Oakland: University of California Press, 2020).

112. Ashley McBride, "Gov. Newsom Orders More DNA Tests in Disputed Kevin Cooper Quadruple-Murder Case," *San Francisco Chronicle*, February 2, 2019, https://www.sfchronicle.com/crime/article/Gov-Newsom-orders-more-DNA-tests-in-disputed-13637172.php.

113. Scott Shafer and Marisa Lagos, "Gov. Gavin Newsom Suspends Death Penalty in California," NPR, March 12, 2019, https://www.npr.org/2019/03/12/702873258/gov-gavin-newsom-suspends-death-penalty-in-california.

114. Michael Levenson, "Golden State Killer Sentenced to Life in Prison without Parole," *New York Times,* August 21, 2020, https://www.nytimes.com/2020/08/21/us/golden-state-killer-sentenced.html#:~:text=Feb.-,Mr.,impose%20and%20meant%20that%20Mr.

115. Megan Cassidy and Jason Fagone, "Coronavirus Tears through San Quentin's Death Row; Condemned Inmate Dead of Unknown Cause," *San Francisco Chronicle,* June 25, 2020, https://www.sfchronicle.com/crime/article/Coronavirus-tears-through-San-Quentin-s-Death-15367782.php.

116. Patt Morrison, "California Is Closing San Quentin's Death Row. This Is Its Gruesome History," *Los Angeles Times,* February 8, 2022, https://drive.google.com/drive/folders/11ai4KjKGt3qusGLud42hg3BPeSx8abtp.

117. Hadar Aviram and Ryan S. Newby, "Death Row Economics: The Rise of Fiscally Prudent Anti Death Penalty Activism," *Criminal Justice* 28, no. 33 (2013): 33–40; George Skelton, "In California, the Death Penalty Is All but Meaningless. A Life Sentence for the Golden State Killer Was the Right Move," *Los Angeles Times,* July 2, 2020.

118. Reiter, *23/7: Pelican Bay Prison*; Terry Allen Kupers, *Solitary: The Inside Story of Supermax Isolation and How We Can Abolish It* (Oakland: University of California Press, 2017); Danielle S. Rudes, "Surviving Solitary," in *Surviving Solitary* (Stanford, CA: Stanford University Press, 2022).

119. Albert Woodfox, *Solitary: Unbroken by Four Decades in Solitary Confinement. My Story of Transformation and Hope* (Melbourne: Text Publishing, 2019); Damien Echols, *Life after Death* (New York: Penguin Random House, 2012).

120. Tehachapi, February 1, 2021, https://staging.prisonpandemic.uci.edu/stories/transfers-stopped/.

121. Wasco, February 22, 2021, https://staging.prisonpandemic.uci.edu/stories/frustration-built-up-2/.

122. Calipatria, February 5, 2021, https://staging.prisonpandemic.uci.edu/stories/relationships-died-2/.

123. Erika Camplin, *Prison Food in America* (New York: Rowan & Littlefield, 2017).

124. *In re Hall*, Nos. SC212933, SC213244, SC213534, and SC212566, slip op. at 86 (Super. Ct. Cal., 2021) (denying petitions for writ of habeas corpus).

125. Chuckawalla, November 6, 2020, https://staging.prisonpandemic.uci.edu/stories/life-in-danger-2/.

126. High Desert, March 3, 2021, https://staging.prisonpandemic.uci.edu/stories/letter-from-high-desert-march-3-2021-8779/.

127. Email exchange with Allison Villegas, March 8, 2020 (on file with authors).

128. José Armendariz, "Humans in Name Only," 52:13, last visited May 21, 2022 (California Correctional Crisis: Mass Incarceration, Healthcare, and the COVID-19 Outbreak, UC Hastings College of the Law, February 5, 2021), https://sites.uclawsf.edu/journal-symposium/symposium-schedule/.

129. *In re Hall*, slip op. at 93–94.

130. *In re Hall*, slip op. at 93; *infra*, Part III(C) (discussing the evidentiary hearing).

131. Avenal, October 30, 2020, https://staging.prisonpandemic.uci.edu/stories /scary-environment-2/.

132. Leah Rorvig et al., "Amend at U.C., S.F., Frequently Asked Questions about the COVID-19 Vaccine: Information for Residents of Correctional Facilities," 2021, https://amend.us/covid/.

133. Field notes from Zoom meeting with #StopSanQuentinOutbreak coalition, August 5, 2020 (on file with author).

134. Avenal, November 5, 2020, https://staging.prisonpandemic.uci.edu/stories /phone-calls-only-2/.

135. Valley State, March 11, 2021, https://staging.prisonpandemic.uci.edu /stories/gross-injustice-2/.

136. Kern Valley, April 30, 2021, https://staging.prisonpandemic.uci.edu/stories /no-inmate-is-safe-2/.

137. CIW, December 3, 2020, https://staging.prisonpandemic.uci.edu/stories /no-fresh-air-2/.

138. Mule Creek, April 29, 2021, https://staging.prisonpandemic.uci.edu /stories/forced-blind-faith-2/.

139. Dale Kasler, "Debit Cards, Illegal Cell Phones: How Inmates Pulled Off Giant California Unemployment Scam," *Sacramento Bee*, November 25, 2017.

140. Norco, February 19, 2021, https://staging.prisonpandemic.uci.edu/stories /nothing-to-do-2/.

141. Throughout the litigation, lawyers asked Judge Tigar to ensure that their clients had access to the phones; this was a repeated theme in the #StopSanQuentinOutbreak meetings throughout July.

142. Avenal, November 10, 2020, https://staging.prisonpandemic.uci.edu /stories/phone-calls-only-2/.

143. Calipatria, February 5, 2021, https://staging.prisonpandemic.uci.edu /stories/relationships-died-2/.

144. New Folsom, April 23, 2021, https://staging.prisonpandemic.uci.edu /stories/very-restricted/.

145. Kern Valley, April 27, 2021, https://staging.prisonpandemic.uci.edu/stories /dont-feel-normal-2/ppe.

146. Riverside County, June 4, 2021, https://staging.prisonpandemic.uci.edu /stories/it-was-awkward/.

147. Chuckawalla, November 27, 2020, https://staging.prisonpandemic.uci.edu /stories/kept-moving-people-2/.

148. Soledad, January 9, 2021, https://staging.prisonpandemic.uci.edu /stories/i-dont-feel-safe-2/.

149. Sam Stanton, "Family of Sacramento Inmate Who Died of COVID at San Quentin Sues California," *Sacramento Bee,* March 16, 2021, https://www.sacbee .com/news/local/article249984909.html.

150. Jason Fagone, "'Disgusting Policy': Prisoners' Families Must Pay for Remains after COVID-19 Deaths," *San Francisco Chronicle*, August 24, 2020, https://www.sfchronicle.com/bayarea/article/It-s-a-disgusting-policy-After-prisoners-15506465.php.

151. "Advancing Public Health Interventions to Address the Harms of the Carceral System," Ending Police Violence, https://www.endingpoliceviolence.com/.

152. Jay Croft, "Prison Deaths Rose Almost 50% When Pandemic Hit, Report Shows," WebMD, February 21, 2023, https://www.webmd.com/covid/news/20230221/prison-deaths-rose-almost-50-percent-when-pandemic-hit-report-shows.

153. Brendan Saloner, "COVID-19 Cases and Deaths in Federal and State Prisons," *JAMA* 324, no. 6 (2020): 602–3, https://jamanetwork.com/journals/jama/fullarticle/2768249.

3. BOTTLENECK

1. Adam J. Hirsch, "From Pillory to Penitentiary: The Rise of Criminal Incarceration in Early Massachusetts," *Michigan Law Review* 80, no. 6 (1982): 1179–269.

2. Ashley T. Rubin, "Prison History," *Oxford Research Encyclopedia of Criminology and Criminal Justice*, 2018, https://oxfordre.com/criminology/view/10.1093/acrefore/9780190264079.001.0001/acrefore-9780190264079-e-455.

3. Ashley T. Rubin, "The Prehistory of Innovation: A Longer View of Penal Change," *Punishment & Society* 20, no. 2 (2018): 192–216; Ashley T. Rubin, "Prisons and Jails Are Coronavirus Epicenters—but They Were Once Designed to Prevent Disease Outbreaks," *The Conversation*, April 15, 2020, https://theconversation.com/prisons-and-jails-are-coronavirus-epicenters-but-they-were-once-designed-to-prevent-disease-outbreaks-136036; "Prisons, Disease, and Medicine" (California Correctional Crisis: Mass Incarceration, Healthcare, and the COVID-19 Outbreak, UC Hastings College of the Law, February 5, 2021).

4. Dolly Stolze, "The Curse of Rowland Jenkins and the Oxford Assize of 1577," *Brewminate*, November 3, 2017, https://brewminate.com/the-curse-of-rowland-jenkins-and-the-oxford-assize-of-1577/.

5. John Howard, *The State of the Prisons in England and Wales* (England, 1777), https://www.google.com/books/edition/The_State_of_the_Prisons_in_England_and/4EhNAAAAYAAJ?hl=en.

6. Ibid.

7. Ashley T. Rubin, *The Deviant Prison: Philadelphia's Eastern State Penitentiary and the Origins of America's Modern Penal System* (Cambridge: Cambridge University Press, 2021), 1829–1913.

8. Michael Meranze, *Laboratories of Virtue: Punishment, Revolution, and Authority in Philadelphia, 1760–1835* (Chapel Hill: University of North Carolina Press, 1996).

9. Jonathan Simon, "The New Gaol: Seeing Incarceration like a City," *Annals of the American Academy of Political and Social Science* 664, no. 1 (March 2016): 280–301.

10. Mariana Valverde, "Seeing like a City: The Dialectic of Modern and Premodern Ways of Seeing in Urban Governance," *Law & Society Review* 45, no. 2 (May 2011): 277–312.

11. *Brown v. Plata*, 563 U.S. 493 (2011).

12. Donald Specter, "Everything Revolves around Overcrowding: The State of California's Prisons," *Federal Sentencing Reporter* 22, no. 3 (2010): 194–99, https://doi.org/10.1111/j.1540-5893.2011.00441.x.

13. Joan Petersilia, "Realigning Corrections, California Style," *Annals of the American Academy of Political and Social Science* 664, no. 1 (March 2016), https://ssrn.com/abstract=2754625.

14. Hadar Aviram, "The Inmate Export Business and Other Financial Adventures: Correctional Policies for Times of Austerity," *Hastings Race & Poverty Law Journal* 11, no. 1 (2014): 111–55.

15. W. David Ball, "A False Idea of Economy: Costs, Counties, and the Origins of the California Correctional System," *Annals of the American Academy of Political and Social Science* 664, no. 1 (2016): 26–42, https://doi.org/10.1177/0002716215601844.

16. Malcolm Feeley and Edward Rubin, *Judicial Policy Making and the Modern State: How the Courts Reformed America's Prisons* (Cambridge: Cambridge University Press, 2000); Bailey Heaps, "The Most Adequate Branch: Courts as Competent Prison Reformers," *Stanford Journal of Civil Rights & Civil Liberties* 9, no. 2 (2013): 281–318.

17. Margo Schlanger, "*Plata v. Brown* and Realignment: Jails, Prisons, Courts, and Politics," *Harvard Civil Rights–Civil Liberties Law Review* 48, no. 1 (2013): 165–215.

18. Ram Subramanian and Ruth Delaney et al., *Incarceration's Front Door: The Misuse of Jails in America* (Brooklyn: Vera Institute of Justice, 2015).

19. Todd D. Minton and Daniela Golinelli, *Jail Inmates at Midyear 2013 - Statistical Tables* (Washington, DC: US Department of Justice, Office of Justice Programs, Bureau of Justice Statistics, 2014).

20. Ryken Grattet, Sonya Tafoya, et al., *California's County Jails in the Era of Reform* (San Francisco: Public Policy Institute of California, 2016).

21. "List of California County Jails," Shouse Law, https://www.shouselaw.com/ca/defense/jails/.

22. In six states—Alaska, Connecticut, Delaware, Hawaii, Rhode Island, and Vermont—both prisons and jails are under the jurisdiction of the state's Department of Corrections. See Barbara Krauth, *A Review of the Jail Function within State Unified Corrections Systems* (Aurora, CO: US Department of Justice National Institute of Corrections Information Center, 1997), 2.

23. Los Angeles County Sheriff's Department, "Jails and Prisons in California," https://apps.lasd.org/iic/maps/Prisons-ALL-MAPS1.html.

24. Board of State and Community Corrections, "About the Jail Population Dashboard," https://public.tableau.com/profile/kstevens#!/vizhome/ACJROctober2013/About. Nationwide, approximately two-thirds of the jail population are under pretrial detention; see Natalie Ortiz, *County Jails at a Crossroads, National Association of Counties* (Washington, DC: NACo Counties Futures Lab, 2015).

25. Board of State and Community Corrections, "About the Jail Population Dashboard."

26. Ashley T. Rubin and Michelle S. Phelps, "Fracturing the Penal State: State Actors and the Role of Conflict in Penal Change," *Theoretical Criminology* 21 (2017): 422–40, https://doi.org/10.01177/1362480617724829.

27. Subramanian et al., *Incarceration's Front Door*, 23.

28. Mark A. Cunniff, *Jail Crowding: Understanding Jail Population Dynamics* (Washington, DC: US Department of Justice National Institute of Corrections, 2002), https://s3.amazonaws.com/static.nicic.gov/Library/017209.pdf.

29. In the defense context, see Tyler Prante and Alok K. Bohara, "What Determines Homeland Security Spending? An Econometric Analysis of the Homeland Security Grant Program," *Policy Studies Journal* 36, no. 2 (April 2008): 243–56; Erica Chenoweth and Susan E. Clarke, "All Terrorism Is Local: Resources, Nested Institutions, and Governance for Urban Homeland Security in the American Federal System," *Political Research Quarterly* 63, no. 3 (April 2009): 495–507.

30. Debra Satz, *Why Some Things Should Not Be for Sale: The Moral Limits of Markets* (New York: Oxford University Press, 2010).

31. Jonathan Simon, *Governing through Crime: How the War on Crime Transformed American Democracy and Created a Culture of Fear* (New York: Oxford University Press, 2007); Victor M. Rios, *Human Target: Schools, Police, and the Criminalization of Latino Youth* (Chicago: University of Chicago Press, 2017).

32. Jeannie Suk, "Criminal Law Comes Home," *Yale Law Journal* 116, no. 2 (2006): 2–70.

33. Loïc Wacquant, *Punishing the Poor: The Neoliberal Government of Social Insecurity* (Durham, NC: Duke University Press, 2009); Angela Davis, *Are Prisons Obsolete?* (New York: Seven Sisters Press, 2003); also see Jordan Camp, *Incarcerating the Crisis: Freedom Struggles and the Rise of the Neoliberal State* (Oakland: University of California Press, 2016).

34. Andrea Miller, "Shadows of War, Traces of Policing: The Weaponization of Space and the Sensible in Preemption," in *Captivating Technology*, ed. Ruha Benjamin (Durham, NC: Duke University Press, 2019), 85–106; R. Joshua Scannell, "This Is Not Minority Report: Predictive Policing and Population Racism," in *Captivating Technology*, ed. Benjamin, 107–29. Walter L. Perry, Brian McInnis, Cart C. Price, Susan C. Smith, and John S. Hollywood, *Predictive Policing: The Role of Crime Forecasting in Law Enforcement Operations* (Santa Monica, CA: RAND Corporation, 2013).

35. Winifred R. Poster, "Racialized Surveillance in the Digital Service Economy," in *Captivating Technology*, ed. Benjamin, 138.

36. Tamara K. Nopper, "Digital Character in 'The Scored Society': FICO, Social Networks, and Competing Measurements of Creditworthiness," in *Captivating Technology*, ed. Benjamin, 170–87.

37. Madison Van Oort, "Employing the Carceral Imaginary: An Ethnography of Worker Surveillance in the Retail Industry," in *Captivating Technology*, ed. Benjamin, 213.

38. Franklin E. Zimring and Gordon Hawkins, *The Scale of Imprisonment* (Chicago: University of Chicago Press, 1991).

39. For commentary on this idea, see Kevin R. Reitz, "Zimring, Hawkins, and the Macro Problems of Imprisonment," *Journal of Criminal Law and Criminology (1973–)* 87, no. 2 (Winter 1997): 604–23.

40. Lynn S. Branham, "Follow the Leader: The Advisability and Propriety of Considering Cost and Recidivism Data at Sentencing," *Federal Sentencing Reporter* 24, no. 3 (2012): 169–71, www.jstor.org/stable/10.1525/fsr.2012.24.3.169; Monica Davey, "Missouri Tells Judges Cost of Sentences," *New York Times*, September 19, 2020, https://www.nytimes.com/2010/09/19/us/19judges.html; Hadar Aviram, *Cheap on Crime: Recession-Era Politics and the Transformation of American Punishment* (Oakland: University of California Press, 2015); Lauren-Brooke Eisen, "Should Judges Know the Costs of Sentencing Options at Their Disposal?," *Think Justice Blog*, Vera Institute of Justice, March 01, 2011, https://www.vera.org/blog/should-judges-know-the-costs-of-sentencing-options-at-their-disposal.

41. Aviram, *Cheap on Crime*.

42. Schlanger, *Plata v. Brown*.

43. Ibid.

44. Marvin Mentor, "Federal Court Seizes California Prisons Medical Care; Appoints Receiver with Unprecedented Power," *Prison Legal News*, March 15, 2006, https://www.prisonlegalnews.org/news/2006/mar/15/federal-court-seizes-california-prisons-medical-care-appoints-Receiver-with-unprecedented-powers/.

45. W. David Ball, "Tough on Crime (on the State's Dime): How Violent Crime Does Not Drive California Counties' Incarceration Rates—and Why It Should," *Georgia State University Law Review* 28 (2013), https://readingroom.law.gsu.edu/gsulr/vol28/iss4/4; W. David Ball, "Defunding State Prisons," *Criminal Law Bulletin* 50, no. 5 (2014): 1060–90; W. David Ball, "A False Idea of Economy: Costs, Counties, and the Origins of the California Correctional System," *Annals of the American Academy of Political and Social Science* 664, no. 1 (2016): 26–42, https://doi.org/10.1177/0002716215601844.

46. Joan Petersilia, "Realigning Corrections, California Style," *Annals of the American Academy of Political and Social Science* 664, no. 1 (March 2016): 8–13.

47. "Meet the 13 Board Members," Board of State and Community Corrections, https://www.bscc.ca.gov/s_thebsccboard/.

48. US Department of Justice, Office of Justice Programs, *Promising Practices in the Use of Data and Justice Information Sharing: A Self-Evaluation Resource for California Counties* (US Department of Justice, Office of Justice Programs, 2016),

https://www.ojp.gov/library/abstracts/promising-practices-use-data-and-justice-information-sharing-self-evaluation.

49. "Jail Profile Survey Querying," Board of State and Community Corrections, https://app.bscc.ca.gov/joq//jps/QuerySelection.asp.

50. Board of State and Community Corrections, "About the Jail Population Dashboard."

51. "BSCC Inspection Reports," Board of State and Community Corrections, https://drive.google.com/drive/folders/16kolLN2nGQreJvoTdaKvLqToRyZa_jpZ.

52. "Office of Research," California Department of Corrections and Rehabilitation, https://www.cdcr.ca.gov/research/.

53. See, for example, "Alameda County Inmate Locator," Alameda County Government, https://www.acgov.org/sheriff_app/.

54. A sense of the "flavor" of a local sheriff's department is discernible from its website: for example, compare the websites for Alameda (https://www.alamedacounty sheriff.org/), Mendocino (https://mendocinosheriff.com/), Ventura (https://www .venturasheriff.org/), and Yolo (https://www.yolocountysheriff.com/) Counties. Notably, all of these websites contain more information and significantly more accessible display and search functions than the BSCC data pages.

55. Among BSCC's lesser known responsibilities, for example, is the tracking of sterilizations performed on incarcerated people, following the shocking exposé of the Center for Investigative Reporting of forced sterilizations at CDCR facilities. See Corey Johnson, "Female Inmates Sterilized in California Prisons without Approval," Center for Investigative Reporting, July 7, 2013, https://revealnews.org/article /female-inmates-sterilized-in-california-prisons-without-approval/. The datasets can be found on BSCC's website: https://www.bscc.ca.gov/m_dataresearch/.

56. Grattet et al., *California's County Jails*.

57. Schlanger, *Plata v. Brown*.

58. Magnus Lofstrom and Brandon Martin, "Proposition 47 Brought Decreases to Both Prison and Jail Populations," Public Policy Institute of California, September 8, 2015, https://www.ppic.org/blog/proposition-47-brought-decreases-to-both-prison-and-jail-populations/.

59. Susan Turner, Terry Fain, et al., *Public Safety Realignment in Twelve California Counties* (Santa Monica, CA: RAND Corporation, 2015), https://www.rand.org /content/dam/rand/pubs/research_reports/RR800/RR872/RAND_RR872.pdf.

60. Robert N. Proctor, Londa Schiebinger, et al., "Agnotology: A Missing Term to Describe the Cultural Production of Ignorance (and Its Study)," in *Agnotology: The Making and Unmaking of Ignorance*, ed. Robert N. Proctor and Londa Schiebinger (Redwood City, CA: Stanford University Press, 2008), 1–33.

61. Daniel Bedford and John Cook, "Agnotology, Scientific Consensus, and the Teaching and Learning of Climate Change: A Response to Legates, Soon and Briggs," *Science and Education* 22 (2013): 2019–30, https://doi.org/10.1007/s11191-013-9608-3.

62. See generally Janet Kourany and Michael Carrier, eds., *Science and the Production of Ignorance: When the Quest for Knowledge Is Thwarted* (Cambridge, MA: MIT Press, 2020).

63. John Hurwitz and Mark Peffley, "Public Perceptions of Race and Crime: The Role of Racial Stereotypes," *American Journal of Political Science* 41, no. 2 (April 1997): 375–401.

64. James F. Quinn, Craig Forsyth, et al., "Societal Reaction to Sex Offenders: A Review of the Origins and Results of the Myths Surrounding Their Crimes and Treatment Amenability," *Deviant Behavior* 25, no. 3 (2004): 215.

65. Franklin E. Zimring, *When Police Kill* (Cambridge, MA: Harvard University Press, 2017).

66. Sarah B. Kaufman, *American Roulette: The Social Logic of Death Penalty Sentencing Trials* (Oakland: University of California Press, 2020).

67. "Population COVID-19 Tracking: CDCR Patients: Covid-19 Cases and Outcomes," California Department of Corrections and Rehabilitation, https://www.cdcr.ca.gov/covid19/population-status-tracking/.

68. Deaths underreported; what does "resolved" mean?

69. Jason Pohl, "California Jail Watchdogs Won't Keep Track of COVID-19 Cases in Lockups. Activists Want Answers," *Sacramento Bee*, April 9, 2020, https://www.sacbee.com/news/california/article241893771.html.

70. Alene Tchekmedyian and Kailyn Brown, "Fateful Choices as Coronavirus Raged through Riverside Jail, Hitting Deputies and Inmates," *Los Angeles Times*, April 27, 2020, https://www.latimes.com/california/story/2020-04-27/riverside-county-jails-coronavirus-outbreak.

71. Ibid.

72. Jason Pohl, "CA Jail Inspectors Decline to Track COVID-19 Infections," *Sacramento Bee*, June 23, 2020, https://www.sacbee.com/news/coronavirus/article243724172.html.

73. Linda Penner, "Launch of Data Collection for BSCC: COVID-19 Dashboard," Board of State and Community Corrections, July 15, 2020, www.bscc.ca.gov/wp-content/uploads/Memorandum-COVID-19-Data-Dashboard-BSCC-7-15-2020.pdf.

74. Board of State and Community Corrections, "About the Jail Population Dashboard."

75. Alexandra Hall, Julie Small, et al., "Why a Massive COVID-19 Outbreak at Fresno County Jail Flew under the Radar," KQED News, August 27, 2020, https://www.kqed.org/news/11835340/why-a-massive-covid-19-outbreak-at-fresno-county-jail-flew-under-the-radar.

76. UCLA Law School, "UCLA Law Builds Databases on Prisons and COVID-19," press release, March 24, 2020, https://law.ucla.edu/news/ucla-law-builds-databases-prisons-and-covid-19.

77. Sharon Dolovich, Aaron Littman, et al., "UCLA Law COVID Behind Bars Data Project," UCLA Law COVID Behind Bars Data Project, https://uclacovidbehindbars.org/.

78. Sharon Dolovich, Aaron Littman, et al., "Methodology," UCLA Law COVID Behind Bars Data Project, https://uclacovidbehindbars.org/methods.

79. Aaron Littman, personal message exchange with author, February 28, 2021.

80. "Covid Cases Rise in Bay Area County Jails and Sheriff's Offices but Vaccination Rates Remain Low," *Davis Vanguard*, July 21, 2022, https://www.davisvanguard.org/2021/02/breaking-down-covid-19-in-ca-jails/.

81. Ibid.

82. Covid-in-Custody Project.

83. Aparna Komarla, "S.F. Jails Are Leading California in COVID-19 Prevention. How Are They Doing It? No One Knows," *San Francisco Chronicle*, November 12, 2021, https://www.sfchronicle.com/opinion/openforum/article/S-F-s-jails-are-leading-California-in-COVID-16613932.php.

84. Darby Aono, "Santa Rita Jail COVID-19 Data," https://docs.google.com/spreadsheets/d/1UfboC8-cRf10glzfnN-mi_hrE1jfdvDYg4KkIuc-VB8/edit#gid=1601012795.

85. Zimring, *When Police Kill*.

86. Michael Barba, "Public Defender Calls for Measures to Prevent a Coronavirus Outbreak in Jail," *San Francisco Examiner*, March 9, 2020, https://www.sfexaminer.com/news/public-defender-calls-for-measures-to-prevent-a-coronavirus-outbreak-in-jail/.

87. Jason Pohl, "California Jails, Prisons on Alert for Coronavirus. Fear It Will 'Spread like Wildfire,'" *Sacramento Bee*, March 6, 2020, https://www.sacbee.com/news/california/article240962761.html.

88. Megan Cassidy, "As Counties Released Inmates amid Coronavirus, Solano County Picked Them Up and Brought Them to Its Jails," *San Francisco Chronicle*, March 30, 2020, https://www.sfchronicle.com/crime/article/As-counties-released-inmates-amid-coronavirus-15167648.php.

89. "Governor Newsom Issues Executive Order on State Prisons and Juvenile Facilities in Response to the COVID-19 Outbreak," Office of Governor Gavin Newsom, March 24, 2020, https://www.gov.ca.gov/2020/03/24/governor-newsom-issues-executive-order-on-state-prisons-and-juvenile-facilities-in-response-to-the-covid-19-outbreak/#:~:text=SACRAMENTO%20%E2%80%94%20To%20reduce%20the%20risks,state's%2035%20prisons%20and%20four.

90. Roy W. Wesley and Bryan B. Beyer, "COVID-19 Review Series, Part Three: California Correctional Health Care Services and the California Department of Corrections and Rehabilitation Caused a Public Health Disaster at San Quentin State Prison When They Transferred Medically Vulnerable Incarcerated Persons from the California Institution for Men without Taking Proper Safeguards," Office of the Inspector General State of California, February 1, 2021, https://www.oig.ca.gov/wp-content/uploads/2021/02/OIG-COVID-19-Review-Series-Part-3-%E2%80%93-Transfer-of-Patients-from-CIM.pdf.

91. Joe Nelson, "ACLU Sues to Reduce California Jail Population, Freeze ICE Transfers amid Coronavirus," *San Bernardino Sun*, April 27, 2020, https://www.sbsun.com/2020/04/27/aclu-sues-to-reduce-california-jail-population-freeze-ice-transfers-amid-coronavirus/.

92. *Barnes v. Ahlman*, 591 U.S. __ (2020).

93. Nigel Duara, "Like a Petri Dish for the Virus: Tens of Thousands of California Inmates Are at Risk," CalMatters, April 13, 2020, https://calmatters.org/california-divide/2020/04/californias-inmates-are-at-high-risk-coronavirus/.

94. Ibid.; José Armendariz and Daisy Ramirez, "The Current State of Medical Access in Prisons" (California Correctional Crisis: Mass Incarceration, Healthcare, and the COVID-19 Outbreak, UC Hastings College of the Law, February 5, 2021), http://sites.uchastings.edu/journal-symposium/.

95. Nadia Lopez, "Tulare County Sheriff Criticized—and Sued by ACLU—for COVID-19 Outbreak at Jails," *Fresno Bee*, January 25, 2021, https://www.fresnobee.com/news/coronavirus/article248669495.html.

96. Dean Growdon, "The Current State of Medical Access in Prisons" (California Correctional Crisis: Mass Incarceration, Healthcare, and the COVID-19 Outbreak, UC Hastings College of the Law, February 5, 2021), http://sites.uchastings.edu/journal-symposium/.

97. Nick Gerda, "How Did OC Sheriff Officials Spend $90 Million in Covid Response Funds? Mostly on Jail Staff," *Voice of OC*, February 18, 2021, https://voiceofoc.org/2021/02/how-did-oc-sheriff-officials-spend-90-million-in-covid-response-funds-mostly-on-jail-staff/.

98. Eric Balaban and Teresa Zhen, "With COVID-19 Raging, Depopulate Los Angeles County Jails," op-ed, *Los Angeles Times*, December 14, 2021, https://www.latimes.com/opinion/story/2020-12-14/los-angeles-county-jail-covid-george-gascon.

99. Ibid.

100. Darrell Smith, "Judicial Council of California Approves $0 Bail for Low-Level Suspects," *Sacramento Bee*, April 6, 2020, https://www.sacbee.com/news/coronavirus/article241817606.html.

101. "Responses to the COVID-19 Pandemic," *Prison Policy Initiative*, July 10, 2020, https://www.prisonpolicy.org/virus/virusresonse.html.

102. Charlotte Scott, "LA County Jail Population Reduced by 5,000 since Outbreak," *Spectrum News 1*, April 30, 2020, https://spectrumnews1.com/ca/la-west/inside-the-issues/2020/04/30/l-a--county-jail-population-reduced-by-5-000-since-beginning-of-coronavirus-outbreak.

103. Jason Pohl, "California Jail Population Plummets during Pandemic. Could This Lead to Long-Term Change?," *Tribune*, May 27, 2020, https://www.sanluisobispo.com/news/california/article242900061.html.

104. Ibid.

105. Greg Moran, "Hundreds Released from Jail under New Bail Rules, but Prosecutors Object to Release of Nearly 200 More," *San Diego Tribune*, April 15, 2020, https://www.sandiegouniontribune.com/news/courts/story/2020-04-15/court-and-jail-releases-draft.

106. Kate Bradshaw, "Hundreds of Inmates Have Been Released from San Mateo County Jails in Recent Weeks," *Almanac*, April 16, 2020, https://almanacnews.com

/news/2020/04/16/hundreds-of-inmates-have-been-released-from-san-mateo-county-jails-in-recent-weeks.

107. Erin Tracy, "COVID-19 Concerns Will Result in Release of up to 300 Stanislaus County Jail Inmates," *Modesto Bee*, April 12, 2020, https://www.modbee.com/news/coronavirus/article241929456.html.

108. Claudia Boyd-Barrett, "COVID-19 Risks Prompt Some California Counties to Ease Jail Populations," *California Health Care Foundation Blog*, April 24, 2020, https://www.chcf.org/blog/covid-19-risks-prompt-some-california-counties-ease-jail-populations/.

109. "Ventura County Deputy Tests Positive for COVID-19, Total Number of Cases Increases to 243," CBS-Los Angeles, April 7, 2020, https://www.cbsnews.com/losangeles/news/coronavirus-ventura-county-deputy-tests-positive-new-cases/.

110. Megan Cassidy, "Spike in Coronavirus Cases at Santa Rita Jail Prompts Clash between Public Defender, D.A.," *San Francisco Chronicle*, April 9, 2020, https://www.sfchronicle.com/crime/article/Spike-in-coronavirus-cases-at-Santa-Rita-Jail-15190792.php.

111. Ibid.

112. Merrill Balassone, "California Counties Keeping COVID-19 Emergency Bail Schedules," *California Courts Newsroom*, July 10, 2020, https://newsroom.courts.ca.gov/news/california-counties-keeping-covid-19-emergency-bail-schedules.

113. "Monitoring Jail Populations during COVID-19," Vera Institute of Justice, https://www.vera.org/projects/covid-19-criminal-justice-responses/covid-19-data.

114. *Ahlman v. Barnes* Order Granting In-Part and Den. In-Part Pls.['] Appl. for TRO or Prelim. Inj. at 694.

115. *Campbell et al. v. Barnes*, No. 30-2020-1141117 (Sup. Ct. Cal. 2020) Order on Writ of Habeas Corpus and Writ of Mandate at 29.

116. *In re Von Staich*, October 5 order.

117. *People v. Duvall*, 9 Cal. 4th 464 (1995).

118. "Orange County District Attorney Todd Spitzer Releases Statement Criticizing Court Ruling to Reduce County Jail Population by 50%," Office of the District Attorney, Orange County, California, December 12, 2020, https://orangecountyda.org/civica/press/display.asp?layout=15&Entry=6087.

119. KJ Hiramoto, "Orange County Sheriff Says Deputies Will Not Enforce Gov. Newsom's New Stay-at-Home Order," Fox 11 Los Angeles, December 6, 2020, https://www.foxla.com/news/orange-county-sheriff-says-deputies-will-not-enforce-gov-newsoms-new-stay-at-home-order.

120. Amy Powell, "OC Sheriff Ordered by Judge to Reduce County's Jail Population by Half amid COVID Pandemic," ABC7 News, December 12, 2020, https://abc7.com/orange-county-jails-inmates-population/8722630/.

121. *In re Von Staich*, 272 Cal. Rptr. 3d 813 (Cal. 2020).

122. Recent order in *Von Staich*, Court of Appeal (from February 2021).

1. "Listings of WHO's Response to COVID-19," World Health Organization, January 29, 2021, https://www.who.int/news/item/29-06-2020-covidtimeline.

2. World Health Organization, "BREAKING: WHO has received genetic sequences for the novel #coronavirus (2019-nCoV) from the Chinese authorities. We expect them to be made publicly available as soon as possible," Twitter, January 11, 2020, https://twitter.com/WHO/status/1216108498188230657.

3. Reuters Staff, "Vaccine for New Coronavirus 'COVID-19' Could Be Ready in 18 Months: WHO," February 11, 2020, https://www.reuters.com/article/us-china-health-who-vaccine-idUSKBN2051ZC?taid=5e42dc55ecb7110001ba6271&utm_campaign=trueAnthem:+Trending+Content&utm_medium=trueAnthem&utm_source=twitter.

4. Vincent Racaniello, Dickson Despommier, et al., interview with Paul Offit, "TWiV 720: With Vaccines, Offit Is on It," *TWiV Podcast*, February 13, 2021, https://www.youtube.com/watch?v=54WDQYvvcCs.

5. Gavin Yamey, Marco Schäferhoff, et al., "Ensuring Global Access to COVID-19 Vaccines," *Lancet* 395, no. 10234 (March 2020): 1405–6.

6. "FDA Approves First COVID-19 Vaccine," Federal Drug Administration, August 23, 2021, https://www.fda.gov/news-events/press-announcements/fda-approves-first-covid-19-vaccine.

7. "Emergency Use Authorization (EUA) for an Unapproved Product Review Memorandum," Federal Drug Administration, November 30, 2020, https://www.fda.gov/media/144673/download; "FDA Takes Additional Action in Fight against COVID-19 by Issuing Emergency Use Authorization for Second COVID-19 Vaccine," Federal Drug Administration, December 18, 2020, https://www.fda.gov/news-events/press-announcements/fda-takes-additional-action-fight-against-covid-19-issuing-emergency-use-authorization-second-covid.

8. "Emergency Use Authorization (EUA) for an Unapproved Product Review Memorandum," Food and Drug Administration, February 4, 2021, https://www.fda.gov/media/146338/download.

9. "COVID-19 Vaccination Plan—Interim Draft," California Department of Public Health, October 16, 2020, https://www.cdph.ca.gov/Programs/CID/DCDC/CDPH%20Document%20Library/COVID-19/COVID-19-Vaccination-Plan-California-Interim-Draft_V1.0.pdf.

10. Hadar Aviram, "Prisons Should Be a Priority for COVID Vaccine," *San Francisco Chronicle*, December 4, 2020, https://www.sfchronicle.com/opinion/openforum/article/Prisons-should-be-a-priority-for-COVID-vaccine-15774745.php.

11. Alexandra Yoon-Hendricks, "California's New COVID Vaccine Plan Leaves Behind Vulnerable Homeless Residents, Inmates," *Sacramento Bee*, January 30, 2021, https://www.sacbee.com/news/equity-lab/article248785125.html.

12. D. L. Davis, "Wisconsin Panel Did Back Vaccinations for Prisoners, but Not Necessarily before Grandma," *Politifact*, January 12, 2021, https://www.politifact

.com/factchecks/2021/feb/11/mark-born/wisconsin-panel-did-back-vaccinations-prisoners-no/.

13. Kimberlee Kruesi and Jonathan Mattis, "Tennessee Panel Deemed Vaccinating Inmates a 'PR nightmare,'" AP, March 6, 2021, https://apnews.com/article/pandemics-prisons-nashville-coronavirus-pandemic-tennessee-35d7e4fb8335fb52f6a5a-8520658bad1.

14. "Guidelines to California's Health Departments Allocation of COVID-19 Vaccine during Phase 1A," California Department of Public Health, December 14, 2020, https://www.cdph.ca.gov/Programs/CID/DCDC/Pages/COVID-19/Allocation-Guidelines-COVID-19-Vaccine-Phase-1A.aspx#:~:text=Recommendation%20A%3A%20Populations%20for%20Phase,or%20long%2Dterm%20care%20settings.

15. Ann Hinga Klein, "25 California Prisons Have Logged More Than 1,000 Infections. None Are in the First Wave of Vaccinations," *New York Times*, January 25, 2021, https://www.nytimes.com/live/2021/01/02/world/covid-19coronavirus.

16. Sara Norman of the Prison Law Office, Zoom conversation with author, January 2021.

17. Emily E. Levitt, Mahmood R. Gohari, et al., "Public Health Guideline Compliance and Perceived Government Effectiveness during the COVID-19 Pandemic in Canada: Findings from a Longitudinal Cohort Study," *Lancet* 9, no. 100185 (2022): 1–11, https://doi.org/10.1016/j.lana.2022.100185.

18. Osagie K. Obasogie, "Prisoners as Human Subjects: A Closer Look at the Institute of Medicine's Recommendations to Loosen Current Restrictions on Using Prisoners in Scientific Research," *Stanford Journal of Civil Rights & Civil Liberties* 6 (2010): 41–82.

19. *Belly of the Beast*, directed by Erika Cohn (Idle Wild Films, 2020), https://www.bellyofthebeastfilm.com/.

20. California State Auditor, *Sterilization of Female Inmates: Some Inmates Were Sterilized Unlawfully, and Safeguards Designed to Limit Occurrences of the Procedure Failed* (Sacramento: California State Auditor, 2014), https://www.auditor.ca.gov/pdfs/reports/2013-120.pdf.

21. "Federal Rules and California Law on Surgical Sterilizations with Federal Funds," Thompson Reuters, 2013, https://www.documentcloud.org/documents/724320-federal-and-state-law-on-sterilization-using.html.

22. "Urgent Memo: COVID-19 Outbreak: San Quentin Prison," AMEND, June 15, 2020, https://amend.us/wp-content/uploads/2020/06/COVID19-Outbreak-SQ-Prison-6.15.2020.pdf.

23. Elizabeth T. Chin, David Leidner, et al., "Covid-19 Vaccine Acceptance in California State Prisons," *New England Journal of Medicine* 385, no. 4 (2021): 374–76.

24. Hadar Aviram, "Friends Want Friends to Take the Vaccine: A Special Message from Ken Hartman," hadaraviram.com, January 11, 2021, https://www.hadaraviram.com/2021/01/09/friends-want-friends-to-take-the-vaccine-a-special-message-from-ken-hartman/.

25. Ibid.

26. Ibid.

27. "Frequently Asked Questions about the COVID-19 Vaccines: Information for Residents of Correctional Facilities," last updated November 11, 2021, AMEND, https://amend.us/wp-content/uploads/2021/11/COVID-Vax-info-for-residents_2021_11_11_Final.pdf.

28. Paige St. John, "California Prisons on Soft Lockdown; Prison Nurses Must Work Overtime, or Else," *Los Angeles Times*, April 8, 2020, https://www.latimes.com/california/story/2020-04-08/coronavirus-prisons-sick-inmates-exhausted-nurses-lockdowns.

29. *Employee Contract Grievance on Behalf of SEIU Local 1000*, https://www.seiu1000.org/sites/main/files/file-attachments/cdcr__cchcs_covid19_grievance.pdf?1596489108; Megan Cassidy, "California Prison Workers File Grievance Alleging Unsafe Conditions to Prevent Coronavirus Outbreaks," *San Francisco Chronicle*, August 6, 2020, https://www.sfchronicle.com/crime/article/California-prison-workers-file-grievance-accusing-15465173.php.

30. State of California, Division of Occupational Safety and Health, "Citation and Notification of Penalty," Department of Industrial Relations, July 24, 2020–January 29, 2021, https://www.dir.ca.gov/dosh/Coronavirus/Citations/02.01.2021-San-Quentin-State-Prison_1480866.pdf.

31. Roy W. Wesley and Bryan B. Beyer, "COVID-19 Review Series, Part Two: The California Department of Corrections and Rehabilitation Distributed and Mandated the Use of Personal Protective Equipment and Cloth Face Coverings; However, Its Lax Enforcement Led to Inadequate Adherence to Basic Safety Protocols," Office of the Inspector, General State of California, October 2020, https://www.oig.ca.gov/wp-content/uploads/2020/10/OIG-COVID-19-Review-Series-Part-2-%E2%80%93-Face-Coverings-and-PPE.pdf.

32. Ibid., 22.

33. California State Assembly hearing on COVID-19, November 10, 2020 (conducted and attended via Zoom). Field notes on file with authors.

34. Erika Tyagi and Joshua Manson, "Prison Staff Are Refusing Vaccines. Incarcerated People Are Paying the Price," UCLA COVID Behind Bars Data Project, August 12, 2021, https://uclacovidbehindbars.org/prison-staff-vaccine-refusals.

35. Josh Page, *The Toughest Beat: Politics, Punishment, and the Prison Officers Union in California* (Oxford: Oxford University Press, 2011).

36. Ben Christopher, "In Attack Ad, California Prison Guards Put Bullseye on Legislator," *Mercury News*, August 24, 2021, https://www.mercurynews.com/2020/09/18/in-attack-ad-california-prison-guards-put-bullseye-on-legislator-2/.

37. Wes Venteicher, "California Prison Guards' Union Spent Big and Lost with Tough-on-Crime Message," *Sacramento Bee*, November 13, 2020, https://www.sacbee.com/article247149034.html.

38. COVID-19 in Custody Project, "Data: County Jails," Covid in Custody, accessed August 24, 2022, https://covidincustody.org/data#data_links.

39. Dean Growdon, "The Current State of Medical Access in Prisons" and panel discussion (California Correctional Crisis: Mass Incarceration, Healthcare, and the COVID-19 Outbreak, UC Hastings College of the Law, February 5, 2021), http://sites.uchastings.edu/journal-symposium/symposium-schedule/.

40. Megan Cassidy, "S.F. Sheriff's Deputies Threaten Resignations over City's Vaccination Mandate," *San Francisco Chronicle*, August 6, 2022, https://www.sfchronicle.com/bayarea/article/S-F-sheriff-s-deputies-threaten-resignations-16370801.php.

5. INCUBATOR

1. Jonathan Simon, *Governing through Crime* (Oxford: Oxford University Press, 2009); Franklin Zimring et al., *Punishment and Democracy: Three Strikes and You're Out in California* (Washington, DC: US Department of Justice, Office of Justice Programs, 2001); C. Crist, "Chain Gangs Are Right for Florida," *Corrections Today* 58, no. 2 (1996): 178; Marie Gottschalk, *The Prison and the Gallows* (Cambridge: Cambridge University Press, 2006).

2. Katherine Beckett, *Making Crime Pay: Law and Order in Contemporary American Politics* (Oxford: Oxford University Press, 1999).

3. Naomi Murakawa, *The First Civil Right: How Liberals Built Prison America* (Oxford: Oxford University Press, 2014); Elizabeth Hinton, *From the War on Poverty to the War on Crime* (Cambridge, MA: Harvard University Press, 2017).

4. Peter K. Enns, "The Public's Increasing Punitiveness and Its Influence on Mass Incarceration in the United States," *APSA 2010 Annual Meeting Paper* (2010): 2–5, http://ssrn.com/abstract=1642977; Peter K. Enns, "The Public's Increasing Punitiveness and Its Influence on Mass Incarceration in the United States," *American Journal of Political Science* 58, no. 4 (2014): 857–72, https://doi.org/10.1111/ajps.12098; Sean Nicholson-Crotty et al., "Dynamic Representation(s): Federal Criminal Justice Policy and an Alternative Dimension of Public Mood," *Political Behavior* 31, no. 4 (2009): 629–55, https://doi.org/10.1007/s11109-009-9085-1.

5. Francis T. Cullen et al., "Public Support for Correctional Rehabilitation in America: Change or Consistency?," in *Changing Attitudes to Punishment: Public Opinion, Crime and Justice*, ed. Julian V. Roberts and J. Michael Hough (London: Willan Publishing, 2002), 128–47; Christopher A. Innes, "Recent Public Opinion in the United States toward Punishment and Corrections," *Prison Journal* 73, no. 2 (June 1993): 220–36, https://doi.org/10.1177/0032855593073002006.

6. Chris Seeds, "Bifurcation Nation: American Penal Policy in Late Mass Incarceration," *Punishment & Society* 19, no. 5 (2016): 590–610, https://doi.org/10.1177/1462474516673822.

7. Brandon K. Applegate et al., "Assessing Public Support for Three-Strikes-and-You're-Out Laws: Global vs. Specific Attitudes," *Crime & Delinquency* 42, no. 4 (October 1996): 517–34.

8. William Samuel and Elizabeth Moulds, "The Effect of Crime Severity on Perceptions of Fair Punishment: A California Case Study," *Journal of Criminal Law and Criminology* 77, no. 3 (Autumn 1986): 931–48, www.jstor.org/stable/1143444; Douglas R. Thomson and Anthony J. Ragona, "Popular Moderation versus Government Authoritarianism: An Interactionist View of Public Sentiments toward Crime Sanctions," *Crime and Delinquency* 33, no. 3 (July 1987): 337–57, doi:10.1177/001112 8787033003002.

9. John Doble, "Attitudes to Punishment in the US—Punitive and Liberal Opinions," in *Changing Attitudes to Punishment: Public Opinion, Crime and Justice*, ed. Julian V. Roberts and Mike Hough (London: Willan Publishing, 2002), 148–62; Jody L. Sundt, "Is There Room for Change? A Review of Public Attitudes toward Crime Control and Alternatives to Incarceration," *Southern Illinois University Law Journal* 23, no. 4 (Winter 1989): 519–37.

10. Julian V. Roberts, "Public Opinion, Crime, and Criminal Justice," *Crime and Justice* 16 (1992): 99–180, www.jstor.org/stable/1147562; Catriona Mirrlees-Black, "Improving Public Knowledge about Crime and Punishment," in *Changing Attitudes to Punishment: Public Opinion, Crime and Justice*, ed. Julian V. Roberts and Mike Hough (London: Willan Publishing, 2002), 184–97.

11. Lynn Chancer and Pamela Donovan, "A Mass Psychology of Punishment: Crime and the Futility of Rationally Based Approaches," *Social Justice* 21 (1996): 50–72; Michael J. Hogan et al., "Economic Insecurity, Blame, and Punitive Attitudes," *Justice Quarterly* 22, no. 3 (2005): 392–412, https://doi.org/10.1080 /07418820500219144; Michael T. Costelloe et al., "Punitive Attitudes toward Criminals: Exploring the Relevance of Crime Salience and Economic Insecurity," *Punishment and Society* 11, no. 1 (January 2009): 25–49, doi:10.1177/1462474508098131; Tom R. Tyler and Robert J. Boeckmann, "Three Strikes and You Are Out, but Why? The Psychology of Public Support for Punishing Rule Breakers," *Law and Society Review* 31, no. 2 (1997): 237–66, www.jstor.org/stable/3053926; David Garland, *The Culture of Control: Crime and Social Order in Contemporary Society* (Chicago: University of Chicago Press, 2002), 148.

12. Arthur L. Stinchcombe et al., *Crime and Punishment—Changing Attitudes in America* (San Francisco: Jossey-Bass, 1980); Mark A. Cohen et al., *Measuring Public Perceptions of Appropriate Prison Sentences, Final Report* (October 2002), ojp. gov/pdffiles1/nij/grants/199365.pdf; Peter D. Hart Research Associates, Inc., *Changing Public Attitudes toward the Criminal Justice System: Summary of Findings* (New York: Open Society Foundations, 2002), www.opensocietyfoundations.org/reports /changing-public-attitudes-toward-criminal-justice-system; Vincent Schiraldi and Judith Greene, "Reducing Correctional Costs in an Era of Tightening Budgets and Shifting Public Opinion," in *Federal Sentencing Reporter* 14, no. 6, Recent State Reforms I: Developments in Sentencing Drug Offenders (May–June 2002): 332–36, www.jstor.org/stable/10.1525/fsr.2002.14.6.332.

13. Hadar Aviram, *Cheap on Crime: Recession-Era Politics and the Transformation of American Punishment* (Oakland: University of California Press, 2015); Katherine

Beckett et al., "The End of an Era? Understanding the Contradictions of Criminal Justice Reform," *Annals of the American Academy of Political and Social Science* 664, no. 1 (March 2016): 238–59; Michael C. Campbell and Heather Schoenfeld, "The Transformation of America's Penal Order: A Historicized Political Sociology of Punishment," *American Journal of Sociology* 118, no. 5 (2013): 1375–1423.

14. Aviram, *Cheap on Crime*.

15. Mona Lynch, *Sunbelt Justice: Arizona and the Transformation of American Punishment* (Stanford, CA: Stanford University Press, 2010); Robert Parkinson, *Texas Tough: The Rise of America's Prison Empire* (New York: Metropolitan Books, 2010).

16. A. Wunder, "The Extinction of Inmate Privileges," *Corrections Compendium* 20, no. 6 (June 1995): 5-24; P. Finn, "No-Frills Prison and Jails: A Movement in Flux," *Federal Probation* 60, no. 3 (September 1996): 35–44.

17. R.J. Bidinotto, "Must Our Prisons Be Resorts?," *Reader's Digest* (1994): 65-71; Michael Welch, "'All the News That's Fit to Print': A Content Analysis of the Correctional Debate in the New York Times," *Prison Journal* 80, no. 3 (September 2000): 245–64.

18. Julian V. Roberts and Mike Hough, "The State of the Prisons: Exploring Public Knowledge and Opinion," *Howard Journal of Criminal Justice* 44, no. 3 (June 2005): 286–306; Katherine Beckett and Theodore Sasson, *The Politics of Injustice: Crime and Punishment in America* (Thousand Oaks, CA: SAGE Publications, 2004); Kathlyn T. Gaubatz, *Crime in the Public Mind* (Ann Arbor: University of Michigan Press, 1995); Belden Russonello & Stewart, *Optimism, Pessimism, and Jailhouse Redemption: American Attitudes on Crime, Punishment, and Over-incarceration* (2001), https://www.prisonpolicy.org/scans/overincarceration_survey.pdf.

19. Kimberly J. Cook and Chris Powell, "Christianity and Punitive Mentalities: A Qualitative Study," *Crime, Law and Social Change* 39 (2003): 69–89, https://doi.org/10.1023/A:1022487430900; John Doble, *Crime and Punishment: The Public's View* (New York: Public Agenda Foundation, 1987); John Doble et al., *Punishing Criminals: The People of Delaware Consider the Options* (New York: Public Agenda Foundation for the Edna McConnell Clark Foundation, 1991); John Doble and Josh Klein, "Punishing Criminals, The Public's View: An Alabama Survey," *Federal Sentencing Reporter* 21, no. 4 (2009): 291–93; Theodore Sasson, *Crime Talk: How Citizens Construct a Social Problem* (Piscataway, NJ: Aldine Transaction, 1995).

20. Paula Bryant and Eugene Morris, "What Does the Public Really Think?," *Corrections Today* 59, no. 1 (February 1998), https://www.thefreelibrary.com/_/print/PrintArticle.aspx?id=20543704; Nygel Lenz, "'Luxuries' in Prison: The Relationship between Amenity Funding and Public Support," *Crime and Delinquency* 48, no. 4 (October 2002): 499–525.

21. Kevin H. Wozniak, "American Public Opinion about Prisons," *Criminal Justice Review* 39, no. 3 (September 2014): 305–24, https://doi.org/10.1177/0734016814529968.

22. Stuart A. Kinner, "Prisons and Custodial Settings Are Part of a Comprehensive Response to COVID-19," *Lancet Public Health* 5, no. 4 (April 2020): e188–e189, https://doi.org/10.1016/S2468-2667(20)30058-X.

23. Brian and Megan Dahle, letter to Ralph Diaz, June 26, 2020. CDCR's letter would later be repurposed in Marin County, as described in the introduction.

24. Matthias Gafni, "State's Largest Ongoing Prison COVID Outbreak Linked to Staff Member; Early Quarantine Release Questioned," *San Francisco Chronicle*, September 24, 2021, https://www.sfchronicle.com/bayarea/article/State-s-largest-ongoing-prison-COVID-outbreak-16483174.php.

25. Austin B. Hill, "The Environment and Disease: Association or Causation?," *Proceedings of the Royal Society of Medicine* 58, no. 5 (1965): 295–300, https:doi.org/10.1177/003591576505800503.

26. Holger Schünemann et al., "The GRADE Approach and Bradford Hill's Criteria for Causation," *Journal of Epidemiology & Community Health* 65, no. 5 (2011): 392–95.

27. Kristen M. Fedak et al., "Applying the Bradford Hill Criteria in the 21st Century: How Data Integration Has Changed Causal Inference in Molecular Epidemiology," *Emerging Themes Epidemiology* 12, no. 14 (September 2015), https://doi.org/10.1186/s12982-015-0037-4.

28. *Los Angeles Times* staff, "Tracking the Coronavirus in California," *Los Angeles Times*, 2020, https://www.latimes.com/projects/california-coronavirus-cases-tracking-outbreak/; "California Coronavirus Data," GitHub, https://github.com/datadesk/california-coronavirus-data.

29. "Population COVID-19 Tracking: CDCR Patients: Covid-19 Cases and Outcomes," California Department of Corrections and Rehabilitation, https://www.cdcr.ca.gov/covid19/population-status-tracking/.

30. "COVID-19 Time-Series Metrics by County and State," California Health and Human Services, https://data.chhs.ca.gov/dataset/covid-19-time-series-metrics-by-county-and-state.

31. Samuel Mwalili, "SEIR Model for COVID-19 Dynamics Incorporating the Environment and Social Distancing," *BMC Research Notes* 13, no. 352 (July 2020): 352, https://doi.org/10.1186/s13104-020-05192-1.

32. Koen Swinkels, "SARS-CoV-2 Superspreading Events around the World," (2020), https://docs.google.com/spreadsheets/d/1c9jwMyT1lw2Pod6SDTno6nHLGMtpheO9xJyGHgdBoco/edit?usp=sharing.

33. Danielle Miller et al., "Full Genome Viral Sequences Inform Patterns of SARS-CoV-2 Spread into and within Israel," *Nature Communications* 11, no. 5518 (November 2020), https://doi.org/10.1038/s41467-020-19248-0.

34. California's jail population hovered between 48,000 and 55,000 daily in 2020. Magnus Lofstrom and Brandon Martin, "California's County Jails," *Public Policy Institute of California* (February 2021), https://www.ppic.org/publication/californias-county-jails/#:~:text=In%20February%202020%20the%20average,between%20May%20and%20September%202020. There are 13 stand-alone federal prisons and 8 federal prison camps within California territory, which housed 11,235 people in 2020. Zoukis Consulting Group, "Federal Prisons in California: California Prisons," Federal Criminal Defense Attorney, https://prisonerresource.com/federal-bureau-prisons/california/. ICE facilities on California soil house

approximately 1,500 people: "Immigration Detention Quick," TRAC, last updated August 15, 2022, https://trac.syr.edu/immigration/quickfacts/.

35. Gregory Hooks and Wendy Sawyer, "Mass Incarceration, COVID-19, and Community Spread," Prison Policy Initiative, December 2020, https://www.prisonpolicy.org/reports/covidspread.html.

36. Gregory Hooks and Wendy Sawyer, "Mass Incarceration, COVID-19, and Community Spread," press release, Prison Policy Initiative, December 2020, https://www.prisonpolicy.org/reports/covidspread.html.

37. Kevin T. Schnepel, Joanna Abaroa-Ellison, et al., *COVID-19 Testing in State Prisons* (Washington, DC: Council on Criminal Justice, April 2021).

38. California State Board of Health and Wilfred H. Kellogg, M.D., *Influenza: A Study of Measures Adopted for the Control of the Epidemic*, Special Bulletin No. 31 (Sacramento: State Printing Office, 1919), 5.

39. L. Stanley, "Influenza at San Quentin Prison, California," *Public Health Reports* 34, no. 19 (May 9, 1919): 996.

40. José M. Carcione et al., "A Simulation of a COVID-19 Epidemic Based on a Deterministic SEIR Model," *Frontiers in Public Health* 8 (May 2020), https://doi:10.3389/fpubh.2020.00230.

41. Derdei Bichara et al., "SIS and SIR Epidemic Models under Virtual Dispersal," *Bulletin of Mathematical Biology* 77 (2015), https://doi.org/10.1007/s11538-015-0113-5.

42. Derdei Bichara and Abderrahman Iggidr, "Multi-patch and Multi-group Epidemic Models: A New Framework," *Journal of Mathematical Biology* 77 (2018): 107–34, https://doi.org/10.1007/s00285-017-1191-9.

43. Yu Duo, "Effects of Reactive Social Distancing on the 1918 Influenza Pandemic," *PLoS One* 12, no. 7 (2017): e0180545, https://doi.org/10.1371/journal.pone.0180545.

44. Bichara et al., "SIS and SIR Epidemic."

6. THE HOUSE ALWAYS WINS

1. Brandon Garrett and Lee Kovarsky, "Viral Injustice," *California Law Review* 110 (2022): 117–78, https://scholarship.law.duke.edu/faculty_scholarship/4110/.

2. Margo Schlanger, "Trends in Prisoner Litigation, as the PLRA Enters Adulthood," *UC Irvine Law Review* 153 (2015): 153–54.

3. Pub. L. No. 104-134, 110 Stat. 1321 (1996) (codified as 42 U.S.C. § 1997e).

4. Sharon Dolovich, "The Failed Regulation and Oversight of American Prisons," *Annual Review of Criminology* 5 (2022): 153.

5. Ibid.

6. Ibid.

7. For example, Margo Schlanger, "*Plata v. Brown* and Realignment: Jails, Prisons, Courts, and Politics," *Harvard Law Review* 48, no. 1 (2013): 153–54.

8. See generally Dolovich, "Evading the Eighth"; Heather Schoenfeld, "Mass Incarceration and the Paradox of Prison Conditions Litigation," *Law & Society Review* 44, no. 3/4 (2010): 731.

9. 445 F. Supp. 3d 557 (N.D. Cal. 2020).

10. See *In re Hall*, Nos. SC212933, SC213244, SC213534, and SC212566 (Super. Ct. Cal., Nov. 16, 2021) (denying petitions for writ of habeas corpus).

11. U.S. Const. amend. VIII; see *Plata*, 445 F. Supp. 3d at 562.

12. Cal. Const. art. 1, § 17; see *In re* Hall, slip op. at 1.

13. 270 Cal. Rptr. 3d 128 (Cal. Ct. App. 2020), *cause transferred with directions to vacate and reconsider, Von Staich on H.C.*, 477 P.3d 537).

14. Complaint at 19, *Plata v. Davis*, 329 F.3d 1101 (9th Cir. 2003).

15. "Tigar, Jon Steven," Federal Judicial Center, last visited March 29, 2022, https://www.fjc.gov/history/judges/tigar-jon-steven.

16. Docket, *Plata v. Newsom*, 2021 WL 5410413 (N.D. Cal. October 27, 2021) (No. 4:01-cv-01351) (showing frequent case management conferences in 2020).

17. Joint Case Management Conference Statement at 16, *Plata v. Newsom*, 445 F. Supp. 3d 557 (N.D. Cal. 2020) (No. 4:01-cv-01351), ECF No. 3389.

18. Ibid.

19. Ibid. at 17–18; see also, generally, "2020 Incident Archive," CAL FIRE, last visited May 27, 2022, https://www.fire.ca.gov/incidents/2020/ [https://perma.cc /H5B3-QJV8] ("The 2020 California wildfire season was characterized by a record-setting year of wildfires that burned across the state of California as measured during the modern era of wildfire management and record keeping").

20. Field notes (on file with author).

21. See Hadar Aviram, "Prisons Should Be a Priority for COVID Vaccine," *San Francisco Chronicle*, December 4, 2020, https://www.sfchronicle.com/opinion /openforum/article/Prisons-should-be-a-priority-for-COVID-vaccine-15774745 .php.

22. Further CMC Transcript, *Plata v. Newsom*, 2021 WL 5410413 (N.D. Cal. October 27, 2021) (No. 4:01-cv-01351), E.C.F. No. 3538.

23. Ibid., 16.

24. Ibid.

25. Ibid., 17.

26. Ibid.

27. Ibid.; field notes (on file with the author).

28. Further CMC Transcript, 2021 WL 5410413, at 20.

29. Ibid., 20–21.

30. Ibid., 19.

31. Ibid., 32–51. The reasons for staff noncompliance, which were not clarified throughout the litigation, can be difficult to tease out given the complete absence of studies about political and social worldviews of correctional staff. Some possibilities involve the law-and-order advocacy and complete political capture of the prison guards' union, the CCPOA, as well as garden variety COVID-19 denialism and

Trumpism among the rank-and-file. For more on the political evolution of the CCPOA, see generally Joshua Page, *The Toughest Beat: Politics, Punishment, and the Prison Officers Union in California* (Oxford: Oxford University Press, 2011).

32. Further CMC Transcript, 2021 WL 5410413, at 25.

33. Ibid.

34. Ibid., 67.

35. Ibid., 29.

36. Ibid., 31.

37. Ibid., 34.

38. Ibid., 35–36.

39. Ibid., 37.

40. Ibid., 41.

41. Ibid., 43.

42. Wes Venteicher, "California Prison Guards' Union Spent Big and Lost with Tough-On-Crime Message," *Sacramento Bee*, November 13, 2020, https://www .sacbee.com/news/politics-government/the-state-worker/article247149034.html.

43. Wes Venteicher, "Update: California Prison Union Headed to Las Vegas for Board Meeting amid COVID-19 Surge," *Sacramento Bee*, January 7, 2021, https:// www.sacbee.com/news/politics-government/the-state-worker/article248318735.html.

44. Ibid., 44.

45. Ibid., 60.

46. Ibid., 64–65.

47. Ibid., 68.

48. Ibid., 68–69.

49. Ibid., 69.

50. Ibid. (quoting *Star Wars: Episode V—The Empire Strikes Back* [20th Century Fox, 1980]).

51. *Plata v. Newsom*, No. 01-cv-01351-JST, 2021 WL 4448953, at *13 (N.D. Cal. Sept. 27, 2021), *vacated*, Nos. 21-16696, 21-16816, 2022 WL 1210694 (9th Cir. Apr. 25, 2022).

52. Ibid., *1.

53. Ibid.

54. Ibid., *7.

55. Byrhonda Lyons, "Judge Requires COVID Vaccines for California Prison Guards," *CalMatters*, March 16, 2022, https://calmatters.org/justice/criminal-justice/2021/09/covid-vaccine-mandate-prison-guards-california/.

56. Notice of CDCR and the Receiver's Submission of a COVID-19 Vaccination Plan for Certain CDCR Workers and Incarcerated People in Compliance with the September 27, 2021 Order at 4, *Plata*, 2021 WL 4448953 (No. 01-cv-01351-JST), ECF No. 3694.

57. Ibid.

58. Emergency Motion to Stay Under Circuit Rule 27-3; Motion for Expedited Briefing at 2, *Plata v. Newsom*, No. 21-16696, 2022 WL 1210694 (9th Cir. 2021); Order, *Plata*, 2021 WL 4448953 (No. 21-16696), discussed in Associated Press,

"Court Blocks COVID-19 Vaccine Mandate for California Prisons," *NBC News*, November 27, 2021, https://www.nbcnews.com/news/us-news/court-blocks-covid-19-vaccine-mandate-california-prisons-n1284800.

59. *Plata v. Newsom*, Nos. 21-16696 & 21-16816, 2022 WL 1210694 (9th Cir. Apr. 25, 2022).

60. Ibid.

61. Ibid., *1.

62. Ibid., *2.

63. See Justin Driver and Emma Kaufman, "The Incoherence of Prison Law," *Harvard Law Review* 135, no. 515 (2021): 542–66.

64. See generally Sharon Dolovich, "Evading the Eighth Amendment: Prison Conditions and the Courts," in *The Eighth Amendment and Its Future in a New Age of Punishment*, ed. Meghan J. Ryan and William W. Berry III (Cambridge: Cambridge University Press, 2020) (discussing how courts apply the Eighth Amendment differently to correctional officers than to other government actors).

65. See generally Aaron Littman, "Free-World Law Behind Bars," *Yale Law Journal* 131, no. 5 (2022): 1385 (discussing how society's failure to enforce regulatory laws within prisons subjects incarcerated individuals to a lower standard of living).

66. Kevin Sawyer, "'They Want to Do Me In': The Prisoner Who Fought COVID Overcrowding," *Filter*, February 8, 2021, https://filtermag.org/prisoner-covid-overcrowding-california/.

67. Supplemental Brief for Petitioner, 270 Cal. Rptr. 3d 128.

68. Bob Egelko, "Court Considers Releasing Inmates Vulnerable to COVID-19 from San Quentin," *San Francisco Chronicle*, August 17, 2020, https://www.sfchronicle.com/bayarea/article/Court-considers-releasing-inmates-vulnerable-to-15490355.php.

69. See Bob Egelko, "California's Top Appellate Judge Retires after 42 Years on Bench, but His Important Rulings Will Live On," *San Francisco Chronicle*, November 12, 2021, https://www.sfchronicle.com/bayarea/article/After-42-years-on-bench-California-s-top-16613822.php (describing Judge Kline's decisions that supported civil rights and the strides he took to change the bail system).

70. *In re Von Staich*, 270 Cal. Rptr. 3d 128 (Cal. Ct. App. 2020).

71. *In re Von Staich*, 270 Cal. Rptr. 3d 128, *cause transferred with directions to vacate and reconsider, Von Staich on H.C.*, 477 P.3d 537 (Cal. 2020).

72. Ibid., 132.

73. Ibid., 134.

74. Ibid., 135.

75. Ibid., 137–38.

76. Ibid., 138.

77. Ibid., 139.

78. Ibid.

79. Ibid., 139, 140–41 (quoting *Williams v. Taylor*, 529 U.S. 420, 436–37 [2000]).

80. Cal. Const. art. 1, § 17. The California constitution forbids "cruel *or* unusual punishment"—a difference that the California Supreme Court relied on in *People*

v. Anderson, 493 P.2d 880, 883, 899 (Cal. 1972), when abolishing the death penalty, but that has since been regarded as largely semantic.

81. *In re Von Staich*, 270 Cal. Rptr. 3d at 140.

82. Ibid.

83. Ibid., 140–50.

84. Ibid., 149.

85. Ibid., 147–50.

86. Ibid., 142 (alteration in original).

87. Ibid.

88. Ibid., 143–44.

89. Ibid.

90. Ibid., 135–36.

91. Ibid., 143–44.

92. Ibid., 146.

93. Ibid., 147.

94. Ibid., 148.

95. Ibid., 153.

96. Ibid., 151.

97. Ibid., 151–52.

98. Ibid., 152.

99. Ibid., 152–53.

100. Ibid., 153 (collecting cases).

101. Ibid., 154.

102. Ibid., 153.

103. *People v. Duvall*, 886 P.2d 1252, 1264–65 (Cal. 1995).

104. *Von Staich on H.C.* 477 P.3d 537, 538 (Cal. 2020).

105. Req. for Depublication, *Von Staich on H.C.*, 477 P.3d 537 (No. S265173).

106. *Von Staich on H.C.*, 477 P.3d at 538.

107. Sawyer, "'They Want to.'"

108. Zoom meeting (on file with authors).

109. Haiyan Ramirez Batlle and John Grant, "Op-Ed: Hard Lessons We Learned from the COVID-19 Tragedy at San Quentin Prison," *Los Angeles Times*, September 4, 2020, https://www.latimes.com/opinion/story/2020-09-04/coronavirus-outbreak-san-quentin-prison.

110. For example, Juan Moreno Haines, "Op-Ed: We Pleaded for Social Distancing Here in San Quentin. The State Refused, and Now COVID Is Raging," *Los Angeles Times*, January 28, 2022, https://www.latimes.com/opinion/story/2022-01-28/covid-prison-san-quentin-ruling; Juan Moreno Haines, "I Got COVID in San Quentin and Watched as Hundreds More Were Infected and 29 Died. Here's Our Story," *San Francisco Chronicle*, October 9, 2021, https://www.sfchronicle.com/opinion/openforum/article/I-got-COVID-in-San-Quentin-and-watched-as-16519424.php.

111. *In re Hall*, Nos. SC212933, SC213244, SC213534, and SC212566, slip op. at 13–70 (Super. Ct. Cal., Nov. 16, 2021) (citation omitted) (quoting *In re Von Staich*,

270 Cal. Rptr. 3d 128, 133 (Cal. Ct. App. 2020), *cause transferred with directions to vacate and reconsider, Von Staich on H.C.*, 477 P.3d 537 (denying petitions for writ of habeas corpus).

112. Ibid., 41–43, 55–57, 92–94.

113. Ibid., 92–95.

114. Ibid., 87–88.

115. Ibid., 111.

116. Ibid.

117. Ibid., 112–15 (emphasis added).

118. Ibid., 115–16.

119. "California Becomes First State in Nation to Announce COVID-19 Vaccine Requirements for Schools," Office of Governor Gavin Newsom, October 21, 2021, https://www.gov.ca.gov/2021/10/01/california-becomes-first-state-in-nation-to-announce-covid-19-vaccine-requirements-for-schools/.

120. This behavior did not go unobserved. Rebecca Bodenheimer, "I Voted against Gavin Newsom's Recall but Can No Longer Be Silent about His Hypocrisy," *SFGATE*, October 27, 2021, https://www.sfgate.com/politics-op-eds/article/Newsom-hypocrisy-on-vaccine-mandates-16565826.php; Sharon Bernstein, "California First in U.S. to Mandate COVID-19 Vaccines for Schoolkids - Governor," Reuters, October 1, 2021, https://www.reuters.com/world/us/california-require-covid-19-vaccines-schoolchildren-governor-says-2021-10-01/.

121. For example, Christina Bravo and Audra Stafford, "Parents Keep Kids Home, Employees Call Out to Protest School COVID-19 Vaccine Mandate," *NBC 7 San Diego*, October 1, 2021, https://www.nbcsandiego.com/news/local/parents-keep-kids-home-employees-call-out-to-protest-school-vaccine-mandate/2750004/; Kevin Kiley (@KevinKileyCA), Twitter, October 1, 2021, 1:24 PM, https://twitter.com/kevinkileyca/status/1443990293926211586?lang=en ("Gavin Newsom just announced a vaccine mandate for K-12 students, days after opposing one for prison guards. California kids made the mistake of not giving millions to his campaigns.").

122. Andrew Sheeler, "California Prison Union Gives to Gavin Newsom's Recall Defense as Bonuses, Raises Take Effect," *Sacramento Bee*, August 2, 2021, https://www.sacbee.com/news/politics-government/the-state-worker/article253144638.html. For an editorial directly linking Newsom's policy to this donation, see "Newsom Bows Once Again to the Prison Guard Union," *Orange County Register*, September 28, 2021, https://www.ocregister.com/2021/09/28/newsom-bows-once-again-to-the-prison-guard-union/.

123. Hadar Aviram, "What Is the CA Attorney General's Job?" hadaraviram.com, October 23, 2021, https://www.hadaraviram.com/2021/10/23/what-is-the-ca-attorney-generals-job/.

124. "Attorney General Kamala D. Harris Issues Statement on Prop. 8 Arguments," Office of the Attorney General, March 26, 2013, https://oag.ca.gov/news/press-releases/attorney-general-kamala-d-harris-issues-statement-prop-8-arguments.

1. Sharon Dolovich, "The Coherence of Prison Law," *Harvard Law Review Forum* 135 (2021): 302–42.

2. See generally Hadar Aviram, *Yesterday's Monsters: The Manson Family Cases and the Illusion of Parole* (Oakland: University of California Press, 2020).

3. See generally B. Jaye Anno et al., *Correctional Health Care: Addressing the Needs of Elderly, Chronically Ill, and Terminally Ill Inmates* (Aurora: US Department of Justice National Institute of Corrections, 2004), https://s3.amazonaws.com/static.nicic.gov/Library/018735.pdf.

4. See generally Michael Massoglia and Christopher Uggen, "Settling Down and Aging Out: Toward an Interactionist Theory of Desistance and Transition to Adulthood," *American Journal of Sociology* 116, no. 2 (2010): 543; see also Caitlin V.M. Cornelius et al., "Aging out of Crime: Exploring the Relationship between Age and Crime with Agent Based Modeling," Agent-Directed Simulation Symposium, no. 3 (2017): 25–26.

5. Jonathan Simon, *Mass Incarceration on Trial: A Remarkable Court Decision and the Future of Prisons in America* (New York: The New Press, 2014), 87–93, 95–97.

6. Christine Vestal, "For Aging Inmates, Care outside Prison Walls," Pew Charitable Trusts, August 12, 2014, last accessed August 8, 2021, www.pewtrusts.org/en/research-and-analysis/blogs/stateline/2014/08/12/for-aging-inmates-care-outside-prison-walls; see generally ACLU, "At America's Expense: The Mass Incarceration of the Elderly," June 2012, https://www.aclu.org/sites/default/files/field_document/elderlyprisonreport_20120613_1.pdf.

7. See generally Human Rights Watch, "Old behind Bars: The Aging Prison Population in the United States," January 27, 2012, https://www.hrw.org/sites/default/files/reports/usprisons0112webwcover_0_0.pdf; KiDeuk Kim and Bryce Peterson, *Aging behind Bars: Trends and Implications of Graying Prisoners in the Federal Prison System* (Washington, DC: Urban Institute, 2014), https://www.urban.org/sites/default/files/publication/33801/413222-Aging-Behind-Bars-Trends-and-Implications-of-Graying-Prisoners-in-the-Federal-Prison-System.PDF.

8. "Surge Reported in Elderly Inmates, Who Cost $72K Annually to House," The Crime Report, August 14, 2010, http://thecrimereport.org/2010/08/14/surge-reported-in-elderly-inmates-who-cost-72k-annually-to-house/; accord E. Ann Carson and William J. Sabol, *Aging of the State Prison Population, 1993–2013* (US Department of Justice Office of Justice Programs, 2016) (indicating the continued rise of the aging incarcerated population).

9. Human Rights Watch, "Old Behind Bars," 6–7.

10. ACLU, "At America's Expense," 5–6.

11. Ronald H. Aday, *Aging Prisoners: Crisis in American Corrections* (Westport, CT: Praeger, 2003), 4–5.

12. Human Rights Watch, "Old behind Bars," 33–34.

13. Ibid., 6.

14. Ibid., 30.

15. Cf. Cyrus Ahalt et al., "Paying the Price: The Pressing Need for Quality, Cost, and Outcomes Data to Improve Correctional Health Care for Older Prisoners," *Journal of the American Geriatrics Society* 61, no. 11 (2013) (indicating that prison costs and the population of the incarcerated elderly continues to rise, and that, in 2013, health care costs made up 10 percent of total costs).

16. Tacara Soones et al., "My Older Clients Fall through Every Crack in the System": Geriatrics Knowledge of Legal Professionals," *Journal of the American Geriatrics Society* 62, no. 4 (2014): 734.

17. Brie A. Williams et al., "Pain behind Bars: The Epidemiology of Pain in Older Jail Inmates in a County Jail," *Journal of Palliative Medicine* 17, no. 12 (2014): 1336.

18. See Monica E. Williams and Robert Vann Rikard, "Marginality or Neglect: An Exploratory Study of Policies and Programs for Aging Female Inmates," *Women & Criminal Justice* 15, no. 3/4 (2004): 135–36.

19. Jordan Segall et al., "Life in Limbo: An Examination of Parole Release for Prisoners Serving Life Sentences with the Possibility of Parole in California," Stanford Criminal Justice Center, September 15, 2011, law.stanford.edu/publications /life-in-limbo-an-examination-of-parole-release-for-prisoners-serving-life-sentences-with-the-possibility-of-parole-in-california/, last accessed August 8, 2021; Dirk Van Zyl Smit and Alessandro Corda, "American Exceptionalism in Parole Release and Supervision: A European Perspective," *American Exceptionalism in Crime and Punishment*, ed. Kevin Reitz (New York: Oxford University Press, 2018), 410–86; Edward Rhine et al., "The Future of Parole Release," *Crime and Justice* 46 (2017): 279–338; Ashley Nellis and Marc Mauer, *The Meaning of Life: The Case for Abolishing Life Sentences* (New York: The New Press, 2018); Aviram, *Yesterday's Monsters*.

20. Rita Shah, *The Meaning of Rehabilitation and Its Impact on Parole: There and Back Again in California* (Abingdon: Routledge, 2017).

21. Albert W. Alschuler, "Sentencing Reform and Prosecutorial Power: A Critique of Recent Proposals for 'Fixed' and 'Presumptive' Sentencing," *University of Pennsylvania Law Review* 126, no. 3 (1978): 550–77; John Pfaff, *Locked In: The True Causes of Mass Incarceration and How to Achieve Real Reform* (New York: Basic Books, 2017); Emily Bazelon, *Charged: The New Movement to Transform American Prosecution and End Mass Incarceration* (New York: Penguin Random House, 2019).

22. Aya Gruber, *The Feminist War on Crime: The Unexpected Role of Women's Liberation in Mass Incarceration* (Oakland: University of California Press, 2020).

23. Aviram, *Yesterday's Monsters*.

24. For background on the Realignment, see Margo Schlanger, "Plata v. Brown and Realignment: Jails, Prisons, Courts, and Politics," *Harvard Civil Rights–Civil Liberties Law Review* 48, no. 1 (2013): 165–215.

25. Henceforth, "the Board."

26. Sullivan, California Criminal Law, § 47.1C, 2014.

27. California Penal Code § 189.

28. W. David Ball, "Heinous, Atrocious, and Cruel: Apprendi, Indeterminate Sentencing, and the Meaning of Punishment," *Columbia Law Review* 109, no. 5 (2009): 893–972.

29. "Board of Parole Hearings," California Department of Corrections and Rehabilitation, www.cdcr.ca.gov/bph/, last accessed August 8, 2021. This is not a California anomaly: it characterizes commissioner appointments throughout the United States. Smit and Corda, "American Exceptionalism in Parole."

30. "Offender Data Points: Offender Demographics for the 24-Month Period Ending June 2019," California Department of Corrections and Rehabilitation, last accessed August 8, 2021, www.cdcr.ca.gov/research/wp-content/uploads/sites /174/2020/10/201906-DataPoints.pdf.

31. William H. Lindsley et al., Penal and Correctional Institutions § 277, 49 Cal. Jur., 3d ed. (2015).

32. Christopher R. Mock, "Parole Suitability Determinations in California: Ambiguous, Arbitrary, and Illusory," *Southern California Review of Law and Social Justice* 17, no. 3 (2008): 889–95.

33. David R. Friedman and Jackie M. Robinson, "Rebutting the Presumption: An Empirical Analysis of Parole Deferrals under Marsy's Law," *Stanford Law Review* 66, no. 1 (2014): 173–90.

34. "Lifer Parole Process," California Department of Corrections and Rehabilitation, https://www.cdcr.ca.gov/victim-services/parole-process/.

35. Cal. Code Regs. Tit. 15, § 2255 (2014).

36. Cal. Penal Code § 3041.5(b) (2014).

37. Aviram, *Yesterday's Monsters*.

38. Because of this, the release rate fluctuates with the winds blowing in the governor's mansion. Davis and Schwarzenegger reversed virtually all parole grants during their tenure. In 2011, as Jerry Brown took office as California governor, he granted parole at a historically high rate, with his reversal rate for murder cases never exceeding 20 percent. Matt Levin, "Behind California's Dramatic Increase in Lifers Freed from Prisons," KQED, May 15, 2014, last accessed August 8, 2021, www.kqed .org/news/135494/behind-californias-dramatic-increase-in-murderers-freed-from-prisons.

39. Michael Brondheim, "Long-Term Incarceration: The Men and Women Who Have Been Locked Away for More than a Quarter Century in California's Prison System," *Elephant Journal*, January 29, 2018, last accessed August 8, 2021, https:// www.elephantjournal.com/now/long-term-incareration-the-men-and-women-who-have-been-locked-away-for-more-than-a-quarter-century-in-californias-prison-system.

40. Friedman and Robinson, "Rebutting the Presumption."

41. Mock, "Parole Suitability Determinations."

42. Ibid., 3.

43. United States Court of Appeal for the Ninth Circuit, In re Powell, 45 Cal.3d 894, 905 (Cal. 1988).

44. Cal. Code Regs. Tit. 15, § 2402(c)(1)-(6).

45. California Supreme Court, In re Lawrence, 44 Cal.4th 1181 (2008).

46. Joey Hipolito, "In re Lawrence: Preserving the Possibility of Parole for California Prisoners," *California Law Review* 97, no. 6 (2009): 1887–98.

47. California Supreme Court, In re Shaputis, 44 Cal.4th 1241 (2008).

48. Robert Sampson and John Laub, "Life-Course Desisters? Trajectories of Crime among Delinquent Boys Followed to Age 70," *Criminology* 41, no. 3 (2003): 301–40; Cornelius et al., "Aging out of Crime."

49. Aviram, *Cheap on Crime*; David Dagan and Steven M. Teles, *Prison Break: Why Conservatives Turned against Mass Incarceration in Postwar American Political Development* (Oxford: Oxford University Press, 2016); Todd Clear and Natasha Frost, *The Punishment Imperative: The Rise and Failure of Mass Incarceration in America* (New York: New York University Press, 2015).

50. Margo Schlanger, "Plata v. Brown."

51. Chris Seeds, "Bifurcation Nation: American Penal Policy in Late Mass Incarceration," *Punishment & Society* 19, no. 5 (2016): 590–610.

52. David Sklansky, *A Pattern of Violence: How the Law Classifies Crimes and What It Means for Justice* (Cambridge, MA: Belknap Press of Harvard University Press, 2021).

53. Susan Turner and Julie Gerlinger, "Risk Assessment and Realignment," *Santa Clara Law Review* 53, no. 4 (2014): 1039–63, https://digitalcommons.law.scu.edu /cgi/viewcontent.cgi?referer=&httpsredir=1&article=2763&context=lawreview.

54. Hadar Aviram, *Cheap on Crime*, chap. 5.

55. Michelle Alexander, *The New Jim Crow: Mass Incarceration in the Age of Colorblindness* (New York: The New Press, 2010).

56. John Pfaff, *Locked In: The True Causes of Mass Incarceration and How to Achieve Real Reform* (New York: Basic Books, 2017); James Forman, *Locking Up Our Own: Crime and Punishment in Black America* (New York: Farrar, Straus and Giroux, 2017); James Forman, "Racial Critiques of Mass Incarceration: Beyond the New Jim Crow," *New York University Law Review* 87 (2012): 101–46.

57. Danielle Sered, *Until We Reckon: Violence, Mass Incarceration, and a Road to Repair* (New York: The New Press, 2019); Michelle Alexander, "Reckoning with Violence," *New York Times*, March 3, 2019.

58. Brett Simpson, "'Governor Newsom, save our lives. We're dying in here': Demonstrators Plea for San Quentin Inmates' Release," *San Francisco Chronicle*, July 10, 2020, https://www.sfchronicle.com/crime/article/San-Quentin-coronavirus-outbreak-Former-inmate-15398062.php; "Activists Call on Gov. Newsom to Address San Quentin Outbreak," ABC7 News, July 9, 2020, https://abc7news.com/san-quentin-prison-outbreak-covid-19-in-prisons-coronavirus-state/6309072/?fbclid=IwAR2rVr-U8gr_xxytcQJC54FIDnoqTSKQRg4vX6v4xfhS_fWTR6Gkj0NteSs.

59. Abené Clayton, "'Make Things Right': Criminal Justice Officials Urge California to Release Prisoners amid Covid-19 Surge," *Guardian*, July 9, 2020, https:// www.theguardian.com/us-news/2020/jul/09/california-governor-urged-release-prisoners-coronavirus-surge.

60. "Urgent Releases due to COVID-19," March 23, 2021, https://docs.google.com /document/d/1ufE5dIl7O2ClDSIL51AM7il5cwoDOUH89m6KxYnzAN4/edit.

61. Jason Fagone, "California Could Cut Its Prison Population in Half and Free 50,000 People. Amid Pandemic, Will the State Act?," *San Francisco Chronicle*, August 13, 2020, https://www.sfchronicle.com/culture/article/Can-California-cut-its-prison-population-in-half-15482084.php.

62. Jason Fagone et al., "Newsom to Release 8,000 Prisoners in California by End of August amid Coronavirus Outbreaks," *San Francisco Chronicle*, July 10, 2020, https://www.sfchronicle.com/crime/article/Newsom-to-announce-8-000-new-prison-releases-15399956.php.

63. Melanie Mason, "When Gavin Newsom Issued Marriage Licenses in San Francisco, His Party Was Furious. Now It's a Campaign Ad," *Los Angeles Times*, May 15, 2018, https://www.latimes.com/politics/la-pol-ca-gavin-newsom-gay-marriage-20180515-story.html.

64. Scott Shafer and Marisa Lagos, "Gov. Gavin Newsom Suspends Death Penalty in California," NPR, March 12, 2019, https://www.npr.org/2019/03/12/702873258/gov-gavin-newsom-suspends-death-penalty-in-california.

65. Richard Winton et al., "Amid COVID-19, California Releases Some Inmates Doing Time for Murder. Advocates Push to Free More," *Los Angeles Times*, August 9, 2020, https://www.latimes.com/california/story/2020-08-09/covid-19-california-releases-violent-crime-murder-prisoners.

66. "Weekly Report of Population as of Midnight July 1, 2020," California Department of Corrections and Rehabilitation, July 1, 2020, https://www.cdcr.ca.gov/research/wp-content/uploads/sites/174/2020/07/Tpop1d200701.pdf.

67. "Weekly Report of Population as of Midnight November 18, 2020," California Department of Corrections and Rehabilitation, November 18, 2020, https://www.cdcr.ca.gov/research/wp-content/uploads/sites/174/2020/11/Tpop1d201118.pdf.

68. It is possible that the COVID High-Risk Medical/Hospice category undercounts the number of high-risk medical people expedited to release because they are also included in the other release cohorts if eligible (though why they would be undercounted here, rather than in the other category, remains unclear). Derived from SOMS as of November 18, 2020, STA322-111920-C19.

69. Aviram, *Yesterday's Monsters*.

70. Ibid.

71. Hadar Aviram, "Leslie Van Houten Could Finally Go Free. Why Does California Leave That Decision to the Governor?," op-ed, *Los Angeles Times*, May 31, 2023, https://www.latimes.com/opinion/story/2023-05-31/leslie-van-houten-california-parole-gavin-newsom; Bill Chappell, "A Former Manson Family Member Is Free, after Her Parole Was Reversed 5 Times," NPR, July 12, 2023, https://www.npr.org/2023/07/12/1187225790/leslie-van-houten-manson-murder-freed-prison-parole; Jeremy Childs, "Newsom Will Not Contest Parole for Former Manson Follower Leslie Van Houten," *Los Angeles Times*, July 7, 2023, https://www.latimes.com/california/story/2023-07-07/newsom-will-not-contest-parole-for-former-manson-follower-leslie-van-houten.

72. Ibid; *People v. Anderson*, 6 Cal.3d 628 (1972).

73. Bob Egelko, "Prospects for California Release of Sirhan Sirhan, RFK's Assassin, Look Unlikely," *San Francisco Chronicle*, September 12, 2021, https:// www.sfchronicle.com/politics/article/Prospects-for-California-release-of-Sirhan-16450649.php.

74. Gavin Newsom, "Op-Ed: Newsom: Why I Will Not Release Sirhan Sirhan on Parole," *Los Angeles Times*, January 13, 2022, https://www.latimes.com/opinion /story/2022-01-13/sirhan-gavin-newsom-parole-decision.

75. Kathryne M. Young and Katie R. Billings, "An Intersectional Examination of U.S. Civil Justice Problems," *Utah Law Review* (2023): 487–543; Kristen Bell, "A Stone of Hope: Juvenile Lifer Parole Decisions," *Harvard Civil Rights–Civil Liberties Law Review* 54 (2018), https://core.ac.uk/download/pdf/326512956.pdf; Rita Shah, *The Meaning of Rehabilitation*.

76. California Department of Corrections and Rehabilitation, Board of Parole Hearings, parole hearing of Gerald Albert Oates, C43300, California Medical Facility, Vacaville, CA, 09/14/2021.

8. THE NEXT PLAGUE

1. Megan Cassidy, "S.F. Inmate with Suspected Case of Monkeypox in Isolation," *San Francisco Chronicle*, August 5, 2022, https://www.sfchronicle.com /bayarea/article/S-F-jail-inmate-has-a-suspected-case-of-17355752.php.

2. Gary Moore, "Mexico's Massacre Era: Gruesome Killings, Porous Prisons," *World Affairs* 175, no. 3 (2012): 61–67.

3. Erving Goffman, "Characteristics of Total Institutions," in *Symposium on Preventive and Social Psychiatry* (Washington, DC: US Government Printing Office, 1958), 43–84.

4. Donald Clemmer, *The Prison Community* (New York: Rinehart & Company, 1958); Lloyd McCorkle and Richard Korn, "Resocialization within Walls," in *The Sociology of Punishment and Correction*, ed. Norman Johnston, Leonard Savitz, and Marvin E. Wolfgang, 2nd ed. (New York: Wiley & Sons, 1970), 409–18.

5. Gresham M. Sykes, *The Society of Captives: A Study of a Maximum Security Prison* (Princeton, NJ: Princeton University Press, 2007); Kevin D. Haggerty and Sandra Bucerius, "The Proliferating Pains of Imprisonment," *Incarceration* 1, no. 1 (July 2020), https://doi.org/10.1177/2632666320936432.

6. Goffman, "Characteristics of Total Institutions"; Clarence Schrag, "Leadership among Prison Inmates," in *Readings in Criminology and Penology* (New York: Columbia University Press, 1972), 600–607; Lloyd McCorkle, "Guard-Inmate Relationships," in *The Sociology of Punishment Correction*, ed. Norman Johnston, Leonard Savitz, and Marvin E. Wolfgang, 2nd ed. (New York: Wiley & Sons, 1970), 419–22.

7. Goffman, "Total Institutions"; Peter G. Garabedian, "Social Roles and Processes of Socialization in the Prison Community," in *The Sociology of Punishment*

Correction, ed. Norman Johnston, Leonard Savitz, and Marvin E. Wolfgang, 2nd ed. (New York: Wiley & Sons, 1970), 484–96.

8. Michel Foucault, *Discipline and Punish: The Birth of the Prison*, trans. Alan Sheridan (New York: Vintage Books, 1975).

9. Graham Burchell et al., *The Foucault Effect: Studies in Governmentality, with Two Lectures by and an Interview with Michel Foucault* (Chicago: University of Chicago Press, 1991); Clifford D. Shearing et al., "From the Panopticon to Disney World: The Development of Discipline," in *Perspectives in Criminal Law: Essays in Honour of John Ll. J. Edwards* (Toronto: Canada Law Book, 1985): 335–49.

10. Malcolm Feeley and Jonathan Simon, "The New Penology: Notes on the Emerging Strategy of Corrections and Its Implications," *Criminology* 30 (1992): 449–74.

11. Rachel Ellis, "Prisons as Porous Institutions," *Theory and Society* 50 (2021): 175–99, https://doi.org/10.1007/s11186-020-09426-w.

12. Coralynn V. Davis and Carol Wayne White, "How Porous Are the Walls That Separate Us? Transformative Service-Learning, Women's Incarceration, and the Unsettled Self," in "Social Justice Action, Teaching, and Research," special issue, *Humboldt Journal of Social Relations* 34 (2012): 85–104.

13. Megan Comfort, *Doing Time Together* (Chicago: University of Chicago Press, 2007).

14. Jeremy Travis, *But They All Come Back: Facing the Challenges of Prisoner Reentry* (Washington, DC: Urban Institute, 2005).

15. Jason Fagone, "California Could Cut Its Prison Population in Half and Free 50,000 People. Amid Pandemic, Will the State Act?," *San Francisco Chronicle*, August 13, 2020, https://www.sfchronicle.com/culture/article/Can-California-cut-its-prison-population-in-half-15482084.php#photo-19797903.

16. Michelle Alexander, *The New Jim Crow: Mass Incarceration in the Age of Colorblindness* (New York: The New Press, 2010).

17. For a critique of the focus on nonviolent drug crimes as a target of reform, see James Forman, "Racial Critiques of Mass Incarceration: Beyond the New Jim Crow," *New York University Law Review* 87 (2012): 101–46; John Pfaff, *Locked In: The True Causes of Mass Incarceration—and How to Achieve Real Reform* (New York: Basic Books, 2017); Christopher Seeds, "Bifurcation Nation: American Penal Policy in Late Mass Incarceration," *Punishment & Society* 19, no. 5 (October 2016): 590–610, https://doi.org/10.1177/1462474516673822.

18. Susan Turner and Julie Gerlinger, "Risk Assessment and Realignment," *Santa Clara Law Review* 53 (2014): 1039–50; Susan Turner, "Moving California Corrections from an Offense- to Risk-Based System," *UC Irvine Law Review* 8, no. 7 (2018): 97–120.

19. Kurt Snibbe, "How Many Homicides Go Unsolved in California and in the Nation?," *Orange County Register*, April 29, 2018, https://www.ocregister.com/2018/04/29/how-many-homicides-go-unsolved-in-california-and-the-nation/.

20. Gabriel Petek, *Improving California's Prison Inmate Classification System* (Sacramento: Legislative Analyst's Office, 2019), https://lao.ca.gov/Publications /Report/4023.

21. Hadar Aviram, *Yesterday's Monsters: The Manson Family Cases and the Illusion of Parole* (Oakland: University of California Press, 2020).

22. Joseph Hayes et al., "California's Prison Population," Public Policy Institute of California, July 2019, https://www.ppic.org/publication/californias-prison-population/.

23. Keith Wattley and the UnCommon Law Team, letter to Governor Gavin Newsom, June 29, 2020, https://static1.squarespace.com/static/5b5f9d4be7494070b92d76f3 /t/5efa2083b1e1f242994281b5/1593451377456/UnCommon+Law%27s+Letter+to+ Governor+Newsom+re.+COVID-19+Release+Levers.

24. Aviram, *Yesterday's Monsters*.

25. "AB-1210, Board of Parole Hearings: commissioners," California Legislature, 2021-2022, https://leginfo.legislature.ca.gov/faces/billNavClient.xhtml?bill_ id=202120220AB1210.

26. Cal. Gov't Code § 8658.

27. Alessandro De Giorgi, "Back to Nothing: Prisoner Reentry and Neoliberal Neglect," *Social Justice* 44, no. 1 (2017): 83–120, www.socialjusticejournal.org/wp-content/uploads/2018/01/147_05_De-Giorgi.pdf.

28. Legislative Analyst's Office, "How Much Does It Cost to Incarcerate an Inmate?," last updated January 2022, https://lao.ca.gov/PolicyAreas/CJ/6_cj_ inmatecost#:~:text=It%20costs%20an%20average%20of,%2432%2C000%20 or%20about%2058%20percent.

29. Ryken Grattet and Brandon Martin, "Alternatives to Incarceration in California," Public Policy Institute of California, April 2015, https://www.ppic.org /publication/alternatives-to-incarceration-in-california/.

30. Emma Kaufman and Justin Driver, "The Incoherence of Prison Law," *Harvard Law Review* 135, no. 151 (2021): 517–84; Sharon Dolovich, "The Coherence of Prison Law," *Harvard Law Review* 135 (2121): 302–41.

31. Margo Schlanger and Betsy Ginsberg, "Pandemic Rules: COVID-19 and the Prison Litigation Reform Act's Exhaustion Requirement," *Case Western Law Review* 72, no. 3 (2022): 533–63.

32. Lee Kovarsky and Brandon Garrett, "Viral Injustice," *California Law Review* 110 (2021), https://www.californialawreview.org/print/viral-injustice/.

33. Aaron Littman, "Free-World Law behind Bars," *Yale Law Journal* 131 (2022): 1385–1490.

34. Ibid., 1450.

35. Ibid., 1397.

INDEX

average daily population (ADP), county
jails, 98*fig.*, 99*fig.*

bare life, 7, 12
Barker, Vanessa, 16, 25
Barnes v. Ahlman, 21, 106, 110
Beety, Valena, 45
Belly of the Beast (documentary), 118
benefits (CARES Act), wrongfully with-
held, 81
Bernal, Jesus G., 110
Bernanke, Ben, 19, 24
Beyrer (doctor and expert witness), in *Von
Staich,* 171
bidirectional causality, burning ranch
analogy, 135–137, 136*fig.*
bifurcation, 41–42; in governor's release
plan, 197; political origins of, 193; of
violent/nonviolent dichotomy, 17, 19,
41–42, 193, 207
biological gradient (Bradford Hill criteria),
138
Black and Filipino people, valley fever
mortality risk to, 34–35
Black Assize of 1577, 14, 88
Block, Diana, 119
Board of Parole Hearings (Board of
Prison Terms), 191–92, 196, 201,
209–210
Board of State and Community Corrections (BSCC), 20, 21, 89, 95–97, 129,
212; database, 102–3, 104
Bonta, Rob, 185–86, 193–94, 194*fig*
Borgeson, Isa, 188, 189
Born, Mark, 116
bottleneck, of populations in county jails,
87, 106, 198, 201
boundaries (prison), 5–6, 7, 49, 56. *See also*
myth of prison impermeability
Bradford Hill criteria, 21, 138–39
Braucher, Richard, 167, 169
Breed, London, 18
Brinkley-Rubinstein, Lauren, 44
Broomfield, Ron, 72, 179
Brown, Jerry, 37, 93, 199
Brown v. Plata, 16, 20, 26, 88, 133; over-
crowding mandate, 60; population
reduction target met, 97; reforms in,

32–34, 42; Supreme Court decision in,
37–40, 38*fig*
BSCC. *See* Board of State and Community
Corrections
Buck v. Bell, 40
Burglar's Guide to the City, A (Manaugh),
11
burning ranch analogy, 135, 137
Burton, Chase, 24
buses, as an extension of carceral space, 8, 9,
68, 92–93, 106

California, apathy from public and authority figures in, 151, 153; disaster mentality
in, 25; political culture in, 25–26; state
population, damage to, from prison
outbreaks, 134–53
California Assembly, 124–26
California Code of Regulations, 191–92
California Constitution, 74, 155, 170, 181,
185, 209
California Correctional Health Care
Services (CCHCS), 74, 120, 123–24,
159, 162. *See also* federal receiver
California Correctional Peace Officers
Association (CCPOA), 21, 164–65, 185;
political capture of, 20, 25, 126–28, 162,
213; vaccination resistance or refusal, 21,
127–28, 130–31. *See also* prison staff
California counties, classified by distance
from CDCR institutions, 141, 143,
142*fig.*
California Court of Appeal, *Von Staich* in.
See *In re Von Staich*
California COVID-19 outbreak, lessons
from, 16–17
California Department of Corrections and
Rehabilitation (CDCR), in COVID-19
crisis, 75, 114, 116–17, 157, 165–66,
184–85; ameliorative actions of, 170, 171,
174–75, 176, 179, 180; data provided by,
22, 23, 101, 103, 138; dismissal of public
health officials' concerns, 4–5, 54–55,
134, 179, 181; failure of leadership in, 125,
158, 181–83; testing and prevention
protocols, systemic failures, 55, 57,
58–59, 62–64, 125–26; trust in, eroded
and collapsed, 21, 69, 85, 118–120, 159,

167, 179. *See also* prison facilities (CDCR)

California Department of Public Health (CDPH), 103, 114–15, 116, 214

California electoral system, reform recommendations, 213

California fires (summer 2020), 68–69

California Government Code, 210

California Institution for Men (CIM), 4, 63, 72, 117, 166, 38*fig.; See also* Chino; San Quentin and Corcoran prison transfer

California Medical Facility (CMF), 68, 72–74, 117, 158

California Penal Code, 76, 86, 172, 209

California Proposition 8, 185–86

California Proposition 20, 128

California Proposition 47, 90, 97–98, 98*fig.,* 99*fig.*

California Proposition 57, 195, 205*fig.*

California State Auditor, 118–19

California Supreme Court, 74, 172–73, 111, 192

CalMatters, 107, 164, 185

Campbell et al. v. Barnes, 111

Campbell, Olivia, 73

capacity, in county jails: and bookings, 99*fig;* releases for, 98*fig. See also* design capacity; rated capacity

capital punishment litigation, expense of, 209

carceral archipelago, 6, 203

carceral geography, 6–10, 11, 15, 85

carceral permeability, 12, 16, 18–19, 23, 44–45, 203–4, 214–15; analytical model (holistic), 6. *See also* boundaries

carceral scholarship. *See* scholarship

carceral space, 7, 8–10, 11, 12, 14, 92

carceral state, 7, 9, 90, 92

carceral suffering, 16, 20, 51, 52, 85. *See also* extreme punishment trifecta; mental anguish; pains of imprisonment

carceral superspreading events, proportion and scale of, 139–40, 140*fig.*

Carson Unit ("the hole"), prisoners isolated in, 66, 69

case management conferences (CMCs), 22, 157–163

cash bail system, risk of, to people awaiting trial, 44–45

causality, epidemiological criteria (Bradford Hill), 137–39

CCHCS. *See* California Correctional Health Care Services

CCPOA. *See* California Correctional Peace Officers Association

CDCR. *See* California Department of Corrections and Rehabilitation

cell phones, 78, 121, 196, 210, 211*fig.*

Center on Prison Law and Policy (UCLA), 46

Centers for Disease Control and Prevention (CDC), 43–44, 65, 129, 163, 215

Central Valley, initial surge of infections in, 140

Chan, Adamu, 59

Chan Zuckerberg Biohub, 58

Chin-Hong, Peter, 84, 193

Chino, 4, 54, 72. *See also* California Institution for Men

CIM. *See* California Institution for Men

civil rights, 112, 117, 128–30, 155

Civil War era, quarantinist approach in, 15

Clarke, Ron, 11

class-action lawsuits, 34, 35–36, 81, 106–7, 108, 109

cleaning, by prisoners, of contaminated spaces and items, 60, 61, 64, 73, 77

cleaning appliances or supplies, lack of, 61, 72, 73, 107, 124, 176

Club Fed," 133

CMCs, in *Plata v. Newsom,* 22, 157–163

CMF. *See* California Medical Facility

Cohen, Lawrence, 10

coherence (Bradford Hill criteria), 138, 144–45

Cohn, Erika, 118

Coleman v. Wilson, 28, 30–32

Commonwealth Scientific and Industrial Research Organization (CSIRO), 113

community support network, for people in reentry, 211*fig.*

commutation of sentences, 209, 195, 205*fig.*

concentric ring model, 146–47, 147*fig.*

confinement, 5, 7, 107, 108. *See also* isolation; quarantine

Howard, Geoffrey, 4, 166, 167, 184, 186; in *Hall,* 173, 180–83
Howard, John, 13–14, 15, 88
human dignity, deprivation of, 39, 182
human remains, receipt of, 84
Human Rights Watch, 190
humanitarian litigation, efficacy of, 154–55, 189
Hutchens, Sandra, 93–94
hydra problem, 20–21, 40, 97, 99, 112
hygiene, 44; lack of, 14, 29, 39, 60, 72–73, 88, 107; testimony on, in *Hall,* 176, 177, 178
hypotheses, to predict Marin County infection rates, 147–49, 148*fig.*
hypothesis, in counterfactual analysis, 138–39

ICE (U.S. Immigration and Customs Enforcement), 4, 90, 91, 195
immunity, qualified, 35–36
impermeability. *See* myth of prison impermeability
incarcerated firefighters, employment of, on release, 210, 212
incarcerated people, animus against, 22, 83, 154–55, 187, 189, 193, 200; family members of, 204, 216; public support and empathy for, 10, 26, 132; at time of vaccine rollout, 120
incarcerated reporter (Haines), 64–65, 72, 178–79
incarceration: alternatives to, 133, 212; crowding standards in, 42; high-cost/low-risk equation in, 189; political accountability for, 95; and public safety, 3, 133; rehabilitative value of, 133
infection data, concentric ring arrangement of, 146–47, 147*fig.*
infection sources, plausible, in correlation analysis, 145–46, 146*fig.*
informed consent requirements, failures in, 119
injunctive relief. *See* relief
Innovative Genomics Institute (Berkeley), 58
In re Hall, 22, 72, 111, 155, 166–67, 173–84, 183–84; evidentiary hearing in, 173–79,

186; medical neglect, in testimony and ruling, 174, 175–177, 178, 181
In re Lawrence, 192
In re Shaputis, 192
In re Von Staich, 22, 55, 156, 167, 168–173; appropriate forum question, 169, 184; decision in, 55, 156, 170–173, 185; order for prisoner release or transfer in, 172–73, 184–85; *Von Staich/Hall,* 156–57, 168–84
"insight" determination, 192, 199, 200
Inspector General (IG), 20, 54, 62, 125
institutional infusion (religion), 203
Interdisciplinary Research Leaders Blog, 46
International Legal Foundation, 44
irreparable harm, 110, 165
isolation: from family and loved ones, 49, 82, 115, 178; guidelines, 43, 55, 66; medical, 44, 50, 68, 108; medical, in punitive spaces, 55, 66–67, 69, 76–77, 177, 182–83
Izadi, Mary, 128–30

Jagiolka, Donald, 167
jail (history), 14, 87–88, 89. *See also* county jails
jail data. *See* county jail data
jail litigation, 21, 41, 89, 97, 106–7, 108, 109–12
Janssen Biotech, vaccine development, 114
Jindia, Shilpa, 119
Johnson & Johnson vaccine, 114, 130
Jones, Nick, 60
journalism, 52, 80, 44, 115, 200; database creation, 104, 105; exposés on outbreaks, 20, 54, 69, 101
Judicial Council of California, 108, 109
judicial discretion in sentencing, 26, 37
judicial psychology, cooperative, 161–62
jurisdictional perspective, 19–20, 90–91. *See also* appropriate forum; "free lunch" problem
jurisdictional shift, under Realignment, 40, 92, 93–94
jurisdictions, interrelated, 91–92, 212
justice delayed is justice denied, 111, 156, 186–87

University of California, Berkeley, 105
University of California, Irvine (UCI), 20, 51
University of California, Los Angeles (UCLA), 20, 46, 85, 103, 105, 127
University of California, San Francisco, 58
Urgent Memo (AMEND), 55, 158, 169–170, 171, 181–82
Urnov, Fyodor, 58, 179
US Justice Department, 95–96

vaccination, 114, 120, 122–23, 127, 143, 184; of county jail populations, 89, 117, 128–30; of prisoners, 21, 69, 115, 116, 117–120, 131, 159–61; of prison staff, 127, 130, 163, 164–65; prison staff refusal (see prison staff, in COVID-19 crisis); vaccine distribution plans, 114–17, 159–60
vaccine emergency use authorization (FDA), 113–14
vaccine refusal report (COVID Behind Bars), 127
vaccines, 114–17, 159–60, 164, 180; development of, 113–14;
valley fever outbreak, 19, 34–36
Van Houten, Leslie, 199
Venteicher, Wes, 126
Ventura County Jail, 109
Vera Institute, 90
victim's rights movement, 25, 190
videos, on COVID-19 preventative measures, 121–22, 130, 162
violent crime, 25, 94, 190, 193, 197–98
violent/nonviolent dichotomy, 2, 17, 19, 41–42, 193, 206, 207. *See also* bifurcation
violent offenders, aging, public safety risk from releasing, 42, 196, 206
visitor policy, suspension of visits, 56, 82

Von Staich, Ivan, 172, 173, 166–67, 169
Von Staich. See In re Von Staich

Wacquant, Loïc, 7, 9
Walnut Street Jail (Philadelphia), 14, 88
Walters, John, 176, 177, 179
Walton, Kathleen, 168–69, 170
warehousing, philosophy of, 16
Warner, Nick, 97
Weisburd, David, 10
When Police Kill (Zimring), 100
White Coats for Black Lives, 193
WHO (World Health Organization), 43, 65, 113
Williams, Larry, 176–77
Willis, Matthew, 4, 54, 179, 181
Wilson, Peter, 110, 111
Witt, John, 13, 51
"wobbler" offenses, 88, 93
Woods, Brendon, 109, 193
World Health Organization (WHO), 43, 65, 113
worthiness, hierarchy of, 12, 18. *See also* bifurcation
Wozniak, Kevin, 134
wrongful death lawsuits, 83, 109

Young, Terell, 101
youth offenders, governor urged to release, 195, 205*fig.*

zero-bail measure, as depressurizing valve, 89, 108–9
zero-sum thinking, 21, 34, 86, 116, 153, 187, 212; impermeability as basis for, 131; moral examination of, 204; and punitive views, 132, 133, 134
"zero tolerance" policy, on COVID insubordination, 123
Zimring, Franklin, 92, 93, 100, 105

Founded in 1893,
UNIVERSITY OF CALIFORNIA PRESS
publishes bold, progressive books and journals
on topics in the arts, humanities, social sciences,
and natural sciences—with a focus on social
justice issues—that inspire thought and action
among readers worldwide.

The UC PRESS FOUNDATION
raises funds to uphold the press's vital role
as an independent, nonprofit publisher, and
receives philanthropic support from a wide
range of individuals and institutions—and from
committed readers like you. To learn more, visit
ucpress.edu/supportus.

www.ingramcontent.com/pod-product-compliance
Lightning Source LLC
Chambersburg PA
CBHW020830270326
41928CB00006B/476